The Origins of Tolkien's Middle-earth For Dummies®

Cheat Sheet

About J.R.R. Tolkien

John Ronald Reuel Tolkien was one of the most beloved authors of the 20th century. He was born in South Africa in 1892 of British parents. When he was two, his mother brought him and his brother back to England, to a village named Sarehole. The idyllic landscape there later inspired his vision of the Shire, home of the hobbits in Middle-earth. By the time he was 12, both of his parents had died, and he was raised under the guardianship of a priest. He remained a devout Catholic the rest of his life. After graduating from Exeter College at Oxford, Tolkien entered the military and served as a lieutenant in World War I, where he took part in the Battle of the Somme. During this time he began working on an invented mythology that later became *The Silmarillion*. After the war, he helped edit the *Oxford English Dictionary* and taught English literature at the University of Leeds. He joined the faculty of Oxford University in 1925, where he was a professor first of Anglo-Saxon and then of English Language and Literature until 1959. He studied and spoke more than a dozen languages, and invented several more for his fantasy world of Middle-earth. In 1937 he published *The Hobbit*. He continued the story of hobbits and other Middle-earth beings in the much larger and more complex *The Lord of the Rings*, which became a best-seller in the decades that followed and is now recognized as a brilliant literary classic. After a long and successful career of writing, scholarship, and teaching, he died in 1973.

Works by J.R.R. Tolkien

The Adventures of Tom Bombadil

Farmer Giles of Ham

The Father Christmas Letters *

Finn and Hingest *

The History of Middle-earth (12 volumes, edited by Christopher Tolkien)*

The Hobbit

The Homecoming of Beorhtnoth

Leaf by Niggle

The Letters of J.R.R. Tolkien *

The Lord of the Rings (*The Fellowship of the Ring, The Two Towers, The Return of the King*)

Mr. Bliss *

The Monsters and the Critics & Other Essays *

On Fairy Stories

Pictures by J.R.R. Tolkien *

The Road Goes Ever On (with Donald Swann)

Roverandom *

The Silmarillion *

Sir Gawain and the Green Knight, Pearl, and Sir Orfeo *

Smith of Wootton Major

Unfinished Tales *

* Published posthumously

Houghton Mifflin is Tolkien's authorized publisher; paperback editions are also available from Ballantine Books.

Books about J.R.R. Tolkien and Middle-earth

The Atlas of Middle-earth by Karen Wynn Fonstad (Houghton Mifflin, 1991)

The Complete Guide to Middle-earth by Robert Foster (Ballantine Books, 1971)

Hobbits, Elves, and Wizards by Michael N. Stanton (Palgrave Macmillan, 2001)

J.R.R. Tolkien: Artist & Illustrator by Wayne G. Hammond, Christina Scull (Houghton Mifflin, 1995)

J.R.R. Tolkien: Author of the Century by Tom Shippey (Houghton Mifflin, 2001)

J.R.R. Tolkien's Sanctifying Myth: Understanding Middle-earth by Bradley J. Birzer (ISI, 2002)

The Magical Worlds of The Lord of the Rings by David Colbert (Berkeley, 2002)

The Master of the Rings by Susan Ang (Totem, 2002)

Tolkien: The Illustrated Encyclopaedia by David Day (Simon & Schuster, 1991)

Tolkien's Ring by David Day (Friedman/Fairfax, 2001)

For Dummies: Bestselling Book Series for Beginners

The Origins of Tolkien's Middle-earth For Dummies

Cheat Sheet

Hobbits

(See Chapter 7)

Bilbo Baggins: "Uncle" to Frodo, finds Sauron's One Ring of Power in Gollum's lair under Misty Mountains

Frodo Baggins: "Nephew" and heir to Bilbo, bearer of Sauron's One Ring of Power, takes up quest to destroy the Ring at Mount Doom

Gollum/Sméagol: Murdered friend to gain One Ring of Power, leads Frodo and Sam to Mordor

Merry Brandybuck: Friend to Frodo, squire to King Théoden, slays the Lord of the Ringwraiths

Pippin Took: Second cousin to Frodo, serves in court of Denethor (Steward of Gondor)

Samwise Gamgee: Faithful servant and friend to Frodo all the way to Mount Doom

Villains

(See Chapter 10)

Balrog: Powerful demon of fire, battles Gandalf in Moria

Melkor/Morgoth: Most powerful of the Ainur, destroyed the Two Lamps and the Two Trees, tutored Sauron in evil

Ringwraiths: Ghouls who serve Sauron, once lords of Men, also called Nazgûl

Sauron: One of the Maiar, Enemy of Middle-earth, served Melkor, forges One Ring of Power to rule over free peoples

Smaug: Last of the fire-breathing dragons of Middle-earth, jealously hoards the Dwarves' treasure under the Lonely Mountain

Men

(See Chapter 5)

Aragorn: Heir to throne of Gondor and Arnor, raised by Elrond, wed to Arwen, also known as Strider and Elessar

Boromir: Son of Denethor (Steward of Gondor), headstrong brother of Faramir

Éowyn: Niece of Théoden, Shield-Maiden of Rohan, wed to Faramir

Faramir: Brother of Boromir, Ranger of Ithilien, wed to Éowyn

Théoden: King of Rohan, uncle of Éowyn, leads Battle of Helm's Deep

Elves

(See Chapter 4)

Arwen: Daughter of Elrond, wed to Aragorn, Queen of Reunited Kingdom, gives up immortality

Elrond: Father of Arwen, Master of Rivendell, chooses immortality

Fëanor: Legendary creator of Tengwar writing script, the palantíri, and the Silmaril jewels

Galadriel: Queen of Lothlorien, keeper of Nenya (the Elven-Ring of Water)

Legolas: Son of Thranduil (king of the Woodland Realm in Mirkwood Forest), friend to Gimli

Wizards and Divinities

(See Chapters 3 and 8)

Ainur: "The Holy Ones," powerful angelic beings who live in the Blessed Realm of Aman

Eru Ilúvatar: "The One All-father," Creator of Middle-earth and the rest of Arda

Gandalf the Grey: One of the Maiar, sent as wizard to Middle-earth to help the free peoples in struggle against Sauron, becomes Gandalf the White

Maiar: The "Lesser" of the Holy Ones, deities who serve higher deities

Saruman the White: Wizard and once leader of Gandalf's order, betrays free peoples of Middle-earth, enters into allegiance with Sauron

Dwarves

(See Chapter 6)

Gimli: Son of Glóin, friend to Legolas the Elf, preserves Glittering Caves

Thorin Oakenshield: Leader of Dwarves in retrieving rightful treasure from Smaug the dragon

Characters in bold type are members of the Fellowship of the Ring

For Dummies: Bestselling Book Series for Beginners

The Origins of Tolkien's
Middle-earth
FOR DUMMIES®

ᚱᛁᚷᛁᛏᚾ ᚠᚢ ᛏᚱᚳᛚᛁᛗᚾ ᛗᛁᚼᚼᛚᛗ ᛦᚱᛈ

The Origins of Tolkien's
Middle-earth
FOR
DUMMIES®

by Greg Harvey

Foreword by Alfred Siewers
Professor of Medieval Literature, Bucknell University

WILEY
Wiley Publishing, Inc.

ᚻ ᚾᚺᚽᚾᛂ ᛒᛂᛁ ᚳᛈᛃᚳᚺ ᛃᛃᛈᚱᛁ ᛒᚨ ᛏᚺᛒᚨᛃᚻᛉᛂ ᚻ

The Origins of Tolkien's Middle-earth For Dummies®

Published by
Wiley Publishing, Inc.
111 River St.
Hoboken, NJ 07030
www.wiley.com

Copyright © 2003 by Wiley Publishing, Inc., Indianapolis, Indiana

Published simultaneously in Canada

For general information on our other products and services or to obtain technical support, please contact our Customer Care Department within the U.S. at 800-762-2974, outside the U.S. at 317-572-3993, or fax 317-572-4002.

Wiley also publishes its books in a variety of electronic formats. Some content that appears in print may not be available in electronic books.

Library of Congress Control Number: 2003105682

ISBN: 0-7645-4186-2

Manufactured in the United States of America

10 9 8 7 6 5 4 3 2 1

 is a trademark of Wiley Publishing, Inc.

About the Author

Greg Harvey was born in Harvey, Illinois, in 1949 and attended the University of Illinois in Champaign-Urbana. There, he achieved the degree of Bachelor of Arts with a major in Classics and Greek and Latin, with a double minor in History and French. After graduation, he pursued a number of careers, including engineering and drafting, teaching (receiving accreditation as a History and Computer Education teacher in secondary and adult education from San Francisco State University), and computer training. He is the author of numerous technical books, including the best-selling *Excel 2003 For Dummies* and *Windows XP For Dummies Quick Reference*. Greg received his Master's Degree in the Humanities in the area of Philosophy and Religion with a concentration in Asian and Comparative Studies from the California Institute of Integral Studies in San Francisco in 2000. Currently, he is working there on his Ph.D. in the same general area. His web site is at www.mindovermedia.com.

Dedication

I dedicate this work to all who've suffered loss and yet refuse to abandon hope.

"For such is the way of it: to find and lose, as it seems to those whose boat is on the running stream."

—Legolas to Gimli upon saying farewell to Lothlórien: *The Fellowship of the Ring* by J.R.R. Tolkien

The Light Within

Oh Elbereth Gilthoniel,
Who set the night-jewels over all,
To rend the darkness that over Middle-earth holds sway,
Till Eärendil's gem appears on high as herald of the day.

Rekindle now the sparks of love in every heart below,
To ignite a flame to guide us on each journey as we go,
So we may be a light to all "when all other lights go out,"
And worthy yet of a hero's tale before our lives are naught.

—Greg Harvey for Ophelia, February 27, 2003

Aiya Elenion Ancalima!

Author's Acknowledgments

Thanking everyone who helped make this project on Tolkien's Middle-earth a reality would leave little room for the text itself. Nevertheless, I will try to acknowledge as many as possible (and to those not mentioned by name who kept telling me this book was a good idea and not to give up on it, just know that you have my unending thanks).

I want to begin by thanking the people whose belief in me and the potential of this project have meant everything in the world to me: Diane Steele, for initially letting me entice her with my renditions of Tolkien's myths and their importance for the everyday world, and Kathy Cox, for her unflagging belief and encouragement in all the stages from inception to printing.

Next, I want to thank the people who actually got into the trenches and helped turn the straw of my rough text into gold ready for publishing: Corbin Collins, the ever-upbeat and creative project editor; Laura Peterson, the ever-vigilant copy editor; Melissa Bennett, editorial assistant and formatter extraordinaire; and Alfred Siewers, our tremendous technical editor. Special thanks to Donald Colby, regional director of gifts at the University of Illinois, for his general encouragement and his help in locating and interesting Professor Siewers in this project.

I also want to thank Melinda Bryant for her great maps of Middle-earth and Michael Bryant for holding down the fort by singlehandedly dealing with a simultaneous revision of one of my technical books.

Finally, I need to acknowledge and thank my professors of Asian Studies at the California Institute of Integral Studies: Steven Goodman, who not only taught me Classical Tibetan, but also how and why to care about the meaning of a text; James Ryan, who taught me the rudiments of comparative religious analysis; and Yi Wu, who not only taught me Classical Chinese, but also opened me wide to the meanings of Zen and Taoist literature *(hsieh hsieh)*.

In conclusion, there's only one yet to thank, one who's last but never least: my partner, Chris, *melindo nin*. Thank you for always being there.

Publisher's Acknowledgments

We're proud of this book; please send us your comments through our Dummies online registration form located at www.dummies.com/register/.

Some of the people who helped bring this book to market include the following:

Acquisitions, Editorial, and Media Development

Project Editor: Corbin Collins

Acquisitions Editor: Kathy Cox

Copy Editor: Laura Peterson

Editorial Project Assistant: Holly Grimes

Technical Editor: Alfred Siewers

Editorial Manager: Michelle Hacker

Editorial Assistant: Melissa Bennett

Cover Photos: Geoffrey Clifford/Getty Images/The Image Bank

Cartoons: Rich Tennant, www.the5thwave.com

Production

Project Coordinator: Nancee Reeves

Layout and Graphics: Amanda Carter, Seth Conley, Heather Ryan, Shae Wilson

Special Art: Melinda Bryant

Proofreaders: TECHBOOKS Production Services

Indexer: TECHBOOKS Production Services

Special Help
Helene Godin

Publishing and Editorial for Consumer Dummies

    Diane Graves Steele, Vice President and Publisher, Consumer Dummies

    Joyce Pepple, Acquisitions Director, Consumer Dummies

    Kristin A. Cocks, Product Development Director, Consumer Dummies

    Michael Spring, Vice President and Publisher, Travel

    Brice Gosnell, Associate Publisher, Travel

    Kelly Regan, Editorial Director, Travel

Publishing for Technology Dummies

    Andy Cummings, Vice President and Publisher, Dummies Technology/General User

Composition Services

    Gerry Fahey, Vice President of Production Services

    Debbie Stailey, Director of Composition Services

Contents at a Glance

Table of Contents

Foreword

By Professor Alfred Siewers, Bucknell University

● ●

J.R.R. Tolkien's writing and drinking buddy C.S. Lewis wrote that reading Edmund Spenser's poem *The Faerie Queene* (the granddaddy of English-language fantasy lit) was therapeutic for the body as well as the mind.

I'll say the same thing here today about Tolkien's own *Lord of the Rings,* for similar reasons (and forgetting about the movies for now).

My first encounter with Tolkien's work was my older sister's dog-eared 1960s paperback version of the trilogy, which I read under the covers with a flash-light as a teenager — and read again and again.

During those years of late-night reading, that same sister was in the next room, suffering from a chronic illness that too soon turned fatal.

Tolkien has helped a lot of us, at different times and in different ways, get through the night. Indeed, I could have had much worse traveling companions growing up. His writing put me in touch with mythic and medieval traditions that helped inform whatever positive patterns of work and faith I rely on today with a sense of the mystery and value of life.

If this sounds like a testimonial, it is. Tolkien's fantasy is often taken as enter-taining escapism, and it is in part, involving as it does the unexpected joy of the fairytales he loved. But in this book that you now hold, Greg Harvey admirably discusses the therapeutic aspect of fantasy while also explaining with helpful clarity and humor the underpinnings of Tolkien's Middle-earth. He delivers the big picture that still escapes those of us who grew up reading just *The Hobbit* and *The Lord of the Rings* and not the posthumously published and edited *Silmarillion* and the multi-volumed *History of Middle-earth*. Harvey does this in part by suggesting unexpected parallels between the unusually interactive effect on readers of Tolkien's project (writing a Catholic epic as English mythology) and experiential spiritual traditions, including Harvey's own Zen Buddhist practice.

It's no coincidence that fantasy literature emerged, as Tolkienologist Tom Shippey observed, as a primary genre of the 20th century. When students in my medieval-literature classes slam the Middle Ages as violent and supersti-tious, I come right back at them with the 20th century: Its atrocities far surpass those of the premodern and traditional cultures we often deride, even when trying to be polite. The horrors of the Holocaust and the persecution of Christians in the Soviet Union are just two prime examples. But fantasy is not merely an escape from such horrors.

The neuroscientist Antonio Damasio has recently and brilliantly illuminated the obvious points that emotion and reason are related and that literature serves a cognitive purpose in developing and stimulating emotion. Herein lies part of the case for fantasy literature: It can help treat the modern bipolarity of heart and mind that enables our hyper-cruelties through a contemplative reading that reconnects intellect and emotion. And key to Tolkien's successful fantasy-therapy is that he moored it in tradition.

In our global consumer society, it is usually considered a good thing to oppose and overturn tradition, or to colonize it smorgasbord-style, picking and choosing from cultures around the world or from the past that with which we like to adorn ourselves.

Tolkien did a good bit of such shopping around himself for the sake of his fantasy storytelling. And yet he did so in three ways that set his work apart: first, as a man who was personally embedded in traditional Catholicism; second, as a scholar who was deeply respectful of early medieval literatures of Europe that emerged in an earlier Christianity engaged with ancient storytelling and myth; and finally, as a thoughtful 20th-century writer who personally had experienced some of the worst warfare in history and saw himself profoundly outside modern life and government.

There is an anti-modernist aspect to tradition, an almost organic wisdom tested over centuries of human interaction in family and community situations, a source of resistance to globalization that need not be exclusionary. Thus, various communitarian traditional cultures — whether they be early Christian, Taoist, Buddhist, Native American, or something else — tend to resist modern Western ideologies and assumptions that seek to turn human beings into abstractions or commodities. Tolkien tapped into this sense of tradition in part through his own religious background. He grew up an orphan in turn-of-the-century industrial Birmingham among a community of Catholic priests founded by the great Victorian retro-medievalist Cardinal John Henry Newman.

With perhaps dim memories in mind of the lush gardens of South Africa, where he was born in 1892, Tolkien also delighted in childhood trips to the green countryside of the West Midlands on the border of Wales, in the old Anglo-Saxon kingdom of Mercia, which he mythically identified as the land of his ancestors. Later, it became the basis for the Shire. In the process, his encounters with Welsh helped inspire his lifelong fascination with words as mythic icons, and also with an earlier Christian tradition.

Tolkien said once in a lecture that *The Lord of the Rings* "contains, in the way of presentation that I find most natural, much of what I personally have received from the study of things Celtic. . . . In *The Lord of the Rings* . . . the names of persons and places in this story were mainly composed on patterns deliberately modeled on those of Welsh. . . . This element in the tale has given perhaps more pleasure to more readers than anything else in it." He would also fondly refer in his famous essay on *Beowulf* to "less severe Celtic learning," in contrast with his main field of study in early English literature.

Here, we get to the heart, I think, of why Tolkien's fantasy appeals so broadly to audiences today, ranging from conservative Christians to neopagan eco-activists. In connecting with early Celtic "fairy" lore of the Otherworld, as found in early medieval Irish and Welsh stories, Tolkien was also connecting with a method of storytelling that was formed, as the Celticist John Carey indicates, in a non-Augustinian Christian view of nature.

Forgive me for slipping on my don's dunce cap to lecture for a moment, but this too is, I think, important to our story. At the time of the fall of Rome, Augustine of Hippo, with his many virtues, set the agenda for a Western view emphasizing nature as distanced from God and corrupt, in which salvation was achieved through grace and not nature, and God's signs in nature were arbitrary objects. By contrast, religious traditions in Wales and Ireland had maintained more of a connection with the emphases of Greek writers and desert ascetics who developed throughout the Middle Ages a sense of how uncreated divine energies flowed through nature. For them, salvation worked iconographically through a synergy of grace and choice, of faith and nature. The views of Augustine's critic John Cassian regarding nature were closer to those of the white and green martyrs of Irish monasticism.

So the early Irish and Welsh Otherworld stories that were ultimately the basis for Tolkien's Elves — central figures in his *Silmarillion* and important to *The Lord of the Rings* — drew on pagan Celtic themes in the context of that older Christianity whose emphases lingered longer in Wales and Ireland than elsewhere in the West, as suggested, for example, by recent historical writings of K.P. Dark on cultural continuity in early medieval Britain.

The immortals of Celtic stories, who ultimately became Tolkien's Elves, were examples of unfallen human beings — of what we could become, through the process of deification opened to us, in this Christian view, through the incarnation of Christ. Nature itself, while mired in mortality by the Fall (in Augustinian overtones) was still in part an icon of the Incarnate God, still with aspects of the original creation, be they Ents or Tom Bombadil. This was the crossroad of faith and myth, of the spiritual and the natural, where Tolkien worked out his fantasy epic and its back story. There, he found his iconographic symbols of integration in words and their histories, real and imagined. In his skillful hands, and despite his own peculiar limitations, words could become, at times, something more than modern metaphor or ideology: a mythic naming *(metonymy)* suggesting the union of mind and heart sought after in many traditions; a grounding of imagination in life; a paralleling in secular story, perhaps, of the spiritual function of visual icons in the Greek Christian world.

Tolkien accomplished all this as someone who had experienced, as a young combatant at the Battle of the Somme during World War I, some of the worst horror of the modern world, and who remained throughout his life something of an outsider in his own beloved Midlands. As a South African native with a German surname, raised a Catholic orphan in a still harshly Protestant and insular England, he was no fan of the British Empire and severely criticized later the apartheid of his native land as well as Nazi anti-Semitism. Yet

he remained an advocate of what he called "unconstitutional monarchy" with anarchistic elements — he was a believer in traditional authority who was nonetheless intensely suspicious of modern states and of trends that today we call globalization.

Most serious writing on Tolkien's fantasy has been by scholars with backgrounds in European medieval studies similar to Tolkien's own, notably Jane Chance and Tom Shippey. Greg Harvey's book was not written to be scholarship but to be a helpful commentary for us readers. It does that job most worthily, and while I may not always agree with all of his connections and interpretations, it is well-informed by knowledge and especially experience: The *For Dummies* title refers to the humility required in approaching Tolkien's complex myth, not to the level of insight herein. The parallels Harvey shows between Tolkien's fantasy and Buddhism, for example, point up the archetypal nature of Tolkien's work and the value of traditional approaches to life already mentioned. This work will have a valued place on my shelf of Tolkien books, and I hope it will on yours as well.

Introduction

●●

*T*his book is the result of serendipity — a happy accident. One day in 2002 as I was returning from a business trip to my publisher (Wiley) in Indianapolis, I happened to turn to an in-flight channel that was playing the National Geographic program *Beyond the Movie: The Lord of the Rings, The Fellowship of the Ring.* In this film, a couple of scenes concern the relationship of Tolkien's Elvish language to Finnish — and, moreover, the relationship of some themes in *The Lord of the Rings* to the Finnish epic poem *The Kalevala.* What was so extraordinary about this was that I had just finished reading *The Key to the Kalevala* by Pekka Ervast, a theosophical analysis of the poem's major themes, as part of my studies in Western philosophy and religion.

Up to that time, I had been aware only of Tolkien's scholarly study of the Old English epic poem *Beowulf* (another text I had been studying) and that it had influenced his Middle-earth mythology. This tie-in with *The Kalevala* sent me off on a new round of research and study, comparing my understanding of Tolkien's Middle-earth with my knowledge of language, mythology, philosophy, and religion. This book is the result of that endeavor.

As a student of comparative philosophy and religion, and not comparative literature, I want to make clear my approach to this material. In place of standard literary analysis, which often emphasizes the author and his or her relationship with the material, I employ *hermeneutics,* a fancy word that means analyzing a text (usually a religious one like the Bible) and figuring out its possible meanings solely from the text itself. Therefore, in this book I'm much more likely to be looking for the internal meaning in Tolkien's books — *The Silmarillion, The Hobbit,* and *The Lord of the Rings* specifically — than for what Tolkien said about the meaning of his own works, although that's important, too.

Adopting this as the primary approach enables me to analyze the possible origins of Middle-earth or, at least, connections between it and other traditional mythologies and religions, without worrying exclusively about whether Tolkien himself was aware of these traditions or possible connections. *Hermeneutics* holds that the work stands apart from its author in such a way that it can be subjected to interpretations that the author neither deliberately intended nor was conscious of. If the work, taken as a whole, suggests a particular interpretation to an audience, then that interpretation is valid, even if the author would not necessarily agree with it. (Interestingly enough, Tolkien took a somewhat similar position in urging scholars to employ an organic rather than piecemeal interpretation of *Beowulf.*)

As mythology, Middle-earth and its lore are as real for me as the mythologies of the Greeks, Romans, Celts, Vikings, Germanic tribes, and Finnish peoples from whom Tolkien so heavily borrowed. I therefore analyze Tolkien's tales with the same eye for meaning that I employ when exploring the meaning of *The Kalevala* or a Taoist philosophical text. It's a testament to the tremendous talent and love that Tolkien poured into his work that it is so full of deep meaning, stands so well in comparison to other mythologies, and is so relevant to our lives.

About This Book

This book is a basic guide to some of the possible linguistic and mythological origins of Tolkien's Middle-earth. It provides a rudimentary analysis of its many themes and lessons for our world. It is not — I repeat, *not* — an encyclopedia or quick guide to the diverse beings, languages, and history that make up Tolkien's Middle-earth. It is also not a set of outlines or notes of *The Hobbit* and *The Lord of the Rings*. If your intention in buying this book is to be able to converse intelligently with your friends or pass a literature course about Middle-earth *without* actually bothering to read *The Hobbit* and *The Lord of the Rings,* you had best put this book back on the shelf right now.

If there's a higher purpose to this book, it is simply to entice you and prepare you to get more enjoyment from reading or re-reading *The Hobbit* and *The Lord of the Rings* and possibly even *The Silmarillion.* This book is intended to enrich your understanding of Tolkien's books on Middle-earth, but it is in no way a replacement for them. It's especially targeted at you *Lord of the Rings* moviegoers who intend to delve into the books.

The basic method I employ to enhance your reading experience of Tolkien is to look at his world's basic components — geography, beings, history, and underlying themes — through the richness of their language and myth. Often, examining the language and myth exposes a little of the hidden structure of Tolkien's Middle-earth and provides a basis on which its meanings may be discussed and understood.

My final purpose in writing this book is to challenge you to think about the themes inherent in Tolkien's stories about Middle-earth and their implications in your own life. I don't really care whether you agree with any particular analysis I make. I will have reached my goal if I simply get you to start thinking about what you think and how you feel about it.

Foolish Assumptions

I have a few assumptions I make about you as a reader and I urge you to check them out before you check this book out at the cash register:

- ✔ You've read *The Lord of the Rings* at least once (even if it was 20 years ago) or have seen Peter Jackson's *Lord of the Rings* movies.

- ✔ The basic storyline of the quest to destroy the One Ring of Power touched you at some level, even if you're not sure why.

- ✔ You're intrigued by the characters, cultures, and languages of Middle-earth, even though they confuse you and border on being overwhelming.

- ✔ You're curious about where this fantasy world came from and why it's so complex and intense, even if you're not sure that you really want to get involved with its detail.

If my first assumption fits, and you can agree with at least one of the other ones, then I think that you've come to the right book. If, on the other hand, you don't fit the profile outlined in the first point and are understandably hesitant to agree with any of the others, then you might want to hold off on this purchase (at least until you've seen the film version of *The Lord of the Rings*).

How to Use This Book

Tolkien's writings rely heavily on new vocabulary, and much of that comes from languages he invented for Middle-earth. Keeping these names straight can be overwhelming to all but the most avid Middle-earth lore masters. I encourage you to make liberal use of this book's index when you come up against an odd name and you're just not sure who or what it is.

Still, I do expect that many of you may feel snowed under by the sheer weight of unfamiliar terms bandied about in the book. For this, I apologize ahead of time. It seems to be the nature of Tolkien's beast to inundate the reader in complex storylines muddied by tons of Elvish names that are almost impossible to keep straight. I know that in my earlier days with *The Silmarillion,* I was fully convinced that I'd never be able to remember the difference between the Kingdom of Gondolin and Doriath — let alone keep Fingolfin straight from Finarfin or tell the Teleri Elves from the Noldor. In time, though, I gained the ability to realize the larger back story without being overwhelmed by the particular names and places involved. Slowly but surely I was able to plug in these details.

I advise you to adopt a similar strategy in dealing with this book's material. As much as possible, don't worry about keeping the character names and place names straight. Just accept that you won't immediately understand all the references (and may not be able to keep them straight even after looking them up in the index). Instead, try to keep your focus on the larger point I'm making about the characters and places. In time, you may be surprised to find that you're beginning to understand who and what and where and, more importantly, how they all fit together into the tapestry of Middle-earth (and when that day comes, if you're like me, you'll be amazed at the intricacy of Tolkien's weaving).

How This Book Is Organized

This book is divided into six parts (so you get to enjoy six Rich Tennant cartoons). Each part addresses a different major component of Tolkien's Middle-earth, from its geography to the major themes and myths it teaches. Two components, the beings and themes of Middle-earth in Parts II and V, respectively, are more complicated than the rest and so contain multiple chapters that you can visit in any order. Three others are two-chapter affairs in which the first chapter gives a more general overview, and the second goes into a little more detail. The last part offers three handy top ten lists.

Part I: The Geography of Middle-earth

This part tries to make you feel at home in Middle-earth by introducing you to its geography. Chapter 1 gives you a general orientation to Tolkien's Middle-earth, including its possible linguistic origin and its existence as a world of fantasy, mythology, history, and language. Chapter 2 looks at specific lands of Middle-earth that feature prominently in Tolkien's tales.

Part II: The Beings of Middle-earth

The eight chapters in this part acquaint you with the many different types of beings that populate the lands of Middle-earth (only some of whom are human), pairing them up with the lands they inhabit and pointing out their place in Tolkien tales.

Part III: The History of Middle-earth

This part gives an outline of the enormous history of Middle-earth. Chapter 11 covers the earlier ages, which appropriately are more like legend and mythology in nature than historical fact. Chapter 12 covers the three major historical ages that Tolkien imagined for his world.

Part IV: The Languages of Middle-earth

This part deals with the role of language in Middle-earth. Chapter 13 investigates Tolkien's general use of language and how his ideas on its importance and power compare with traditional ideas held by ancient peoples. Chapter 14 examines the characteristics of the actual languages that Tolkien invented for the various races of Middle-earth.

Part V: The Themes and Mythology of Middle-earth

This part forms the core of the book. These nine chapters explore the major themes and mythologies embodied in Tolkien's stories about Middle-earth. The topics here are diverse as the stories themselves: good and evil, death and immortality, true love, heroism, fate and free will, the Ring and its relation to other ring myths, environmental concerns, and gender and sex.

Part VI: The Part of Tens

This last part gives you a few at-a-glance chapters filled with facts for easy ingestion. Chapter 24 gives a blow-by-blow account of the top ten battles in the War of the Ring chronicled in *The Lord of the Rings*. Chapter 25 is a list of my top ten Web sites for learning more about Tolkien's Middle-earth. Chapter 26 gives you my top ten differences between Tolkien's book and Peter Jackson's movie versions of *The Lord of the Rings*.

Icons Used in This Book

Icons warn of information of very narrow or specific interest. Most of them occur in front of the sidebars that are strewn throughout the text. They quickly identify the following types of extraneous information:

Indicates some sort of idea, character, symbol, or meaning that recurs in Tolkien's Middle-earth.

Denotes obscure or strange facts about origins or connections that may or may not be of interest (depending on how deep you're into this stuff).

Points out heavy-duty language associations that I'm trying to make. Stay clear if language isn't your thing.

Signals a place where there is lot of specific detail or history. When you're dealing with Tolkien, who revels in cross-associations and fine points, it can be a bit much for all except hardcore Tolkien enthusiasts.

Where to Go from Here

The immediate answer to this question is simple: Before you do anything else, check out the cartoons at the beginning of the six parts of the book. After that, it depends on what you want to know. Unlike Tolkien's books, this one isn't meant to be read from cover to cover. You can pick and choose according to what you're keen to know about Middle-earth. If you tend not to skip around, I hope you find the progression of topics a natural one that gets you primed and ready to explore the major themes and mythologies. Enjoy!

Part I
The Geography of Middle-earth

The 5th Wave   By Rich Tennant

AFTER SEVERAL DAYS OF ARDUOUS TREKKING, FRODO AND SAM GET A SIGN THAT THEY'RE APPROACHING THE FORTRESS OF SAURON.

MORDOR HOUSE OF PIZZA

In this part . . .

Where exactly is Tolkien's Middle-earth, and what kind of world is it anyway? Part I provides answers to these questions by giving you a general introduction to the many realms and lands that Middle-earth encompasses and, in so doing, orients you to the rest of the book. This part investigates the relationship between the world of Middle-earth and our world, while giving you an overview of the wide and varied landscape that this world entails.

Chapter 1
The Worlds of Middle-earth

*1*n its broadest sense, geography is the study of the physical features of the world as well as its biological and cultural characteristics. When attempting to deal with the "geography" of a fantasy world like Middle-earth, as envisioned by J.R.R. Tolkien, you're almost compelled to use this wider definition, even if your only goal is to get an overview of its many features. For Tolkien's Middle-earth is never just one of physical geography filled with strange lands, weird creatures, and unfamiliar cultures. As Tolkien conceived it over the better part of his life, Middle-earth is also a world rich in its own mythology, history, and languages.

This chapter gives an overview of the various worlds that await you in your journey to Tolkien's Middle-earth, while at the same time familiarizing you with how these realms are covered in the rest of the book. It opens by exploring the questions of where exactly Middle-earth is located and why Tolkien chose the name Middle-earth for his fantasy world. The chapter then looks at Middle-earth as a fantasy realm in light of Tolkien's ideas on the importance of fairy-tale in our lives. The chapter concludes with an overview of the creatures, history, and languages with which Tolkien filled his world of Middle-earth.

Where in the World Is Middle-earth?

You may well wonder why it's important at all to locate Middle-earth. Does it really matter whether Middle-earth is a future world in another galaxy or a Europe long gone? Would it really detract from your enjoyment of Bilbo's journey to the Lonely Mountain or Frodo's quest from the Shire to Mount Doom if you found out that Middle-earth were nowhere on this earth?

I happen to feel that Tolkien drew Middle-earth so well in *The Hobbit* and told the story of *The Lord of the Rings* so tightly that it wouldn't matter a whit if he had started off either story with the now famous declaration from George Lucas' *Star Wars* saga, "Long, long ago in a galaxy far, far away . . ." On the other hand, coming to know how much Middle-earth owes to past European sagas, legends, and languages can only enhance appreciation of his works and deepen understanding of their many lessons.

Associating Middle-earth with our world and not some alien planet or invisible dimension was very important to Tolkien. When pressed for the location of Middle-earth (as fans and critics continually did), Tolkien often replied that Middle-earth most definitely refers to lands of this world. In his letter commenting on a review of *The Lord of the Rings* by W. H. Auden, he wrote, "Middle-earth is not an imaginary world." He then declared that his Middle-earth is "the objectively real world" as opposed to an imaginary world such as Fairyland or invisible ones such as Heaven or Hell.

In another letter responding to a draft of a *Daily Telegraph* article for which he was interviewed, Tolkien said that the stories in *The Hobbit* and *The Lord of the Rings* take place in the "north-west of 'Middle-earth,' equivalent to the coastlands of Europe and the north shores of the Mediterranean." He then went on to fix some of the primary locations in his books by stating that if you placed Hobbiton and Rivendell at the latitude of Oxford (which was his intention), then Minas Tirith, some 600 miles south in Gondor, would be at approximately the same latitude as Florence, Italy. This puts the Mouths of the river Anduin and the ancient Gondorian city of Pelagir at about the same latitude as the fabled city of Troy (made famous in Homer's heroic epic poem the *Iliad* and located on the west coast of modern-day Turkey).

To get an idea of these spatial relationships, see Figure 1-1, which shows the western coastline of Middle-earth and points out the specific parallel locations that Tolkien pinpointed in his letter. From this map, you'd be hard pressed to match any of Middle-earth's physical features with those of modern-day Europe. Tolkien would have explained this obvious discrepancy as the result of changes in coastal geography during the time that has elapsed since his epic adventures took place. To me, it's sort of like the difference between Earth's Jurassic age and the Middle Ages — not too much looks the same, but it's the same old Earth.

Figure 1-1:
Middle-
earth's
coastline
super-
imposed on
Western
Europe.

The Meaning of Middle-earth

In the letter commenting on a *New York Times* book review, Tolkien stated that the name *Middle-earth* is a "just a use of Middle English *midden-erd* (or *erthe*), altered from Old English *Middangeard,* the name for the inhabited lands of Men 'between the seas' . . ."

The origin of the term "Middle-earth"

Midden-erde (or *erthe*), however, is good old Middle English for "middle-earth." As Tolkien pointed out, it hails from an earlier form, *middangeard,* which literally means the "middle yard" in Old English or Anglo-Saxon, the language Tolkien taught at Oxford University. *Middangeard* was taken to mean, like *oikumenos,* the "inhabited world." It is rumored that Tolkien first happened upon this term as an undergraduate student when he read the following lines in *Crist (Christ)*, an Old English poem attributed to a bard named Cynewulf:

```
∞ala ∞arendel engla beorhtast ofer middangeard monnum sended
```

In my translation, this reads, "Hail, Earendel, the brightest of angels sent to the world of men!" In this early form, Middle-earth was not only the inhabited lands in the midst of the encircling seas, but also the middle ground between Heaven above and Hell below. This vertical dimension of the early European Christian Middle-earth is entirely missing from Tolkien's — even though you'd be hard pressed to find a more devout Catholic Christian.

"Stuck in the middle again . . . "

At the time when *The Hobbit* and *The Lord of the Rings* take place, the inhabited lands of Middle-earth are surrounded on three sides by wastelands and on the west by open sea. To the north lies the Ice Bay of Forochel, and beyond that is the frozen Northern Waste; to the east is Rhûn, populated by the barbaric Easterlings. To the south you find the vast deserts of Harad, populated by dark-skinned peoples called the Haradrim ("Southerns"). In *The Lord of the Rings,* both Easterlings and Southrons often make war on the free peoples of Middle-earth and are allied with Sauron, Dark Lord of the eastern realm of Mordor, who is the greatest threat to freedom in Middle-earth.

On the west, many of the lands of Middle-earth, just like many lands of Europe, have borders that adjoin the sea. According to Tolkien's thinking, at the time of *The Hobbit* and *The Lord of the Rings,* you could sail west and not find any other land masses (you certainly wouldn't discover the Americas). In earlier ages, though, sailing directly west would bring you to the island of Númenor, the ancient homeland of the people who end up settling the northern and southern coasts of Middle-earth. And west of Númenor lay the continent of Aman — the so-called Blessed Realm or Undying Lands (see Chapter 2). Aman is where two types of immortal beings, the Valar and Elves, dwell together. By the Third Age, the one in which *The Hobbit* and *The Lord of the Rings* take place, the island of Númenor has sunk beneath the sea, and Aman, removed from the physical plane of the world, is accessible only by the magic White Ships of the Elves (see Chapter 12).

Viewed from this perspective, you can start to understand how the peoples of Tolkien's Middle-earth perceive their lands as being encircled by limiting forces, some of which are hostile. This viewpoint is perhaps not so unlike the Anglo-Saxons before they came to Britain, when they still dwelt along the northwestern coast of Europe in the lands now known as Denmark and north-west Germany. At that time, they were surrounded on three sides by poten-tially hostile tribes and the open sea on the other. The situation didn't change much when they got to England, except that the sea was mostly at their back with the hostile Celts in front and on either side of them. I think that much of the orientation of Middle-earth's geography is rooted in the perspective of Tolkien's Anglo-Saxon ancestors, whose language he knew so well.

Middle-earth as a Fantasy World

Fantasy is an attempt to create a complete, imaginary world with its own crea-tures, cultures, and lands that are governed by their own set of physical laws and guided by their own morals and principles. For Tolkien, fantasy was defi-nitely akin to the world of the fairies. *Fairy* comes from the Middle English *faerie,* perhaps related to Old English *faeger,* meaning "beautiful," "lovely," and "fair." Tolkien's fairy world, although certainly containing its share of Elves and Dwarves, diverges greatly from the modern view of fairies as diminutive folk — the "little people" of many fairytales. In Tolkien's Middle-earth, you find no brownies, pixies, Tinkerbell-like fairies, or Snow White-type Dwarves. Moreover, his trolls don't charge to cross their bridges, although his dragons do breathe fire and his wizards have magic staffs.

In place of pointy-shoed Elves dressed in green like bonnie leprechauns and Dwarves in floppy stocking caps shouldering pickaxes and singing "Heigh-Ho, Heigh-Ho," Tolkien presents tall, shining Elves with a complex, not altogether beautiful history side by side with serious Dwarves who not only delve into caves but create magnificent underground cities

Interestingly enough, Tolkien's mythology may well explain the modern, Disneyesque view of Elves and Dwarves as the natural outgrowth of the great stresses to which his fairy world had been subjected. For the Middle-earth of *The Hobbit* and *The Lord of the Rings* is in the throes of a great upheaval, a battle between good and evil that threatens to foist the race of Men (Tolkien's term, not mine) onto center stage as the dominant culture at the expense of the other beings of Middle-earth.

As a result of this transition, the fairy or magic aspect of Middle-earth in the Third Age — especially as embodied in the Elves — is in danger of disappear-ing and being replaced by an age of almost total reliance on science and tech-nology, a world as rich in know-how as it is poor in spirit. This is, of course, an age we can all readily recognize, for it is the one we live in.

On the nature of the fairytale

Tolkien had definite ideas about the essential nature of fairytales, which he set forth in a 1939 lecture at St. Andrew's University entitled "On Fairy-Stories." In this lecture, he argues against the demotion of the fairytale to an insignificant tale fit only for children (or very childish adults). Doing so, he argues, is neither fair to the stories nor the children.

According to Tolkien's lecture, a good or successful fairytale exhibits three important structural characteristics:

- **Recovery** of the appreciation of the simple and humble things in our world
- **Escape** from one's narrow and distorted view of the world
- **Consolation** that leads to a kind of joy even in the face of continuing evil in the world

In Tolkien's three features of a good fairytale, I see also the essential qualities of religion. This should come as no surprise — Tolkien was a devout Catholic all his life. Anyone who has read Tolkien's *The Lord of the Rings* or seen Peter Jackson's astounding films inspired by the book will instantly recognize the themes of recovery, escape, and consolation in them.

To many readers, including me, *The Lord of the Rings* is a fantasy or fairytale of the highest order simply because it so successfully and completely fulfills the tasks of recovery, escape, and consolation described by Tolkien. Through its heroic tales, we recover a deep appreciation of life's simple pleasures, especially the power of the love and fidelity inherent in fellowship. In this deepened appreciation, we temporarily escape the fetters of our self-centered desires that so constrict our idea of the world and distort our place in it. As a result of this escape, however brief, we find consolation in our broader outlook on the world, one that puts evil in a place where it is neither understated nor exaggerated. From that vantage point, we have the chance to experience a type of joy that transcends the cares of the world by celebrating life's simple pleasures. See Part V for my thoughts on the particular themes in Tolkien's works that employ these elements and bring them to life.

Many criticize Tolkien's works as escapist, unrealistic fantasies that promote the avoidance of responsibility in the real world. I think that these critics confuse the escape the works are intended to provide with a more general *escapism*. In my opinion, a work such as *The Lord of the Rings* primarily provides an escape from the distorted viewpoint of utter hopelessness and pessimism that so often threatens to overtake us in this postmodern age. But it is a far cry from a call to escape our responsibilities in the world — *The Lord of the Rings* is rather a work that enables us to see that each of us can and does make a difference in the world.

The fairytale as "sub-creation"

In the same "On Fairy-Stories" lecture, Tolkien describes the good fairytale as a product of "sub-creation," where the author successfully creates a secondary world that has its own "inner consistency of reality." As a Christian, Tolkien saw the primary world (what we so often refer to as the "real world") as the creation of God. Because man specifically was created in the image of God, he inherited the ability to create imaginary or secondary worlds such as Middle-earth. The key to this sub-creation is the power of human language, which, of course, as a linguist, was Tolkien's specialty.

Tolkien argues that "sub-creation" stems from two basic human needs:

- **To survey** the depths of space and time
- **To heal** the separation of mankind from nature

It's no wonder, then, that Tolkien's Middle-earth is rich in languages and detailed geography and history — all of which enable us to explore the depths of both space and time. Mankind's need to heal our alienation from nature is often expressed in Western culture as the need to return to the Garden of Eden (as in Joni Mitchell's song "Woodstock": ". . . we've got to get ourselves back to the Garden").

Middle-earth as a Mythic World

Myths are a culture's attempt to express in story form the ideas that are most important to it. Most myths deal with cosmic subjects such as the creation and ultimate destruction of the world system. They also deal with universal themes like heroism and love (see Part V).

Because myths are often just as concerned with meaning as with plot line, they rely heavily on symbolism and poetic language to convey their meanings. The myths of many cultures appear as epic poems or songs (sometimes referred to as *lays*) that were sung by troubadours and wandering minstrels long before they were ever committed to paper.

Unfortunately, today when you refer to something as a myth, you normally mean that it's some sort of illusion or fiction — some kind of "tall tale." When some people refer to something as a myth, they usually mean a naive story that our "primitive" forebears told to explain some phenomenon that they couldn't otherwise explain (because they weren't yet equipped with logic). Myth in this sense is a childish explanation of a phenomenon that is ultimately to be replaced by a more learned and accurate account.

For Tolkien, a myth was no more an illogical fable than the fairytale was an escapist fantasy. For him, myths were the best way to convey certain truths — especially those of a religious nature — that would otherwise be inexpressible. Myths, of course, use very different language than logical discourse does. They tend, especially the older ones, to be couched in poetic language coming as they often do in lyric poems (odes) or ballads (lays).

Poetry, unlike most prose, is rich in symbol and relies heavily on metaphor (a figure of speech implying a similarity between two unlike things, as in "drowning in sorrow") and simile (a figure of speech using "like" or "as" to compare two unlike things, as in "life is like a bowl of cherries").

For example, say I were writing an autobiography and wanted to start it off by expressing the opinion that my life had been no bed of roses (note the metaphor). I could do this through either of the following sentences:

- ✔ In my life, I've had many dragons to slay.
- ✔ In my life, I've had many obstacles to overcome.

The first sentence is more poetic because "dragons to slay" conjures up the image of a knight in shining armor displaying extraordinary bravery and strength in valiantly battling a huge reptilian monster. The second sentence expresses the same thought, but much, much more abstractly and less evocatively. Yet both statements make essentially the same point and are readily understood even though none of us (or, at least, just a very few) believes in the existence of dragons.

"Fortunate" calamities in myth and legend

Tolkien coined the term *eucatastrophe* to describe the unforeseen twists and turns that often take place at the end of our favorite fairytales and legends. For example, the villain's evil becomes an instrument in his own downfall (what I call, "when bad things go good"). This sort of "fortunate" calamity (*eu* is a Greek prefix that means "sweet" or "good") is a favored element in many of Tolkien's myths and legends.

The Lord of the Rings, for example, delivers its fair share of "fortunate" calamities — Sauron's forging of the One Ring, for example (see Chapter 21). Placing so much of his power in this external object gives the heroes a chance to do away with him once and for all simply by destroying his Ring.

Another important "fortunate" calamity occurs in the story of Gollum, who, it turns out, becomes instrumental in the Ring's destruction (and therefore Sauron's as well). This act, which ends up saving all of Middle-earth, is the culmination of Gollum's betrayal of Frodo at Cirith Ungol and his later attack on him at Mount Doom — despicable acts all stemming from Gollum's uncontrollable need to have the Ring for himself.

Background myths of "The Lord of the Rings"

Most of Tolkien's great mythological content, however, occurs in the so-called "back story" told in *The Silmarillion,* a book that was published posthumously by his son Christopher. In fact, the story of the War of the Ring chronicled in *The Lord of the Rings* is but a small part of the history of Middle-earth recorded in *The Silmarillion.*

The Silmarillion is essentially a compilation of many of Tolkien's writings (some of them very early) about the ancient history of Middle-earth, to which is appended the myth of the downfall of Númenor in the Second Age and the War of the Ring in the Third Age (detailed in *The Lord of the Rings*).

The Silmarillion is a very important book for understanding Middle-earth; but many find it not nearly as easy to read as *The Hobbit* and *The Lord of the Rings* — a number of its tales read more like fleshed-out outlines than actual stories. It begins with Tolkien's beautiful creation myth (see Chapter 11) in a book called the *Ainulindalë,* and then accounts for the coming of the immortal beings the Valar into Middle-earth in a book entitled *Valaquenta.*

The bulk of *The Silmarillion,* however, is taken up by the next book, *Quenta Silmarillion,* which tells of the creation of the most beautiful jewels ever made by Man or Elf: the Silmarils. It recounts their subsequent theft and the war waged for their recovery. Many of the tales in this particular book deal with traditional mythic elements such as heroism, true love, and tragic fate, but with what I've come to call the "Tolkien twist," where Tolkien preserves some of the basic mythic storyline but reverses key elements, perhaps because he felt that the original myth somehow got it wrong or that his telling improved upon its moral (see Part V for multiple examples).

The great battle that ended this long and involved war over the Silmarils also drastically altered the geography of Middle-earth. Almost all of the western land mass called Beleriand was submerged in a great cataclysm that created Middle-earth's western coastline. In fact, all that's left of Beleriand by the time of *The Lord of the Rings* is a small strip of land west of Ered Luin ("Blue Mountains"). This means the geography that you take so much for granted in *The Lord of the Rings* is in fact, according to *The Silmarillion,* rather recent.

On the heels of the *Quenta Silmarillion* comes Tolkien's version of another persistent myth in Western civilization: that of Atlantis and its sinking beneath the sea. What's so fascinating about Tolkien's version, entitled the *Akallebêth,* or the Downfall of Númenor, is that Númenor's destruction is tied directly into the storyline of *The Hobbit* and *The Lord of the Rings*. Instead of just another interesting version of the Atlantis myth, Tolkien wove his account directly into the story of Sauron's attempt to subjugate Middle-earth, which is what *The Hobbit* and *The Lord of the Rings* are all about.

Underscoring this connection is the fact that the last book of *The Silmarillion* is entitled *Of the Rings of Power and the Third Age*, which is basically a 19-page outline of the events told in much fuller story form in *The Hobbit* (300-plus pages) and *The Lord of the Rings* (more than 1,000 pages).

Middle-earth as a World of Diverse Beings

Much of the appeal of Tolkien's Middle-earth comes from the charm of the diverse beings and races in it. As you discover in Part II, which is devoted to the main types of Middle-earth beings, Tolkien's creatures literally run the gamut from angels (the Ainur, or "Holy Ones," discussed in Chapter 3) to devils (Sauron and his Orc hordes, dealt with in Chapter 10).

In between these two extremes are the more fascinating and endearing creatures of Middle-earth: Elves, Dwarves, hobbits, Ents, and, oh yes, Men. What some readers find most appealing about *The Lord of the Rings* (I know I'm in this crowd) is the way Tolkien combines the action of the story with a sort of hobbit travelogue. The four hobbit compatriots — Frodo, Sam, Pippin, and Merry (see Chapter 7) — make first contact with all types of beings, many of whom they've heard about only through legend and who have likewise heard of hobbits only in their wildest myths. Tolkien surely had fun, for example, having the hobbits Merry and Pippin explain the nature of their kind (and the etymology of the term *hobbit*) to such different creatures as the tree-like Ents (see Chapter 9) and the Horse Lords of Rohan (see Chapter 5).

This approach enables readers to experience many of the unfamiliar creatures of Middle-earth just as the hobbits do. Readers get to become more intimate with the hobbits and their ways while simultaneously seeing how the hobbits' contacts with wondrous and frightening creatures enlarge the scope of their world beyond the safe and narrow confines of the Shire. At the same time, Tolkien enlarges our worldview well beyond its normal boundaries. In this way, he provides an effective avenue for us to experience first the discovery and escape aspects of the story and ultimately the consolation aspect as well — all of which he considered so important to a successful fantasy tale (see the section "On the nature of the fairytale" earlier in this chapter).

Middle-earth as a Historical World

History attempts to answer the essential questions of who, what, when, and where. So to make his world as realistic as possible and, perhaps, more palatable to contemporary readers schooled in the rudiments of historical analysis, Tolkien endowed Middle-earth with a very rich history in addition to its abundant mythology (see Part III for timelines of the most important events in Tolkien's various historical ages).

Tolkien establishes Middle-earth as a historical world through a convenient fiction in which all the stories of Middle-earth and its various ages come from a single written source: the Red Book of Westmarch (so called because it was bound in red leather). It's in this book that Bilbo recorded his adventures with the Dwarves on the quest to recover their treasure at the Lonely Mountain, a tale he gave many titles to, including *My Diary, My Unexpected Adventure,* and *There and Back Again,* but which we all know best as *The Hobbit.*

Frodo, Bilbo's heir, takes over the Red Book and upon his return to the Shire after his adventures fills most of its remaining pages with his story and that of his compatriots Sam, Pippin, and Merry. Frodo entitles this part of the Red Book "The Downfall of the Lord of the Rings and the Return of the King." Once Frodo finishes chronicling the War of the Ring and the better part of the Third Age, he turns the book over to his faithful servant and friend Sam, the last Ring-bearer. Sam records his own part of the story and the first part of the history of the Fourth Age that is now dawning.

In *The Lord of the Rings,* when Sam finally leaves Middle-earth to sail west to Aman (see Chapter 2), following Bilbo and Frodo, he leaves the Red Book in the care of the wardens of the Shire. In the prologue to *The Lord of the Rings,* Tolkien underscores the historical nature of the Red Book by telling us about other versions of the book, which contain different and even conflicting stories that were supposedly prepared by Pippin's descendents and from other sources provided by Merry.

It's difficult to adequately evaluate the value of this historical veneer that Tolkien created. For many readers, it just adds a superfluous layer to an already complicated subject. For others, it provides yet another example of the almost unbelievable amount of thinking and detail that Tolkien put into this fantasy world.

For me, the historical evolution of Middle-earth — starting with the almost prehistorical "days of yore" of the Valarian Ages and progressing to the daily and even hourly historical recording of the Third Age and the War of the Ring — is in harmony with the underlying story. It mirrors Tolkien's story of transition from the fairy realm of the Elves to the historical dominion of Men, when the accurate record-keeping of science and technology ultimately submerges and reigns supreme over myth and epic poetry.

Middle-earth as a World of Language

When contemplating the many worlds that Middle-earth contains, you'd be wise to never overlook the fact that whatever else Middle-earth is, it is first and foremost a world of language. This is something that anyone who starts reading *The Lord of the Rings* discovers almost immediately. In fact, for many a reader, the cascade of foreign names and places, often made more confusing by Tolkien's insistence on giving each character and land several names, is a very tall stumbling block.

Diverse terminology is, of course, only one example of the magnitude of language in Tolkien's Middle-earth. In addition, you actually encounter bits and pieces of languages that he invented for the various beings (see Chapter 14). It's not at all unusual in *The Lord of the Rings* to be reading along only to have one of the hobbits or Aragorn suddenly spout off in Elvish — only some of which Tolkien bothers to translate into English. I've always presumed that Tolkien didn't translate those remarks where understanding them had no bearing on the story — that they just add to the realism of the situation, because so few of us speak good Elvish anymore.

As a linguist who was accomplished in many languages, Tolkien found his true passion in languages. Indeed, his curiosity over the etymology of particular terms itself is no doubt the real origin of Tolkien's Middle-earth. (Etymology is the study of the history and roots of a word.) His delight in such origins motivated and enabled him to devise complex stories to explain particular names and words. He was an "etymological mythmaker," if you will. We probably owe all of Middle-earth's wondrous beings, inspiring myths, and fascinating histories to Tolkien's passion for language and his need to explain why things are named as they are.

Chapter 2

The Lands of Middle-earth and Beyond

*T*olkien's worlds are as varied as their inhabitants, only some of whom are humans. The existence and configuration of these lands change through the various ages of the world (see Part III for details on Middle-earth history).

In the Third Age — during which *The Hobbit* and *The Lord of the Rings* take place — the lands of Middle-earth extend from the frigid wastelands of the north known as Forodwaith ("Land of the North People") or Forochel ("Northern Ice") to the sweltering deserts of the south known as Haradwaith ("Land of the South People"). In between these two extremes, you find the wide-ranging lands where the stories told in those two books take place.

This chapter gives you a geographic overview of the most important lands of Middle-earth. These lands extend from the Shire, beloved home of the Hobbits in the northwest, south to the kingdom of Gondor, the last realm of the ancient kings of the Westernesse, and over east to Mordor — the dreaded domain of the Enemy. In addition, this chapter covers three realms that are no longer physically a part of Middle-earth in the Third Age, but which are often referred to in *The Lord of the Rings* and have bearing on its story. They are

  ✔ **Aman,** the realm of the Valar ("Holy Ones") in the Uttermost West that has been removed from the Circles of the World

✔ **Beleriand,** a western region that contained many significant Elf and Dwarf kingdoms until it was flooded and sank at the end of the First Age

✔ **Númenor,** the island continent of the Dúnedain ("Men of the Westernesse") that was sunk after their vainglorious attack on Aman

When Númenor sank (Tolkien's version of the Atlantis myth), Aman was removed from the physical plane of the world, and the ancestors of Men such as Aragorn and Boromir sought refuge in Middle-earth where they established Arnor and Gondor.

Eriador, the Home of the Shire

Eriador ("Land of the Single Expanse") comprises the northwestern region of Middle-earth between the Blue Mountains (Ered Luin) on the west and the Misty Mountains on the east. Eriador begins just south of the Forodwaith, the Northern Wastes, and extends south to the White Mountains that form the northern border of Gondor. Eriador encompasses many places that are crucial in *The Hobbit* and *The Lord of the Rings*, the most important of which just happens to be the Shire.

Arnor, the Land of the King

Arnor, the Royal Land, is the name given the northern kingdom founded by Elendil after he and his sons Isildur and Anárion fled Númenor before its destruction near the close of the Second Age (see Chapter 12). Arnor's original royal city (or capital) was Annúminas, located on the southern shore of Lake Evendim. Eventually, the city of Fornost ("Norburg") became the capital, and in that year Arnor was split into three separate kingdoms by the sons of King Eärendur, the tenth king after Elendil. These new kingdoms of Arnor were called Arthedain, Cardolan, and Rhudaur.

Arnor was home to three of the seven palantíri, the Seeing Stones, which were brought from Númenor. The Seeing Stones enable the user to see things through its fellow stones — kind of like a multiple video feed. They were placed in diverse parts of Arnor and Gondor to keep an eye on their borders. One palantir was placed in the watchtower called Elostirion upon Emyn Beraid ("Tower Hills") in the west of Arnor near the Grey Havens, another in Annúminas, and a third in the watchtower of Amon Sûl ("Weathertop").

Arnor is also the home of the Shire, where hobbits live (discussed later in this chapter). King Argeleb II of Arthedain granted permission to the hobbits to cross the River Baranduin ("Brandywine") and settle there in the year 1601 of the Third Age (which became the year 1 in Shire Reckoning).

TRIVIA

Arnor and Charlemagne's Empire

The subdivision of Arnor into Arthedain, Cardolan, and Rhudaur for the three sons of King Eärendur is reminiscent of the story of Charlemagne and the founding of the original Holy Roman Empire. Charlemagne left behind a great empire that encompassed almost all of western and central Europe, including modern-day France, Germany, and Italy. Charlemagne's empire was billed as the Christian successor to the Western Roman Empire (hence, Holy Roman Empire). However, it didn't survive long intact. Upon the death of his only son Louis in 840, the empire was divided among Charlemagne's three grandsons (similar to Arnor's division upon the death of King Eärendur). This division set up the separate kingdoms of West Francia, the Middle Kingdom, and East Francia — very much like the Arnorian kingdoms of Arthedain, Cardolan, and Rhudaur.

Angmar, the Witch Kingdom

Angmar is the kingdom at the northern base of the Misty Mountains that arose in the year 1300 of the Third Age (see Chapter 12 for more on the dating systems). It is often referred to as the Witch Kingdom because it was ruled by a king known as the Witch-king or Witch-lord.

Angmar made almost constant war on Arnor. Although Angmar shattered the power of Arnor's kingdoms and eventually captured Fornost, it was ultimately defeated by a combined army of Men and Elves in the Battle of Fornost (T.A. 1975). Unfortunately, the Witch-king escaped the destruction of Angmar. He fled to the south and later laid siege to Minas Ithil ("Tower of the Moon"), where his true identity as the Lord of the Nine Ringwraiths was exposed (see "Minas Morgul, the Tower of Sorcery" later in this chapter).

The Shire, home of the hobbits

The Shire is the beloved home of the hobbits. *Shire* comes from the Old English *scir,* meaning "district," usually administrative such as a county. The hobbits themselves call it Súza (see Chapter 14 for more on this).

The Shire is rather centrally located in Arnor between the Brandywine River on the east and the Far Downs on the west, and just south of Annúminas. The Shire is divided into four Farthings, with the very original titles of East, West, North, and South.

The Shire as our touchstone in Middle-earth

The Shire surely evokes the quaintness and charm of 19th century English villages. In so doing, it functions as our touchstone in Middle-earth, enabling the reader to judge the strangeness of other lands and beings and become involved emotionally in the outcome of the tales. In *The Lord of the Rings,* we're deeply concerned over the possible victory of Sauron and Saruman because it would be the death knell of idyllic life in the Shire.

Many of the most important locations in *The Lord of the Rings* are located in the West Farthing of the Shire, including the villages of Hobbiton, Bywater, and Michel Delving. Bag End, the burrowed home of Bilbo and Frodo Baggins, is right above the village of Hobbiton.

As described by Tolkien in *The Hobbit* and *The Lord of the Rings,* the Shire is blessed with rich farmland, which provides the hobbits with an idyllic way of life (see Chapter 7). Life in the Shire is pretty much free of the general strife found elsewhere in Middle-earth — until the War of the Ring.

Tolkien's naming of the four districts of the Shire as Farthings is a play on words. The word *farthing* denotes something of small value, or "a quarter of a penny." Modern English *farthing* comes from the Old English *feorthung,* which simply meant a fourth, so that the four Farthings of the Shire are simply its four fourths (which, let's hope, do make a whole).

The Barrow-downs

The Barrow-downs are the great barrow (mound) graves that house the dead of Arnor, located east of the Old Forest and Buckland on the east side of the Brandywine River, near Bree. With the rise of Angmar, ruled by the Witch-lord, evil spirits called Barrow-wights came to haunt the Barrow-downs. These spirits attack Frodo, Sam, Merry, and Pippin and nearly end their quest.

A *barrow* refers specifically to a mound of earth or stones over the remains of the dead. It comes from the Old English *beorg,* meaning "hill." *Barrow,* therefore, is often part of the names of hills in England. The word *wight* (pronounced like "white") is also Old English for "anything" or "something." Eventually, *wight* came to mean a "creature" or "thing."

The village of Bree

At the crossing of the Great East Road and the North Road, well east of the Shire beyond the Barrow-downs, lies the village of Bree. One of the main towns of Bree-land, Bree is inhabited by Men and hobbits. Bree is important to the plot of *The Lord of the Rings* because of its famous inn, the Prancing Pony. This is where Frodo, Sam, Merry, and Pippin meet Strider (Aragorn), who helps them make it to the Elf stronghold of Rivendell.

Rivendell, the Last Homely House

Rivendell, called Imladris ("Valley Cleft" in Elvish), is the home of Elrond Half-elven (see Chapter 4). In *The Hobbit,* Tolkien refers to Rivendell as the Last Homely House west of the Mountains — meaning the Misty Mountains. As such, Rivendell is a stronghold for the Elves who live there. It's also a refuge for travelers such as Bilbo and his Dwarf party in *The Hobbit* and later Frodo and his comrades in *The Lord of the Rings*. Rivendell lies at the foot of the western side of the Misty Mountains, in a valley bordered by two tributaries of the Loudwater River. Rivendell is protected from its enemies by Elven spells that cause the river to rise on Elrond's command, washing away invaders, such as the Ringwraiths in *The Lord of the Rings*.

Rivendell is important in *The Lord of the Rings* because it is where a great council of Elves, Men, and Dwarves decide that the One Ring of Power must be destroyed in the fires of Mount Doom in Mordor.

Eregion, the Land of Holly

After most of Beleriand was destroyed in the War of Wrath at the end of the First Age (see Chapter 12), many of the surviving Elves made their way to Eregion ("Land of Holly," called Hollin by Men). Eregion is in Eriador, west of the Misty Mountains, near the Dwarf kingdom of Khazad-dûm, and east of Rhudaur below the Loudwater River.

The Elves of the Second Age established a single city in Eregion named Ost-in-Edhil ("Fortress of the Elves"). This city was connected to Khazad-dûm by the Old Moria Road that led to Moria's west gate.

Eregion has the dubious honor of being the place where Sauron tricked the smiths of Ost-in-Edhil into crafting the Rings of Power. When the Elf-smiths kept the Three Elven-rings after learning of the One Ring that would control theirs, Sauron made war on Eregion. He laid waste to the entire region and ultimately slew the Elf-smiths, including the master craftsman Celebrimbor. (See Chapter 21 for more on Sauron's Ring and the other Rings of Power.)

Khazad-dûm, or the Mines of Moria

Khazad-dûm ("Mansions of the Dwarves") is the oldest Dwarf kingdom in Middle-earth. It lies due east of Ost-in-Edhil in Eregion and consists of a series of vast caverns tunneled under the Misty Mountains connecting the east and west sides. Here, the Dwarves mined mithril ("grey brilliance"), a rare ore of inestimable value used to make chain mail (Bilbo brings back a mithril vest from his adventures and gives it to Frodo to wear on his quest). Also called Moria ("Dark Abyss"), Khazad-dûm is the ancestral home of Durin the Deathless, one of the seven Dwarf Fathers (see Chapter 6). Durin began delving its caverns after discovering natural caves on the east side of the Misty Mountains. After the destruction of most of Beleriand at the end of the First Age, Dwarf survivors from Belegost and Nogrod dwelt in Khazad-dûm.

During the Second Age, as Sauron made war on the Elves of Eregion after they forged the Rings of Power for him, the Dwarves sealed the west door to Khazad-dûm. During the Third Age, the Dwarves delved too deep and released a demon called a Balrog (see Chapter 10). This Balrog, with the help of Orcs, overcame the Dwarf kingdom and slew Durin. This same Balrog confronts the Fellowship on their passage through Moria to Lothlórien. Gandalf battles it to the death after being dragged down from Durin's Bridge.

Rhovanion, the Wilderland

Rhovanion ("Wilderland") is the wide expanse of land east of the Misty Mountains and west of the Sea of Rhûn ("East Sea"). Rhovanion extends approximately as far north as the Grey Mountains and south to about the Ash Mountains, Mordor's northern border. Rhovanion encompasses the great Mirkwood forest, the Lonely Mountain, and Lake Town in the north, and Lothlórien and Fangorn Forest to the south.

The Lonely Mountain and Lake Town

Erebor, the Lonely Mountain, is a solitary peak due east of the north end of Mirkwood Forest, before the Iron Hills. Lake Town, just south of the Lonely Mountain, was built on pilings in the middle of the Long Lake, into which feeds the Forest River and out of which flows the Running River.

The Lonely Mountain and Lake Town figure prominently in *The Hobbit*, Tolkien's story of Bilbo and his adventure with the Dwarves to regain the vast treasure of the Dwarf King Thráin that is hoarded by the dragon Smaug the Golden inside the Lonely Mountain. (It's during this journey that Bilbo finds the One Ring in Gollum's cave in the Misty Mountains.)

Mirkwood

Formerly known as Greenwood the Great, Mirkwood is east of the Misty Mountains that runs roughly from the Lonely Mountain down to Lothlórien. In the year T.A. 1050, an evil power — known originally as the Necromancer and later identified as Sauron — came to Greenwood and established his base of operations in a southern fortress named Dol Guldur. Upon his return to Middle-earth, Sauron brought with him foul creatures, including giant spiders, Orcs, and wolves. That's when Greenwood became known as Mirkwood.

The Woodland Realm of King Thranduil

Despite the growing shadows in Mirkwood, a single community of Wood-elves remained free: the Woodland Realm of Mirkwood, ruled by King Thranduil. Thranduil led the Elves in the Battle of the Five Armies at the Lonely Mountain. He also sent his son, Legolas, to the Council of Elrond in Rivendell that decides the fate of the One Ring. Legolas becomes part of the Fellowship of the Ring that accompanies Frodo.

Dol Guldur, the Hill of Sorcery

Dol Guldur was located at the southern end of Mirkwood on the west side. Its fortress tower became Sauron's refuge until he abandoned it in favor of Barad-dûr in Mordor (see "Barad-dûr, the Dark Tower" later in this chapter). After that, three Ringwraiths used Dol Guldur as their base of operations.

During the War of the Ring, the dark armies of Dol Guldur repeatedly attack Lothlórien and the Northern Elves of Mirkwood. Eventually these armies are defeated, and the tower is finally torn down (see Chapter 24).

Emyn Muil and the Argonath

Emyn Muil is a rather bleak hill formation on the east side of the River Anduin, north of the Dead Marshes. At its southern end lies Nen Hithoel ("Lake of Mist"). This lake, fed by the Anduin River, is guarded by the Argonath, the massive stone statues of Isildur and Anárion, the first Kings of Gondor, marking Gondor's one-time northern border. South of the lake is the island of Tol Brandir, above the entrance of Rauros Falls. On either side are two hills: Amon Hen ("Hill of Sight") and Amon Lhaw ("Hill of Hearing").

Lothlórien, the Golden Wood of Galadriel

Lothlórien ("Flower Dream"), the Golden Wood of Galadriel, is the fairest Elf-kingdom in Middle-earth. It is a small woodland located between the Misty Mountains on the west, the Anduin River on the east, and the Celebrant River, which runs through part of it, on the south. Filled with beautiful mallorn trees bearing golden leaves and silver bark, Lothlórien is also often known by the shorter name, Lórien ("Dreamland").

Lothlórien has but one city: Caras Galadon, or the City of Trees, built on a high hill encircled by a wall of huge trees and ruled by King Celeborn and Queen Galadriel. The Elves of Lothlórien, known as the Galadrim ("Tree People"), dwell on platforms in the trees.

Fangorn, or Treebeard's Forest

Fangorn Forest is what is left of the most ancient forest in Middle-earth. It is located on the eastern side of the Misty Mountains just north of Isengard and Rohan. The people of Rohan call it Entwood Forest because of legends of the last of the ancient race of Ents. These Ents are giant, treelike beings who act as the shepherds of the forest. The Elves call it Fangorn ("Beard of Tree") after Ent leader, Treebeard, the oldest of his race (see Chapter 9).

The Dead Marshes

The Dead Marshes are located between Emyn Muil and the Black Gate of Mordor. They lie west of the battlefield of Dagorlad, where the Last Alliance of Men and Elves fought at the end of the Second Age (see Chapter 12).

The Dead Marshes are natural bogs and fens that over time spread eastward until they began to incorporate part of the Dagorlad battlefield. When Frodo and Sam traverse the Dead Marshes, guided by Gollum, on their way to the Black Gate, they come upon the Mere of Dead Faces. These are pools in the swamps containing the preserved corpses of warriors felled in the Battle of Dagorlad. These dead soldiers hold little corpse-candles with flickering lights that beckon to the hobbits as they pass. Tolkien's thought here may be that the bogs of Dagorlad have worked like the peat bogs in parts of Northern Europe where ancient mummified bodies have been found.

Isengard, the Iron Enclosure

Isengard is the name given to the fortifications immediately below the last peak at the south end of the Misty Mountains. It consists of a very tall, man-made tower called Orthanc ("Forked Height") built from a massive stone in the middle of a natural ring-wall of rock known as the Ring of Isengard.

Isengard: Tolkien tips his hat to Stonehenge

The great megalithic standing stones and stone circles such as Stonehenge that dot the English countryside are well described in the Old English phrase *Orthanc enta geweorc,* meaning the "ingenious work of giants." In his letters, Tolkien wrote that this phrase inspired the name of Isengard's tower, Orthanc, which is an Old English adjective meaning "ingenious" or "skillful," and the name for his race of tree-shepherds, the Ents, who live in nearby Fangorn Forest (*Ent* means "giant" in Old English). Considering the fact that Orthanc was constructed by the men of Gondor from gigantic stones which were already raised and set in the center of a vast ring of stones, the Ring of Isengard looks more and more like a Middle-earth version of Salisbury's Stonehenge.

The tower of Orthanc — more than 500 feet from base to tip — is so named because of the four prongs that jut from its top. Built by the Men of Gondor at the beginning of the Third Age, the tower was fashioned from an enormous rock that rises in the middle of the Ring of Isengard and ends in four spires (making the horns of Orthanc). This fortress hewn from rock is strong enough to withstand any attack.

In T.A. 2759, Saruman the Wizard took possession of the Tower of Orthanc with the permission of the King of Rohan and the Steward of Gondor. As Orthanc was home to one of the seven palantíri (Seeing Stones), Saruman used its power to probe the land of Mordor — and so comes under the spell of Sauron, with whom he becomes allied in *The Lord of the Rings.*

Saruman fortifies Isengard and begins raising an army to attack Rohan: He rids the Ring of Isengard of all vegetation (including the old trees), drains the natural pools, and builds underground forges and armories. After the destruction of Saruman's army at the Battle of Hornburg (see "The Hornburg Fortress of Helm's Deep" later in this chapter), the Ents attack and overcome Isengard by tearing down the ring-wall of stones and flooding the basin of Orthanc. At the end of the War of the Ring, the Ents dismantle Isengard's underground defenses and plant a new forest called the Treegarth of Orthanc.

Rohan, Land of the Horse-lords

Rohan is the name of the vast grasslands and plains that are home to the Rohirrim. The Rohirrim call themselves the Éothéod (Old English for "horse people") and their land the Riddermark — *mark* coming from the Old English *mearc,* meaning "a land within a boundary."

Rohan: A veritable Anglo-Saxon word-hoard

Tolkien really showed off his Anglo-Saxon chops when it came to naming the people and places of Rohan. *Edoras,* Rohan's capital, is an Old English word for "dwellings." *Théoden* is Old English for "prince, chief, or lord." Our dear friend Gríma Wormtongue, King Théoden's treacherous counselor, gets his first name from *grimm,* Old English for "fierce or savage." The last name Wormtongue in its Old English form was a compound used to describe a person whose speech was acerbic or cynical (*wyrm* being Old English, meaning "serpent" rather than the creepy-crawly worms you and I think of). Finally, *Meduseld,* King Théoden's hall, just happens to be the name given to a mead-hall in *Beowulf,* Tolkien's favorite Anglo-Saxon poem.

Rohan is bounded by the White Mountains on the lower west and along the south, the Misty Mountains on the upper west, Fangorn Forest and the Limlight River to the north, and the Anduin River to the east. Rohan is divided into five districts:

- **Wold ("Open Hills"):** The hilly area below the Limlight River is due east of Fangorn Forest on the west side of the River Anduin. (This reference probably comes from the Weald, a region of domed hills in southwestern England.) The Wold stretches to the east side of the Anduin, where it is known as the Brown Lands, formerly the great garden of the Entwives (see Chapter 9).
- **Eastemnet ("East Plain"):** This plain lies east of the Entwash River.
- **Westemnet ("West Plain"):** This one lies west of the Entwash.
- **Westfold ("West Earth") Vale:** This valley or basin at the western foot of the White Mountains contains the fortress of Helm's Deep.
- **Eastfold ("East Earth") Vale:** This valley at the eastern foot of the White Mountains holds the royal city of Edoras.

There is a break between the end of the Misty Mountains (where Isengard stands) and the beginning of the White Mountains. The Isen River flows through this break, known as the Gap of Rohan. The Gap connects Rohan with the western lands of Arnor called Dunland, where the wild men known as Dunlendings live.

Edoras, the royal city of Rohan

The capital of Rohan is Edoras, a fortified city high on a green hill in a vale at the base of the White Mountains. The city is surrounded by a dike, a wall, and a palisade (a fence of stakes). To reach it, you must ford the River Snowbourn and follow a road with two lines of barrows on either side that contain the tombs of the past kings of Rohan.

In the middle of Edoras stands Meduseld, the golden hall of King Théoden. Meduseld contains a vast meeting hall at the center of which is a dais with the king's throne. The hall serves as both feasting hall and official reception area.

The Hornburg and the Glittering Caves of Helm's Deep

Although somewhat protected, Edoras is not defensible against any great enemy. For the safety of the people in time of crisis or great attack, the Rohirrim seek refuge in the fortresses of Helm's Deep, northwest of Edoras and just below the Gap of Rohan. The fortress is named for the man who built it: King Helm, once king of Rohan.

Located in a deep and narrow gorge, Helm's Deep contains a walled citadel known as the Hornburg because a trumpet sounded from it echoes throughout the Deep and into the gorge, calling all its defenders to arms. The Hornburg holds the high honor of having never been taken by an enemy.

Behind Helm's Deep lie the caves of Aglarond, the so-called "Glittering Caves," which are full of gems, crystal, and precious ore. These caves so impress Gimli the Dwarf while he is there during the Battle of the Hornburg (see Chapter 24) that he returns there to develop its mines after the conclusion of the War of the Ring.

Dunharrow and the Púkel-men

Like Helm's Deep, the Hold of Dunharrow (probably from Old English *dun hearg,* for "hill temple") also provides a refuge for the Rohirrim in time of need. Dunharrow is both hard to reach and mysterious in its history. To reach it, you must traverse a winding road with many switchbacks called the Stair of the Hold. It is here that Merry, while accompanying King Théoden to Dunharrow, sees the statues of the Púkel-men.

Beyond the Stair of the Hold is the Firienfeld, a green field of grass and heath at the end of which is a great black Standing Stone called the Dimholt. Beyond the Dimholt is a cleft in Mount Dwimorberg ("Haunted Mountain") called the Dark Door, leading to a passage known as the Paths of the Dead.

Merry Puck, and those menacing Púkel-men

It may be odd to think of Tolkien's statues of the misshapen Púkel-men along the Stair of the Hold at Dunharrow as somehow related to Puck, Shakespeare's merry sprite in *A Midsummer Night's Dream,* but it's probably true. Old English *pucel* (Middle English *puckle*) denotes some sort of goblin or demon, and it is almost certainly related to the Welsh *pwca* and the Irish *puca,* both of which refer to a malevolent spirit. As

Robin Goodfellow in Shakespeare's comedy, Puck is more much benign, a merry trickster who's quite unlike the scary Púkel-man. Nevertheless, we know that before Shakespeare gave his Robin a fairy-makeover in play, he was well known in legend as a hobgoblin (*Hob* being a nickname for Robin) whose mischief was much less benign.

Both the purpose of Dunharrow and its builders are shrouded in mystery. The Rohirrim don't know whether Dunharrow was built as some sort of temple or a series of tombs for ancient kings. Tolkien also says that Dunharrow was built by unknown men long before the coming of the Dúnedain from Númenor. These men have now vanished without a trace — except for the strange statues of the Púkel-men (see nearby sidebar).

Gondor, the Land of Stone

Gondor is the southern kingdom founded and ruled by the sons of King Elendil, Isildur and Anárion. This kingdom was founded upon their arrival to Middle-earth, having escaped from Númenor after its sinking. Gondor is located south of the White Mountains and east of the Mountains of Shadow, which form the western border of Mordor. The great River Anduin running through Gondor divides the region known as Ithilien from the main area. Gondor is bordered on the west by the tremendous Bay of Belfalas and in its heyday extending all the way south to the port of Umbar, the city of the Corsairs. The River Anduin turns west in South Ithilien and reaches the sea right around the Lebennin plain in a delta area known as the Ethir Anduin, which divides Gondor into north and south.

Late in the Third Age, both Gondor's power and holdings dwindle. By the time of *The Lord of the Rings,* South Gondor and the lands of Ithilien are abandoned, along with the cities of Umbar, Osgiliath (the former capital), and Minas Ithil — renamed Minas Morgul and home to Sauron's Ringwraiths.

Osgiliath, Fortress of the Stars

In its heyday, Osgiliath was the greatest city of Gondor, built over the River Anduin with some of its structures actually built on the bridges that span the river. The original capital of Gondor, Osgiliath is located midway between Minas Anor (renamed Minas Tirith) to the west and Minas Ithil (renamed Minas Morgul) to the east. It was home to the palantir, or Seeing Stone, to which the ones located at Orthanc, Minas Anor, and Minas Ithil responded.

In T.A. 2745, Orcs from Mordor sacked Osgiliath. It remained abandoned even after the end of the War of the Ring.

Minas Tirith, the Tower of the Guard

Minas Tirith became the capital of Gondor after the fall of Osgiliath. Originally named Minas Anor ("Tower of the Sun"), Minas Tirith was renamed when Minas Ithil ("Tower of the Moon") fell to Sauron in T.A. 2002. Minas Ithil was then renamed Minas Morgul ("Tower of Sorcery").

Located at the base of Mount Mindolluin in the White Mountains, Minas Tirith sits on the Hill of the Guard, a terraced hill with seven levels. Its citadel is dominated by a white tower called the Tower of Ecthelion, the King's House, and several other buildings, including Merethrond, the Feast Hall. At the Place of the Fountain in front of the Tower of Ecthelion stood the Withered Tree, the dry remnant of the seedling of the White Tree that Isildur secretly brought from Númenor before it sank beneath the waves.

Minas Tirith is surrounded by a much longer wall called the Rammas Echor ("Encircling Wall") that defines a large enclosed area around the city called the Pelennor ("Fenced Land"). Pelennor lends its name to the great battle in which Minas Tirith is defended during the War of the Ring (see Chapter 24).

Minas Tirith is home to one of the seven palantíri — the one used by Denethor, the Steward of Gondor. Through this Seeing Stone Sauron shows Denethor events that make him fear that the quest of the Ring-bearer has failed and despair of Gondor's fate (see Chapter 20).

Minas Ithil/Minas Morgul

Minas Ithil ("Tower of the Moon") is east of the Anduin River at the base of the Mountains of Shadow, Mordor's western border. At the time of its founding, it was the home of Isildur, the elder son of King Elendil. Isildur cut the One Ring from Sauron's hand with the shards of his father's sword Narsil at the Battle of Dagorlad in S.A. 3441 (see Chapter 12).

The origin of the Woses?

At one point in *Sir Gawain and the Green Knight,* the poet describes Gawain as having to battle with all sorts of unpleasant creatures, including serpents, wolves, bears, boars, ogres, and of all things, a *wodwos.* Tolkien thought that the term *wodwos* was derived from the Old English compound *wudu-wása,* which signified some kind of wood-troll. Interestingly enough, Tolkien's office at the University of Leeds was just off Woodhouse Lane that leads to Woodhouse Moor, a densely forested area. Of course, in some British dialects the word "Woodhouse" is pronounced exactly as though it were spelled "Wood-'os" — this is almost the same way a good old Anglo-Saxon would pronounce Gawain's "wodwos." Knowing Tolkien's love of word origins and word-play, we may well have Woodhouse Moor to thank for Drúadan Forest and those wild Woses.

Minas Ithil was originally the capital of the fiefdom of Gondor known as Ithilien ("Land of the Moon"), renowned for its beautiful gardens and woodlands. In T.A. 2002, after a two-year siege, Minas Ithil fell to the Ringwraiths and became known as Minas Morgul ("Tower of Sorcery").

After the fall of Minas Ithil, its palantir passed to Sauron at Barad-dûr who used it to keep tabs on enemies and communicate with Saruman at Orthanc.

Drúadan, forest home of the Woses

Drúadan Forest is a small woodland nestled against the northern slopes of the White Mountains just above the Grey Wood near Minas Tirith. It is the home of the Woses — the Wild Men of the Woods. These men are also called Woodwoses and are ruled by the chieftain Ghân-buri-Ghân. The Woses are renowned for helping the Rohirrim reach Gondor in time to help lift the siege by the host of Mordor. At the end of the War of the Ring, King Aragorn grants Drúadan Forest to Ghân-buri-Ghân and his people in perpetuity in thanks for their help in the Battle of Pelennor Field (see Chapter 24).

Pelargir, the harbor of the royal ships

Pelargir, a port city, is the oldest city in Gondor. It is located at the confluence where the River Sirith meets the River Anduin not far from its mouth. Pelargir is where King Elendil landed his ships after the destruction of Númenor. Ever after, it served as a haven for all the royal ships of the kings of Gondor. This port is important in the War of the Ring for it is here that Aragorn is able to overcome the Corsairs of Umbar with the help of the Dead of Dunharrow. He commandeers their black ships and sails up the River Anduin to the Harlond harbor, right below the Pelennor, and turns the tide of the siege of Minas Tirith (see Chapter 24).

Mordor, the Land of Shadow

Mordor ("Dark Land" in Elvish and "murder" in Old English) is, of course, the home of Sauron, the Enemy of the Free Peoples of Middle-earth. Appropriately, it is a desolate and arid land, almost completely devoid of vegetation because of volcanic activity and limited precipitation.

Mordor is located in southeastern Middle-earth. It is surrounded by mountains on three sides with the Ash Mountains (Ered Lithui) forming the north border and the Mountains of Shadow (Ephel Dúath) forming both its western and southern borders. At the junction of these mountains lies a semi-circular plateau called Udûn, before which stands the tremendous Black Gate — called Morannon in the language of the Elves — that guards the Enemy's realm.

To the south of the Udûn plateau is a great lava plateau called Gorgoroth ("Place of Horror"). Atop Gorgoroth stands the volcanic mountain affectionately known as Mount Doom, also known as Orodruin, ("Mountain of Red Flame"). South of Gorgoroth lie two regions: Lithlad, below the Ash Mountains to the north, receives copious ash from Mount Doom's frequent eruptions. And the vast plain of Nurn to the south contains Sauron's slave fields, which lie between the Mountains of Shadow and the bitter inland Sea of Núrnen ("Dark Water").

The Ash Mountains and Mountains of Shadow are formidable natural barriers that prevent unwanted entry into Mordor from either the north or west. These ranges provide only two mountain passes: Cirith Gorgor at the junction of the Ash Mountains and Mountains of Shadow, where stands the tremendous Black Gate, and Cirith Ungol, which is farther south near Minas Morgul in the Mountains of Shadow.

Mount Doom

Mount Doom is the volcano in whose fires Sauron secretly forged the One Ring of Power. It stands in the Plateau of Gorgoroth, west of Barad-dûr. Mount Doom is accessible by Sauron's road that winds around the mountain to Sammath Naur ("Chambers of Fire"), Sauron's fire pit, accessible by a causeway known as the Crack of Doom. This is where Frodo must go in his quest to destroy the Ring.

Barad-dûr, the Dark Tower

To the east of Mount Doom at the base of an outcropping of the Ash Mountains, Sauron built a formidable fortress called Barad-dûr. Because this tower was raised with the help of the sorcery of the One Ring of Power, its foundations are invincible as long as the Ring exists.

In S.A. 3434, the Last Alliance of Men and Elves laid siege to Barad-dûr. After seven years, it was overthrown, and Sauron was defeated when Isildur cut the One Ring from his hand. However, because Isildur did not destroy the One Ring in the fires of Mount Doom when he had the chance, the alliance was able to dismantle all but the foundations of Barad-dûr (see Chapter 12).

In T.A. 2941 (the year Bilbo finds the One Ring in Gollum's cave), Sauron returns to Mordor and rebuilds Barad-dûr to its former strength. His tower is once again indestructible until the One Ring is unmade in the fires of Mount Doom — which happens on March 25, 3019. At that time the entire tower, including its foundations, collapses into ruin.

Cirith Ungol, the Spider's Pass

Cirith Ungol is the name of the narrow pass through the Mountains of Shadow that leads from Ithilien, the eastern region of Gondor, to Mordor. It is guarded by the monstrous spider Shelob, who attacks and usually devours anyone who tries to pass from Gondor to Mordor.

On the west (Ithilien) side of Cirith Ungol stands Minas Morgul, taken over by Ringwraiths. On the east (Mordor) side of the pass stands the Tower of Cirith Ungol, built by the men of Númenor to keep an eye on Sauron's realm. It is via this pass that Gollum leads Frodo and Sam into Mordor in hopes that Shelob will dispose of them both and enable him to regain the One Ring.

Aman, the Western Paradise

Aman is the name given to the western paradise in Tolkien's mythology. Like the Western Paradise of Buddhism and the Garden of Eden in Judaism, Christianity, and Islam, Aman is a place of pristine beauty and goodness. In Tolkien's stories Aman is often referred to as the Undying Lands not because it bestowed immortality upon its inhabitants (like Paradise) but because it was the abode of Tolkien's immortal races.

Although originally housing only the two races of immortal ones, the Valar and Maiar, Aman later became the western home for the immortal Elves of

Middle-earth. The Elves began referring to Aman as Eldamar ("Elvenhome") after the Valar summoned them to come and live in Aman during the Ages of the Trees (see Chapter 11). As a result of this summons, the continent of Aman became divided into two rather indistinct realms: Valinor, the land of the Valar, and Eldamar, the home of the Elves (see Figure 2-1).

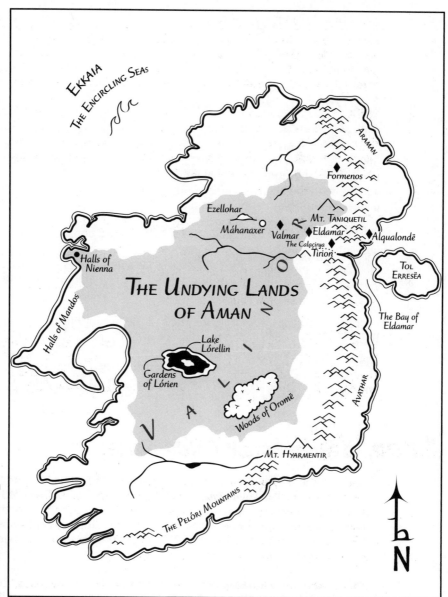

Figure 2-1:
The Blessed Realm, The Undying Lands of Aman.

By the time of *The Lord of the Rings,* Aman no longer lies within the physical realm of Middle-earth (see Chapter 12 for why). Although the Elves of this time still regard Aman as somewhere to the west of Middle-earth, it can now only be reached by special White Ships of the Elves that are able to sail the so-called Straight Road. The idea for the Straight Road connecting Middle-earth to Aman may well be Tolkien's version of Bifrost, the Rainbow bridge of Norse mythology, that connects Midgard (Middle-earth) to Asgard (the realm of the Gods). The major difference is that you ride on horseback on Bifrost to reach Asgard, whereas you sail a White Ship on the Straight Road to reach Aman (see the section on the fate of the Ring-bearers in Chapter 19).

Valinor, home of the gods

Valinor is by far the largest region of Aman. On the eastern shore, it is surrounded by a mountain range known as the Pelóri. This range includes two tall peaks. One of them is Mount Taniquetil in the north, the highest mountain in Valinor. At the top of this mountain sits Ilmarin, a marble watchtower and home to the king and queen of the gods, Manwë and Varda. The other peak is Mount Hyarmentir far to the south.

Valmar is reputed to contain many vast structures, courtyards, and gardens. Immediately outside the golden gates of this fair city are two very important areas: The Máhanaxar ("Ring of Doom"), containing the thrones of the Valar where they sat in judgment, and Ezollahar ("Green Mound"), on which the light-giving Two Trees grew.

On the west side of Valinor lie the Halls of Nienna ("Mourning") and the Halls of Mandos, also called the Halls of Awaiting or the Halls of the Dead. In between the Halls of Mandos and the woods of Oromë ("Horn-blower," Lord of Trees) are the golden gardens of Lórien. In Lórien is an island in the midst of a lake called Lórellin ("Gold Star Lake"). A certain Maia named Olórin came from that island — he is better known as Gandalf to you and me.

The Elvenhome (Eldamar)

The Elvenhome of Eldamar is confined primarily to the east coast of Aman and the island called Tol Erresëa (the "Lonely Island"). Tol Erresëa stands at the mouth of a bay formed by a ravine known as Calacirya ("Cleft of Light"). This ravine breaks the Pelóri mountain range and thus allowed the light of the Two Trees to shine on Tol Erresëa (see Chapter 11).

The Elves of Aman dwelt in several beautiful cities: Avallónë, built on the western harbor of Tol Erresëa nearest Valinor; Alqualondë ("Swan Haven"), built on a northern harbor above the Calacirya pass; and Tirion, the great watchtower, built atop the green hill of Túna in the Calacirya ravine.

Avallónë as Tolkien's Avalon

In *The Silmarillion,* Tolkien says that the city of Avallónë is so named because of all the Elvish cities on Tol Eressëa, it is the "nearest to Valinor." (Avallónë is a compound name from *a,* meaning "to" or "toward," *vala,* meaning "the Valar," and *lonn,* meaning "haven" or "harbor.") He also says that its tower is the first sight that any sailor sees as he approaches the Undying Lands from the east. Of course, the name sounds suspiciously like an Elvish pronunciation of Avalon, the mythical isle in the west where King Arthur was taken after he fell in battle with Mordred. In Avalon, Arthur will be healed and will one day return to save the Isle of Britain in its time of need.

Taniquetil, the Mount Olympus of Aman

Tolkien's version of Mount Olympus, home of the Greek gods, is Mount Taniquetil ("High White Peak"). Atop this highest mountain in Aman is Ilmarin, the mansions of Manwë and Varda (Tolkien's equivalent of Zeus and Hera or Jupiter and Juno in Roman mythology). However, unlike Mount Olympus where all the Greek gods dwell together, most of the Valar dwell in the flats, in the city of Valmar. Only the king and queen live so high up in Ilmarin. Tolkien seems to have borrowed this idea from Norse mythology where Odin and his Frigg, king and queen of their pantheon, dwell in the highest hall of Asgard called Valaskjalf. This hall's throne allows Odin to view the entire world and all its goings on, which is precisely the way Tolkien describes Manwë's throne in Ilmarin.

Beleriand, the Original Western Middle-earth

Beleriand means "the Lands of Balar" and is so named because of its proximity to the Bay of Balar, which contained an island of the same name. Beleriand encompassed all the land between the then western coast on the Great Sea (Belegaer in Elvish) extending east to Ered Luin ("Blue Mountains"), which separated it from other lands that are more familiar from *The Hobbit* and *The Lord of the Rings.*

Beleriand and all its kingdoms feature prominently in the stories in *The Silmarillion,* but are only the stuff of legend in the time of *The Lord of the Rings.* This is because by that time most of the land mass of Beleriand has sunk due to the ruinous War of the Silmarils (see Chapter 12).

At the far north of Beleriand, you find Helcaraxë ("Ice Jaws"), the icy strait that once connected Beleriand with Aman. South of this strait, Ered Engrid ("Iron Mountains") run east/west to intersect the Ered Luin ("Blue Mountains") that run north/south and form Beleriand's eastern border. The Iron Mountains became the fortress of Melkor, the mighty but fallen Vala, who was to be called Morgoth by the Elves. Beneath these mountains, Morgoth tunneled Angband, a tortuous series of underground dungeons. On the south side of the mountains, at the end of a tunnel, Morgoth constructed a tower called Thangorodrim from the slag and ash of his Angband hells.

South of the Ered Engrid, Beleriand was divided into several regions:

- **Hithlum,** the Land of Mist, bordered on the west by Ered Lómin ("Echoing Mountains") and on the east by Ered Wethrin ("Shadowy Mountains")

- **Dor-lómin,** the Echoing Land, immediately east of Hithlum

- **Ard-galen,** a great grassy plain beneath Thangorodrim to the east of Hithlum

- **Dorthonion,** a great highland with many pine forests directly beneath Ard-galen and towering above the protected Elf kingdom of Doriath

- **Nevrast,** the Hither Shore, that encompassed the coastal region of Beleriand between the Firth of Drengist and Mount Taras at the end of Ered Lómin ("Echoing Mountains")

- **Nargothrond,** also known as West Beleriand, the area below Ered Lómin ("Echoing Mountains") bordered on the west by the seacoast and on the east by the great River Sirion

- **East Beleriand,** the region south of the kingdom of Doriath, bordered on the west by the River Sirion and the east by the River Gelion

- **Ossiriand,** the Land of the Seven Rivers, the region between the River Gelion and Ered Luin

In its heyday, Beleriand was home to many Elvish kingdoms and the two Dwarvish kingdoms of Belegost and Nogrod, both of which were located in Ered Luin. Beleriand was also the theater of the War of the Jewels, the Silmarils, for which *The Silmarillion* is named, and the War of Wrath and the Great Battle that resulted in the flooding and ultimate sundering of Beleriand (see Chapter 12 for details).

Númenor, Tolkien's Atlantis

Númenor ("Western Land" or "Westernesse") was the island that, at the beginning of the Second Age, the Valar prepared as a dwelling place for the Men of Middle-earth who had allied themselves with the Elves during the War of the Jewels (see Chapter 12). It was also known by the name Elenna, the Land of the Star, because of its star shape, and after its fall as Atalantë, The Downfallen.

Númenor was important for a couple of reasons: It is often mentioned in *The Lord of the Rings,* especially in the third volume, *The Return of the King.* The story of Númenor's sinking beneath the sea is very obviously Tolkien's version of the myth of Atlantis — thus the Elvish name, Atalantë. Atlantis has fired the Western imagination since it was first mentioned by Plato.

The arms of the star-shaped island of Númenor came together at a central mountain peak known as Meneltarma ("Pillar of Heaven"). Here stood the so-called Hallow of Eru Ilúvatar (The One All-father), a sacred high place dedicated to Mankind's Creator. It was said that from Meneltarma on a clear day one could see west all the way to Aman. This fact would have disastrous consequences for both Aman and Númenor (see Chapter 12).

Númenor had three major cities: Andunië ("Sunset"), a harbor city on the westernmost side of the island; Armenelos, (the "Golden"), the royal city built on the slope of Mount Meneltarma; and Rómenna ("Sunrise"), a harbor on the east coast of the island.

It was from Andunië that the Númenóreans launched their armada of ships that sailed west in a vain attempt to take Valinor by force, which resulted in the Valar's sinking of Númenor. And it was from Rómenna that the survivors, called the Faithful and led by Elendil and his sons Isildur and Anárion, sailed east to seek refuge and a new life in Middle-earth. There, they established the kingdoms of Arnor in the north and Gondor in the south.

Table 2-1 lists some of the more important places in Middle-earth.

Table 2-1	Some Places in Middle-earth	
Place	*Also Known As*	*What It Is*
Aman	Blessed Realm, Uttermost West	Island continent of the Valar (gods) and home of migrated Elves
Arda	The Realm, Eä	The earth, created by Eru Ilúvatar
Arnor	Land of the King	Kingdom in Eriador
Bag End		Hobbit hole home of Bilbo and Frodo
Barad-dûr	Dark Tower	Sauron's tower in Mordor
Barrow-downs		Ancient burial mounds near Old Forest
Belegaer	The Great Sea	Sea between Aman and Middle-earth

(continued)

Table 2-1 *(continued)*

Place	*Also Known As*	*What It Is*
Beleriand		West Middle-earth of the First Age, sank under the sea
Black Gate	Morannon	Huge gate at Cirith Gorgor in Mordor
Cirith Ungol	Spider Pass	Pass to Mordor near Shelob's lair
Crack of Doom	Sammath Naur	Fissure in Mount Doom where the One Ring was forged and only place it can be destroyed
Dol Guldur	Hill of Sorcery	Sauron's underground Mirkwood fortress
Edoras		Capital city of Rohan, home of Théoden
Eldamar	Elvenhome	Region of Aman where the Elves dwell
Entwood	Fangorn	Forest home of Ents, north of Isengard
Erebor	The Lonely Mountain	Mountain containing a Dwarf kingdom
Eriador		Region containing Arnor and the Shire
Gondor	Stone Land	South Middle-earth Dúnedain kingdom
Grey Havens	Mithlond	Elf harbor where ships depart for Aman
Halls of Mandos	House of the Dead	Where Elves, Dwarves go after death
Helm's Deep		White Mountains fortification in Rohan
Hobbiton		Frodo and Bilbo's home village
Isengard	Angrenost	Saruman's fortress near Rohan
Khazad-dûm	Moria	Dwarf mine under Mount Caradhras
Lothlórien	Lórien	Elf forest kingdom ruled by Galadriel
Middle-earth	Endor	Main land area for Men, Dwarves, Elves
Minas Tirith	Tower of the Guard, Minas Anor	Tower built by the Dúnedain in Gondor
Mirkwood	Greenwood the Great	Great forest east of Misty Mountains

Place	Also Known As	What It Is
Misty Mountains		Mountain range in Middle-earth
Mordor	Dark Land	Southeastern land, home to Sauron
Mount Doom	Orodruin	Volcano in Mordor, Sauron's forge
Númenor	Westernesse	Island home of Men in First Age
Old Forest		Remnant of great forest near the Shire
Orthanc		Isengard's tower, home to Saruman
Rivendell	Imladris	Elf community, home of Elrond
Rohan	Riddermark	Land of the Rohirrim, north of Gondor
The Shire		District of Eriador, home of the hobbits
Valinor	Land of the Valar	Land inhabited by the Valar in Aman

Part II
The Beings of Middle-earth

The 5th Wave   By Rich Tennant

"I'm sure he's a very nice lumberjack. I just don't like the idea of our daughter dating one."

In this part . . .

Who exactly are the beings that populate Tolkien's Middle-earth? Part II provides the answers to this question by giving you an overview of each of the major types of creatures who live there. These run the gamut from the magical Elves to the horrible Orcs, from the heart-warming hobbits to the chilling Ringwraiths. It's here, in the diverse and wonderful characters that populate the many lands and worlds of Middle-earth, that you see Tolkien's genius at its finest.

Chapter 3

The Divine Ainur

The Ainur — meaning "Holy Ones" in Elvish — are Tolkien's angelic beings of Middle-earth. Some of the more powerful characters in *The Lord of the Rings* are Ainur, among them Gandalf, Saruman, and Sauron. They are fascinating for a couple of reasons. On one level, they appear to be Tolkien's attempt to reconcile the monotheism of Christianity with the many gods and immortals of Norse and Celtic mythology. On another level, they appear to be his take on teachings, such as Christian Gnosticism and the Jewish Kabbalah, that endeavor to explain how a completely spiritual entity such as God can create and interact with the physical world.

The Ainur figure prominently in *The Silmarillion,* Tolkien's collection of stories about the Elder Days of Middle-earth, edited by his son Christopher. The Ainur are introduced in the first book of *The Silmarillion,* called the *Ainulindalë* (Music of the Ainur), and are then chronicled at length in its second book entitled the *Valaquenta* (Account of the Valar).

This chapter explores the nature of the Ainur in light of their likely dual function in Tolkien's Middle-earth and chronicles the individual powers assigned to them in their guise as the Valar of Aman. It also takes a good look at the more important of the so-called "lesser" Ainur, the Maiar, who figure prominently in *The Lord of the Rings.*

Eru and His Angelic Ainur

Despite his extensive background in the languages and mythology of the Nordic peoples, Tolkien as a good Christian was unwilling to give Middle-earth over entirely to their polytheistic view of the universe. Accordingly, the Creation Myth as told in the *Ainulindalë* of *The Silmarillion* blends in monotheism so that God in the form of Eru Ilúvatar (The One All-father) creates the "gods" — the Ainur.

The Ainur emanated directly from the thoughts of Eru Ilúvatar. They existed with him in a purely spiritual sense before the creation of the world, which is called Arda (Elvish for "The Realm"). Hence, Tolkien's Ainur may be closer to the conception of angels in Christianity and Judaism (the messengers of God) than the gods in the pantheons of Norse, Greek, and Roman mythology. This is all the more true when you consider that the hierarchy maintained by Christianity and Judaism between angels and archangels corresponds nicely to Tolkien's two classes of Ainur: the Maiar, or lesser Ainur (angels), and the Valar, or greater Ainur (archangels). See "The Mighty Valar" and "The Valiant Maiar" later in this chapter for more on these two classes of Ainur.

Eru's purpose in creating the Ainur was to make them the designers of this world of Arda that he was about to create. Eru intended to model the various aspects of Arda after the themes sung together by the Ainur. These themes were to counterbalance each other, and in their harmony, the full promise of his creation was to be realized.

After leading this heavenly choir through the Music of Creation, Eru showed the Ainur a vision of the world that their music would create. He then actualized this vision and brought Arda into being by uttering the prophetic word *Eä* (Elvish for "It is" or "Let it be") — a word that thereafter became synonymous with the Creation itself. See Chapter 13 for more on the relationship between Tolkien's creation myth and other theories on the connection between sound and creation.

The Ainur and the Sefirot of the Kabbalah

In the mystical tradition of the *Kabbalah* in Judaism, the essence of God is named *Ein Sof* (Without End). From Ein Sof radiate ten emanations called the *Sefirot* (Countings), which not only represent the qualities (such as Wisdom, Understanding, Mercy, Strength, and so on) by which we can know God, but also the powers through which He both creates and interacts with the physical world. The Sefirot then are intimate both with the particular qualities of Ein Sof and with His created world in somewhat the same way that Tolkien's Ainur, as the product of Eru's thoughts, are intimate with both him and his vision of Arda.

The Mighty Valar

Eä, as initially created by Eru Ilúvatar, was far from complete. To achieve the complete plan envisioned by the music of the Ainur, Eru invited the Ainur to enter into Arda. Those Ainur who decided to go to Arda dwell in the Blessed Realm of Aman (see Chapter 2) till its end were thereafter known to the Elves as the Valar, meaning "Powers." To Men, they became known as the gods.

Tolkien states that when the Valar entered the world, they took on shapes and colors according to the knowledge they had of their powers and their roles in the Music of Creation. They also assumed either a male or female gender according to their basic temperament (see Chapter 23 for my thoughts on how Valar gender selection relates to human gender). The Valar toiled together to bring order to the world and to fulfill the vision that Eru had shown them.

The powers of the Valar

Each Vala (the singular of Valar) is associated with a particular power or set of characteristics. There are seven Lords and seven Queens among the many Valar. Table 3-1 lists the seven Lords of the Valar, their associated realms, the names of their spouses (if any), and their special powers and pleasures.

Table 3-1	The Seven Lords of the Valar
Name	**Who He Is**
Manwë	King of the Valar and spouse of Varda, with whom he dwells atop Mt. Taniquetil, the highest peak in Arda. He delights in the winds and the clouds and all swift birds.
Ulmo	Lord of the Waters. He loves the Elves and Men and speaks to them in the music of water.
Aulë	The Master Smith and spouse of Yavanna. He delights in fashioning things and is lord of all substances and crafts in Arda.
Oromë	The Horn Blower, Hunter of the Fell (Creatures), Lover of Trees, and spouse of Vána. He loves to hunt monsters and evil creatures in Middle-earth and delights in horses and hounds.
Námo	Also known as Mandos, the name of the realm over which he rules, the Judge and the Keeper of the Halls of Mandos or the Halls of Awaiting, one of the Fëanturi ("Masters of Spirits") with his brother Irmo, and spouse of Vairë. He summons the dead and pronounces judgments (dooms) at the command of Manwë.

(continued)

Table 3-1 *(continued)*	
Name	*Who He Is*
Lórien	Irmo, the Master of Dreams, one of the Fëanturi with his brother Námo, and spouse of Estë. He is the master of visions and dreams.
Tulkas	The Valiant and spouse of Nessa. He has the greatest strength among the Valar and delights in wrestling and contests of strength.

Table 3-2 lists the seven Queens of the Valar, along with notable characteristics, names of their spouses (if any), and what is special to them.

Table 3-2	The Seven Queens of the Valar
Name	*Who She Is*
Varda	The Lady of the Stars and spouse to Manwë. She has the light of Iluvátar in her face, and light is her delight and joy.
Yavanna	The Giver of Fruits and spouse to Aulë. She loves all things that grow in the earth.
Nienna	The Lady of Mourning and sister of the Fëanturi, Námo and Irmo. She mourns for every hurt done to the world of Arda and brings strength to the spirits of those waiting in Mandos who call upon her.
Estë	The Gentle and spouse of Irmo (also known as Lórien). She is the healer of hurts and the giver of rest.
Vairë	The Weaver and spouse of Námo (Mandos). She weaves into her storied fabrics all things that have ever been. These fabrics hang in the Halls of Mandos.
Vána	The Ever-young and spouse of Oromë. Flowers open at her glance, and birds sing at her coming.
Nessa	The Fleetfooted, sister of Oromë and spouse of Tulkas. She is swifter than an arrow and delights in deer and dancing.

The Valar and the gods of mythology

Although it's tempting to compare the Lords and Queens of the Valar with the traditional gods of the Norse, Greek, or Roman pantheons, there actually are very few one-to-one correlations. Many of the gods from classic mythology are similar to various Valar, but in keeping with Tolkien's love of improving on a tradition or changing it to fit his needs, few are definite equivalents.

The closest correlations between Tolkien's Valar and particular Norse or Greco-Roman gods seem to be the following:

- **Manwë and Varda** with **Odin and Frigga** and with **Jupiter/Zeus** and **Juno/Hera**, King and Queen of the gods in Norse and Greco-Roman mythology, respectively
- **Ulmo** with **Neptune/Poseidon,** the god of the sea in Greco-Roman mythology
- **Aulë** with **Vulcan/Hephaestus,** the god of the forge in Greco-Roman mythology
- **Mandos** with **Pluto/Hades,** the god of the underworld in Greco-Roman mythology

The connection between Manwë and Odin is especially close. Just as Odin ascends Hlidskiaf, his high throne in Asgard (the upper realm of the gods) from which he overlooks the entire world and keeps tabs on the other gods, so too does Manwë ascend his throne in the tower on Mt. Taniquetil, the tallest mountain in Arda. From here Manwë overlooks the world and watches for the evil doings of his wayward brother, Melkor (see "Melkor, the Rebel Vala" later in this chapter).

The Valar as the Aeons of the Gnostics

Gnostic Christianity is primarily centered around the belief that matter is inherently sinful and that salvation comes from *gnosis* (knowledge, especially knowledge of spiritual truth). It envisions a world created by deific beings known as *Aeons,* from the Greek word *aeon,* meaning "the ages," "eternity," or "ever-existing." Aeons emanate directly from God as the Eternal Being and are intermediaries between the invisible spiritual world *(Pleroma)* and the visible physical world *(Kenoma).* They not only manifest qualities of the Divine, but are also able to work His will in the world, particularly by being able to interact with and counter evil in ways that He cannot. Tolkien's Valar are reminiscent of the Gnostic Aeons in how they interact directly with the physical world of Arda — they are, in fact, tied to its fate. The Valar can openly counter the evil that Melkor, the Fallen Vala, introduces into Arda (see "Of Melkor, the Rebel Vala" later in this chapter).

Eru and Odin, the two "All-fathers"

One of the most common names for Odin, the king of the gods in Norse mythology, is Alfaðr (All-father). Eru's most common title, Ilúvatar, literally means "All-father," too. Tolkien could not give the title All-father to Manwë, his king of the gods, despite Manwë's close connection to Odin, without compromising the monotheism that Tolkien as a Christian felt was essential to any mythology he developed.

Oromë the Horn Blower seems to be a composite of more than one Norse and Greco-Roman god. His closest correspondent in Norse mythology seems to be Heimdall, the Horn Blower, who with a blast of his horn (called Gjallerhorn) will announce the coming of Ragnarok, the final battle leading to the Twilight of the Gods. (Heimdall, though, possesses the keenest eyesight and hearing, and in his mythology Tolkien gives these attributes to Manwë and Varda, sitting together on their thrones.) Oromë also shares much in common with the goddess Diana/Artemis and her love of the woods and the hunt — although in Oromë's case, it's a love of hunting monsters rather than game.

As you look over the pantheon of Tolkien's Lords and Queens of the Valar in Tables 3-1 and 3-2, you may notice one god conspicuously absent: There's no Vala who delights in love. Norse mythology offers Freya as the goddess of love, just like Venus/Aphrodite in Greco-Roman mythology. Although Tolkien created many Valar who give respite from the hurts of the world and who delight in nurturing its elements and its creatures, he did not create a Vala who is the Lord of Love or who delights in its passion. In Tolkien's world, love is always of a higher order — it either partakes of the code of chivalry (see Chapter 18) or is intimately involved with the quest for the light (see Chapter 15). The sensuous side of love is conspicuously absent from Middle-earth (see Chapter 23).

The Valiant Maiar

Tolkien describes the Maiar as being in the same order as the Valar but to a "lesser degree" — it seems the Maiar are servants to particular Valar and generally act as their helpers. Why it is that Tolkien found it necessary to have two classes of Ainur, the greater Valar and the lesser Maiar, is unknown.

The only counterpart to this arrangement that I'm aware of is in the Norse pantheon where the gods of Asgard were divided into two tribes: the Aesir and the Vanir (not to be confused with Tolkien's Valar). The Aesir were the more bellicose group, including such high ranking deities as Odin, his queen Frigg, and his son Thor. The Vanir were the tribe of gods associated more with peace and prosperity. These deities dwelt in an upper realm separate from Asgard called Vanaheim and fought a long war with the Aesir. At the end of this war some of the Vanir such as Niörd (see the sidebar "Ossë and Ulmo as Niörd and Aegir" later in this chapter) and his son Freyr were sent to live in Asgard, and in exchange some of the Aesir went to dwell in Vanaheim. The Norse division of their gods into the Aesir and Vanir tribes may well have inspired Tolkien to divide his Ainur into the Valar and Maiar classes.

The most important fact about the Maiar is that they do not all remain in Aman, serving their individual Vala — they often come to Middle-earth. Once there, they interact with its creatures, especially the Elves and Men, and thereby influence the course of history.

In the following sections, you meet several Maiar who are the most important to the Elves and Men of Middle-earth. These include Ossë and Uinen, who serve Ulmo, Lord of the Seas; Melian, who serves Vána and Estë; and Olórin — better known in Middle-earth as Gandalf the Wizard — who serves Irmo and studies with Nienna.

As with the Valar, not all the Maiar remain good and true. Sauron began as a good Maia, serving Aulë the Smith, but later went astray and became the servant of Melkor, the Fallen Vala. And there are the Valaraukar, better known in Middle-earth as Balrogs — powerful spirits corrupted by Melkor to serve only him.

Ossë and Uinen, Maiar of Ulmo

Ossë is a vassal of Ulmo, Lord of the Seas. He does not wander into the deeps, though, but rather hugs the shores of Middle-earth and the coastlines of islands. He delights in the winds of Manwë and loves the roar of waves.

Ossë's spouse is named Uinen. She is revered especially by mariners who cry out for her help when Ossë makes the waves wild. She loves all that live in salt streams and all the weeds that grow there — which are likened to her long hair floating in the water. The Númenóreans held Uinen in the highest regard and considered her to be their special protector among the Ainur.

Ossë is one of the Maiar whom Melkor attempted to corrupt and turn to darkness. At one time, he promised to give Ossë Ulmo's realm of the sea if he would swear Melkor his allegiance. As a result of Melkor's corruption of Ossë, he raised a great tumult in the seas that threatened to overcome the shores of Middle-earth.

Ossë and Ulmo as Niörd and Aegir

Tolkien may well have gotten his idea for Ossë and Ulmo from the pair of Norse gods Niörd and Aegir. Both Niörd and Aegir are gods of the sea, but with a special distinction: Niörd is the guardian of the coastline and oversees sailing and fishing grounds, whereas Aegir is the lord of the deep ocean, far from the safety of land.

Aegir dwells with his wife, Ran, in a golden underwater palace in the depths of the ocean. They keep themselves apart from the other Norse gods who live in Asgard. In this regard, Ulmo is similar to Aegir, as Ulmo stays away from the other Valar in Aman, preferring instead the silent depths.

Fortunately, Aulë prayed to Uinen, who restrained Ossë and brought him to Ulmo for justice. Ossë repented to Ulmo and once more swore allegiance as his loyal vassal, a vow to which Ossë has remained true. It is said, though, that after this incident Ossë sometimes becomes capriciously violent and raises the waves even when Ulmo does not command it. Since then, sailors and those who live by the sea have never again fully trusted Ossë, no matter how much they revere him (see the nearby sidebar for a comparison of Ossë and Ulmo to Norse gods).

Melian, Maia of Vána and Estë

Melian is the handmaiden of two Valar: Vána and Estë. Estë the Gentle is the spouse of Irmo, in whose gardens of Lórien ("Land of Dreams") Melian dwells. In Lórien, she tended flowering trees, and it is said that nightingales sang around her wherever she went in the gardens.

Melian is noteworthy in the annals of Middle-earth because she left Aman and came to live in Middle-earth. There, she married the Elf-king Thingol, lord of Doriath who built the stronghold of Menegroth (see Chapter 4).

Olórin, Maia of Lórien and Nienna

Olórin is the wizard Gandalf's name as a Maia. In Aman, he serves Irmo and dwells in his gardens of Lórien. He also frequents the house of Nienna, the Lady of Mourning, from whom he learns the virtues of pity and patience. He is considered to be among the wisest of the Maiar.

He left Aman and came to Middle-earth as a wizard, becoming a great friend to all the races of Middle-earth, with a special fondness for the hobbits of the Shire (see Chapter 8 for more on Gandalf).

Sauron, Maia of Aulë and Melkor

Sauron, the great Enemy of Middle-earth in *The Lord of the Rings,* began his life in Aman as a good Maia who served Aulë, the Lord of the Forge. Under Aulë's tutelage, Sauron learned the subtle arts of blacksmithing — skills that enabled him much later in Middle-earth to forge the One Ring of Power.

Sauron, however, was ultimately corrupted by Melkor. Tolkien says that once Sauron started serving Melkor, he became part of all of Melkor's evil doings, both in Aman and Middle-earth. Sauron is only slightly less evil than his master and that is only because of the years he served as Aulë's apprentice. However, after long years of serving Morgoth (Melkor's name after his fall), Sauron became his master's shadow, embodying all Morgoth's malice and continuing his evil in Middle-earth long after Morgoth was annihilated (see Chapter 10).

The Valaraukar, those nasty Balrogs

The Valaraukar ("Demons of Might") are Maiar, but they are better known to readers of *The Lord of the Rings* as Balrogs, those whip-cracking, fire-breathing denizens of the deep.

The Fellowship of the Ring encounter one of these Balrogs in the mines of Moria, and Gandalf fights this fellow Maia all the way through the abyss under Durin's Bridge and all the way up the Endless Stair to Durin's Tower at the top of Mount Silvertine, where he finally vanquishes the demon by throwing it from the mountain pinnacle.

According to *The Silmarillion,* the Valarauker are among those Maiar whom Melkor corrupted and brought into his service through lies and treacherous gifts, which may include their fire whips. The Valar consider them to be among the most dreadful spirits in Middle-earth and refer to them as "scourges of fire." Quite unlike any other demons of mythology, the Balrogs remain one of Tolkien's most original creatures — see Chapter 10 for more on them.

Chapter 4

The Fair Race of Elves

*Y*ou don't have to read too far into Tolkien's works to know that he's really keen on Elves. They are without a doubt his favorite creatures in Middle-earth. He positively waxes eloquent, describing them as slender and tall with very fair faces that are said to shine or glow with unearthly beauty.

This chapter explores some of the possible origins of Tolkien's Elves and looks at the very important function they serve in his tales of Middle-earth. Here, you become acquainted with the struggles that formed the background to the great conflict that takes place in *The Lord of the Rings*. And you get a chance to meet some of the more legendary Elves whose lives and fates have an important bearing on the history of Middle-earth.

The Role of the Elves

In considering the role that the Elves play in Tolkien's Middle-earth, you need to be aware of their special nature when compared to the other creatures. Two significant factors stand out:

   ✔ **Elves are immortal.** They don't die from natural causes such as old age and sickness, although they can be slain in battle or die from "weariness" of being in the world.

   ✔ **The fate of the Elves is closely linked to that of Middle-earth.** Should Elves die, they remain in the Halls of Mandos in Aman or are reborn and return to Middle-earth until the end of the world.

Elves as the Bodhisattvas of Middle-earth

A Bodhisattva (Sanskrit for "Light-being") is a special being in Mahayana Buddhism who vows to postpone individual enlightenment and continue being reborn in this world until it's entirely emptied of all suffering beings. As with the Elves of Middle-earth, the Bodhisattva's fate is intimately tied to that of the world. And like the Elves, who bring beauty and grace to Middle-earth, the Bodhisattvas bring wisdom and tireless compassion to our world. The big difference is that Bodhisattvas commit themselves to the final destiny of the world by individual choice, whereas Elves are committed to the final destiny of Middle-earth by their collective fate.

In these two ways, the Elves are similar to the Valar. The Valar entered the world as caretakers until it either ends or is remade. Unlike the Valar, however, who can clothe themselves in whatever types of bodies they please, Elves are flesh and blood and are tied to their particular bodies. And because we know from the history of Middle-earth that Elves can reproduce with Men, they must share our physiology and a similar anatomy.

In contrast to the immortal Elves, mortal Men seem weak and, in some ways, cursed. However, according to Tolkien, Ilúvatar gave mortality to his second-born children as special gift. This gift enables Men to go beyond the "Circles of the World" at death, something which is not possible for the Elves.

The destinies of the Elves are inseparable from the fate of Middle-earth, while Men's destinies remain at all times in their own hands, making them creatures of free will. This is not to say that Elves can't make individual decisions independent of what's happening in the world around them — they can and do, sometimes with dreadful consequences. Likewise, Men can't ignore the condition of the world around them when deciding how to act individually, although some Men try to do just that, with equally bitter results.

(For more on immortality and mortality, see Chapter 16. And for more on fate versus free will, see Chapter 19.)

The Great Journey to the Blessed Realm

In the *Quenta Silmarillion* (The History of the Silmarils), you get the definite impression that the Valar's decision to summon the Elves to Aman to live in the light of the Two Trees was, to the say the least, not their best decision.

Tolkien says that in making this judgment, the Valar were motivated by two things: Their fear for the Elves in the dangerous twilight world of Middle-earth and their desire to be near such beautiful beings.

In the council of the Valar, a small group led by Ulmo, the Lord of the Sea, argued against taking the Elves away from their homes in Middle-earth and depriving them of their freedom "to walk as they would" throughout their lands. Nevertheless, the council went ahead and decided that they should come to Aman forever, which Mandos pronounced as a doom or irrevocable judgment on the Elves.

The summoning of the Elves to Aman is one of Tolkien's examples of lack of faith (in "providence") leading to a fatal mistake. The Valar didn't fully understand Ilúvatar's Firstborn or their purpose in the grand scheme of things. Rather than trust in his plan as revealed in the second theme of the Music and let the Elves on their own in Middle-earth, the Valar interfered out of fear and desire. This combination of a lack of faith and fear and desire caused the division among the Elves that ultimately led to their long string of troubles both in Aman and Middle-earth.

The mustering of the Elves

The Valar had to convince the Elves to make the long trek west. This was not so easy — they were asking the Elves to leave their homes for a new land sight unseen. Even after hearing the testimony of their leaders Ingwë, Finwë, and Elwë about the beauty of the light of the Two Trees and the wonders of Valinor, some Elves were unwilling and resisted. These are the Avari.

If you were to consider the Great Journey as a metaphor for the spiritual quest for enlightenment, as some Tolkien critics do — the deeper meaning of "living in the light of the Blessed Realm" — then I suppose that the response of the Elves to the summons can be seen as symbol of the way modern people respond to the spiritual aspects of their lives. Many of us, like the Avari, refuse even to consider making the journey at all and convince ourselves that our day-to-day existence provides enough light for anything we need to do.

Of those who do undertake the Great Journey, it seems that only the smallest group, like the Vanyar, ever make it all the way to the Blessed Land *and* live happily ever after at the foot of the gods. Far more common, like the Noldor, are those who reside in the Blessed Land for a limited time before finally returning to their original way of life. Last but never least, you find the largest group, like the Teleri, uncertain of their destination and so easily distracted along the way that many never make it even close to the Blessed Land. (See later in this chapter for more on the Vanyar, Noldor, and Teleri.)

The dividing of the Elves

The worst consequence of summoning the Elves to Aman was that they became divided and started judging one another. This judging became especially pronounced among the Three Kindred of the Light Elves, who rate each other according to the order in which their individual groups arrived in Aman and by how close they dwell to the light of the Two Trees.

The Vanyar or Fair Elves consider themselves the most blessed not only because they were the first to arrive in Aman but because they live at the foot of the king and queen of the gods, literally basking in the light of the Two Trees. The Vanyar are the smallest group and the most comfortable dwelling among the Valar, extending Eldamar (Elvenhome) to the edge of Valinor.

The Noldor or Wise Elves are the middling group in all ways. Their numbers are larger than the Vanyar but fewer than the Teleri. The Noldor settled in the coastal valley halfway between the Two Trees and the sea to the east. Like the middle child, the Noldor became over-achievers, acquiring knowledge (they invented the Elvish writing scripts), building glorious structures (such as the city of Tirion with the lighthouse of Mindon), and making beautiful things.

The Teleri or the Latecomers were the largest group to set off from Middle-earth and the most fractured. Many in their company, including Elwë, one of their leaders, never made it to the Blessed Realm. As latecomers, they mostly remain on the fringe of the Blessed Realm, either on Tol Eressëa ("the Lonely Isle") or in their city of Alqualondë ("Haven of the Swans") on the Bay of Eldamar. They remain connected to the sea, building and sailing their beautiful white ships.

The Origin of Tolkien's Elves

Tolkien's idea of Elves as the *fair* race — the word that gives us *fairies,* another term sometimes applied to Elves — certainly did not originate with him. In fact, the Celtic tradition as well as the old Norse and Germanic sagas are full of stories of immortal beings like the Elves, some of whom are described as the fairest of beings. "Fair as an Elf" was a fairly common Anglo-Saxon compliment given to beautiful babies. Some speculate that the word "Elf," spelled *aelf* in Old English and *alfr* in Old Norse, comes from the Latin *albus,* meaning "dazzling white."

But alongside the idea of Elves as delightful, beautiful beings comes a long tradition of Elves as somewhat malevolent creatures. Some Anglo-Saxon tribes believed that Elves caused certain diseases, and in the epic poem *Beowulf,* Elves are lumped together with such baddies as ogres and goblins (called *orcneas,* which is where Tolkien got the name for his Orcs). However, the spelling used for Elves in *Beowulf* is *Ylfe,* which has an evil connotation.

Thus, it should come as no surprise to learn that in Norse mythology Elves are of two basic types:

- ✔ **Light Elves,** who are more beautiful than the sun and dwell in Alfheim, which is on the same high level as Asgard, the home of the gods
- ✔ **Dark Elves,** who are darker than pitch and dwell in Niflheim, at the lowest level under Midgard (Middle-earth)

Tolkien was well aware of this sharp distinction between Light and Dark Elves in mythology. In keeping with his fondness for taking traditional elements from folklore and giving them his own explanations, his Middle-earth has its own Light and Dark Elves.

For Tolkien, Elves represent a type of higher being in Middle-earth, but the distinction between Light and Dark Elves has nothing to do with either beauty or essential nature. Both are beautiful and inherently good, although they are capable of doing evil. In Middle-earth, Light Elves are simply those who have literally "seen the light," and Dark Elves are the ones who have not.

The light here is the light of the Two Trees that grew in Aman, the Blessed Realm (see Chapter 2). During the Ages of the Trees (see Chapter 11), the Valar invited the Elves to leave Middle-earth and come west to dwell with them in Aman where they could enjoy the light of the Two Trees. Many groups of Elves undertook the long westward trek from their homeland, which they call the Great Journey, but not all of them made it all the way to Aman.

Those Elves who took the long trek west and saw the light of the Two Trees in Aman, whether they stayed or not, call themselves the Light Elves (Calaquendi). Those Elves who did not undertake the Great Journey or who didn't make it all the way there are called the Dark Elves (Moriquendi).

More on what makes an Elf dark

In addition to the Úmanyar, who attempted the Great Journey but did not make it to Aman, Tolkien mentions a group of Elves who refused to even attempt the westward migration. This group is called the Avari ("the Unwilling"). Both the Úmanyar and the Avari are called Moriquendi ("Dark Elves") because none of them actually saw the light of the Two Trees.

Those Noldorin Elves such as Fëanor and Galadriel, who eventually left the Blessed Realm and returned to Middle-earth to live, even though they dwell outside the Blessed Realm, are still Calaquendi ("Light Elves") because they *once* saw the light of the Two Trees. For Tolkien, it's not so much about where you currently dwell as whether you've *ever* seen the light.

The Downfall of the Elves

The divisions among the Light Elves in the Blessed Realm led to their downfall both in Aman and back home in Middle-earth. Tolkien chronicles this fall in great detail in the *Quenta Silmarillion,* part of *The Silmarillion.* The downfall of the Elves is tied to the fate of the Silmarils, the three jewels crafted by Fëanor (a Noldor Elf) from the light of the Two Trees.

As is common in mythologies about falls from grace, Tolkien's tales in the *Quenta Silmarillion* revolve around failed attempts to possess something of great value — in this case, the light of the Two Trees. In keeping with Tolkien's idea of the Elves as the fated race of Middle-earth, these stories often explore how personal desire leads to overreaching pride and hastens a personal downfall that affects the fate of the entire group. The Greeks called this tragic idea *hubris,* meaning "pride before a fall."

In Tolkien's myth of the Silmarils, you can certainly see the influence of other legends such as *The Volsung Saga* of the Norsemen and the Finnish collection of epic poems *The Kalevala.* In *The Volsung Saga,* the thing of value is a magical gold ring crafted by the dwarf Andvari. This ring, called Andvarinaut ("Andvari's Loom"), produces untold treasure, making it a thing which all desire to possess. But its possession only brings catastrophe.

In *The Kalevala,* the thing of great value is called the Sampo, a mill that continually grinds out riches in the form of flour, salt, and money. This magic mill is stolen by the people of the Far North. The Sons of Kaleva, the saga's heroes, must steal it back. This is reminiscent of Bilbo Baggins helping the Dwarves steal back their treasure from the dragon Smaug in *The Hobbit.*

The big difference between Tolkien's Silmarils and the Andvarinaut and the Sampo is the spiritual rather than physical benefits that the Silmarils bestow. Rather than increasing material wealth, as the ring and the mill do, the Silmarils, containing the light of the Two Trees, have only the power to illuminate the darkness. The problem is that light, the gift that the Silmarils impart, is not something you can possess. As they say in *The Sound of Music,* "How can you hold a moonbeam in your hand?" However, by encasing this light in crystal jewels, the Silmarils do give the unfortunate illusion of possessing the light of the sacred Trees. Also, by encasing their light, Fëanor made it possible for someone to withhold it by hiding the Silmarils or stealing them away — both of which happened during their history.

The danger of this situation is brought home when Melkor and the spider Ungoliant (see Chapter 10) destroyed the Two Trees and stole the Silmarils, setting in motion a series of tragic events for the Elves of Aman and Middle-earth (see Chapter 19).

Legendary Elves of Middle-earth

The *Quenta Silmarillion* is chock-full of important myths concerning the fate of the Silmarils and the exiled Noldor in Middle-earth. This section covers some of the more legendary Elves in the history of Middle-earth. You can also find some related information in Chapter 5, in the biographies of famous Men in Middle-earth, such as Eärendil and Beren. In addition, you may want to take a peek at the story of Túrin Turambar in Chapter 19. Túrin, though a mortal man and not an Elf at all, got all tangled up in the wars to regain the Silmarils and ended up combating Morgoth's favorite weapon — a dragon.

Fëanor, the maker of the Silmarils

Fëanor was heralded as the most creative and skilled of all the Noldor, which makes the story of his downfall all the more tragic (see Chapter 19). Fëanor was the only son of Finwë, King of the Noldor, and Míriel, his first queen.

Originally named Curufinwë ("Finwë's Skill"), his mother called him instead Fëanor ("Spirit of Fire"). Shortly after his birth, his mother Míriel wasted away, having given all of her strength to her only son. As a result, Fëanor grew up motherless and, when his father took a second wife, Indis of the Vanyar, he had to share his father's love with two half-brothers, Fingolfin and Finarfin. See Figure 4-1.

The House of Finwë of the Noldor

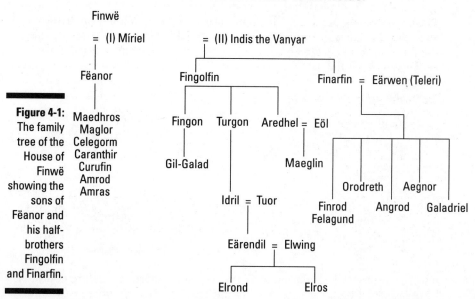

Figure 4-1: The family tree of the House of Finwë showing the sons of Fëanor and his half-brothers Fingolfin and Finarfin.

Fëanor became estranged from his step-mother and brothers and wandered about Aman. During this time, he improved upon the original script designed by an Elf named Rúmil by creating his own script for writing Elvish, which is used ever after by all Elves (to see Fëanor's script, see Chapter 14).

Fëanor later married Nerdanel, with whom he had seven sons (see Figure 4-1), although they later became estranged. Nerdanel was the daughter of the great smith Mahtan, who made Fëanor his apprentice and taught him metalworking skills. After working with Mahtan, Fëanor got the idea of creating the Silmarils to preserve the light of the Two Trees within crystal jewels — a long, arduous project he began in secret.

When finished, the Silmarils were the pride and joy not only of Fëanor, but of all who dwelt in Aman. The Vala Varda blessed them so that no unclean hands could hold them without being "scorched and withered." The Vala Mandos declared that the Silmarils had the fate of the elements of the earth, sea, and air of Arda locked within them.

See Chapter 11 for a rundown on the history of Fëanor and the Silmarils, Chapter 12 for a chronology of the war fought over the Silmarils in Middle-earth, and Chapter 19 for an analysis of Fëanor as a tragic character.

Elwë, King Thingol of Doriath

The story of Elwë ("Starry One") is a tale of someone who saw the light at one time in his life and then, when he set out to find it again as the leader of the Teleri Elves, became waylaid (in this case by love for the Maia Melian). Instead of later completing the journey to the light in Aman, Elwë became comfortable living outside of the light in the section of Middle-earth known as Beleriand. This may account for his title, Singollo, or Thingol, meaning "Grey-cloak" in the two dialects of Elvish — he lived under the gray cloak of the starlight over Middle-earth.

Elwë and the Maia Melian

When the Teleri Elves reached eastern Beleriand, their leader Elwë became separated from his brother Olwë and the rest of his people in the valley known as Nan Elmoth ("Valley of Star-Dusk"). Here, he heard the singing of the Maia Melian who had left the gardens of Lórien in Valinor to wander Beleriand in Middle-earth.

Elwë was enchanted by Melian's voice — as soon as he came upon her in a glade under the stars and saw that she had the light of the Blessed Realm in her face, he fell instantly in love with her. Elwë took her hand, and neither spoke a word as they stood in silence under the stars for untold years.

In the meantime, Olwë searched everywhere for his brother before continuing on and leading the greater part of the Teleri to Aman, where he became

King of the Teleri at Alqualondë. Elwë, on the other hand, dwelt in Beleriand for the rest of his life with Melian. He built the fortress Menegroth in the land of Doriath, which was protected from evil by Melian's magic defensive barrier (called "Melian's girdle"). There, he ruled as King Thingol over the Teleri who remained in Middle-earth. These Elves became the Sindar, or Grey-elves.

The House of Elwë

King Thingol's family tree, shown in Figure 4-2, is renowned for a couple of reasons. First, his union with the Maia Melian is the only known union between an Elf and a being of Valinor. Second, he and Melian were the ancestors of a proud line that included several rare and important unions between Elf and mortal:

- ✔ **Lúthien,** Thingol and Melian's only daughter, and the mortal **Beren**

- ✔ **Elwing,** the daughter of King Dior and Queen Nimloth of Doriath, with **Eärendil,** who became the parents of Elrond the Elf and Elros the mortal

- ✔ **Arwen,** only daughter of Elrond, and the mortal **Aragorn,** who restores the line of Númenoréan kings in Gondor as detailed in *The Lord of the Rings* (see Chapter 5)

The House of Elwë of the Sindar

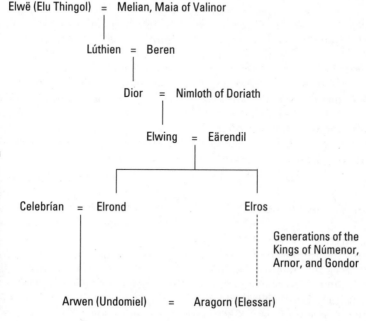

Figure 4-2:
The family tree of the House of Elwë showing the descent of Arwen and Aragorn.

Elwë and the ban on the language of the Noldor

After King Thingol found out about Fëanor and the Kinslaying of his kinfolk in Alqualondë (see Chapter 19), he forbade the use of the language of the Noldor, a dialect of Elvish known as Quenya, or High Elvish. Thereafter, all the Elves of Doriath were required to use the dialect called Sindarin, or Grey Elven. This ban on the language of the Light Elves began a process in which Quenya became a "dead" language, like Latin during the Middle Ages, used in official written communications but no longer spoken (see Chapter 14).

You can see one result of the ban on the High Elven language in the way the king was hailed. Originally, in the Quenya dialect of Elvish, his name was pronounced Elwë Singollo. In the Sindarin dialect, *Elwë* is pronounced *Elu*, and his title *Singollo* is pronounced *Thingol*, so that henceforth he was called King Elu Thingol (or just King Thingol, for short).

Thingol and the recovery of the Silmarils

King Thingol's downfall came when he involved himself and his daughter in the struggle for the Silmarils. Ultimately, this quest for Fëanor's jewels and Thingol's desire to possess their light destroyed him and the protected kingdom of Doriath.

King Thingol's possession of the Silmaril sealed his downfall and that of Doriath as well. As his desire for the Silmaril grew, he yearned to have its light about him at all times. To this end, he commissioned some of the finest craftsmen of the Dwarf-kingdom of Nogrod to set the Silmaril in a golden necklace called the Nauglamír ("Dwarf Jewel"), which their kinsmen had originally made for King Finrod of Nargothrond (see "Finrod Felagund" later in this chapter).

Unfortunately, the beauty of the Silmaril proved to be too much of a temptation for the Dwarves, who slew King Thingol rather than hand over the refashioned Nauglamír. They were in return slaughtered by Thingol's Elves. As a result, Queen Melian left Doriath after a time of mourning and returned to Valinor forever more. After Melian left, her magic barrier no longer protected Doriath from her enemies. The Dwarves of Nogrod ransacked the Thousand Caves of Menegroth in vengeance for the killing of their kinsmen and in a vain attempt to recapture the Nauglamír.

Thingol and the light of Aman: to have and to hold

After seeing the original light from the Two Trees in Aman, King Thingol sought it ever afterward in things outside of himself. Initially, he was waylaid on his return journey to the Blessed Realm because he recognized the light of the Trees shining in Melian's face. Later, he tried to protect the light he saw in the beauty of his only daughter, Lúthien, whom he calls his jewel, by offering her hand to Beren in return for one of the Silmarils. Once he possessed the Silmaril, he had to have it set in the Nauglamír necklace so that he could have the light, as Tolkien says, when "both waking and sleeping."

King Thingol's recognition of the light in Melian and Lúthien led to a strong desire to be near them in order to partake of their light. This desire was repeated in his "fatal attraction" to the Silmaril, manifested by his need to partake of its light at all times by wearing it in the necklace. For some unknown reason, it wasn't possible for Thingol to be like Melian and Lúthien, who radiated the light from within; rather he was always someone who beheld the light in a source outside of himself.

Elrond Half-elven

Elrond, the Half-elven, is well known to readers of *The Lord of the Rings*. He is the son of the mortal hero Eärendil (himself half-Elven and half-human) and the Elf-princess Elwing, daughter of King Dior and Queen Nimloth of Doriath. He is the twin-brother of Elros, who is also known as Tar-Minyataur, the first king of Númenor (for more on Eärendil and Elros, see Chapter 5).

Elrond married Celebrían, the daughter of Celeborn of Doriath and Galadriel of Lothlórien (see the following section) and had two sons and a daughter with her: Elladan, Elrohir, and Arwen. During part of the Second and all of the Third Age, Elrond is the master of Rivendell (Imladris in Elvish), a refuge at the foot of the Misty Mountains.

Elrond is famous for being the one who, when given the chance by the Valar to choose between the immortal life of Elves and the mortal life of Men, chose immortality — unlike his brother Elros, who chose to be mortal (see Chapter 5). Elrond is also famous for aiding Men countless times during the tumultuous Second and Third Ages and for offering Rivendell as a refuge for the weary and the hunted. Among these are Bilbo Baggins and the Dwarves on their quest to the Lonely Mountain and Frodo Baggins and the Fellowship of the Ring on their quest to Mount Doom. Elrond is able to offer this refuge in large part because he is the keeper of one the three Elven Rings of Power: Vilya, the Ring of Air (see "Celebrimbor, the Maker of the Rings of Power" later in this chapter).

Elrond took in Gilraen and her son Aragorn, Isildur's heir to the throne of Gondor, and brought up Aragorn as his own in Rivendell. Later, Arwen, Elrond's only daughter, fell in love with Aragorn when they met in Rivendell. Elrond opposed this union until Aragorn proved himself worthy of her hand by retaking the throne of Gondor.

Galadriel, Queen of Lothlórien

Galadriel is widely known as the beautiful and good Elf-queen who aids the Fellowship of the Ring after they lose Gandalf in Moria in *The Lord of the Rings*. She is more than that, however. She's what you'd call a lady with a past. Her story goes all the way back to the Blessed Realm and the flight of the Noldor to Beleriand at the beginning of the First Age (see Chapter 12). In this way, Galadriel is one of the few female Tolkien characters who do not readily accept the expected gender role that their society bestows on them — see Chapter 23 for more on this theme.

If you look at the genealogy charts in Figures 4-1 and 4-3, you can see that Galadriel is the daughter of Finarfin, the third son of Finwë, King of the Noldor, and Eärwen, only daughter of Olwë, King of the Teleri in Aman. Olwë became king because his older brother Elwë, also known as Thingol, stayed in Beleriand with Melian.

In the Blessed Realm, Galadriel became somewhat notorious for her decision to support her half-uncle Fëanor and her brother Finrod in rebelling against the Valar and returning to Middle-earth to seek revenge for the wrongs Melkor did to the Noldor. Fortunately for her, she stopped short of taking Fëanor's terrible oath of vengeance on anyone who touched the Silmarils and so escaped the calamities that befell so many of her Noldorin kin (see Chapter 19). Tolkien says, though, that Fëanor's words urging the Noldor to return to Middle-earth kindled in her a desire to see the wide open spaces of that land and to rule over a kingdom of her own.

The House of Olwë of the Teleri

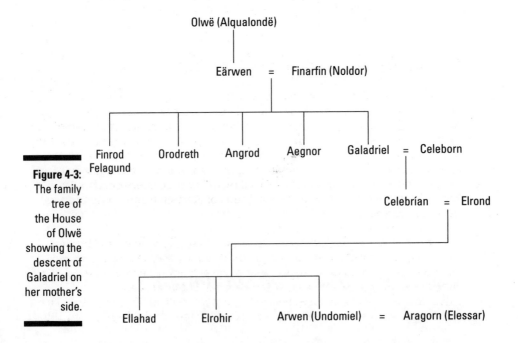

Figure 4-3: The family tree of the House of Olwë showing the descent of Galadriel on her mother's side.

After leaving Aman, Galadriel remains in Middle-earth till the end of the Third Age, after the War of the Ring. For a long time, she dwelt in the land of Doriath, which was ruled by King Thingol and Queen Melian. It's there that she met and fell in love with Celeborn, one of Thingol's kinsmen.

After the sinking of most of Beleriand during the War of Wrath at the end of the First Age, Galadriel and Celeborn established the wooded kingdom of Lothlórien on the east side of the Misty Mountains not far from the edge of Mirkwood. After Celebrimbor forged the nineteen Rings of Power, she became the keeper of Nenya, the Ring of Water, one of three Elf-rings not touched by the hand of Sauron. Through the power of this ring, Galadriel is able to keep Lothlórien hidden from the Enemy and safe from his minions, as well as slow down the ravages of time and ward off weariness of the world (one of the few sicknesses fatal to Elves). See Chapter 21 for more on the role of these Rings of Power in Tolkien's writings.

At the end of the War of the Ring and the Third Age, the Valar pardon Galadriel for her part in the rebellion of the Noldor — in large part because of her long fight against Sauron and her refusal to take the One Ring when Frodo offers it. This enables Galadriel to return to Aman with her son-in-law Elrond, accompanied by Gandalf and the Ring-bearers Bilbo and Frodo.

Galadriel's husband Celeborn elects to stay in Middle-earth when she returns to Aman. He guides the Elves of Lothlórien to live in the new land of East Lórien, located in Eryn Lasgallen, the Wood of Greenleaves — which is the new name for the once foul Mirkwood after it's cleansed of evil.

Gil-galad, the legendary Elf

Gil-galad ("Star of Radiance") was the only son of Fingon and thereby the grandson of Fingolfin (the second son of Finwë, original leader of the Noldorin Elves in Aman). Upon the death of his uncle Turgon at the fall of his hidden Kingdom of Gondolin in Beleriand, Gil-galad became the last High King of the Noldor in Middle-earth. At the end of the War of the Silmarils, when most of Beleriand sank beneath the sea, Gil-galad did not return to Aman but instead settled in Lindon on the newly created northwestern coast of Middle-earth. There he ruled as king of the regions of Forlindon and Harlindon and the Grey Havens.

Near the end of the Second Age, when Sauron's threat to western Middle-earth resurfaced, Gil-galad and King Elendil formed the Last Alliance of Men and Elves. At the end of the seven-year siege of Sauron's tower of Barad-dûr, after the victory of the Alliance at the Battle of Dagorlad, Sauron slew Gil-galad in hand-to-hand combat before slaying Elendil and, in turn, having the One Ring cut from his hand by Isildur (see Chapter 12 for details).

That, in a nutshell, is all that Tolkien tells us of the life and death of this Elf hero of *The Silmarillion*. In *The Lord of the Rings*, Gil-galad is mentioned in only two places (he's long dead by the time of those events).

The first time we hear anything about Gil-galad is when Aragorn is leading the hobbits to Weathertop (the watchtower of Amon Sûl) and Merry questions him about the history of the road they're taking. Aragorn explains that it is an ancient road leading to Amon Sûl, where Elendil watched for the coming of Gil-galad during the Last Alliance of Men and Elves. When Merry asks who Gil-galad was, Sam recites three stanzas of a poem from the lay (song) called *The Fall of Gil-galad* that he's learned from Bilbo. The second and last time we hear of Gil-galad in *The Lord of the Rings* is at the Council of Elrond when Elrond recounts his eyewitness account of the fall of Gil-galad and Elendil at the hands of Sauron (which astonishes Frodo, as it does the rest of us — to think of anyone living through thousands of years of history, let alone remembering any of it).

By all accounts, certainly including the two in *The Lord of the Rings*, Gil-galad is the stuff of legends rather than a robust Elven character. Tolkien makes him into the quintessence of the legendary hero, one whose courage is captured and remembered in a heroic poem. Gil-galad is never a real character in either *The Silmarillion* or *The Lord of the Rings* in the same way, for example, that Elrond or Galadriel are. For Tolkien, Gil-galad is an ideal of the fallen hero remembered in epic song whose mighty deeds are meant to inspire and encourage later generations.

Legolas, Prince of the Woodland Elves

Legolas ("Green Leaf") is the son of King Thranduil, King of the Woodland Elves in Mirkwood. As his father's representative at the Council of Elrond, Legolas becomes a member of the Fellowship of the Ring.

As part of this company, Legolas becomes firm friends with the Gimli the Dwarf (see Chapter 6) as well as comrade-in-arms to the future king, Aragorn. After the death of Boromir and the breaking of the Fellowship, Legolas fights alongside Gimli and Aragorn at the Battle of the Hornburg and accompanies them through the Passes of the Dead to the fight with the Black Corsairs at the port of Pelargir and at the Battle of the Pelennor Fields.

As warned by Galadriel, after Legolas first comes upon the sea in Gondor, he is never again content to dwell in the woods of Middle-earth. After the passing of King Aragorn, Legolas builds a grey ship and sails it with his dear friend Gimli down the great River Anduin and west to the Undying Lands of Aman.

In the story of the friendship that grows between Legolas and Gimli, Tolkien shows the reader an example of how tolerance is possible between people from widely divergent and naturally mistrustful backgrounds (the Elves never completely forgive the Dwarves for the murder of Thingol — see "Thingol and the recovery of the Silmarils" earlier in this chapter). As we experience Legolas in this story of growing friendship with Gimli, he becomes, like Elrond, another example of the nobility and selflessness that Elves are capable of achieving. Their examples contrast with those of Elves like Fëanor and Thingol who seemingly are incapable of rising to this level and, as a result, come to tragic ends.

Table 4-1 lists some of the more important Elves in Middle-earth.

Table 4-1	Some Important Elves of Middle-earth	
Name	*Translation*	*Who They Are*
Aredhel	Noble Elf	Turgon's sister, married to the Dark Elf Eöl
Arwen Undomiel	Daughter of Twilight	Elrond's daughter, Aragorn's Queen, chose mortal life for his sake
Avari	The Unwilling	Elves who refused summons to live in Aman
Calaquendi	Light Elves	Elves who've seen the light of the Two Trees in Aman
Celeborn	Silver Tree	Lord of Lothlórien and husband of Galadriel
Celebrimbor	Hand of Silver	Grandson of Fëanor, forged Rings of Power
Círdan	Shipwright	Master of the Grey Havens
Dior / Eluchíl	Elu's Heir	Son of Beren and Lúthien
Elrond	Star Dome	Master of Rivendell, father of Arwen Undomiel
Elwë Thingol	Elu Singollo, Elwë Greymantle	Leader of the Teleri Elves, forbade Quenya
Elwing	Star-spray	Eärendil's wife, helped him go to Aman
Fëanor	Spirit of Fire	Created Tengwar script, palantíri, Silmarils
Finarfin	Royal (Golden) Hair	Leader of the remaining Noldor at Tirion

(continued)

Table 4-1 (continued)

Name	Translation	Who They Are
Fingolfin	Cloak of Hair	High King of the Noldor, slain by Morgoth
Finrod Felagund	Champion of Golden Hair	Aided Beren in recovering the Silmaril
Finwë	Hairy One	Fëanor's, Fingolfin's, and Finarfin's father, leader of the Noldor
Galadriel	Radiant Garland Maiden	Ruler of Lothlórien, keeper of an Elven-Ring
Gil-galad	Star of Radiance	Formed the Last Alliance of Men and Elves
Laiquendi	Green Elves	Elves of Beleriand and Mirkwood Forest
Legolas	Green Leaf	Elf member of Fellowship of the Ring
Lúthien Tinuviel	Nightingale	Helped husband Beren recover Silmaril
Nandor	Those Who Turn Back	Teleri who refused journey west to Aman
Noldor	Wise	Elves led by Finwë to Aman
Sindar	Grey Elves	Elves who stayed in Beleriand under Thingol
Teleri	Lastcomers	Largest group of Elves, last to leave for Aman
Thranduil	Hall of Star Shadow	Legolas's father, King of the Woodland Realm
Turgon	Master Commander	Founded Hidden Kingdom of Gondolin
Vanyar	The Fair	Smallest group of Elves, first to leave for Aman

Chapter 5

The Mortal Race of Men

*I*n Tolkien's Middle-earth, Men — which is what he calls people of both genders — are the second-born of Eru Ilúvatar, the Creator. This makes the Firstborn Elves the Elder Kindred. As the "babies" of Ilúvatar's family, Men literally wander onto the scene in Beleriand and are quickly embroiled in the conflicts between Morgoth and the Elves (see Chapters 11 and 12 for the blow-by-blow details of these conflicts).

This chapter explores the role of Men in Middle-earth and compares it with that of Tolkien's favorites, the Elves. This exploration looks closely at the relationship between Men and Elves, especially those rare, but very significant, Elf/human unions. This chapter also acquaints you with the different tribes of Men found in Middle-earth and the significance of the Age of Men in *The Lord of the Rings* — plus it gives short biographies on some of the greatest heroes among Men, one of whom is a woman.

Mankind's Role in Middle-earth

Tolkien's idea of Men as the second-born children of God (Ilúvatar), rather than the *only* children is quite exceptional. The Christian worldview normally admits of no other earthly creatures on a par with humanity — let alone superior, as Elves seem to be.

This has led to speculation by some critics of Tolkien's work that Elves represent a superior form of "humanness," a brighter, more evolved, more spiritual form. That, of course, would make Men a younger, less evolved, and in some ways less spiritual form of humanness (or "Elfness," rather).

As appealing as this idea may be, I find it hard to believe that this was Tolkien's purpose for creating two similar yet very different races of beings and putting the Elves ahead of humans as the elder race. For one thing, humans were presumably his intended audience. For another, Tolkien makes it clear that Ilúvatar is not only the sole creator of both races (they were not influenced by the Valar), but that both races were planned for from the beginning in the themes in the Music of Creation.

So it's hard to understand why Ilúvatar would create a less spiritually evolved form of humanity after creating a more evolved one in the Elves. Although many ancient cultures such as the Greeks and the Chinese have myths in which a Golden Age of Mankind is followed by successive ages of cultural degradation, none involves the creation of a secondary, less-perfect form of humanity.

In Tolkien's world, neither race avoids trouble. The Elves experience theirs when they rebel against the Valar in Aman and become embroiled in the war over the Silmarils in Beleriand. Men fall into the hands of Sauron — first in Númenor in his convincing them to storm Aman, and later in Middle-earth when they are corrupted by his Rings of Power.

The history of Tolkien's world involves a kind of cyclical decline — what Galadriel at one point calls "the long defeat." But Tolkien gives no indication that this is the result of Men's inferiority to Elves. In fact, *The Silmarillion* consistently implies that Men are secondary only in the literal sense that Ilúvatar created the Elves first — who are always the "elder brothers."

Mortality as God's gift to Men

Ilúvatar gave Men a special gift that neither the Ainur (the Holy Ones, see Chapter 3) nor the Elves get: a mortal life. As immortals, the destinies of the Ainur and the Elves are tied to that of Arda, so that they are all fated to exist in one form or another until the world ends. Elves in particular either remain in the Houses of the Dead or return to the world in some sort of reincarnation.

This contrasts greatly to the fate of Men, who die after a relatively short number of years (although the early kings of Men lived into their hundreds). When they die, Men first go to the Houses of the Dead in the Blessed Realm of Aman, just as the Elves do. But after a time, their spirits leave the Houses of the Dead and the physical world. Where exactly they go is a secret that Tolkien never reveals.

In Middle-earth, the greatest among Men accept this gift of mortality as the bittersweet part of being human and use their limited lifespan to discover and attain their individual destiny. The weakest reject and fear this gift and spend their time denying its reality or, in some instances, fighting against it. (For more on mortality and immortality, see Chapter 16.)

The freedom of mortal Men

To the Elves of Middle-earth, the race of Men seems especially frail and weak, falling prey to sickness, old age, and ultimately natural death. The Elves know nothing of these particular human ailments. They can only die through being slain or by contracting a disease known as "weariness of the world" (a kind of Elven ennui).

When you compare the human lot — riddled as it is with the pain of disease, old age, and death — with that of the Elves and their world-weariness, the fate of humanity doesn't seem so horrible. Ilúvatar's gift isn't such a bad deal in the end. After all, each Elf faces an eternity of either fighting and defeating evil only to see it reappear or waiting in the Houses of the Dead for the world to end. Men face a similar fight but only for a short while and with the knowledge that through death they will be freed from the struggle. By pairing the immortal race of Elves with the mortal race of Men, Tolkien can play off the difference between those whose lives are linked to the fate of the world with those whose lives can be free of it.

Some of Tolkien's mortal characters despair at the brevity of Men's years and how little they can accomplish within that time, as well as envy the immortality of the Firstborn. For other Men, the awareness of their capacity for surpassing the fate of the world enables them to fulfill their own destinies. These Men who make their limited number of years valuable way beyond their count become the heroes of Middle-earth.

The Awakening of Men

In the *Quenta Silmarillion* (History of the Silmarils, one of the books of *The Simarillion*), Tolkien tells us that Ilúvatar awoke his younger children, the race of Men, at the dawn of the very first sunrise in the far eastern regions of Middle-earth called Hildórien ("Place of the Followers") — *Followers* being one of the designations that Elves give the second-born Men. Tolkien also says that because this first sunrise occurred in the west, and the opening eyes of Men were turned toward it, ever after Men tend to stray toward the west.

Unlike the Elves, whom the Valar summoned to the Blessed Realm in the far west, no Valar came to meet or summon the second-born children of Ilúvatar in Hildórien. As a result, the race of Men know little of the Valar. They think of them as "gods" and, as often as not, fear them. Indeed, Men's mistrust of the Valar is only reinforced through their interaction with the Dark Elves (see Chapter 4). The Dark Elves only knew the Holy Ones of Aman through secondhand reports and through the servants of Morgoth, the Dark Enemy, who purposely misled them about the true nature and motives of the Valar.

Is the Garden of Eden in Hildórien?

Tolkien never actually accounts for the biblical fall of Man in any of his writings about the awakening of Men in the far east of Middle-earth. In the story of how Men wandered west into Beleriand and met the Elves, however, he does allude to a darkness that weighs on the hearts of the Men "on which they have turned their backs" and of which they have no memory. Many readers and critics interpret this as a veiled reference to the Fall of Adam and Even and their banishment from the Garden of Eden. Note that Eden means "East" in Hebrew.

According to Tolkien, the Elves say that when Men awoke in the east, Morgoth left Beleriand

for Hildórien to spy on them and, of course, to make trouble. If Hildórien is really Eden, this puts Morgoth in the role of the serpent who tempted Adam and Eve and caused their downfall there.

Tolkien is not alone in thinking that human death is not a punishment for the Fall. Many Jewish theologians do not attribute mortality to the Fall either, though St. Paul disagrees. I find the Hebrew text far from conclusive on this point, so Tolkien's view is as good as anyone's.

The Different Tribes of Men

The Elves first encountered the race of Men in the eastern part Beleriand known as Ossiriand. King Finrod came upon them on a hunting trip in that area. Finrod befriended the leader of the group, whom he named Bëor (meaning vassal) because this leader eventually pledged his unending loyalty to Finrod and the House of Finarfin (see Chapter 4 for details on Finrod).

Tolkien says the language of Men resembles the language of the Dark Elves east of the Misty Mountains, with whom Men first had contact. Finrod not only learned the language of Men, but also invited them to take up residence west of Ossiriand because the Men's presence was bothering the Wood-elves who dwelt in Ossiriand. Bëor moved his people to an area known as Estolad ("Encampment"), west of the River Gelion on the eastern shores of the River Celon, below Nan Elmoth.

In addition to Bëor's people, another group known as the Haladin, who spoke a different dialect of human speech, came to eastern Beleriand. They first settled in a more northerly region called Thargelion east of Estolad only to later move to the Forest of Brethil west of the Elven kingdom of Doriath.

A third group of Men migrated into Beleriand led by their chief Marach, who was a friend to Bëor and spoke a similar dialect of human speech. He settled his people southeast of Estolad. (See Chapter 14 for more on languages.)

The Edain

Atani is what the Valar call the race of Men, in the high Elvish dialect of Quenya. But the Dark Elves of Beleriand named them the Edain, the plural of Adan, meaning Man. Over time, Edain came to refer only to the groups of humans considered to be part of the three kindreds of Elf-friends — the Haladin and the groups under the leadership of Bëor and Marach.

Many of the descendents of the Edain became key figures in the history of Middle-earth, greatly aiding the Elves in their struggles against Morgoth during the wars of the First Age (see Chapter 12 for details). Figures 5-1 and 5-2 give the partial genealogy of the Houses of Bëor, Hador (descended from Marach), and the Haladin.

The House of Bëor
(and the mortal descent of Elrond and Elros)

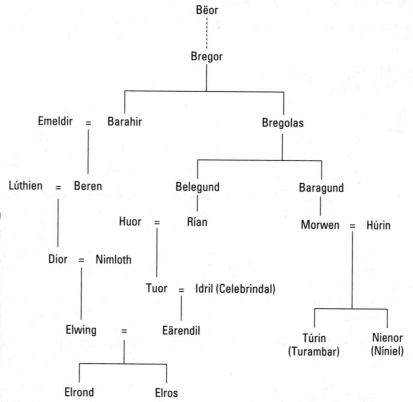

Figure 5-1:
The House of Bëor showing the paternal lineage of Beren and maternal lineage of Tuor and Túrin.

The House of Hador
(and the Haladin of Brethil)

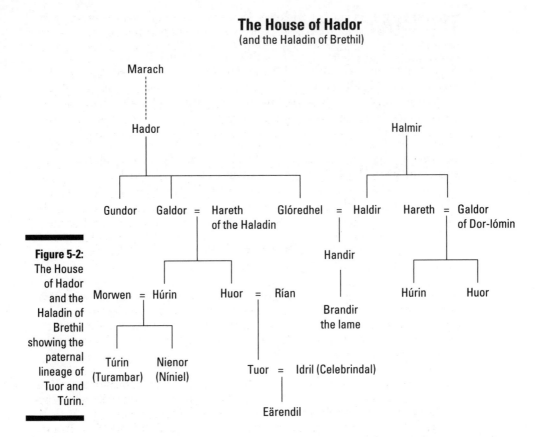

Figure 5-2:
The House
of Hador
and the
Haladin of
Brethil
showing the
paternal
lineage of
Tuor and
Túrin.

From these three houses came great heroes such as Beren who, with the help of the Elf princess Lúthien, wrested one of the Silmarils from Morgoth (see Chapter 18 for their story). Tuor, son of Huor, tried to save the hidden Elf-kingdom of Gondolin, and Túrin, son of Húrin, slew the dragon Glaurung, who had destroyed Finrod's kingdom of Nargothrond.

From the Houses of Hador (Haladin) and Bëor came possibly the most important hero in the history of Middle-earth: Eärendil, the Blessed Mariner who brought an end to the War of the Jewels. As you can see in Figure 5-1, Eärendil was the son of the hero Tuor and the father of the twins Elrond and Elros. Eärendil's wife, the Elf-princess Elwing, also descended from the House of Bëor. She was the granddaughter of Beren and his Elven wife, Lúthien. See "Eärendil the Blessed Mariner" later in this chapter for details.

The Dúnedain

The Dúnedain ("Men of the West") are the descendents of the Edain of Beleriand, loyal Men who fought alongside the Elves in the War of the Jewels.

For their service in helping to defeat Morgoth, the Valar rewarded them with the beautiful, star-shaped island kingdom of Númenor at the beginning of the Second Age. This kingdom lay in the midst of the Great Sea Belegaer, between Middle-earth and Aman.

The Valar forbade the Dúnedain to sail to the Blessed Realm, but the Elves of Tol Erresëa were permitted to sail east to Númenor and in friendship they provided the Dúnedain with gifts, including a seedling from the White Tree, that grew on Tol Erresëa (see "The lore of the White Tree" sidebar).

The Dúnedain were renowned as great sailors who often visited Middle-earth and eventually established colonies there, becoming very wealthy and powerful. Ar-Pharazôn, the most powerful of Númenor's twenty-odd kings, was so powerful, in fact, that he went to Middle-earth and subdued Sauron in his dark tower in Mordor and took him back to Númenor as a hostage. But once there, Sauron poisoned Ar-Pharazôn's mind, convincing the Dúnedain that if they took over the Undying Lands of Aman, they could then rule the entire world and partake in the land's gift of immortality.

But when Ar-Pharazôn's armada arrived in the Blessed Realm, Manwë called upon Ilúvatar, who opened a great chasm in the sea that swallowed up the armada. Ilúvatar then removed Aman from the physical plane of the earth, but in doing so, he opened such a wide trench that the island of Númenor sank beneath the waves.

The wealth and influence of Dúnedain island kingdom of Númenor, as well as its sinking, has many parallels to the ancient myth of Atlantis, which has captured the Western imagination ever since the tale first appeared in Plato's *Critias.* Atlantis was an island just beyond the pillars of Hercules (the Straits of Gibraltar) and ruled by Poseidon, the god of the sea (and the Greek equivalent of the Vala Ulmo). The kingdom of Atlantis became so rich and influential that it turned into a colossal empire that eventually colonized most of the Mediterranean.

For a long time, the kings of Atlantis, in whose veins divine blood flowed, upheld the laws and were virtuous — an exceedingly important thing to Plato — especially where their wealth was concerned. Eventually, however, they became corrupt and were filled, as Plato puts it, "with an unjust lust for possessions and power." As a result, Zeus, the king of the gods, punished them through a series of earthquakes that sunk the island of Atlantis under the sea. This sinking, Socrates claimed, made the Great Ocean (which we call, significantly, the Atlantic) impossible to navigate. Apparently because the rubble from the sunken island produced a vast sea of mud that mariners couldn't get beyond.

The sinking of Númenor wasn't the end of the Dúnedain, though. A few, called the Faithful, refused to join Ar-Pharazôn and escaped to Middle-earth. Under the leadership of Elendil of the royal house of Númenor and his two sons, Isildur and Anárion, the Dúnedain established the separate kingdoms of Arnor and Gondor. These two kingdoms are restored as the Reunited Kingdom by their descendent, Aragorn son of Arathorn, after the successful conclusion of the War of the Ring.

The Rohirrim

The Rohirrim ("Horse-Lords" in Elvish) came down in the Third Age from the northernmost parts of Mirkwood to settle a large tract of land in the vale of the Anduin between the River Isen and the River Anduin. They call themselves Éothéod (which is "horse people" in Old English) and they delight in the plains of the land they call the Riddermark and the horses that they raise there. The Elves call this land Rohan.

Tolkien's descriptions of the Rohirrim and how they live give the distinct impression of Viking-like Norsemen who just happen to adopt a land-locked lifestyle. Instead of roaming the sea in ships, they roam the plains on their horses. This Viking flavor is reinforced by Tolkien's extensive use of Old English in naming the people and places in the Riddermark. The word *Riddermark* itself comes from an Old English compound, *Riddena-mearc,* which means "the Territory of the Knights." In some ways you can think of the Rohirrim as Beowulf's distant cousins.

The Rohirrim live in simple villages, with thatched roof cottages reminiscent of Viking coastal settlements. Their only fortified "town" is Edoras, which means "Courts" in Old English. Edoras contains the royal hall Meduseld, which seems to be a cross between a traditional Viking mead-hall and a king's council chambers.

The simple, rural lifestyle of the Rohirrim contrasts greatly to the more sophisticated, urban way of life practiced by their neighbors in Gondor. This distinction is also born out in Tolkien's depictions of the major characters from Rohan and Gondor who appear in *The Lord of the Rings*. King Théoden of Rohan, for instance, is a salt-of-the-earth warrior who contrasts sharply with the calculating and complicated Denethor, Steward of Gondor and father of the major characters Boromir and Faramir.

The melding of the two very different cultures of Rohan and Gondor occurs in the romance and eventual marriage of Éowyn, Théoden's warrior niece, to Faramir, the very educated and somewhat pacifistic son of Denethor. See Chapter 23 for analysis of how the romance between this mismatched pair is an example of gender role reversal.

Great Heroes of Middle-earth

Human heroes abound in Tolkien's works. This section looks at a few of the more important ones in history of the first Three Ages. These include the First Age heroes Beren, Tuor, and Túrin and the Second Age heroes Elendil, Anárion, and Isildur. All the rest of the heroes covered in this section are from the Third Age and figure prominently in *The Lord of the Rings*. Of these only one, Éowyn, is not a man — a fact that is crucial to her story.

Beren, son of Barahir

Beren is an example of the mortal hero who accomplishes the impossible task — like David slaying the giant Goliath in the Bible. In Beren's case, the task was to recover one of the stolen Silmaril jewels from the iron crown of Morgoth, the Lord of Darkness. He was aided in his task by his beloved, the Elf-princess Lúthien, without whose magical help he would never have succeeded (for details on their love story, see Chapter 21).

The quest of Beren is very similar to the Greek tale of Jason and the Argonauts. In that story, Jason assumed the impossible task of recovering the Golden Fleece of the flying ram that carried his ancestor Phrixus to safety in the barbaric land of Colchis at the end of the earth. The Golden Fleece of the ram, which Phrixus sacrificed to the gods in thanksgiving for his safe journey, hung on a tree guarded by, of all things, a dragon.

Jason was sent on this impossible errand by an evil uncle who had usurped Jason's throne and wished him to fail. In Beren's story, King Thingol set the recovery of the Silmaril as the price for Lúthien's hand in marriage, hoping that Beren would fail, and his Elven daughter would never be wed to a mortal.

Medea, daughter of Aeëtes, King of Colchis, fell instantly in love with Jason and used her magic potions to help him accomplish the impossible tasks that her father set before him. She finally put the guardian dragon to sleep so that Jason could steal the Golden Fleece. Likewise, Lúthien used the magic of her voice to cast spells that put Morgoth to sleep, so that his crown containing the three Silmarils slipped from his head, enabling Beren to cut one of the three jewels free before he was awakened.

For the end of the heroic tale of Beren and Lúthien, Tolkien also borrowed from the Greek myth of Orpheus and Eurydice. In this myth Eurydice, the beloved of Orpheus, the famed lyre-player and singer, died and went to the realm of the god Hades (similar to Tolkien's Mandos). Distraught, Orpheus traveled to the land of the dead — the equivalent of the Halls of Mandos in

Tolkien. There, he sang and played such a beautiful and mournful tune that Hades relented and allowed Eurydice to return with Orpheus to the land of the living.

Tolkien uses the basic theme of this myth, although with his much-loved role-reversal, to bring his story to a close. Beren died of wounds sustained in recovering the Silmaril. A distraught Lúthien abandoned her body and sent her spirit to the Halls of Mandos, beyond the western edge of Valinor, in an attempt to bring him back. There, she sang for the Vala Mandos a sad lament that wove together the sorrow of Elves and Men. So moving was her song that Mandos felt pity and begged Manwë, King of the Valar, to intervene.

Manwë gave Lúthien the following choices: She could dwell with the Vala in Valinor without worry, but without Beren until the world's end; or she could return to Middle-earth with Beren and live in the uncertain joy of a mortal. Lúthien, of course, chose the latter. She and Beren returned to Middle-earth and dwelt on Tol Galen, an island in the midst of the River Adurant in south-eastern Beleriand.

At Tol Galen, Lúthien and Beren had a single son, Dior Eluchíl, who eventually inherited his grandfather's kingdom of Doriath, along with the Silmaril jewel that his father recovered in his quest for Luthien's hand.

Túrin, son of Húrin

Túrin is an example of the hero who slays the dragon, like Saint George, patron saint of England. In this case, the dragon was Glaurung, the Father of Dragons and the Worm of Morgoth (remember, *worm* denotes serpent in Old English). Unfortunately, Túrin's tale is as much a tragedy of one who falls prey to his cursed fate as it is a tale of the courageous knight who slays the evil dragon (for the tragic, Oedipus-like aspects, see Chapter 19).

When Túrin was very young, he was sent to live in Menegroth under the care of King Thingol and Queen Melian. Much later, after assuming many different identities, Túrin came to dwell in the Elf-kingdom of Nargothrond, now ruled by Orodreth, the brother of Finrod who was killed helping Beren recover the Silmaril. There, Túrin was hailed as Adanedhel (Elf-Man) because his bearing was so much more like an Elf than like a mere Man.

Morgoth unleashed the dragon Glaurung on Nargothrond. The serpent slew King Orodreth and laid waste to the underground fortress. Túrin met the beast on the fortress's stone bridge, which bore Túrin's name ever after, but came under the spell of the dragon's words — much as Bilbo nearly did when conversing with Smaug under the Lonely Mountain (see Chapter 10 for more on dragons and their devious ways). Glaurung then let Túrin go free to bring about his own downfall through unknowingly marrying his own sister (see Chapter 19 for details).

Some years later, Túrin encountered Glaurung again, this time at a place called Nen Girith ("Shuddering Water"). Here he slew Glaurung, but not before the dragon could exact revenge.

In a page right out of *Romeo and Juliet* (with that good old Tolkien role-reversal), Túrin swooned from the venom in the dragon's blood and appeared dead when Nienor, his sister and wife, found him. With his last breath Glaurung revealed to Nienor the true identity of her brother-husband. When she heard someone coming, she killed herself by jumping into the River Teiglin. Túrin then awoke and asked for the whereabouts of his beloved Nienor. Once the dreadful truth about Nienor his long-lost sister, whom he knew only as his dear wife Niniel, was revealed to him, Túrin fell on the sword he had used to slay Glaurung (see Chapter 19 for the entire sad story).

Tuor, son of Huor

Tuor is an example of the unknown hero whose mode of dress reveals his true identity as a messenger of the gods, as in the Greek myth of Jason and the Argonauts. In that myth, an oracle warned the King of Iolcus, who had usurped his brother's throne, that he would lose the throne to a messenger who appeared before him wearing only one sandal. When Jason was on his way to reclaim this throne, Hera, queen of the gods, disguised herself as an old woman who needed help crossing the river. In carrying her across the river, Jason lost a sandal in the torrent and so appeared before the king as Hera desired — wearing only one shoe. Revealed to the king as the one who threatened his throne, the king then challenged Jason to prove himself worthy by undertaking the arduous quest to retrieve the Golden Fleece.

In Tuor's story, it is Ulmo, the Lord of the Sea, who chose him to be his messenger to warn King Turgon that his kingdom of Gondolin would fall and to urge Turgon and his people to flee to the sea. To mark Tuor as his messenger, Ulmo revealed to him the whereabouts of weapons and a tunic that Ulmo had made Turgon hide away many years before he went to dwell in Gondolin.

Tuor was fostered by the Grey-elves of the eastern region of Beleriand known as Mithlum. At age sixteen, he was taken captive by a band of Orcs and wild men, known as Easterlings. After three years of servitude, Tuor escaped and lived as an outlaw.

Ulmo then found Tuor and led him to Nevrast, on the western coast of Beleriand, to a cave beneath Mount Taras where, many years earlier, Ulmo had asked King Turgon to hide away a shield, hauberk (a tunic of chain mail), sword, and helmet. Tuor took up these arms, and Ulmo guided him to the secret entrance of Gondolin.

King Turgon saw Tuor approaching the white walls of his city dressed in this tunic and bearing the arms that he had hidden away at Ulmo's command — a sure sign that Tuor was Ulmo's messenger. Tuor delivered Ulmo's warning to flee Gondolin, which King Turgon ignored to his peril. Fortunately, Turgon's daughter Idril — who just happened to fall in love with Ulmo's messenger — took his words to heart and prepared, over time, a secret exit from Gondolin. Through this secret passage, Idril and Tuor, as her husband, later escaped the sack of Gondolin with their seven-year old son Eärendil and a handful of others and made their way to the relative safety of the havens of Sirion.

Eärendil, the Blessed Mariner

Eärendil is an example of the mortal hero who journeys to the home of the gods and confronts them directly. In this, Eärendil is somewhat reminiscent of Gilgamesh, the Mesopotamian hero who sought out the garden of the heavenly gods in a quest for immortality. In Eärendil's case, he sought out the Valar in the Blessed Realm of the Uttermost West to request their aid against Morgoth and in ending the devastating War of the Silmarils between the Elves of Beleriand.

Eärendil's tale began with the building of a ship named Vingilot with the help of the famed shipbuilder, Círdan the Shipwright (see Chapter 4). Eärendil sailed Vingilot west in search of his father and mother, Tuor and Idril, who had sailed into the west some years earlier, and to plead the case of Elves and Men against Morgoth before the Valar in Aman.

Having found neither his parents nor Aman, Eärendil was heading back to his wife Elwing and his twin sons Elrond and Elros at the same time that Maedhros and Maglor, the sons of Fëanor, were attacking the havens of Sirion in a vain attempt to wrest the Silmaril from Elwing. (She had kept it from their grasp when they murdered her parents Dior and Nimloth in their attack on Menegroth years before.)

Rather than relinquish the jewel to the sons of Fëanor, now engaged in the third "Kinslaying" of Elves for the sake of the Silmarils, Elwing cast herself into the sea, wearing the Silmaril around her neck. But Ulmo had mercy upon her, bore her up into the air, and cloaked her in the likeness of a great white bird. In this guise, she flew to Eärendil and fell exhausted on the deck of the Vingilot. Together, they sailed again for Aman, guided by the light of the Two Trees in the Silmaril jewel Eärendil wore on his brow (see Chapter 4).

Finally, the Vingilot reached the Bay of Eldamar. When Eärendil and Elwing stepped onto the shore of the Blessed Realm, they were met by Eönwë, the herald of Manwë. He hailed Eärendil as the most renowned of mariners who, although looked for, came unexpectedly, and although longed for, came "beyond hope." (See Chapter 20 for more on the role of hope in Middle-earth.)

Eärendil came before all the Valar in the Halls of Valimar and pled for mercy upon Men and pardon for the Elves in Middle-earth. The Valar then pardoned the rebellion of the Noldor and decided to save Middle-earth by making war on Morgoth. To Eärendil and Elwing and their sons Elrond and Elros, the Valar offered the choice of which kindred to be associated with: mortal Men or immortal Elves. Elwing decided to be judged as one of the Eldar and Eärendil joined in this fate for her sake.

The Valar sanctified the Vingilot, causing it to rise in the heavens where Eärendil, as its mariner with the Silmaril on his brow, sails across the heavens. Ever after, the elder and younger of Ilúvatar's children in Middle-earth hail him as Gil-Estel, the Star of Hope, appearing as he does around sunrise or sunset with the light of the Silmaril shimmering brightly in the waxing or waning sunlight.

Then the host of the Valar accompanied by the Elves in Aman came to Middle-earth and cast down Morgoth's fortress of Angband. They captured Morgoth and bound him with his own iron crown, from which they took the remaining two Silmarils. Finally, the Valar heaved Morgoth into the Timeless Void, locked beyond the walls of the world, which is henceforth guarded by Eärendil in his heavenly rounds.

Unfortunately, this Last Battle in the War of Wrath did not end the curse of the Silmarils. Maedhros and Maglor, the last living sons of Fëanor, stole the Silmarils from Eönwë, who had removed them from Morgoth's iron crown for safekeeping. Because of their participation in the Elven Kinslaying, the Silmarils burned their unclean hands, causing Maedhros to jump into a fiery chasm and Maglor to cast himself into the sea. So, the War of the Jewels ended with each of the three Silmarils in different realms of the world: the Silmaril carried by Eärendil in the air above, the one stolen by Maedhros in the depths of the earth, and the one stolen by Maglor at the bottom of the sea.

Tolkien's myth of Eärendil, the Blessed Mariner, on one level explains how the planet Venus — known to us as the Morning and Evening Star — became a beacon of hope called Gil-Estel for the Elves and Men of Middle-earth. As I mention in Chapter 1, Tolkien was much taken with a line from the Old English poem *Crist* (Christ) in which the poet Cynewulf writes, "Hail, Earendel, the brightest of the angels over Middle-earth sent to men." Some scholars believe that the Earendel (meaning "First Dawn" in Old English) hailed in the poem really refers to the Morning and Evening Star — though it's very unusual for a Christian poet to hail a "star" as one of God's angels. Yet Tolkien, perhaps like Cynewulf, was aware that near the very end of the Book of Revelation, Christ likens himself to the Morning Star when St. John hears him declare, "I am the root of David, the bright and Morning Star."

Just as Earendel is the Star of Hope for Christians — a *messenger* (the original meaning of *angel*) proclaiming the ultimate return of Christ — Eärendil is the Star of Hope for Middle-earth, proclaiming ultimate deliverance from Morgoth. Given how deeply religious Tolkien was, it may not be too much of a stretch to suggest that this deliverance from the Lord of Darkness will eventually come to the descendents of these Men in Middle-earth in the form of Christ, the "bright and Morning star."

Elendil, Isildur, and Anárion

Elendil and his two sons Isildur and Anárion are the heroes who escape the sinking of Númenor and continue the struggle against Sauron in Middle-earth. As the leaders of the Faithful, a small contingent of Númenóreans who resisted the corruption of Sauron and didn't support the king's assault on Aman, these heroes represent both a kind of political and spiritual righteousness.

Elendil and his sons preserved the people of Númenor by leading most of the Faithful to Middle-earth (known collectively as the Exiles). They took with them the symbols of its greatness and learning, scrolls with the lore of their forefathers, the seven Seeing Stones from the Eldar, and — most important of all — the scion of the White Tree, Nimloth the fair, grown from its fruit stolen by Isildur and nurtured by the hands of Amandil.

Elendil and his sons not only attempted to reestablish Númenor in the new lands of Middle-earth, but also sought justice against Sauron, who helped perpetrate its downfall. They spearheaded the Last Alliance of Men and Elves with Gil-galad, last great king of the Elves in Middle-earth (see Chapter 4).

This great alliance defeated Sauron's army at the Battle of Dagorlad and then lay a seven-year siege to Sauron's dark tower, Barad-dûr, during which Anárion was slain. At the end of this siege, Sauron came down from his tower to battle Kings Elendil and Gil-galad. He slew both of them. Isildur then cut the One Ring from Sauron's hand with the hilt-shard of Elendil's sword, Narsil, which had broken when Elendil fell in battle.

With the loss of the Ring, Sauron's evil spirit fled his body and hid in the wastelands. The alliance eventually routed Sauron and leveled the Dark Tower to its foundations, bringing an end to the Second Age. Isildur returned to Gondor bearing Sauron's One Ring as an heirloom of his family, but he was slain by Orcs near the Gladden Fields while traveling north to take up residence in his father's kingdom of Arnor. The Ring — which abandoned Isildur by coming off his finger as he tried to swim away in the River Anduin, thus revealing him to the Orcs and leading to his death — became lost in the river. Thus began the Third Age and the final struggle with Sauron chronicled in *The Lord of the Rings*.

TRIVIA

Isildur's Bane

When Isildur cut the One Ring from Sauron's hand, Elrond and Círdan the Shipwright urged Isildur to destroy it by casting it into the fires of Mount Doom. Isildur refused, claiming the One Ring was *weregild* (man-gold) for his father and brother. Weregild (often spelled *wergeld*) was the value set in Anglo-Saxon law on a person who was slain to be paid as compensation to that person's kindred or lord, the amount varying according to the rank of the slain person. Presumably, because both Elendil and Anárion were kings, the weregild due for them was among very highest, making the One Ring the most "precious" to Isildur and a great "heirloom" of his kingdom. Of course, Isildur's weregild soon became his bane as well. The word *bane* comes from *bana*, Old English for "slayer" or "murderer."

Théoden, King of Rohan

Théoden is a perfect example of the warrior king and hero who literally throws himself into battle against his enemies against all odds. He is a fearless warrior on horseback who utters stirring words such as "Forth Eorlingas!" before leading a valiant charge on Snowmane, his beautiful white horse.

Entwined with the story of Théoden is the story of Gríma Wormtongue, his treacherous counselor (stories of treacherous ministers who poison the minds of their leaders and undermine their confidence abound in tales ancient and modern). Gríma is surreptitiously helping the wizard Saruman who is secretly in league with the Enemy, Sauron (see Chapter 8). Under the spell of Wormtongue, Théoden lacks his natural courage and becomes a recluse in his golden hall of Meduseld, far from his troops at the battlefront. It is only after Gandalf breaks Gríma's hold on Théoden that he returns to his old vigor, becoming a force to be reckoned with in the War of the Ring.

As the renewed king of the Rohirrim, Théoden features prominently in the later battle scenes of *The Lord of the Rings,* especially in the Battles of the Hornburg and Pelennor Fields (see Chapter 24 for details). He falls in the latter battle and is crushed under the weight of Snowmane, who is brought down by the Lord of the Nazgûl. This is perhaps the most proper way Tolkien could have him die. (See the following section on Éowyn for more.)

After his death in battle, King Théoden is arrayed in his battle gear and buried in a fashion that any Viking lord would fancy, to the cries of "Théoden King!" by his loyal horse-lords.

Éowyn, Lady of Rohan

Éowyn, King Théoden's neice, is known alternately as the shield-maiden and the Lady of Rohan. In many ways, Éowyn is a female version of the King of the Riddermark. She is frustrated at not being allowed to partake in the honor and glory of battle with the other, male horse-lords. To that end, she disguises herself as the male knight Dernhelm (meaning "Secret Helmet" in Old English) and bears the hobbit Merry, acting as King Théoden's squire, into the Battle of Pelennor Fields in Gondor.

On the field, Éowyn distinguishes herself by facing down the Lord of the Ringwraiths and slaying his winged-serpent steed in her attempt to protect the mortally wounded King Théoden. As she stands between the Ringwraith and Théoden, the Lord of the Ringwraiths warns her not to stand in his way, saying, "no living man may hinder me." Éowyn then unnerves the Ringwraith by removing her helmet to show her long golden hair — as a woman, she is indeed no "man" standing in his way. Then Merry and Éowyn slay the Ringwraith. Merry stabs him first with the blade retrieved the Barrow-downs (see Chapter 9) crafted in earlier ages by the Lords of the Dúnedain who fought the Lord of the Nazgûl when he was the Witch-king of Angmar. Éowyn then gives him the final blow by driving her sword in the space beneath his crown and the mantle of his cloak where his head ought to be, which shatters her sword into a million pieces, causing the wraith's spirit to rise into the wind and disappear forever.

TRIVIA

"None of woman born shall harm Macbeth"

Tolkien had a bone to pick (actually a couple) with Shakespeare's play *Macbeth*. He felt that the Bard of Avon got off a little too easy when it came to the predictions given to Macbeth. One prediction that has bearing on the story of Éowyn and her battle with the Lord of the Nazgûl is that given by the ghost who tells Macbeth that no one born of woman shall ever be able to harm him. In the play, Macduff is able to kill Macbeth because he was born by Caesarean section — technically he's not "of woman" born, in the sense of a normal birth.

Tolkien supposedly wasn't happy at all with this explanation and thought it was a big copout on Shakespeare's part. He wove what he thought was a better version of this prediction into his tale of Éowyn and the Lord of the Nazgûl. When the Ringwraith challenges Éowyn with the line "no living man may hinder me," she pulls off her helmet and reveal herself as a woman. As far as I'm concerned, Tolkien's linguistic trick is only a little less technical than Shakespeare's — besides, who was Tolkien to talk when he used the gender-specific term *Men* to refer to humans of both sexes?

Gravely injured after her battle with Ringwraith Lord, Éowyn is taken to the Houses of Healing in Minas Tirith where she is tended to and healed by Aragorn (see "Aragorn, son of Arathorn, King of the Reunited Kingdom" later in this chapter). While recovering, she renounces her life as a shield-maiden and takes up the path of a healer. She also falls in love with Faramir, who is also healing from a wound and from the suicide of his father, Denethor (see "Faramir, son of Denethor, Steward of Gondor" that follows). At the end of *The Lord of the Rings,* they marry and dwell in Ithilien, where they work at restoring the "garden of Gondor."

Faramir, son of the Steward of Gondor

Faramir ("Jeweled Hunter") is not what you'd call a conventional warrior hero. The fact that he — son of the Steward of Gondor and younger brother of Boromir (of the Fellowship of the Ring) — doesn't fit into any standard mythological "hero" molds makes him all the more interesting.

Faramir is the captain of a band of Rangers who patrol the borders of Gondor in the ruined land of Ithilien, engaging in a kind of guerilla warfare against their enemies, the Southrons and Orcs. When Faramir and his band come upon Frodo and Sam and interrogate them in the cave at Henneth Annûn, they are wearing green and brown jerkins and equipped with bows and green arrows — very reminiscent of Robin Hood and his merry men.

Although Faramir lives a life more suited to the outlaws of Sherwood Forest, he is well educated in the history and lore of his people. He is even taught some of the writing of the old characters by none other than Gandalf the Wizard (known in Gondor as Mithrandir, the Grey Pilgrim — see Chapter 8).

Faramir, although forced into the role of a warrior, is really a pacifist at heart and longs for the days of peace and the return of the rightful king. He makes it clear in his speech to Frodo and Sam that he has no love for the weapons of war and the glory of the warrior, only a love for the things that they defend. This very modern view of war puts Faramir at odds with the likes of King Théoden, Éowyn the shield-maiden, and especially his elder brother Boromir.

In comparison to Boromir, Faramir is neither quick to action nor to judgment. Boromir wants things done quickly — he criticizes his father for not seizing the throne of Gondor after so many years as the Steward and the Council of Elrond for not using the Ring against the Enemy. Faramir, on the other hand, wants to study the situation and analyze all the facts before rushing to judgment and taking action.

Faramir's slow, studied approach ends up a key element in the success of the quest to destroy the One Ring. Instead of taking the Ring back to Minas Tirith in Gondor as his duty commands, Faramir recognizes it as Isildur's Bane and lets Frodo and Sam free to complete their appointed task in Mordor. In this way, Faramir's restraint, so sorely lacking in his brother Boromir, helps to bring down and destroy the overconfident and overeager Sauron. (See Chapter 20 for details on Boromir's fall and redemption.)

In the Houses of Healing, Faramir, recovering from a wound and his father's suicide (during which he nearly died), falls in love with Éowyn. Here is another example of a Tolkien role-reversal: Instead of the mild-mannered woman who restrains the bellicose nature of her warrior lover, Tolkien creates an educated, peace-loving man attempting to temper the battle-lust of his rough-and-tumble shield-maiden of Rohan.

Fortunately, Faramir's love and Éowyn's conversion from ways of war to ways of healing enable them to become a happily-ever-after storybook couple who, through their dedication to healing the wounds of war, help restore the gardens of Ithilien to their former beauty. In some ways, the story of Faramir and Éowyn is a veritable "Beauty and the Beast" tale with the old Tolkien twist so that Faramir plays the part of Beauty and Éowyn (at least, in her shield-maiden days) the Beast. See Chapter 23 for more on Faramir and Éowyn as examples of gender role reversal.

Aragorn, son of Arathorn, King of the Reunited Kingdom

Aragorn is an example of the unknown king who must prove himself worthy to regain his throne. In this way, he is very much Middle-earth's equivalent of King Arthur of Camelot. Like Arthur, who was fostered in Sir Ector's castle and whose royalty is concealed from him, Aragorn is fostered in Rivendell by Elrond Half-elven and only later told of his royal ancestry.

Aragorn's mother Gilraen ("Wandering Star") is widowed early when Orcs ambush and slay her husband, Arathorn. She then seeks refuge for herself and her son in Rivendell under Master Elrond's protection. There, she gives Aragorn the name Estel ("Hope" in Elvish) and keeps from him his true name of Aragorn and his lineage as the sole living heir of Isildur.

When Aragorn turns twenty, Elrond reveals to him his true name and identity and gives him the heirlooms of his house: the ring of Barahir (the Elven King Finrod's ring given as token of friendship) and the shards of the sword Narsil with which Isildur cut the One Ring from Sauron's hand. Elrond withholds the Scepter of Annúminas, the royal emblem of the kings of Arnor, until Aragorn earns it by defeating Sauron and reclaiming his throne. Before Aragorn leaves the safety of Rivendell to seek his fame and fortune, he meets and falls in love with Arwen, Elrond's only daughter, who has just returned home from her stay in Lothlórien with her mother's kin.

Elrond cautions Aragorn that he is fated to wed no woman, Elf or human, until he achieves his destiny of either outshining all of his ancestors or falling well below them. So Aragorn sets out and becomes an unknown wanderer — a Ranger of the North known by the name of Strider.

During this time Gandalf the Wizard befriends Aragorn, preparing him to achieve his greatness. This is also when Gandalf and Aragorn discover that the One Ring has indeed been found and become involved in the quest to destroy it.

Just as a big part of the myth of King Arthur has to do with Merlin the Magician, who attempted to train Arthur in the ways of being a just and noble king, Gandalf the Wizard befriends Aragorn and aids him in regaining his throne and achieving his destiny. The biggest difference is that Gandalf does not mentor Aragorn as a youth as Merlin did Arthur — this role is left to Elrond, who fosters Aragorn. Also, unlike Merlin, who stayed at Arthur's side well after he was crowned king, Gandalf leaves Aragorn shortly after he is crowned and sails to the Blessed Realm with Frodo and his company, leaving the new king to figure out all on his own how best to put the wizard's lessons into practice.

Aragorn leads the Fellowship of the Ring as they set off from Rivendell to Mount Doom. When the Fellowship breaks on the shores of Nen Hithoel, he leads Legolas and Gimli to Rohan in search of the hobbits Merry and Pippin.

To help Aragorn when he becomes the leader of the Fellowship of the Ring, the Elves reforge the pieces of Narsil into a new sword named Andúril (Elvish for "Flame of the West"). Andúril is the sword Aragorn uses to do battle in the War of Ring.

During the rest of the War of the Ring, Aragorn distinguishes himself as a natural-born leader not just on the field in the Battles of the Hornburg, Pelargir, and Pelennor Fields (see Chapter 24), but also in the Houses of Healing, where in healing both Faramir and Éowyn he fulfills the ancient prophecy, "the hands of the king are the hands of a healer" (check out Chapter 17 for more about Aragorn as the classic hero).

At the end of the War of the Ring, Aragorn is crowned King of the Reunited Kingdom, which combines the territories of Arnor and Gondor. He also weds Arwen, who for him chooses a mortal life over the Elven, immortal life (see Chapter 18 for more on Aragorn and Arwen).

TRIVIA

The lore of the White Tree

The White Tree Nimloth ("White Flower") the fair — a descendant of the original White Tree fashioned by Yavanna as "an image" of Telperion (one of the Two Trees that illuminated Arda until they were destroyed by Melkor) — became inextricably tied to the fate of the Númenórean kings after the seer-king Tar-Palantir prophesied that when Nimloth perished, the line of Númenórean kings would perish as well.

When the last king of Númenor fell under Sauron's spell, Isildur secretly saved one of Nimloth's fruits, which his grandfather planted. Isildur took the resulting sapling Isildur to Middle-earth when he fled Númenor, saving both the White Tree and the Númenórean line. Eventually, a seedling from this tree was planted in the Court of the Fountain beneath the White Tower of Ecthelion in Minas Tirith, and a representation of this White Tree blossoming beneath seven stars became the herald of the ruling houses of Gondor. In time, however, the White Tree withered, and the bloodline of Isildur's brother failed, signaling what appeared to be the end of the line.

But Aragorn (and fate) came to the rescue. Just as Arthur's ability to remove the Sword of Kings from the stone in which it languished confirmed his legitimacy as King of England, the newly crowned King Aragorn at the end of the War of the Ring finds a sapling from Nimloth growing high on the mountain behind Minas Tirith. Nimloth hadn't died out after all, and the line of Númenórean kings lived on. Aragorn replants the sapling in the Court of the Fountain as a sure sign that the rightful king had returned to the throne.

Table 5-1 lists some of the more important Men (and woman) in Middle-earth.

Table 5-1	Some Important Humans of Middle-earth	
Name	*Translation*	*Who They Are*
Anárion	Lord of the Sun	Younger son of Elendil, first King of Gondor
Aragorn	Lord of the Trees	Member of Fellowship of the Ring, wed to Elf Arwen Undomiel, crowned King of the Reunited Kingdom, also called Strider and Elessar
Argeleb II	Silver King	Eriador king who granted the Shire to hobbits
Ar-Pharazôn	The Golden	Last king of Númenor, attacked Aman
Atani	The Second People	Elven name for the race of Men
Barahir	Tower Lord	Beren's father, saved King Finrod Felagund

Name	Translation	Who They Are
Bëor	Vassal	Leader of the first Men to go west to Beleriand
Beren		Recovered a Silmaril from Morgoth's crown
Boromir	Jeweled Hand	Member of Fellowship of the Ring, elder son of Denethor II (Steward of Gondor)
Denethor II	Water Torrent	Last Steward of Gondor, suicide by immolation
Dernhelm	Secret Helmet	Alias of Éowyn when she fought as a man
Dúnedain	Men of the West	Númenóreans who came to Middle-earth after sinking of Númenor near end of Second Age
Eärendil	Lover of the Sea	Wed to Elf-princess Elwing, sails the skies bearing Silmaril on his brow
Elendil	Elf-friend/Star-lover	1st king of Arnor, father of Anárion and Isildur
Elros	Star Foam	Son of Eärendil and Elwing, Elrond's brother, chose mortal life, first king of Númenor
Éomer	Horse Mare	Nephew, successor to King Théoden of Rohan
Éowyn	Horse Friend	Niece of Théoden, fought as a man in Battle of Pelennor Fields, wed to Faramir
Faramir	Jeweled Hunter	Younger son of Denethor II, wed to Éowyn
Gríma Wormtongue	Serpent Tongue	Treacherous counselor to King Théoden, later assistant and murderer of Saruman
Isildur	Lover of the Moon	Elder son of Elendil, cut the One Ring from Sauron's hand
Nienor	Mourning	Sister/wife of Túrin, also called Níniel
Rohirrim	Masters of Horses	People of Rohan
Théoden	People/Nation	King of Rohan during War of the Ring
Túrin Turambar	Master of Doom	Tragic hero, brother/husband of Nienor

Chapter 6

The Hardy Race of Dwarves

Talk of Dwarves invariably brings to mind those seven stouthearted fellows who sing, "Heigh ho, heigh ho, it's off to work we go" as they march off to the mines in Walt Disney's *Snow White and the Seven Dwarfs*. Tolkien's Dwarves share few characteristics with Disney's — besides the fact that they tend to be employed in the mining profession.

This chapter looks at Tolkien's Dwarves and the role they play in Middle-earth. It investigates the way in which Dwarves are traditionally depicted in Norse mythology and discusses how Tolkien adapts this portrayal in *The Hobbit* and *The Lord of the Rings*. It also looks at why Tolkien insists on calling them Dwarves rather Dwarfs and how in Tolkien's mythology they would have been awakened before the Firstborn Elves if it hadn't been for the intervention of Eru Ilúvatar.

This chapter also investigates the story of the Dwarves of Nogrod and Belegost in Beleriand, who become embroiled in the Elves' conflict with Morgoth (see Chapter 4), and their relationship with the Elves in Middle-earth later on as the lords of Khazad-dûm (the Mines of Moria). Finally, it looks at two of the more legendary Dwarves in Middle-earth, namely Thorin Oakenshield, the King under the Mountain in *The Hobbit,* and Gimli, son of Glóin, who joins the Fellowship of the Ring in *The Lord of the Rings*.

The Origin of Tolkien's Dwarves

In Germanic mythology, Dwarves are not very clearly differentiated from the Dark Elves who dwell beneath the ground of Midgard (Middle-earth) in a realm known as Svart-alfa-heim (Dark Elves' home). These Dark Elves are immediately turned to stone the moment they are caught in sunlight. As I discuss in Chapter 4, Tolkien's Dark Elves have nothing to do with the nether regions of Middle-earth. The only creatures in his mythology that turn into stone in sunlight are Trolls (see Chapter 10).

Unlike the Dwarves of Germanic legend, the Dwarves of Middle-earth are completely unaffected by sunlight. They can dwell above ground with no problem at all, if they so choose. Dwarves are also completely distinct from the race of Elves, both the Light and Dark varieties, although they do frequently interact with Elves both in Beleriand and Middle-earth proper.

Also, Dwarves of Germanic mythology are not only small beings, perhaps even smaller than Tolkien's hobbits (see Chapter 7), but are also reputedly very ugly, with dark complexions, green eyes, huge heads, stubby legs — and they're pigeon-toed. Because of their small stature, they also are said to be very nimble and love to hide behind rocks and eavesdrop on people's conversations, repeating only the last words — called "dwarfs' talk." To make them invisible so that they can't be seen by people when eavesdropping and from being turned into stone by the sun, Dwarves wear a tiny red cap called a Tarnkappe, which may be familiar from the lawn variety of Dwarf or gnome statuary.

Tolkien's Dwarves are not nearly so short, being somewhat taller than your average hobbit. Neither are they particularly ugly, nor do they wear red caps to make themselves invisible (only the One Ring does that). On the subject of their looks, Tolkien says that when the Elves first encountered Dwarves in Beleriand, they named them the Naugrim, which means "the Stunted Ones" in Elvish. Needless to say, Dwarves didn't take that as a compliment. They call themselves the Khazâd in their own tongue.

Why Dwarves and not Dwarfs?

Tolkien was well aware that the correct plural of dwarf is dwarfs. Nevertheless, he insisted on using the plural *Dwarves* rather than *Dwarfs*. The reason was that as a linguist he knew that modern English tends to add a simple *s* to words that end in the letter *f* so that the plural of *cliff* is cliffs. But words of great antiquity in English which end in *f*, such as *life* and *elf*, form their plurals by changing the final *f* to *ve* and adding *s*, so that *lives* and *elves* are the plural forms rather than *lifes* and *elfs*.

Using this reasoning, Tolkien imagined that the word *Dwarf* is one of great antiquity (it was spelled *dwerf* in Middle English). For Tolkien, it was every bit as old as *elf* and, therefore, its plural should be formed in the old way — hence *Dwarves*.

Tolkien's Dwarves do share some important characteristics with the underground creatures of Germanic mythology. For one thing, Dwarves are highly skilled in the smithing arts — both metallurgy and the jeweler's arts. And Tolkien's Dwarves, like the ones who dwell in Svart-alfa-heim, are miners par excellence, spending most of their time exploring caves, excavating underground strongholds, and extracting precious metals and gemstones.

The Awakening of Aulë's Children

In the second chapter of the *Quenta Silmarillion* (The History of the Silmarils), which appears in *The Silmarillion,* Tolkien relates that the Vala Aulë fashioned the Seven Fathers of the Dwarves in secret under the mountains of Middle-earth — before the awakening of Elves or Men.

Aulë is the Master Smith, similar to the Roman god Vulcan (Hephaestus in Greek), god of the forge and metalworking, except that Aulë is the lord of all types of crafts and skills, not just metalworking. Aulë not only loves to make things — he fashioned the mountains of Middle-earth, the Lamps of Arda, and even the vessels that contain the light of the sun and moon — but he also loves to teach these crafts.

One of the major reasons that Aulë fashioned the Dwarves was so that they could be his students and learn all his lore and crafts. However, Aulë ran afoul of Ilúvatar because he did not consult with him prior to fashioning the Dwarves in secret. As a result, Ilúvatar forbade the coming of the Dwarves prior the awakening of his Firstborn Children, the Elves. To placate Ilúvatar, Aulë put the Dwarf Fathers to sleep under the mountains until after Ilúvatar awakened the Elves.

TRIVIA

Aulë and Father Abraham

The Dwarves know Aulë as Mahal, the Maker. They consider him their father and teacher, rather than Ilúvatar. When Ilúvatar challenged Aulë's right to make the Dwarves, Aulë took up his hammer, ready to destroy his creation at Ilúvatar's command. But Ilúvatar stayed Aulë's hand, much as the Angel of the Lord restrained Abraham, the father of the Jewish nation, when he was about to sacrifice his son Isaac to God. Ilúvatar restrained Aulë as soon as the Dwarf fathers recoiled in fear and begged for mercy, demonstrating to Ilúvatar that they were creatures with a life of their own. In the case of Abraham, God restrained his hand as soon as He saw that Abraham's faith in His demand to sacrifice his firstborn was beyond doubt.

Tolkien tells us that Aulë made the Dwarves strong and unyielding so that they could resist the evil that Melkor was spreading in Middle-earth. Therefore, when Ilúvatar did re-awaken them they came forth "stone-hard" and "stubborn." As a people, they are quick to become either friend or foe, and they can withstand great physical duress, including toil, hunger, and bodily injury. As a rule, Dwarves live well beyond the age of Men, though they are by no means immortal like the Elves.

The Role of Dwarves in Middle-earth

Tolkien's role for the Dwarves in Middle-earth is probably best understood by reviewing their major characteristics:

- Dwarves exhibit much of their father Aulë's impatience. In his eagerness for beings to love and teach, Aulë could not wait for Ilúvatar's design for the Firstborn Elves to come to fruition.

- Dwarves are skilled in all the arts of their father Aulë, especially the skills of the forge, metalworking, and stone carving.

- Dwarves take great pride in all the things they fashion.

- Dwarves were made physically sturdy and psychologically stubborn to resist Melkor's evil.

- Dwarves are quick to make friends and enemies alike and slow to forgive the wrongs done to them.

Missing from this list is the Dwarves' short physical stature: just over that of a hobbit's (between two and four feet). As I argue in Chapter 7, for Tolkien, physical stature is not just a matter of size. Dwarves stand just below Men — who stand just below the Elves. This ordering could possibly reflect each race's relationship to Ilúvatar: Elves as the Firstborn, Men as the secondborn, and Dwarves as the adopted children.

However, the differences in physical stature among Tolkien's peoples may also reflect their relationship to desire and how it influences their aspirations and their abilities to realize them. As I maintain in Chapter 7, hobbits' small stature reflects their small-scale ambitions — to live happily, eating, drinking, and smoking their pipe-weed in peace. Dwarves dwell deeper in the earth than hobbit-burrows go, are more ambitious in their delving, and more covetous of Arda's riches.

On the positive side, their sturdiness gives the Dwarves the kind of driven personalities and energy required to perform great engineering feats, such as the excavation and carving of underground fortresses like Nargothrond in Beleriand

and Khazad-dûm in the Misty Mountains. Their stubbornness gives them the steadfastness and courage to be formidable warriors in fighting against Morgoth and later Sauron.

On the negative side, their pride in their skills makes the Dwarves very possessive of their work. When this strong sense of ownership is coupled with their somewhat volatile nature, it can lead to conflict, as it does when they try to seize the Silmaril from the Elves in Doriath. At that point, the Dwarves' stubbornness, instead of leading them in the resistance of evil, leads them to murder and theft (see "The fashioning of the Nauglamír" later in this chapter for details).

The Death and Rebirth of Dwarves

Although Dwarves typically live to be over 200 years old, they are mortal beings like Men and do eventually die from natural causes. Tolkien tells us that it is generally believed that when Dwarves die, they turn into the earth and stone from which they came. Here, perhaps, are shades of the Nordic myth about Dwarves turning to stone in sunlight.

The Dwarves themselves say that when they die, they go to a special part of Mandos (the Halls of Waiting) prepared by their father, Aulë. Here, it is said, they wait until the end of the world. At that time, after what is referred to as the Last Battle, the Dwarves will join Aulë and help him to rebuild Arda. Also in the end, Ilúvatar will bless them and set them in their rightful place alongside his other children (Elves and Men).

The Last Battle and Ragnarok of the Norse gods

In describing what the Dwarves believe happens to them when they die, Tolkien makes a casual reference to the Last Battle at the end of the world. Knowing Tolkien's Christian beliefs, you might be inclined to identify this Last Battle with the Battle of Armageddon described in the Bible's book of Revelation.

However, given that the Dwarves help Aulë rebuild the world after this Last Battle, chances are that, if anything, Tolkien is alluding to the final battle of the Norse gods, called Ragnarok.

In Ragnarok, the forces of chaos — personified by the giants — destroy both the gods and their abode in Asgard, the heavenly realm, and the realm of men in Midgard (Middle-earth). At the end of the catastrophe brought on by Ragnarok, Modi and Magni, the sons of Thor (who is the closest match to Aulë in the Norse pantheon), will still be alive along with the sons of Odin (king of the gods) to help rebuild the world for the new Adam and Eve (called Lif and Lifthrasir).

Dwarves also believe that the Seven Fathers of the Dwarves originally fashioned by Aulë are reborn again and again among their own kin, assuming their original names each time. The eldest of the Seven Fathers — and the only one Tolkien mentions by name — is Durin, also known as Durin the Deathless because of his long age. In the Third Age, when the action of *The Lord of the Rings* takes place, Durin the Deathless who disturbed the Balrog in Moria is in his sixth incarnation.

The Downfall of the Dwarves

Like the Elves in Beleriand and the Dúnedain in Númenor, the Dwarves experienced their own downfalls in Middle-earth. The first occurred in Beleriand when the Dwarves became mixed up with the Elves' battle for possession of the Silmaril that Beren retrieved for King Thingol of Doriath (see Chapter 4). This tragic tale involves not only the green-eyed dragon of greed but also the venom of vengeance, which helped to poison future relations between Elves and Dwarves.

In Middle-earth proper, the Dwarves faced ruin in the form of dispossession from their early homes under Erebor, the Lonely Mountain in eastern Rhovanion and from their most ancient dwelling of Khazad-dûm under the Misty Mountains. In their struggle to repossess and rebuild these ancient dwellings, they come face to face not only with the Enemy's minions (Smaug the dragon, countless Orcs, and even a Balrog), but also with the special strength of the Rings of Power forged for them by the Elves of Eregion under the leadership of Sauron and given to the Seven Dwarf Fathers.

The fashioning of the Nauglamír

It is during the Noontide of the Blessed Realm (see Chapter 11) that the Dwarves established first the great kingdom of Khazad-dûm in the Misty Mountains and the later the underground kingdoms of Nogrod and Belegost in Blue Mountains. The Dwarves from Belegost then helped King Thingol and Queen Melian of Doriath realize their vision of the Thousand Caves of Menegroth. They excavated the underground caverns and carved the plant and animal relief sculptures that adorn its many pillars. For this, the Elves called the Dwarves the Gonnhirrim ("Masters of Stone").

In addition to their work on the caves of Menegroth, the Elves of the Blue Mountains also aided King Finrod in creating his underground fortress at Nargothrond. At that time, Fingon also employed a group of Dwarves to fashion a necklace of gold for him and to set in it all kinds of gems that he had brought from the Blessed Realm. This golden collar — called the Nauglamír ("Necklace of the Dwarves") — was considered the Dwarves' finest work. It was of such exquisite quality that it hardly weighed anything and always rested on the wearer perfectly.

Unfortunately, the history of the Nauglamír is not nearly as lovely as its design. Upon the destruction of Nargothrond by the Glaurung the dragon, Húrin, the father of Túrin Turambar (Glaurung's slayer), took the Nauglamír to King Thingol of Menegroth as payment for the safekeeping of his children and wife (see Chapter 19 for details).

Thingol then decided to have the Silmaril jewel — recently recovered by his son-in-law Beren son of Barahir (see Chapter 18) — set in the Nauglamír so that he could wear it day and night and have its light with him at all times. The Dwarves of Nogrod marveled at the craftsmanship of the Nauglamír and the unparalleled beauty of the Silmaril. They consented to undertake the work, but secretly lusted after both the necklace fashioned by their fathers *and* the Silmaril gem — the product of the Elf Fëanor's unparalleled skill.

When the Dwarves finished setting the Silmaril in the Nauglamír, they were so overwhelmed by its beauty, which combined their skill with that of the Elves, that they refused to hand it over to King Thingol and demanded it for their own. When Thingol not only refused their demand but ridiculed them for asking, the Dwarves became enraged and killed him to steal the Nauglamír. This monstrous crime set in motion a terrible vendetta between the Elves and the Dwarves.

This vendetta began when the Elves caught up with Thingol's murderers and slew all but two of them. These two Dwarves returned to Nogrod and spread the story that Thingol ordered the slaying of their kin to cheat them out of their rightful fee for remaking the Nauglamír. The Dwarves of Nogrod then rose up to seek vengeance upon Menegroth, which then lay unprotected while Queen Melian returned in grief to Aman.

After the sacking of Menegroth, the victorious Dwarves retook the Nauglamír and attempted to return to their fortress in Nogrod. The Green Elves of Ossiriand, however, received the news of the sack of Menegroth and advance word of the coming of the Dwarf host. They planned to seek their vengeance for the slaying of their kin as Beren and his son Dior led the Green-elves in an ambush. In this battle, Beren slew the King of Nogrod and recovered the Nauglamír from him, upon which the Lord of the Dwarves had lain his curse. The Nauglamír therefore carried a double whammy, as it contained the Silmaril that was already cursed by Fëanor.

That ended the vendetta between the Dwarves and Elves of Beleriand. However, ill-feelings and mistrust caused by this terrible bloodletting continued to taint the relations between the two races even into the Third Age, when *The Hobbit* and *The Lord of the Rings* take place.

Freya's necklace and the Nauglamír

Norse mythology also has a story about a golden necklace made by Dwarves that is of such fine quality that is desired by many. This was the necklace of the Brisings made by four Dwarf craftsmen. This necklace became the property of Freya, the goddess of love, when she finally agreed to the Dwarves' price, which was to spend a night of love with each of the four of them. Later, Loki, the trickster of the gods, in the form of a flea tried to steal the necklace of the Brisings while Freya slept. Fortunately, Heimdall, the sentinel of the gods, spied this theft and fought with Loki (each assuming a number of different forms). Heimdall ultimately regained the necklace and returned it to Freya. In the Norse myth, the necklace of the Brisings was just as highly prized as the Nauglamír in Tolkien's story. The major difference is that its theft did not result in the same type of tragedy that followed the Nauglamír, due undoubtedly to the curse on the Silmaril jewel it contained.

The Dwarf-Rings and the downfall of Moria

Khazad-dûm — also known as the mines of Moria — is the oldest of the Dwarf dwellings. It was here that the Seven Fathers of the Dwarves, fashioned by Aulë, slept until they were awakened by Ilúvatar. During all the ages of the Dwarves, Khazad-dûm has been a rich and productive mine.

When the Sindarin Elves came from Beleriand and settled in Ost-in-Edhil in nearby Hollin, also known as Eregion, the Dwarves of Moria befriended them. These Elves included the smiths who, under the guidance of Celebrimbor and the help of Sauron, forged the Rings of Power with which Sauron intended to enslave all the various races of Middle-earth. As the Fathers of the Dwarves numbered seven, so Sauron had the Elves forge seven Rings of Power for their lords. Remember that even though Dwarves are mortal, their leaders continue to be reborn, returning to lead their people through the ages (for a modern reincarnation parallel, see the sidebar "The Dalai Lama and the Dwarf Fathers").

In *The Hobbit* and *The Lord of the Rings,* Tolkien relates the story of Durin the Deathless, one of the Seven Dwarf Fathers. According to the Dwarves, this is actually Durin III, the third incarnation of the original Durin, who received one of the seven Rings of Power from the Elves.

Durin's Ring of Power was responsible for much hardship in his lineage and among his people. However, because Aulë made his children strong in their ability to resist domination by the Dark Lord, Melkor (Sauron's mentor in evil), the Rings' evil doesn't work on the Dwarf-lords in the same way it does on other creatures.

Instead of putting the Dwarf-lords' wills under Sauron's direct control — as the Men's Rings do for the race of Men — the Rings only arouse in the Dwarf-lords a lust for gold and precious things. So great is this desire that if the Dwarf-lords lack these kinds of riches, then they regard all other good things in their lives as worthless. And if they think anyone else is trying to prevent them from having these treasures, they become filled with the desire to strike back at the ones they see as foes.

From this special influence that the Rings of Power holds over them comes the expression among the Dwarf-lords that the Ring "needs gold to breed gold." This need is first felt by Durin VI who lived during the middle of the Third Age (see Figure 6-1) just as Sauron's influence was beginning to creep back into the Mirkwood forest (see Chapter 12).

Under the direction of Durin VI, the Dwarves began to excavate much deeper under Mount Caradhras in search of the precious and very rare metal mithril, which was becoming harder and harder to find.

Unfortunately, in their delving they disturbed a Balrog, a Maia demon who escaped the destruction of Morgoth's fortress in Beleriand and took refuge in the dark of Moria (see Chapter 10 for more on Balrogs). This Balrog killed both Durin VI and his son Náin I (refer to Figure 6-1) and chased the rest of Durin's people from Khazad-dûm. Known ever after as Durin's Bane, this is the same Balrog that Gandalf ends up facing in *The Lord of the Rings*.

The Dalai Lama and the Dwarf Fathers

Tolkien's idea of Dwarf leaders being continually reborn to guide their people has a real-world parallel in the country of Tibet. According to Tibetan beliefs, the man known as the Dalai Lama — who was the spiritual and political leader of Tibet until his exile in 1959 — is the reincarnation of one of their original political and spiritual leaders.

Originally the title *Dalai Lama* (meaning "Ocean of Wisdom Guru" in Mongolian) was conferred on the monk Sonam Gyatso in 1578 by the Mongol ruler Altan-khan, to whom he was a spiritual mentor. Sonam Gyatso is now known as the third Dalai Lama because the title was conferred posthumously on two of the teachers in his spiritual lineage from whom he believed he was reincarnated. In 1642, the Mongol leader Gushri-khan set up the monk now known as the fifth Dalai Lama to be the spiritual and political leader of Tibet. The current Dalai Lama (Tenzin Gyatso) is believed to be the fourteenth reincarnation of the original monk in this spiritual lineage.

Lineage of the Dwarves of the Lonely Mountain
(as related by Gimli son of Glóin)

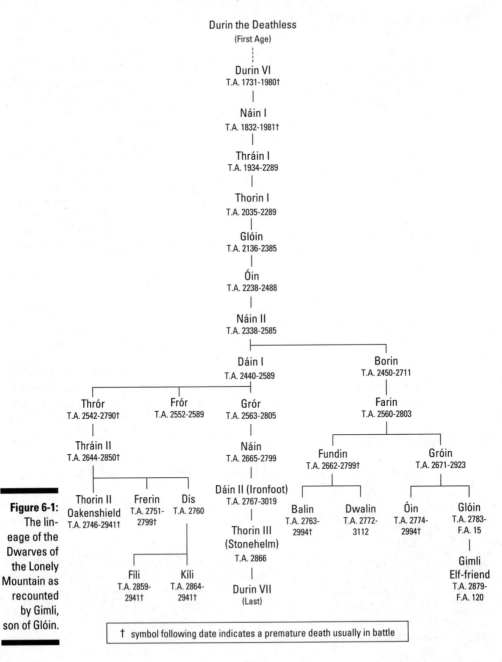

Figure 6-1: The lineage of the Dwarves of the Lonely Mountain as recounted by Gimli, son of Glóin.

Durin the Deathless
(First Age)

Durin VI
T.A. 1731-1980†

Náin I
T.A. 1832-1981†

Thráin I
T.A. 1934-2289

Thorin I
T.A. 2035-2289

Glóin
T.A. 2136-2385

Óin
T.A. 2238-2488

Náin II
T.A. 2338-2585

Dáin I
T.A. 2440-2589

Borin
T.A. 2450-2711

Thrór
T.A. 2542-2790†

Frór
T.A. 2552-2589

Grór
T.A. 2563-2805

Farin
T.A. 2560-2803

Thráin II
T.A. 2644-2850†

Náin
T.A. 2665-2799

Fundin
T.A. 2662-2799†

Gróin
T.A. 2671-2923

Thorin II
Oakenshield
T.A. 2746-2941†

Frerin
T.A. 2751-2799†

Dís
T.A. 2760

Dáin II (Ironfoot)
T.A. 2767-3019

Balin
T.A. 2763-2994†

Dwalin
T.A. 2772-3112

Óin
T.A. 2774-2994†

Glóin
T.A. 2783-F.A. 15

Thorin III
(Stonehelm)
T.A. 2866

Fíli
T.A. 2859-2941†

Kíli
T.A. 2864-2941†

Durin VII
(Last)

Gimli
Elf-friend
T.A. 2879-F.A. 120

† symbol following date indicates a premature death usually in battle

Legendary Dwarves in the History of Middle-earth

Of the many legendary Dwarves in the lore of Middle-earth, two names stand out: Thorin Oakenshield, Durin's heir, who leads Bilbo on the great adventures to the Lonely Mountain in *The Hobbit,* and Gimli, son of Glóin, who becomes a member of the Fellowship of the Ring and thus a major character in *The Lord of the Rings.*

It is interesting to note that both Thorin and Gimli are in the lineage of the Durin the Deathless (refer to Figure 6-1), one of the Seven Dwarf Fathers originally fashioned by Aulë, and both their stories involve Erebor, the Lonely Mountain. In Thorin's case, he is on a quest to take the Lonely Mountain from the dragon Smaug and thus to earn his ancestors' title, King under the Mountain. Gimli, after the death of Smaug, dwells in Erebor with his father Glóin, an important lord there. Together, Glóin and Gimli travel to Rivendell to represent the Dwarves at the Council of Elrond in deciding what is to be done with the One Ring of Sauron.

Thorin Oakenshield, King under the Mountain

Tolkien makes much of a simple chance encounter between Thorin Oakenshield and Gandalf the Grey Wizard (see Chapter 8 for details). In the village of Bree — perhaps at the Inn of the Prancing Pony? — Thorin and Gandalf hatch a plan by which Thorin and a company of twelve loyal Dwarves, with the help of the hobbit Bilbo Baggins, might bring an end to the dragon Smaug and regain Thorin's family's treasure under the Lonely Mountain.

Gandalf's motive in arranging the destruction of Smaug the Golden is to prevent Sauron from making use of the evil beast in the war he is plotting against Middle-earth. Thorin's motive is, of course, to avenge the exile of his grandfather Thrór and his father Thráin from the Lonely Mountain and to regain their treasure, including the priceless Arkenstone.

Gandalf is on his way to visit the Shire after a twenty-year absence at the time he meets Thorin and he just happens to stay in Bree because he is fatigued from the journey. The most amazing thing about this chance encounter is that part of Gandalf's plan involves bringing along Bilbo — who just happens to find the One Ring of Sauron during *his* chance encounter with Gollum in his cave under the Misty Mountains.

TRIVIA

When is a chance meeting the hand of fate?

You can be sure that Tolkien's chance meeting between Gandalf and Thorin Oakenshield at Bree is anything but chance. If you need proof, it may interest you to know that the date of this chance meeting is March 15, 2941 of the Third Age. In case you've forgotten your Roman history, March 15 is what the Romans called the Ides of March — the date on which Julius Caesar (although forewarned by the augurs not to go anywhere near the Forum) strode into the Senate where, instead of being declared King of Rome, he was murdered by a number of Senators, including his dear friend Brutus, using knives that they hid underneath their togas.

Chance encounters such as this in Tolkien's Middle-earth can be interpreted as a nudge by the hand of fate, although the author never makes clear whether this hand belongs to one of the Valar such as Ulmo or Aulë or to Eru Ilúvatar himself. It is interesting to note that Gandalf, himself a Maia — a lesser Vala, but from the Blessed Realm nonetheless — knows no more than we do about the source of these encounters. He just knows that there are powers at work for good in the world as well as for evil.

Gandalf's "chance-meeting" (see sidebar) with Thorin Oakenshield then not only deprives Sauron of Smaug's destructive power in his conquest of Middle-earth but also puts the One Ring into the hands of the hobbits, the only creatures in Middle-earth capable of withstanding its power long enough to bring it to Mount Doom — the only place it can destroyed.

Unfortunately, although Thorin and Company are able to destroy Smaug — through the skill and courage of Bard the Bowman, a Man, and with inside information from Bilbo on how to slay the beast — Thorin himself is not able to escape the evil of the Dwarf-Ring of Power. Its "gold-needs-gold" influence prevents him from being able to share the Dwarf treasure with the Men of Dale. Thorin is therefore prepared to fight Men rather than share the Dwarf-treasure of Erebor, when instead he should be preparing for an upcoming attack by Orcs and wolves.

When the attack finally comes, Thorin is mortally wounded in the Battle of the Five Armies. He is buried in traditional Dwarf fashion, in a hewn stone tomb, with the much treasured Arkenstone on his breast. Thorin's kingdom under the Mountain then goes to his cousin Dáin, also known as Ironfoot, who rules Erebor as King Dáin II (for more on Dáin's role in the War of the Ring, see Chapter 24).

Gimli, Son of Glóin

Gimli grows and evolves into a very special member of his race. In Gimli, Tolkien familiarizes readers with the average Dwarf sensibilities, their likes and dislikes, strengths and weaknesses. Through Gimli's growth as part of the Fellowship of the Ring, these typical Dwarf qualities are enhanced when they are in service of others and not in the service of hoarding riches. Gimli is not under the influence of "gold needs gold."

When Tolkien introduces Gimli and his father Glóin in *The Lord of the Rings,* they've arrived in Rivendell from Erebor to take part in the Council of Elrond assembled to decide the fate of the One Ring of Power. Elrond chooses Gimli to be one of the nine members of the Fellowship of the Ring — nine to counter Sauron's Ringwraiths, disguised as Nine Black Riders, who are looking everywhere for Frodo, the Ring-bearer.

Tolkien often contrasts Gimli, the only Dwarf in the Fellowship, with Legolas, the only Elf. One of the most poignant of these moments occurs when the Fellowship (minus Gandalf, who has fallen in Moria at the hands of the Balrog) arrives in Lothlórien, the Elven land of Celeborn and Galadriel.

Because of the ancient mistrust of Dwarves, the Elves initially refuse Gimli entrance to Lothlórien. They later relent if he is blindfolded, so that he cannot betray the way to the dwellings of the Galadrim. Gimli refuses this indignity, which singles him out from all other members of the Fellowship, and Legolas chides Gimli for his stubbornness. Aragorn suggests that all members of the Fellowship be blindfolded, to which Gimli replies that he will be satisfied if only Legolas is blindfolded as well. Legolas bristles in anger at this suggestion, causing Aragorn to chide Legolas for *his* stubbornness, which is quite equal to Gimli's. In the end, Aragorn has the Elves blindfold everyone in the Fellowship.

Through situations such as these, Gimli and Legolas begin to better understand each other emotionally and slowly become friends. In battle, they compete for the number of Orcs killed — an adolescent type of rivalry that ultimately helps them bond as well. By the end of their adventures during the War of the Ring, Gimli and Legolas are inseparable.

Gimli is known as Elf-friend, though, not only for his close relationship with Legolas but also for his great love for Galadriel, whom Gimli declares is far fairer than "all the jewels that lie beneath the ground." Gimli falls under Galadriel's spell when they first meet and she defends him against Celeborn's rebuke of the Dwarves' re-awakening the Balrog that fells Gandalf in Moria (see Chapter 20 for details).

In the adventures of the War of the Ring with Aragorn and Legolas, Gimli is every bit a hero and stalwart compatriot — even conquering his great fears by accompanying Aragorn on the Paths of the Dead (see Chapter 19). At the conclusion of the War of the Ring, Gimli becomes an important part of healing Middle-earth in the Fourth Age.

As I argue in Chapter 20. Gimli functions as a redeemer of the Dwarves' reputation when he becomes known as the Elf friend and later takes on the role of the protector the Glittering Caves of Aglarond as leader of the Dwarves. After the death of King Aragorn, Gimli is said to have joined his old friend, Legolas, when he sails out of Middle-earth west to the Blessed Realm of Aman. If this is true, it marks the first time that a living Dwarf ever comes to Aman, surely a testament to Gimli's special role as the friend of the Elves in the Third Age and the redeemer of the Dwarves at the beginning of the Fourth Age.

Chapter 7

Those Homespun Hobbits

"In a hole in the ground there lived a hobbit." So reads the first line of *The Hobbit,* wherein Tolkien sets in motion his entire saga of Middle-earth during the Third Age. In this chapter, you learn about these amazing creatures who continue to delight today's readers every bit as much as they did the author who created them.

I begin this exploration of hobbit lore by investigating the nature of hobbits followed by a discussion of their origin in Tolkien's imagination and his close relationship with his beloved "halflings." I continue with a look at the various breeds of hobbits and their history in the Shire. I also acquaint you with the most famous hobbits of Middle-earth, those being Bilbo and Frodo Baggins, Samwise Gamgee, Peregrin (Pippin) Took, and Meriadoc (Merry) Brandybuck.

I end this chapter on a bit of a sour note, however, in my examination of Gollum, the terribly conflicted hobbit, who although gone terribly wrong, plays a pivotal role in the history of Middle-earth.

Concerning the Nature of Hobbits

Tolkien seems to have regarded the Elves as his favorite creatures of Middle-earth, but most of his readers seem to be hobbit-lovers at heart. They find hobbits to be the most likeable and also to be the most like themselves, despite some obvious differences (for most people) in the height and furry-footedness departments. Even Tolkien referred to himself as a hobbit ("in all but size") for his love of pipe-smoking, gardens, plain and simple food, peace and quiet, his dislike of mechanized farmlands and traveling, and his fondness for wearing ornamental waistcoats on particularly dull days.

Before considering what hobbits really meant to Tolkien, you need to picture them as Tolkien designed them. In the Prologue to *The Lord of the Rings,* Tolkien asserts that hobbits are distantly related to humans and acquaints readers with all their vital statistics. According to this Prologue, hobbit characteristics include:

- A height of between two and four feet
- Feet with tough, leathery soles covered in hair (they seldom wear shoes)
- Long skillful fingers
- A tendency towards chubbiness
- Little or no facial hair (except for the Stoors — see "The Different Breeds of Hobbits" later in this chapter)
- An ability to disappear swiftly and silently
- Excellent hearing and sharp eyesight
- No understanding of machinery more complicated than the watermill, forge bellows, and the hand loom
- A delight in wearing bright colors, particularly yellow and green
- A love of food and drink (especially ale), eating a mere six times a day on average
- A love of laughter, jests, games, and celebrations
- A love of peace and quiet and "good tilled" earth
- A particular love for the smoking of tobacco in small clay pipes

For many readers, one of the more important hobbit characteristics is missing from this list — namely, their tendency to live in burrows or what Tolkien so ignobly calls a hole.

In fact, Tolkien is quite clear that only extremely rich or poor hobbits live in burrows (sometimes referred to in *The Lord of the Rings* as *smials* from the Old English *smygel,* meaning a "burrow" or "place to crawl into"). Because Bilbo and Frodo are such major characters in *The Hobbit* and *The Lord of the Rings,* and are fairly well-to-do, you are probably more accustomed to hobbits dwelling in very well-appointed holes (none of your wet, smelly rabbit holes, mind you). The more middle-class hobbits, Tolkien assures you, dwell above ground in houses of wood, brick, or stone.

Hobbits are deeply contented with their way of life. Understanding the level of this contentment is important to comprehending their central role in *The Lord of the Rings* and *The Hobbit.* Tolkien therefore spends a good deal of time introducing the reader to the way hobbits party and hang out together, thus ensuring that his readers understand the depth of this contentment.

Does Bilbo cheat to win the riddle-game?

Bilbo's thoughts on the sacredness of the riddle-game and the reluctance of even the wicked to cheat at it is ironic because he wins the riddle-game with Gollum on a technicality (a nice way of saying he cheated). According to the rules of their riddle-game (and where these rules came from is anybody's guess) the game continues until one player either can't correctly guess his opponent's riddle after three tries or can't come up with a riddle to ask his opponent. Bilbo is actually just about to forfeit the game (and his life) because he can't think of another riddle to ask Gollum when, fiddling about in his pocket, he feels the ring he found (Gollum's lost ring and Sauron's One Ring of Power) and simply asks out loud, "What have I got in my pocket?"

Technically speaking, this simple question (which Gollum takes a bona fide riddle) is not a riddle at all — at least not in the same league as the Sphinx's ("What creature walks on four feet in the morning, two feet in the afternoon, and three feet in the evening? Answer: Man, because he crawls as a baby, walks in adulthood, and uses a cane in old age) or Gollum's ("What has roots as nobody sees, is taller than trees, up, up it goes, and yet never grows?" Answer: a mountain). Compared to these true enigmas, Bilbo's simple question just does not pass muster, and so is actually a form of cheating — which even the wicked like Gollum wouldn't dare to do. Further, the answer to Bilbo's riddle is Gollum's golden ring, which Gollum has yet to discover he's lost. In a certain sense, these actions make Bilbo both a cheat and a thief — not exactly the noblest qualities you normally find in a hero.

A great part of the overall contentment with the hobbit way of life comes from their deep love of the Shire (from Old English *scir* meaning a "district"). The Shire is the region where most hobbits live, in the northwest section of the land of Eriador. Tolkien, like many English authors before him, is in love with his own "shire" (the Midlands in his case) and therefore naturally fosters in his hobbit characters a parallel love for their homeland.

In the tradition of English villagers at the turn of the nineteenth century, the hobbits of the Shire are very distrustful of any kind of stranger. They think it quite "queer" when they run into hobbits such as Bilbo and Frodo who go off on foreign adventures. Because everything any hobbit could desire is found right in the Shire, why would any hobbit *in his right mind* want to go off to some strange, far-off land in search of adventure, of all things! They often say that this isn't natural and trouble will come of it. And it often does.

So hobbits are Tolkien's "Everyman" in Middle-earth — creatures who just want to mind their own business and live a simple life. But the hobbits' simple life, just the like the one that Tolkien knew as a boy in the village of Sarehole (a hamlet just outside Birmingham), is being threatened by the outside world. Just as Tolkien saw the urban sprawl from Birmingham threaten the isolation and idyllic rural existence of Sarehole, the Shire in the Third Age faces its own menace from without that threatens to end its isolation from the rest of Middle-earth and endanger the hobbits' very way of life (see Chapter 22 for details).

Lao-tzu's description of an ideal hobbit life

Believe it or not, one of the best ways to understand Tolkien's hobbits and how they feel about life in the Shire is by reading Chapter 80 of the ancient Chinese classic *Tao Te Ching* ("The Way and Its Virtue") by Lao-tzu. This book extols the way of nature and the virtue of emulating that nature. Chapter 80, for all intents and purposes, could be describing the hobbits and their Shire when it says

> A small country has few people.
>
> Although they have machines a hundredfold, no one uses them.
>
> As people treat death as important, they do not migrate far.
>
> Even if they have boats and chariots, they do not ride them.
>
> Even if they have armor and weaponry, they do not display them.
>
> Let the people again tie knots and use them for reckoning.
>
> Their food is sweet and their clothes pleasing.
>
> Their dwellings are peaceful and their customs happy.
>
> Neighboring countries face each other from a distance; though the sounds of the chickens and dogs are within earshot, their people grow old and die without coming and going to see each other.

This quote as I translate it from the Chinese more or less sums up the attitudes and feelings hobbits have towards life, with one big exception. In the fourth line, Lao-tzu makes reference to boats and chariots. Whereas you might cajole a hobbit into getting into a carriage or chariot (they're generally way too short to ride horses), you'd rarely see them getting into a boat. Tolkien brings this fact home by relating how big a scandal the knowledge of the drowning of Frodo's parents, Drogo and Primula, in a boating accident on the Brandywine (Branduin) River causes in the Shire.

Hobbits and their homespun wisdom

Among the many delightful aspects of hobbits is their great homespun wisdom. Tolkien puts a number of pithy sayings, proverbs, and aphorisms into the mouths of the hobbits of the Shire. On the surface, the wisdom of these sayings appears commonsensical, but becomes a bit more complex when examined further. In Middle-earth, hobbits could write the equivalent of Ben Franklin's *Poor Richard's Almanac* — they achieve contentment by living their lives according to truisms.

One of the first of these sayings comes from the Gaffer, Sam's dad. At one point, the Gaffer warns his son about queer folk such as Bilbo Baggins by telling him not to get mixed up in the affairs of *"your betters"* or *"you'll land in trouble too big for you."*

When the hobbit fellowship of Frodo, Sam, Merry, and Pippin are making their way to the Bucklebury Ferry, Frodo suggests cutting across country to save time and avoid the roads (and the Black Riders who are following them). Pippin responds, *"Short cuts make long delays."*

A couple of my favorite aphorisms come from the incident in which Frodo finally gets Gandalf's letter at the inn of the Prancing Pony in Bree, warning him to make sure that he's dealing with the "real" Strider. Frodo tells Strider that if he (Strider) were a spy of the Enemy, he would somehow *"seem fairer and feel fouler."* Then, after Strider wryly observes that his looks are against him, Pippin quotes the old saying of the Shire, *"handsome is as handsome does"* — words of wisdom that many a mother tries to pass on to her daughters.

As you can see, these commonsensical hobbit sayings are cautions when making judgments about the truth of a situation. They are forewarnings of the troubles that come your way when you can't effectively make these determinations. This makes them typical of the kind "folk" wisdom and truisms that that abound not only in faraway legends but also in today's small communities all around the world.

A pocketful of riddles

Along with a natural knack for homespun wisdom, the hobbits seem to have an abiding love for riddles. This is borne out most clearly in the chapter called "Riddles in the Dark" in *The Hobbit* where Bilbo and Gollum engage in a rather long and drawn out riddle-game. Gollum suggests the game to buy time while deciding if Bilbo is good to eat and if he's hungry enough to eat him. Bilbo plays the game basically to gain time while sizing up Gollum and how best to escape him and his cave.

The most astonishing thing about Tolkien's account of the riddle-game is the general characterization that Tolkien makes about the riddle-game right after Bilbo's has bested Gollum and is waiting for him to pay up (by showing Bilbo the way out of his cave). At that point Bilbo says to himself, "He knew, of course, that the riddle-game was sacred and of immense antiquity, and even wicked creatures were afraid to cheat when they played at it."

Tolkien is correct at least in his assessment that the riddle-game is of great antiquity (I have my doubts about the cheating part), at least as far as legends and myths are concerned. One of the oldest and most famous riddle contests is the one that occurs between Oedipus (the Greek tragic hero who inadvertently kills his father and marries his mother) and the Sphinx (a monster with the face of a maiden and the body of a winged lion sent by Hera the queen of the gods to afflict Thebes). Like Bilbo and Gollum's riddle contest, the one between Oedipus and the Sphinx is one whose stakes are the highest of all in that if Oedipus wins, he lives, and if he loses, he dies.

Another similarity between these two riddle contests is that in winning their contests along with their lives, each of the heroes (Oedipus and Bilbo) gains some completely unforeseen winnings, not all of which are positive. When Oedipus wins against the Sphinx by correctly answering the Sphinx's riddle, he not only destroys the Sphinx, thus setting the city-state of Thebes free from the monster's evil, but also wins its throne and consequently the hand of the widowed queen Iocasta (who is his mother, unbeknownst to both of them). When Bilbo wins against Gollum, he not only escapes Gollum's cave life, but also carries away Sauron's One Ring of Power. Bilbo uses this magic Ring to great advantage in saving his own life and that of his companions in subsequent adventures with Gandalf and the Dwarves in *The Hobbit*. He also hands the Ring down to his heir Frodo, thus unintentionally laying on Frodo's shoulders the heavy burden of saving the Shire and the rest of Middle-earth.

Bilbo's riddle-game in *The Hobbit* is not the only example of the hobbits' riddle-solving ability. In *The Lord of the Rings*, the hobbit Merry is the one who helps Gandalf solve the riddle that prevents him from opening the Doors of Durin, the western entrance to Moria (Peter Jackson puts Frodo in this role in the *Fellowship* movie's version of this scene).

In the book, after Gandalf translates the writing on the Doors of Durin for the Fellowship, Merry asks him what is meant by the words "speak, friend, and enter." Gandalf immediately jumps to the conclusion that they indicate a riddle to be solved, in the sense that if you're a friend, you say the password (kind of like Ali Baba's "Open sesame"), and the doors magically open. In fact, after trying all sorts of exotic Elvish passwords to no avail, Gandalf discovers that opening doors is not a matter of guessing the secret password but of correctly interpreting the inscription plainly written on the doors. Merry was correct to question the meaning of the words for it is in their very interpretation that the secret to opening the doors lies. As soon as Gandalf properly translates the Elvish as "speak '*Friend*' and enter," he realizes that he has only to repeat the word "Mellon" — the Elvish word for "friend," written right there in the inscription — to open the doors.

This episode about getting the Doors of Durin to open offers a solid lesson in how best to interpret Tolkien's meanings in *The Lord of the Rings* and his other fantasy works. Instead of approaching his characters and stories as riddles to be solved, having definite correct and incorrect answers, I think you're much better off approaching them as expressions whose meanings are to be construed according to their context and that are open to many, sometimes divergent interpretations.

Hobbit-sized heroes

Despite their short stature and relatively conservative nature, at least when it comes to traveling and going on adventures, hobbits are the heroes of *The Hobbit* and *The Lord of the Rings*. In the case of *The Hobbit*, Bilbo Baggins saves the day for the Dwarves of the Lonely Mountain, even though it is a Man, Bard the Bowman, who slays Smaug the dragon, and even though it takes a host of Men, Elves, Dwarves, eagles, plus Gandalf to defeat the army of goblins and wolves. In the case of *The Lord of the Rings*, it's the hobbits Frodo, Sam, Pippin, Merry, and yes, even Sméagol/Gollum, who save Middle-earth from the domination of Sauron (see Chapter 17).

On the one hand, you may find it strange that Tolkien calls upon the "wee" folk of his fantasy world to carry the day. On the other hand, if you consider the hobbits' diminutive stature as a sign not of a lack of courage or steadfastness, but rather as a lack of towering ambition and desire, their heroic role makes perfect sense. In *The Lord of the Rings*, the Men, Elves, Dwarves, and wizards in the story, for all their might, are not able to handle the One Ring. Only Bilbo, Frodo, Sam, and Gollum are able to bear it, each with differing amounts of harm to their personalities (see Chapter 17 for more on the harmful aspects of the Ring to Frodo).

All those "greater" in stature than the hobbits, including the Dwarves because of their greater stoutness, are hampered by their high aspirations and the great purposes to which they would put the One Ring. To be sure, those purposes are noble ones, such as defending their people and defeating the Enemy. But most hobbits lack any overarching goals (other than a pint of beer and a good meal) that the One Ring could amplify and distort and in turn use to control them. The hobbit who suffers the most in bearing the Ring is Frodo, because he carries the ambition of destroying the Ring in the fires of Mount Doom — a noble goal but one that the Ring itself naturally resists.

The hobbits' way of life also suggests the "common person" who does his or her duty without any greater goal than a job well done and seeing the matter through to its conclusion — the ideal of any good infantryman, as Tolkien's experience on the front in World War I confirmed. By contrast, the high and the mighty seldom, if ever, do anything for its own sake. They are always working for a "greater" goal that inevitably colors the endeavor and that often can work against the very thing they want so badly to accomplish.

Viewed in this light, Tolkien's selection of hobbits as the true heroes of *The Lord of the Rings* and *The Hobbit* marks these works as very contemporary in outlook. For it seems to me that in contemporary history — the modern democratic age — the common man is the hero. This was especially true in the two World Wars (Tolkien fought in the first one, and his son Christopher fought in the second). In Tolkien's opinion, it wasn't the lieutenants, colonels, and commanders who were the true heroes of the war, but rather the common soldier — especially the foot soldier, the nameless infantryman. (See Chapter 17 for more on the common man as hero in *The Lord of the Rings*.)

Concerning the Origin of Hobbits

The origin of hobbits, with their odd names, small statures, fuzzy feet, and other wonderful characteristics, remains a mystery despite a number of interesting theories that are circulated.

One of the most well-known stories is the one that Tolkien himself propagated. One day while marking a batch of School Certificate papers (which he did to supplement his income as a professor), Tolkien turned a page in one of the examination booklets to find that the student had left it blank. Tolkien then impulsively wrote there the sentence that later became the first line of *The Hobbit:* "In a hole in the ground there lived a hobbit."

Tolkien became immediately curious as to the nature of this thing called a "hobbit" and how and why it lived in a hole. The result, as they say, is history. He then went about creating a geography, culture, and history to explain hobbits and, eventually, the entire Middle-earth mythology.

I like this story almost as much for what it *doesn't* say as for what it says. First, it appears highly likely that the sentence Tolkien meant to jot down on the student's blank paper was "In a hole in the ground there lived a rabbit" — because "a hole in the ground" is exactly where a "rabbit" is likely to live. Somehow, out of the musing or daydreaming fostered by the boredom of grading, the word popped out as "hobbit" instead of "rabbit," much to his surprise.

Of course, no one later denied that hobbits have anything to do with rabbits more fervently and consistently than Tolkien himself. I imagine that he would vigorously dispute my contention that he intended to write "rabbit" instead of "hobbit." He would insist, in his best Gandalf voice, that he always wrote down precisely what he intended to write down.

But the fact remains that rabbits live in holes and have furry feet with soles tough as leather, so that they rarely, if ever, wear shoes or boots (not even the ones in cartoons). Even more to the point, *The Hobbit* contains many references to Bilbo Baggins either acting or appearing like a rabbit. At one point, as he is carried down by an eagle to the grasslands below, the eagle chides him for holding on so tightly. The eagle says that there's no need to be "frightened like a rabbit even if you look rather like one." Later, Beorn (see Chapter 9 of this book) pokes Bilbo in the stomach and remarks that the "little bunny is getting nice and fat again on bread and honey."

Even if Tolkien's characters in *The Hobbit* hadn't sometimes compared Bilbo's looks and actions to those of a bunny rabbit, I'm afraid that many readers, including myself, would still make this connection. The biggest reason I can't entirely dissociate hobbits from rabbits is because Tolkien's depiction of Bilbo dressed in his waistcoat (with his furry hobbit feet) is just a little too reminiscent of the worried and shoeless white rabbit who arouses Alice's curiosity by taking his pocket watch out of his waistcoat in Lewis Carroll's *Alice's Adventures in Wonderland.*

King Théoden and the *Holbytlan*

Tolkien tries awfully hard to deflect the rabbit/hobbit connection by inventing a really convoluted etymology for the word "hobbit" that he hoped would settle the question. In Book Three of *The Lord of the Rings,* when King Théoden first meets Merry and Pippin at Isengard, Théoden refers to them as the *holbytlan* of folk legend (by which he means "hole-dwellers").

Near the end of Appendix F in the third volume of that book, Tolkien gives the etymology of *hobbit,* saying that it is an invention, and that everyone in the book who refers to hobbits actually uses his own translation of *halfling.* The only exception to this is King Théoden with his term *kûd-dûkan* ("hole-dweller" in Westron — see Chapter 14 for details). Tolkien says that he translates this *kûd-dûkan* term into the invented word *holbytla* from which *hobbit* might just have been derived if *holbytla* had ever existed in the ancient language (*hol-bytla* is a made-up Old English compound meaning "hole-dweller").

Personally, I think it would have been a heck of a lot easier if Tolkien hadn't bothered with this tortured word origin, had just owned up to the rabbit/hobbit association, and let it go at that!

Concerning Hobbit Clans and Government

According to the Prologue of *The Lord of the Rings,* hobbits are an ancient people who only recently settled the area of northwestern Middle-earth that they call the Shire. Supposedly, they know very little about this ancient past, which they refer to as the Wandering Days.

The hobbits' earliest legends put them in the upper valleys of the Anduin River on the eastern side of the Misty Mountains. Tolkien says that by the time they decided to migrate west across these mountains (for reasons unknown), they were already divided into three distinct clans or groups. Tolkien calls these "breeds" (a term more fitting to a race of rabbits than humans). The three "breeds," or clans, of hobbits are as follows:

- **Harfoots** are the darkest skinned and shortest of the three. They are also beardless and shoeless, and prefer highlands and hillsides.

- **Stoors** are broadest and heaviest, with the largest hands and feet. They prefer flat land and riversides.

- **Fallohides** are fairest of skin and hair, tallest, and slimmest. They prefer woodlands.

The Harfoots ("Hair-foots") clan is the most numerous. In ancient times they had a lot of dealings with the Dwarves in the mountains. These hobbits came across the mountains and settled for a time only as far west as Weathertop, the hill between Bree and Rivendell, before entering the Shire. Most of the hobbits in the Shire are Harfoots.

The Stoors tended to remain along the banks of the great River Anduin. They are more comfortable near water and less apt to be shy of Men (Big Folk).

The Fallohides ("Pale Hides") are the least numerous and most northerly branch of hobbits and are friendliest with Elves. Tolkien describes them as being more skilled in language and song than in other handicrafts and as originally preferring hunting to farming. They were the last group to cross the Misty Mountains, but because they are a bit bolder and more adventurous than the other two clans, they tend to become leaders. Tolkien tells us that even in Bilbo's time, a strong Fallohidish strain can be detected in the great families of the Shire, including the Tooks, to whom Bilbo and Frodo are related and of whom Pippin is a member, and the Masters of Buckland (Merry's family).

It is interesting to compare Tolkien's three clans of hobbits to his three Elf Kindred (see Chapter 4). In the case of hobbits, the things that differentiate the three clans are all physical characteristics: relative size, height, and coloring. For Elves, what differentiates the three kindreds is completely non-physical: the order in which each group arrived in the Blessed Realm. The physical differences between the hobbit clans obviously mix and fade as the different families intermarry, but the division among the Elven kindreds never goes away, no matter where the groups go or whom they marry. As a race, the Elves are burdened by their differences in ways that the hobbits are not.

Official history and Shire Reckoning

The "official" recorded history of the Shire begins in the Third Age, in the first year that the Fallohide brothers Marcho and Blanco crossed the Bridge of the Stonebows over the Brandywine River. They went forth with a large following of hobbits and the permission of the high king of Fornost (Norbury in the language of the hobbits, thought to be King Argeleb II of the northern kingdom of Arthedain).

The king granted them the land between the Brandywine River on the east and the Far Downs on the west, a land they dub the Shire. In return, the hobbits swear fealty to the King and promise to maintain the Bridge of the Stonebows.

The year that the hobbits first settle the Shire becomes known as Year 1 in their dating system, called Shire Reckoning. Because this year is counted as 1601 of the Third Age in the dating system used by the Kings of Fornost, to obtain the Third Age date from a Shire Reckoning date, add 1600. Subtract 1600 to go the other way. Things really get interesting when dealing with Fourth Age dates because the Shire keeps counting its years from the founding of the Shire, even after the year when the Third Age closes, the year T.A. (Third Age) 3019 and S.R. (Shire Reckoning) 1419, and the year when the Fourth Age begins, the year F.A. 1 and S.R. 1420. See Chapter 12 for more on what is known about Fourth Age events and the reason that hobbits hold to Shire Reckoning while at the same time acknowledging the change from the Third to the Fourth Age.

The management of the Shire

The way Tolkien presents it, the Shire appears like an anarchist's paradise, with little or no government in existence. In place of government institutions, well established and important families bring order to the different areas, known as the East, West, North, and South Farthings.

The sole real official in the Shire is the Mayor of Michel Delving, a town in the East Farthing. He is also known as the Mayor of the Shire. This official is elected every seven years at the Free Fair held on the White Downs on midsummer's day. This is the post to which Sam, Frodo's faithful servant and friend, is elected for a total of seven terms after his return to the Shire at the end of the War of the Ring.

Although the Mayor's main duty is to preside over the various banquets given on Shire holidays, he also oversees the management of the only two services offered in the Shire: the Office of the Postmaster, providing a letter courier service, and the First Shirriff (Sheriff), employing the 12 Shirriffs who patrol the Four Farthings. These Shirriffs are the closest thing to policemen in the Shire, although they wear no uniforms (only a feather in their caps á la Yankee Doodle Dandy). Their primary duty is to redirect wayward beasts.

In addition to the 12 Shirrifs, the Shire also employs a group of hobbits to patrol its borders, called Bounders because they "beat the bounds" (that is, patrol the boundaries on foot). The number of Bounders varies depending on the number of border disturbances reported, these being definitely on the rise during the years covered in the *The Hobbit* and *The Lord of the Rings*.

The only other vaguely governmental office in the Shire is the Thain (related to Old English *Thegn* and Middle English *Thane,* a feudal baron who holds lands and performs military service for a king). Traditionally, the Thain represents the high king's interest in the Shire and sees to it that his laws are obeyed. These laws are known simply as The Rules to the hobbit folk.

As there has not been a high king in Fornost in over a thousand years at the time of *The Hobbit,* the post of Thain has become purely ceremonial and usually falls to whoever is the head of the Took clan. The one remaining duty of the Thain is, as the master of the moot and muster, to call all able-bodied hobbits to service during times of extreme emergency — which also has not occurred in more than a thousand years. This is the office that Aragorn appoints Pippin to after Aragorn is crowned King of the Reunited Kingdom.

The terms *moot* and *muster* are very old words referring to different types of assemblies. In the olden days, *moot* referred to a meeting of a deliberative body for the administration of justice, and *muster* to the assembling of knights for a formal military inspection.

The Shire as Tolkien's utopia

In many ways, Tolkien's description of the history and the management of the Shire is about as utopian and idealistic as you can get. Where else can you find a situation in which a group peacefully migrates into a fertile and central region of an established realm without displacing the indigenous population? Just as astounding is the simple land grant that King Argeleb II gave the hobbits: the land of the Shire in return for general fealty to the king and the promise to maintain the stone bridge over the Brandywine River.

This is indeed a fantasy world. In the real one, migrating peoples almost inevitably displace indigenous peoples, and royal land grants are made, even in years long after medieval times, to particular nobles rather than general populations. Moreover, in medieval times, fealty sworn to a king involved far more than a promise to perform routine maintenance on a bridge — it entailed total devotion to the lord and his lands, which often meant taking up arms in his defense. Given the history of the kingdom of Arthedain in its struggle against the Witch-king of Angmar, this is exactly the kind of promise King Argeleb II would have needed instead of a bridge maintenance agreement.

No less fantastic is the laissez-faire government the hobbits established soon after their peaceful migration into the Shire. Here is a perfect example of a utopian government whose only functions seemingly are to secure the land's boundaries against the occasional intruder and to deliver letters among its peaceful, honest citizens. Tolkien makes no mention of taxes to support these governmental functions (not to mention the occasional bridge maintenance). The Shire seemingly also has no need of courts, judges, or jails, as its citizens never engage in illegal or illicit behavior, despite living in a world surrounded by rampant evil — see Chapter 10 for some examples.

One has to wonder why Tolkien made the Shire so utopian. Surely, he was not so naïve as to suggest that this kind of minimal governmental structure was workable, even in rural communities such as the one he knew as a child in England. I, for one, think that the Shire didn't need such a utopian spin in order to win the reader over to the view that the hobbits led an idyllic life and were a good people whose way of life was worth fighting for. I mostly attribute Tolkien's extreme idealism regarding the Shire to the free reign of his "what-if" imagination that is usually not as evident in his depiction of the other peoples of Middle-earth. I see in his description of the Shire's workings what Tolkien would have liked to see happen between people in the best of all possible worlds, though it was quite impossible in the world he lived in.

Legendary Hobbits of Middle-earth

Hobbits of any great renown are relatively unknown until well into the Third Age when one Bilbo Baggins is cajoled into joining Gandalf the Wizard and a band of thirteen Dwarves. Bilbo is employed as a burglar to help recover the Dwarves' stolen treasure under the Lonely Mountain, far east of the Misty Mountains. Bilbo's big adventure might have been the last of its kind had it not been for the fact that, along with an Elven blade named Sting and a tunic of mithril (a light, strong metal), he also brings back a magical gold ring that he finds (or that finds him) as he's being chased by goblins (Orcs) through the deep caverns of the Misty Mountains.

This gold ring, of course, turns out to be the One Ring of Power forged by none other than The Dark Lord, Sauron of Mordor. It was cut from his finger by Isildur at the end of the Second Age and lost centuries ago in the River Anduin. The ring came next to a Stoor-type hobbit, originally named Sméagol and later nick-named Gollum, where it resided until abandoning him for Bilbo to retrieve in Gollum's cave.

At Gandalf's urging, Bilbo leaves the Ring along with the rest of his estate to his adopted heir Frodo (a cousin twice-removed on his mother's and father's side who refers to Bilbo affectionately as his uncle). This seeming act of generosity actually burdens Frodo with the overwhelming task of having to destroy the Ring in the fires of Mount Doom in the faraway land of Mordor. Accompanying Frodo in this desperate quest to save Middle-earth from slavery under the Dark Lord Sauron are his gardener, Samwise Gamgee (Frodo's first cousin on his mother's side), Peregrin (Pippin) Took, and his very close friend Meriadoc (Merry) Brandybuck.

In the end, Frodo must seek the aid of the strange hobbit-like creature Gollum in order to complete his quest. Gollum becomes Frodo and Sam's guide, and his help is crucial to their being able to enter Mordor and make their way to Mount Doom. In the end, Gollum's need for the Ring becomes the key element in the completion of the quest and the saving of Frodo and Sam's lives. See Chapter 17 for my analysis of Bilbo, Frodo, Sam, and even Gollum as different types of "common" heroes.

Bilbo Baggins of the Shire

Bilbo Baggins is a very well-to-do hobbit who lives in a large, well-furnished burrow consisting of many tunnels and rooms, called the Hill at Bag End or just Bag End for short. (*Bag end* is a literal English translation of the French *cul-de-sac.*) Bag End is right outside the tiny village of Hobbiton in the Shire. The local folk are convinced it is stuffed with treasure.

Bilbo is unusual among his fellow hobbits for a number of reasons:

✔ He is a confirmed bachelor who lives alone at Bag End with his adopted heir, Frodo Baggins, also a confirmed bachelor.

✔ He seems untouched by aging and at 111 reaches what is considered in even hobbit terms a respectable old age.

✔ He willingly leaves the Shire to see strange places and hobnob with weird creatures, including wizards, Dwarves, and Elves.

In addition to his many unusual habits, Bilbo possesses one very important and positive quality: his generous and compassionate nature. This makes Bilbo popular among the folk of Hobbiton, despite his "queer" ways.

This compassion plays an important role in *The Lord of the Rings* in that it is the reason that Bilbo restrains himself from slaying Gollum during their encounter in *The Hobbit* when Bilbo finds the Ring. Bilbo's decision to spare him enables Gollum to play his pivotal part in guiding Frodo and Sam to Mount Doom and finally ridding Middle-earth of the Ring when Frodo is no longer able to do so.

Bilbo's character undergoes extraordinary growth and development. When you first meet him in his hobbit hole at Bag End in *The Hobbit,* he's a fairly fussy, self-absorbed, and timid gentleman. He is very concerned about the legal terms of his deal with the Dwarves and is worried to death by the potential danger of the enterprise. By the end of the book, though, Bilbo has become genuinely concerned with more than just saving his own hide. He finds his courage, which hovers somewhere between his natural hobbit reserve and his great desire to help his friends.

Through Bilbo's growth and development in *The Hobbit,* you get your first glimpse of the complexity in the hobbit mentality and how the deep appreciation and love of life's simple pleasures can fuel determination to come to the aid of others and see a job through to the end, no matter how unpleasant. These qualities of Bilbo's are developed more fully in the other hobbit characters in *The Lord of the Rings* and are key elements in their quest to stop Sauron from overpowering Middle-earth and destroying the way of life in the Shire (see Chapter 17 for more on Bilbo's heroic qualities).

Frodo Baggins, the "famousest of the hobbits"

In some ways, Frodo Baggins — from the Old English *frōd*, meaning wise or experienced — the protagonist of *The Lord of the Rings*, is the least complicated of Tolkien's hobbit characters. In other ways, he is the most complex. Frodo, like Tolkien, is an orphan (Frodo's parents drowned in a freak boating accident). He is adopted by his distant cousin Bilbo Baggins. However, Frodo looks on Bilbo more as a dear uncle than a cousin because of the wide difference in their ages: Bilbo is 60 years older to the day, for they were both born on September 22nd.

As Bilbo's sole heir, Frodo inherits Bilbo's estate (including his magic ring) when the older hobbit decides to leave the Shire and stay with the Elves at Rivendell. As part of its magic, the ring renders its wearer invisible and pro- longs life by slowing down and stretching out one's allotted lifespan.

Later, Frodo learns from Gandalf that the ring is the Ring — the One Ring of Power — and that it is sought by its maker, the Dark Lord Sauron, as the key element in his bid to conquer and rule Middle-earth. Frodo takes it on himself to dispose of the Ring in the fiery innards of the volcano Mount Doom (where it was forged and therefore the only place it can be destroyed).

Frodo in part bears the burden of the One Ring simply as a duty laid upon him as part of his duty to Bilbo and out of a wish to save the Shire and its way of life. However, in addition to his sense of duty, Frodo yearns to follow in Bilbo's footsteps by having faraway adventures of his own. He also says he wants to get away from the Shire and its narrow-minded folk.

In Frodo, you clearly see the tension between craving security, as only an orphan can, and longing for recognition — maybe even fame. Frodo's all-too- human conflict is to remain safely anonymous and, at the same time, stand out. It haunts him throughout the quest to Mount Doom as he tries to evade Sauron's Ringwraiths and roving, all-seeing eye. For just as wearing the One Ring makes Frodo invisible and hides him from his peers, it exposes him to these wraiths and the Enemy's gaze. (See Chapter 17 for more on Frodo as a conflicted hero.)

Upon his return to the Shire, Frodo garners none of the recognition and thanks he's due from his fellow hobbits. Even worse, he cannot really partake of the peace that he worked so hard to restore to the Shire. He becomes an exile who must leave Middle-earth to try to find peace in the Blessed Realm of the Uttermost West.

The question of whether Frodo finds peace in the Blessed Realm or remains an exile there continues to engage many readers of *The Lord of the Rings*. It's a crucial question to many who want reassurance that good is ultimately rewarded, even if it is not always recognized. But Tolkien does not give any such assurance. He leaves it to each reader to do his or her duty just like Frodo, without any guarantee of success or acknowledgment. (See Chapter 19 for more on the fate of Frodo as the Ring-bearer.)

Samwise Gamgee, the stouthearted

Tolkien indicates in his letters to his son Christopher that as he was writing *The Lord of the Rings*, he began more and more to see Sam as its hero. Sam, whose full name is Samwise Gamgee, is first Bilbo's and then later Frodo's gardener at Bag End. He is the youngest son of Hamfast Gamgee, known as the Gaffer and from whom he inherits the gardening position.

Samwise (from Old English *sam wís,* for "half-wise") is well treated in Mr. Bilbo's employ, learning his letters from Bilbo, as well as lore, legends, and songs about the strange and beautiful creatures of Middle-earth. Bilbo's instruction fosters in Sam a wish to visit the Elves someday and see exotic creatures. Sam joins Frodo's quest to destroy the Ring as both devoted servant and dear friend. Tolkien, however, clearly draws a class distinction between the working-class Sam and upper-class Bilbo and Frodo — this friendship is not one between equals. During much of *The Lord of the Rings,* Sam seems more like Frodo's valet than friend. By the end, though, having faced the fire of Doom together, this master/servant, upper-/lower-class distinction gives way to a deep and abiding friendship that admits no difference in rank.

Sam is Tolkien's hero probably because he shows loyalty that never waivers, no matter how dire the situation. Frodo can always count on Sam to encourage him, guide him, and chide him when necessary to keep him going. Sam's determination is such that near the very end of the quest, he actually carries Frodo and the Ring on his back to reach the Crack of Doom. See Chapter 17 for more analysis of Sam as a common hero and Chapter 19 for more on Sam's ultimate fate as short-time Ring-bearer.

Peregrin (Pippin) Took

Peregrin Took (from the Latin *peregrinus,* meaning "pilgrim" or "wanderer") is most often called Pippin (from the French *pepin,* an "admirable person or thing"). He is Frodo's devoted and stalwart second-cousin, once removed on his mother's side, and is a plucky, unstoppable hobbit.

Pippin is one hobbit you can't keep down. He is less intimidated by Big Folk than the other hobbits on the quest. It is he who speaks out loudly when Elrond is about to name his own people to fill the last two spots in the Fellowship of the Nine, protesting that it would leave no room for Merry and him to go. Elrond relents when Pippin tells him that the only way to prevent him from going would be to "lock me in prison, or send me home tied in a sack." His enthusiasm on the quest gets him into trouble with Gandalf the Wizard, often bringing out Gandalf's gruffness (making him a *pip* in the British sense of an irritant or minor annoyance).

Pippin, however, shows his more serious side when swearing his allegiance to Denethor, Steward of Gondor. In this role, Pippin saves Faramir's life when his despairing father, Denethor, tries to immolate himself and the ailing Faramir on a funeral pyre. Pippin persuades Gandalf to attempt to rescue both of them from Denethor's madness. Unfortunately, the wizard can only save Faramir, as Denethor is determined to commit suicide rather than face the bleak future he believes to be inevitable.

After returning to the Shire and cleaning out Saruman's ruffians in the Battle of Bywater (see Chapter 24), Pippin settles down, marries, and has a family. He is eventually named Thain by King Aragorn Elessar (see "The management of the Shire" earlier in this chapter for more on this office). In his old age, he and his fellow traveler, Merry Brandybuck, leave the Shire together. Pippin travels south to Gondor where he passes the rest of his days. When Pippin dies, he is laid to rest in the Tombs on Rath Dínen (the "Silent Street") behind Minas Tirith, among the great of Gondor. (See "The roles of Merry and Pippin in *The Lord of the Rings*" later in this chapter for more.)

Meriadoc (Merry) Brandybuck

Meriadoc Brandybuck, most often called Merry, is one of Frodo's closest friends. In many ways, Merry is a typical hobbit who is unsure of himself around the Big Folk in Middle-earth, not at all clear on what he can do or how he can help. Nevertheless, friendship leads him to join Frodo's quest to destroy the One Ring and enables him to overcome fears and uncertainties.

Merry is a hobbit of superior wisdom and common sense. However, he also at times feels inadequate beside the Men he encounters in his travels, because of the difference in size. He often tries to find ways of proving his worth despite his shorter stature. When he encounters the horsemen of Rohan, he does this by swearing fidelity to King Théoden and becoming an esquire of Rohan and of the household of Meduseld. Théoden becomes a second father to Merry — and Merry a second son to the King, succeeding Théodred, this king's only son who was slain in battle.

Merry shows his courage when he sneaks onto the field at the Battle of Pelennor Fields and with the help of Éowyn slays the Lord of Nazgûl with the very knife with which he swore fealty to King Théoden. The king meanwhile is mortally wounded when the Nazgûl's winged-serpent spooks his horse. Because of Merry's service to Théoden, Éomer, the new King of Rohan, gives Merry the title Master Holdwine ("true friend" in Old English).

At the end of the War of the Ring, Merry returns to the Shire where he becomes the Master of Buckland and is dubbed Meriadoc the Magnificent. At the ripe age of 102, he journeys south with his old friend Pippin. He stays with King

Éomer in the courts of Rohan until the king's death, at which time he goes to Gondor to stay with Pippin. Upon his death, Merry, like Pippin, is laid to rest in the Tombs on Rath Dínen among the great heroes of Gondor.

The roles of Merry and Pippin in The Lord of the Rings

When examining the roles of Merry and Pippin in *The Lord of the Rings,* one must be careful to differentiate between the caricatures of these two presented in Peter Jackson's movie versions and the characters in Tolkien's book. For some reason, Jackson felt compelled to flatten these good-natured and generally upbeat hobbits into the buffoons who provide the major comedy in an otherwise fairly serious story. If your only exposure to Merry and Pippin is through the movie version of *The Lord of the Rings,* it may come as some surprise to find out that their characters provide much more than comic relief.

In *The Hobbit,* Bilbo is the lone hobbit character and provides the reader's sole example of hobbit life and mannerisms. When Tolkien wrote the much longer and more complex *The Lord of the Rings,* he expanded the major hobbit characters by four — Frodo, Sam, Merry, and Pippin (with Bilbo introducing the story and then playing a much more limited role).

With four hobbits, Tolkien could further develop their individual and heroic characteristics. He was also able to advance the theme of companionship by dramatizing how much stronger the hobbits are when they work together, a theme that is important to all members of the Fellowship of the Ring.

Frodo's character is seriously narrowed by the tremendous role placed on him as the bearer of the One Ring — Tolkien once complained about how uninteresting Frodo's character was. Sam's character, too, is limited by his primary function as the Ring-bearer's totally devoted and selfless servant (see Chapter 17 for more on their respective roles).

With Merry and Pippin's characters, however, Tolkien was not working under the same kinds of restrictions. He was able to use them to illustrate how typical hobbit characteristics fare in the wider world of Middle-earth while developing them into far-from-typical hobbits. While all four hobbits exhibit plenty of pluck, loyalty, and fortitude, Merry and Pippin add a level of high curiosity and stratagem to the mix.

Pippin exhibits these characteristics by excelling at stealth and subterfuge: He spies Bilbo using his Ring to disappear from the Sackville-Bagginses, has a look at Bilbo's secret diary of his adventures, and steals the palantír from Gandalf while he's sleeping.

Merry, on the other hand, exhibits these characteristics by excelling at planning and looking ahead: He sets up the new house in Buckland for Frodo to cover his leaving the Shire and guides Pippin into Fangorn Forest, having studied Elrond's maps of it in Rivendell.

In addition to the smarts and craftiness displayed by each of them, expressed in individual ways, they both show a certain level of humor — and not the burlesque kind as in *The Lord of the Rings* movies — and apprehension. The fun-loving side of Merry and Pippin is evident in the songs they sing as they make their way to the village of Bree (they also encourage Frodo and Sam to sing less familiar ones by Bilbo).

The apprehensive side of Merry and Pippin becomes especially evident after they all are joined by Strider at Bree and head for Rivendell. They are particularly terror-stricken by the Ringwraiths on Weathertop, falling flat on their faces and giving Frodo no help at all. After they join the Fellowship of the Ring and leave Rivendell towards Mordor, they are still quick to express their fear (which is probably felt by all in the company).

Only after the breakup of the Fellowship at Parth Galen, and their abduction by Uruk-hai Orcs, do Pippin and Merry begin to find their courage again and once again employ cunning that not only keeps them alive but later makes them so valuable as servants to King Théoden and Denethor, Steward of Gondor.

I find it fitting that over the course of their adventures Tolkien has Merry and Pippin grow to become the tallest hobbits in history (because of the Ent drinks that Treebeard gives them). This physical growth on their part mimics the growth of their personalities as they mature by overcoming fear and mastering their innate abilities to help the quest succeed however they can.

Far from being the simple buffoons of the movie versions, Merry and Pippin strike me as among the most complex and personally inspirational characters in Tolkien's *Lord of the Rings*. I find much to emulate in their optimism, innate humor, intelligence, and conquering of their fears.

Sméagol/Gollum, hero and villain

Sméagol, better known as the despicable creature, Gollum, is a hobbit gone terribly wrong. Sméagol is part of the Stoor clan that is cut off from those who dwell in the Shire. Originally, Sméagol dwelt in the flatlands at the foot of the Misty Mountains.

Sméagol's original downfall occurred when he and his friend Déagol went out on a fishing trip down the Anduin River to the Gladden Fields. Déagol caught a fish so big it dragged him underwater, where he discovered a shiny, gold ring — the One Ring of Power that betrayed Isildur to his death many years earlier.

Sméagol immediately coveted the Ring. When Déagol refused to surrender it, Sméagol strangled him and buried him on the shore. Upon Sméagol's return home, he was pleasantly surprised to find that no one could see him as long as he wore the Ring. Soon, however, he was banished by his kin after causing much trouble. (He was nicknamed Gollum for the gurgling sounds that he made in his throat.)

After his exile, Gollum becomes a solitary soul who finds his sole refuge and comfort in the Ring. He disappeared into a deep cave at the roots of the Misty Mountains, where he lives undisturbed until Bilbo happens upon him.

In the character of Gollum, Tolkien depicts a classic schizophrenic. One part of Sméagol remains alive but completely split off from the Gollum creature that he's become. So deeply is his mind split that Sméagol usually refers to himself in the third person as "he" or "Sméagol" or even "Precious" — his name for the Ring and by extension, his Gollum side created by the Ring's power over him.

Despite the Ring's corroding and evil influence, a small part of Sméagol lives on, a testimony to his kinship with hobbits and their many virtues and strengths. This is the part of Gollum that Frodo is able to touch when he tames him and uses him as a guide into Mordor. This is also the part of Gollum that Sam has so much trouble seeing, causing him to despise Gollum and in some ways even mistreat him.

However, it is Sam who asks the $64,000 question regarding Gollum, namely: What part is Gollum to play in the myth — hero or villain? The answer, of course, is that in Sméagol/Gollum Tolkien gives the reader both — a cowardly villain and a corrupted hero who, through his intense desire to possess the Ring, ends up destroying both it and himself. (See Chapter 17 for more on Gollum as the fallen hero.)

Chapter 8

The Wily Wizards

*N*owadays when you mention the term *wizard,* most folks either think of the Wizard of Oz or King Arthur's Merlin. Tolkien's wizards are much more like Merlin, who helps to crown the rightful king and restore peace to the land, than they are like Oz, a humbug interested primarily in eliminating his enemies. Gandalf was sent (presumably by the Valar) to help guide Elves, Men, and Dwarves in their struggle against Sauron, much as Merlin tutored and mentored King Arthur in the legends of Camelot.

This chapter looks at Tolkien's wizards with an eye towards explaining their overall function in the lore of Middle-earth. It explores their possible sources by taking a detailed look at Merlin in the Arthurian legends. It then goes on to investigate the particular part each of the three wizards, Saruman, Gandalf, and Radagast, plays in the War of the Ring.

The Wizards of Middle-earth

The Silmarillion and *The Lord of the Rings* tell similar stories of how the wizards (called Istari by the Elves) came to Middle-earth: Five wizards arrived in Middle-earth sometime after the first thousand years of the Third Age. This was around the time when evil started creeping into the Greenwood Forest, which was thereafter known as Mirkwood.

According to the Elf, Círdan the Shipwright, these five wizards sailed into the Grey Havens on a ship from the Blessed Realm. Each looked like an old man (although they aged very slowly), had a long white beard, carried a staff, and wore a tall pointed cap and a colored cloak.

These wizards came to Middle-earth to contend with the growing power of Sauron and to aid others in struggling against him. Tolkien makes it clear, however, that the wizards were forbidden to confront Sauron's power directly or to dominate the races of Middle-earth by force or intimidation.

Of the five wizards who came to Middle-earth, only three played any role in its history — without any explanation, Tolkien sent the other two off to eastern areas of Middle-earth where they played no part in the War of the Ring. The three are

- ✔ **Saruman the White** of Isengard, leader of the order to which all wizards belong and considered the most knowledgeable and powerful

- ✔ **Gandalf the Grey**, special friend to Elves and hobbits and considered the wisest and most compassionate

- ✔ **Radagast the Brown** of Rhosgobel (on the western edge of Mirkwood Forest), closest to nature and able to communicate with all living creatures

Of these three, Gandalf is the only one definitely identified as having been a Maia in the Blessed Realm. There, he was known as Olórin (see Chapter 3 for details). Saruman and Radagast may or may not have existed as Maia before coming from the Blessed Realm to Middle-earth as wizards — Tolkien never makes it clear one way or the other.

A tale of three Maiar: Gandalf, Sauron, and the Balrog of Moria

Gandalf, Sauron, and the Balrog unearthed by the Dwarves in Khazad-dûm (see Chapter 6) are all equally powerful in the sense that they are all three Maiar. The Maiar are the lesser order of Powers who originally served the Valar in the Blessed Realm of Aman. Of course, in this group, only Gandalf stands out as a good egg — both Sauron and the Balrog are rotten to the core.

As Maiar, Gandalf served the Vala Lórien, and Sauron served first the Vala Aulë and then the Vala Melkor, later called Morgoth. It is while serving Melkor that Sauron turned to evil and earned the chummy nickname Gorthaur the Cruel (Gorthaur means "Dread Abomination"). The Balrog — Valarauko in Elvish, meaning "Demon of Might" — is one of the many Maiar who were corrupted by Melkor's lies and gifts. Both Sauron and the Balrog followed Melkor when he fled the Blessed Realm for his stronghold of Thangorodrim in Beleriand. When the Valar destroyed Melkor and his stronghold, Sauron and the Balrog high-tailed it east to what was left of Middle-earth, the Balrog heading to the depths of Khazad-dûm and Sauron to Barad-dûr in Mordor. Of his two enemies, Gandalf faces only the Balrog directly, and in that battle both are destroyed at the bottom of Mount Barazinbar. Fortunately for Middle-earth, the Valar send Gandalf back to continue in the struggle against Sauron.

Merlin and Odin: Possible sources for Tolkien's wizards

The wizard Merlin, made familiar from the more popular forms of the King Arthur legends, is one possible source for Tolkien's Middle-earth wizards, and comes from two divergent sources. One is a Welsh Celtic source that identifies Merlin with a mythic wild man named Myrddin who gained the gift of prophecy after going mad and running wild through the woods. The other is an Anglo-Saxon source that identifies him with Ambrosius, a man with prophetic powers who is notorious for being "fatherless" — it seems that Ambrosius's mother, the daughter of a king, was impregnated by an incubus, a male demon who has sexual intercourse with women while they sleep, while she was staying at a convent (how rude!).

In the Arthurian legends, Merlin is a crafty, prophetic, and powerful magician. He uses his powers to engineer Arthur's conception, aid him in gaining and holding the throne of England, and even, according to some tales, move the great stones of Stonehenge into place.

None of Tolkien's three wizards is quite as powerful or prophetic as Merlin. Each is, however, quite crafty in his own way and uses his special knowledge to counsel leaders of Middle-earth and guide the course of events. In the case of Saruman, though, much of his later counsel is colored by his towering ambition to find the One Ring of Power and wield its power himself.

Another source for Tolkien's wizards comes from Norse mythology. Odin (*Woden* in Old English) is the Norse chief, or "All-father," of the gods, but in these legends, he appears less like a father and more like one of Tolkien's wizards. For one thing, Odin is pictured as a rather tall, bearded man clad in a grey robe with a blue hood (remind you of anyone?). He is said to carry a very special spear called Gungnir — any oath sworn on its tip can never be broken. When Odin walks among men, he is also said to don a broad-brimmed hat pulled down over his forehead to hide the fact that he has only one eye. If not for the missing eye and the spear (though remove the metal point and it's pretty darn close to a staff), Odin could easily be mistaken for a wizard — in particular, Gandalf the Grey.

More important, perhaps, than Odin's physical characteristics are his under-standing of the runic characters used in divination, his knowledge of magical spells, and his ability to speak in verse. Odin gains knowledge of the runic char-acters by hanging upside-down in the ash tree Yggdrasil. (This tree is some-times called the World Tree because its roots link all three levels of the world: Asgard, the realm of the gods; Midgard, the realm of men; and Niflheim, the realm of Dark Elves and of the dead.) After nine days and nights of suffering, hanging on the ash tree and wounded by his own spear, Odin, finally reaches down and seizes the magic runes, which he can then understand and later inscribes on Gungnir, his spear. After this incident, Odin's wisdom increases so much that he masters 18 previously unknown magical spells and hankers after the gift of the poet, which he achieves later by stealing and drinking the mead that inspires poetry (see Chapter 14 for more on Tolkien's use of runic characters).

Odin, then, is as much a man of knowledge as he is a sorcerer — especially in terms of language, in spoken incantations and in reading characters. In this respect, both Gandalf and Saruman resemble Odin quite a bit. They are both very knowledgeable in the languages and lore of Middle-earth and often pore through old records, searching for answers to the mystery surrounding Sauron and the One of Ring of Power.

The Role of Tolkien's Wizards

On the surface, the role of Tolkien's wizards is to champion the rights of the Free Peoples of Middle-earth and help them defend against Sauron's coming assault during the War of the Ring. However, only two of them — Gandalf and, to a much lesser extent, Radagast — actually do this. Saruman, in fact, spends most of his time working *against* this goal, first by competing with Sauron for power over Middle-earth and then by joining him in alliance.

One way to understand the role that the wizards play is by analyzing what sets them so much apart from the other beings of Middle-earth. The big difference between Elves, Men, and Dwarves and the wizards has to be the wizards' overriding interest in knowledge. This interest runs the gamut from the lore and languages of Middle-earth to the knowledge of natural science, to magic or sorcery.

Each wizard is primarily interested in a different area of knowledge:

- **Saruman the White** wants external knowledge — that is, **science** (from the Latin *scientia,* meaning "having knowledge"), similar to the medieval alchemy of metals.

- **Gandalf the Grey** is interested in self-knowledge — that is, **wisdom,** the more contemplative alchemy of the soul.

- **Radagast the Brown** seeks visionary and healing wisdom — in other words, *shamanism,* a form of knowledge that relies on deep communication with all forms of life.

Each wizard, then, personifies a type of learning: Saruman the scientist, Gandalf the sage, and Radagast the shaman. Tolkien uses the three wizards to show us how these three types of knowledge can be applied — or in the case of Saruman, misapplied — to life.

Saruman the White

The name *Saruman* means "crafty-man," from the Old English *searu,* denoting a craft, device, or wile. This idea of Saruman as a crafty old man is reinforced by his name in Elvish, Curunír, meaning "Man of Skill." When introducing Saruman in *The Silmarillion,* Tolkien characterizes him as "subtle in speech" and skilled in "all the devices" of the smith.

These names do much to create the conception of Saruman as a consummate scientist — especially in the area of applied science or technology. Saruman clearly loves technology and has little regard for nature.

After settling at Orthanc (which means "Cunning Mind"), the tower at Isengard, and destroying its gardens, Saruman creates underground furnaces and forges to make a cache of weapons. He also comes up with a breeding program to create Orcs who can travel in the sunlight (regular Orcs, like Trolls, can't bear direct sun). Treebeard the Ent, who cares for Merry and Pippin in Fangorn Forest, at one point says of Saruman, "he has a mind of metal and wheels."

Saruman and the ends justifying the means

Saruman goes over to evil through a combination of pride and fear stemming from reliance on his great knowledge. What begins as research into the lore and history of the One Ring to prevent Sauron from ever recovering it again ends up becoming Saruman's quest to secure the Ring for himself. In this, Saruman reveals not only his great political ambition to rule Middle-earth in place of Sauron, but also his enormous hubris in thinking that he can wield the power of Sauron's Ring when no one else in Middle-earth can.

When Saruman fails to recover the Ring, and when he gets wind of the strength Sauron has developed even without the Ring, he changes very quickly from Sauron's rival to Sauron's collaborator. After tricking Radagast into luring Gandalf to Orthanc, Saruman argues that he and Gandalf should join forces with Sauron. His argument here is pure political expediency: The combined hope of being rewarded as Sauron's ally in the short term and of directing the course of Sauron's rule over Middle-earth in the long term.

Saruman's reasoning begins with "if you can't lick 'em, join them" and concludes with "the ends justify the means." According to Saruman's latter argument, the deplorable evils that may come from aiding Sauron's conquest are justified by the higher goals of "Knowledge, Order, and Rule" that he and Gandalf have long championed in Middle-earth.

Saruman, it seems, rationalizes his compromise with evil by believing that he is using his great body of knowledge in the service of greater goals; in reality he simply seeks power and justifies it as his right because of his extensive knowledge — at one point, he refers to Gandalf and himself as "the Wise." Of course, Gandalf is not taken in by Saruman's arguments any more than, presumably, Sauron would be (except that Sauron is more than willing to take Saruman's help until he achieves domination).

Saruman of Many Colors

At an earlier point in this same conversation between Saruman and Gandalf, Saruman bristles when Gandalf refers to him as Saruman the White. Saruman reveals his contempt for Gandalf as merely the "Grey" wizard and Radagast as merely the "Brown" by declaring himself Saruman of Many Colors. When Gandalf replies that he prefers Saruman the White, Saruman answers that white can easily be colored just as white cloth is dyed, white paper is written upon, and white light is broken (into the color spectrum with a prism). Gandalf responds that in these cases the thing is no longer white and goes on to say that "he that breaks a thing to find out what it is leaves the path of wisdom."

Saruman's claim to be a wizard of "Many Colors" begs the question of just what the wizards' different colors symbolize. Are they grades that indicate the relative rank of each of the wizards? Or could they be instead indicative of the kind of knowledge that each wizard possesses? My feeling from the preceding conversation is that the colors symbolize one thing to Saruman and quite another to Gandalf.

I believe that Saruman firmly sees the colors as a ranking system with white naturally at the top, grey in the middle, and brown at the bottom. Further, I think that Saruman sees his "white" wizardry in terms of vastly superior knowledge that he connects with his relative power. His reference to becoming a wizard of Many Colors seems to point toward his ability to put his extensive knowledge to use in the pursuit of particular applications (such as breeding Uruk-hai, creating incendiary devices, and making underground machinery at Isengard).

Gandalf, on the other hand, seems to respond to Saruman of Many Colors with the idea that knowledge put to the use of a particular application is no longer pure knowledge (white) but more what one would call skill (particular colors in the spectrum of white light). Applied knowledge is no longer pure, which Gandalf says he prefers, and a wizard seeking it is in danger of leaving the path of wisdom (something Saruman is guilty of in contrast to Gandalf).

Gandalf's other comment about breaking a thing "to find out what it is" may also be Tolkien's way of criticizing scientists who investigate aspects of nature without first considering possible ramifications, necessity, or morality of such inquiry. Here, Tolkien reminds us that although knowledge is power, it is not necessarily wisdom. In the person of crafty old Saruman, you see that when knowledge is wedded to expediency and lacks wisdom, it can all too easily be made to serve evil and, indeed, may become evil itself.

Certainly if my interpretation of Tolkien's color symbolism for his wizards is correct, this begs the further question of why, after dying in his struggle with the Balrog, is Gandalf sent back as a white rather than grey wizard? For many readers and critics alike, this rebirth as Gandalf the White is a clear indication that the colors represent rank, that Gandalf is sent back by the Valar stronger, and is now an equal of Saruman in terms of knowledge or, at least, power.

I see the meaning of Gandalf's change from "Grey" to "White" somewhat differently. I've always regarded the greyness of Gandalf as indicating his wisdom and compassion, acquired from great experience over time, in the same way that our greying elders can be sources of such understanding and caring.

Gandalf's transformation may symbolize purification — sacrificing his life to save those of his companions and refining his goal of aiding the free peoples of Middle-earth. He then starts his new life as a "White" wizard, from exactly the position where Saruman once started his. By contrast, Saruman allowed his preference for knowledge over wisdom to denigrate his original caring and transform him from White into Many Colors.

Saruman as Sharkey of the Shire

In the end, Saruman's stratagems for rivaling Sauron and converting Gandalf to his cause come to nothing. His disregard of the natural environment cause the Ents to make war on Isengard and imprison him in his own tower. However, Saruman escapes imprisonment and goes on to make trouble in the Shire, where he appears as the lowly and reprehensible Sharkey (the new name probably coming from Sharkú, meaning "Old Man" in the Orcs' Black Speech).

Saruman as Sharkey, with ruffians as his "brute squad," makes himself Chief of the Shire and attempts to impose on the hobbits' beloved home many new "rules." Saruman/Sharkey makes Frodo's home, Bag End, his center of control, justifying his occupation and corruption of the Shire as his just due for the hobbits' part in his downfall at Isengard. In the end, Sharkey is murdered by his own mistreated servant, Grímá Wormtongue, and his spirit, rising above his body as a grey mist in the shape of a shrouded figure, dissipates into nothing before the west wind.

Thus, Saruman the White, the most knowledgeable wizard in Middle-earth, ends his days as a petty boss murdered by one of his own henchmen. Saruman's story is Tolkien's cautionary tale about mistaking knowledge for wisdom. He squanders his considerable skills because of overriding pride and fear. Because he's unable to see the logic in helping others — his original mission in Middle-earth — Saruman never comes close to realizing his awesome potential.

Gandalf the Grey

Gandalf is, of course, one of the most beloved characters in *The Hobbit* and *The Lord of the Rings* and possibly the most beloved wizard in all of fantasy fiction (no offense to you *Harry Potter* fans!). Called Mithrandir (Grey Pilgrim) by the Elves, Gandalf is remarkable for taking his mission in Middle-earth so seriously. He never waivers in his allegiance to those who sent him from the Blessed Realm — obviously the Valar, although which of them is not certain.

Gandalf takes no fixed abode in Middle-earth, preferring to travel freely in various lands to better check up on Sauron and his minions. He even refuses an offer (pushed by Galadriel, who really doesn't trust Saruman) to become the head of the White Council of Elves and wizards set up to investigate the whereabouts of Sauron and his One Ring of Power. Gandalf refuses this honor, which then falls to Saruman despite Galadriel's misgivings, saying that he would prefer to have no ties or allegiance to any but those who sent him to Middle-earth.

Although Gandalf can be a crotchety old man, especially around Pippin, who really knows how to push his buttons, he is mostly a gentle and wise counselor. In his role as sage, Gandalf uses his knowledge to guide people such as Frodo and Aragorn into making correct decisions and supports them in carrying them out.

Gandalf's considerable wisdom and compassion stem from several sources. One is his previous life in the Blessed Realm as a Maia, serving the Vala Lórien in his gardens and learning compassion from the Vala Nienna, the Lady of Mourning who tends to the needs of the dead sent to the Halls of Mandos. The others are his special roles as servant of the Secret Fire and bearer of the Elven-Ring of Power called Narya (the Ring of Fire that Círdan the Shipwright entrusted to him when he arrived at the Grey Havens).

Gandalf's special relationship to fire is not terribly unusual for a wizard. After all, many wizards of ancient lore and fiction have been servants of the so-called *alchemical fire* that transforms base elements into gold. The fire Gandalf serves, however, is the Flame Imperishable that Ilúvatar kindled within the divine Ainur at the time of their creation (see Chapter 3 for details). This Flame is much closer in nature to the indwelling spirit of Christianity than to the alchemical fire. Saruman, on the other hand, would be much more interested in transmuting iron into gold than elevating and transforming his spirit.

Tolkien also refers to Gandalf's Secret Fire as the "flame of Anar" (the Sun), which he contrasts with the "dark fire" of the Balrog that Gandalf confronts in Moria. Tolkien refers to this "dark fire" as the "flame of Udûn." Udûn refers both to Melkor's underground fortress of Utumno in the far north of Middle-earth during the First Age and to the plain in Mordor below the Black Gate (see Chapter 2). Obviously, the supportive fire of the sun, which illuminates and reveals everything, is here contrasted to the destructive fire of an underground fortress which the Enemy (first Melkor and then Sauron) uses to his dark purposes and whose veiled light casts deep shadows.

In addition to Gandalf's wisdom, Tolkien also shows him as a very loving, compassionate person. Because he is so devoted to saving Middle-earth, and because he is full of this love, he lays down his life for his companions when he single-handedly battles the Balrog on Durin's bridge in Moria. In the Christian tradition, Jesus refers to giving your life for someone as the greatest form of love.

Gandalf the Dwarf?

You may be surprised to know that Gandalf got his name from a section of an ancient Norse poem called the *Dvergatal* ("Tally of the Dwarves") inside a poem named the *Völuspá.* This particular section contains a rather long list of Dwarf names, many of which found their way into *The Hobbit,* including Thór, Fíli, Kíli, Nóri, Bífur, Bombur — and *Gandálfr.* In early drafts of *The Hobbit,* Tolkien made Gandalf the name of the Chief Dwarf who comes to visit Bilbo Baggins.

In later drafts of the book, Tolkien described Gandalf (still a Dwarf) as a little "old man with a staff," presumably because he interpreted *Gandalfr* to mean "staff-Elf" in Old Norse. From there, Gandalf turned into a tall, Elf-like old man with a staff, and then — because his staff identifies him more as a wizard than an Elf — into the Gandalf the Wizard, who organizes the Dwarves in their quest to regain their treasure under the Lonely Mountain (see Chapter 6).

This struggle between the Secret Fire and the "dark fire" results in the deaths of both the Balrog and Gandalf. Because of Gandalf's self-sacrifice and devotion to his mission, though, the Valar promote him and send him back to Middle-earth — this time as Gandalf the White. This new Gandalf is even more powerful in terms of his counsel, guidance, and ability to battle evil.

When at last Gandalf completes his mission by setting in motion Sauron's demise and installing King Aragorn on the throne of the Reunited Kingdom (made up of the old kingdoms of Arnor and Gondor), he is ready to return home. At the Grey Havens, Círdan the Shipwright prepares a white ship to bear him with the other Ring-bearers, Elrond, Galadriel, Bilbo, and Frodo, west across the sea to the Blessed Realm.

Radagast the Brown

Radagast the Brown appears so briefly in *The Lord of the Rings* that he is more of a plot device than an actual character. Like the legendary Elf-lord Gil-galad, Radagast is one of those characters you hear talked *about,* but never actually meet first-hand.

In fact, Tolkien's only mention of Radagast is at the Council of Elrond when Gandalf is telling the story of Saruman's treachery. He meets the Brown wizard by chance outside the village of Bree. Radagast is on his way to the Shire to warn Gandalf that the Nine Nazgûl, disguised as Black Riders, are looking for the Shire. During this meeting Radagast reveals that Saruman sent him to find Gandalf and ask him to come quickly to Isengard if he desires Saruman's help in the matter.

Gandalf tells the Council that Radagast is a member of his order who normally dwells in Rhosgobel on the western border of Mirkwood Forest and that he is a "master of shapes and changes of hues." He also says that Radagast is a close friend to the birds and beasts of the woods and is well versed in the uses of herbs (most likely for healing).

From this description, Radagast seems more shaman than Merlin. Shamans are renowned for their affinity with all living creatures, their ability to communicate with them, and, in some cases, to actually assume their shapes. In addition, shamans also heal physical and psychological ailments.

Radagast's knowledge contrasts sharply with Saruman's — Saruman ridicules Radagast's simplicity, his brown color, and his affinity with birds. Radagast possesses the intimate knowledge of nature that is so lacking in the "skilled" knowledge that Saruman possesses. Radagast maintains an intimate relationship with the earth (thus, his brown color) and all her creatures that is unknown to the Saruman the scientist and technocrat (see Chapter 22 for more on environmental issues raised in *The Lord of the Rings*).

Chapter 9

Beorn, Tom Bombadil, and Treebeard

At first glance, Beorn, Tom Bombadil, and Treebeard the Ent may seem like a hodgepodge. After all, Beorn appears in *The Hobbit,* and Bombadil and Treebeard are from *The Lord of the Rings.* But all three are, in fact, very deeply tied to nature. Most importantly, all three are *very* ancient, predating the arrival of Elves, Men, and Dwarves in Middle-earth and are indicative of the importance that Tolkien placed on nature.

Although these characters are not central to the plots of their respective books, they all play important parts and all three make a definite impression on first-time readers. I have always found Tom Bombadil and Goldberry to be among the most memorable and inspiring characters in *The Fellowship of the Ring* without ever really knowing why. And I know that I stand with many readers in my love of the Ents and concern about the whereabouts of the wayward Entwives — where have those girls gotten to, anyway?

Understanding Tolkien's Nature Beings

Beorn, Tom Bombadil, and the Ents all seem like something out of a Grimm's fairytale. This is probably because as purely natural creatures, like fairies, they're all associated to one extent or another with the forests or woods. The Ents practically *are* the woods. In the case of Beorn and Bombadil, even though they don't actually live in the woods (Bombadil lives at their very edge), they're unintimidated by the frightening creatures, such as wolves, Orcs, and the like, who live there and threaten Tolkien's heroes.

All three of these nature beings not only provide refuge and comfort to the various heroes of the books, but rescue them from immediate danger:

- **Beorn** gives refuge to Gandalf, Bilbo, and Thorin and Company after their encounter with the goblins in the Misty Mountains and rescues them near the end of *The Hobbit* during the Battle of the Five Armies.

- **Tom Bombadil** gives refuge to Frodo, Sam, Merry, and Pippin after rescuing them from Old Man Willow in the Old Forest and later rescues them from the Barrow-wights at the Barrow-downs.

- **Treebeard and the Ents** give refuge to Merry and Pippin in Fangorn Forest and protect them from harm during the Ents' assault on Isengard.

These children of Mother Nature are more than mere plot devices, though. Each in his own way represents the ancient spirit of Middle-earth, reminding the reader of the primordial relationship between man and nature that existed before civilization — be it of Elves, Men, or Dwarves. They are also all "out of time," in the sense of being from a time long past and headed for extinction during the coming Dominion of Man in the Fourth Age. For Tolkien, the world is poorer spiritually for the loss of this relationship.

Beorn, the Skin Changer

Beorn (Old English for "man," "hero," and "warrior" and a cognate of Old Norse *bjorn,* meaning "bear") is the original Middle-earth mountain man. It's to his house near the great rock hill Carrock that Gandalf leads Bilbo and Thorin's Dwarf Company after their encounter with the ferocious wolves called the Wargs on the eastern slopes of the Misty Mountains.

Beorn lives in a low, wooden house, on a large farmstead with bee pastures, flower gardens all enclosed within a circle of oak trees, and a thorn-hedge. His house has a large hall with an open fire pit in the middle and openings in the ceiling to let out the smoke. The design of this hall, which Tolkien himself illustrated for *The Hobbit,* is reminiscent of a Viking hall where great feasts were held, lots of mead was drunk, and heroes recounted great tales.

And this is exactly what transpires as Beorn turns out to be a wonderful, if reluctant, host who loves hearing of the group's adventures on the road, even if he's initially skeptical. The odd thing about their feast is that because Beorn lives alone without human company, his animals — with whom he communicates with no problem — do all the cooking and serving. Nature comes to the rescue and provides care and comfort, too.

So, why does he call it "the Carrock"?

Tolkien, for all his fussy linguistic studies and preoccupation with the etymology of every term under the sun, did have a sense of humor about it all. Consider the incident when Bilbo pesters Gandalf to tell him why Beorn calls the rock formation *the Carrock*. Gandalf irritably replies that Beorn calls it that because *Carrock* is his word for things like that, and that this particular Carrock is *the* Carrock because it just happens to be the one closest to his house.

This response seems to imply that things are called what they're called just because that's what we call them — a complete retreat from Tolkien's usually detailed etymological meanings. Yet it is an inside joke, because the word *Carrock* is an artificial compound made up of *carr + rock. Carr* is Old English for "rock," so *rock* is Modern English for "carr." The real question is why does the word *rock* mean rock — and the answer is because that's what we call things like that.

Beorn the berserker

In this stressful world, everybody knows what it's like to go berserk (sometimes once or twice a day). You may even be aware that this term for going bonkers applied to Viking warriors, known as *berserkers,* who dressed up in bearskins and attacked their enemies like crazy people. *Berserker* is in fact an Old Norse compound, *bjorn + serkr,* which literally means "bear shirt." Some thought they actually changed into bears, and most probably believed they got extra-human strength from the bears whose skins they wore.

Tolkien was not unaware of these connections when he created Beorn. Rather than just dress up his warrior hero in a bear shirt, he made Beorn a full-fledged skin-changer who *literally* changes his hide into a bear's, apparently at will, though Tolkien didn't make this clear. So, when Beorn goes berserk, he doesn't just emulate a bear's fierceness — he becomes it body and soul.

Beorn and the Wargs

Beorn may be as fierce as an old brown bear, but he is an accommodating host and a stalwart ally to Bilbo and Thorin's Company, coming to their aid and turning the tide in the Battle of Five Armies.

Beorn's dual animal/human nature contrasts with that of the Wargs, terrible wolf-like creatures that Gandalf, Bilbo, and the Dwarves encounter shortly before coming to Beorn's home. These Wargs are so large that the goblins (called Orcs in *The Lord of the Rings*) ride them into battle. Wargs also exhibit a human-like intelligence in their ability to plan and communicate with each other, making them a bit like werewolves.

Wearg in Old English originally meant "criminal," but eventually came to mean "wolf," the criminal animal that raids homesteads. The German *wargwulf* means "werewolf" in the sense of a man who changes into a wolf and thus makes himself a criminal (at least to civilized people).

Beorn acts as a kind of master of animals, protecting them from abuse at the hands of other races (including his own). He is fierce in their defense but otherwise harmless. The Wargs, though, are "criminal" animals that viciously attack humans and serve the Dark Lord. As Gandalf says in *The Lord of the Rings*, Wargs are "no ordinary wolves hunting for food in the wilderness."

The Role of Tom Bombadil

Tom Bombadil is one of the most delightful characters in *The Lord of the Rings*, if for no other reason than his wonderful poetry and his lovely lady Goldberry. He is a joyful, nature-boy character with a long brown beard, great yellow boots, bright blue eyes, blue coat, and a feather in his cap. Tom Bombadil as a character precedes *The Lord of the Rings* — he is supposed to have been a doll that one of Tolkien's children had, and about whom Tolkien made up stories and rhymes for the children's amusement.

Tom is in tune with all living things and, like Beorn, is in close communication with all animals. He has the power of naming animals (like father Adam, methinks). After he names the hobbits' ponies, they ever after answer only to the names Tom gave them. Of course, who wouldn't come running when called Sharp-ears, Wise-nose, White-socks, or, of all things, Bumpkin?

The very first time I read *The Lord of the Rings,* I found Tom Bombadil so vital to the story, not because he contributed that much to the plotline (although he does save Frodo and the other hobbits from the Willow Man and thereby saves the Ring quest). He's vital because he sets the tone of what is right in Middle-earth and worth saving from Sauron.

Still, even Tolkien admitted that in some ways Tom Bombadil seems stuck into the first book of *The Lord of the Rings* without really being integral to its plot. He is left completely out of Peter Jackson's movie *The Fellowship of the Ring.*

In a letter to one of his proofreaders, Tolkien defended Bombadil's place in the book, saying that although he is not an important person to the narrative, he is important as a comment on the conflict between good and evil that is central to the book.

Tom Bombadil as a "natural" pacifist

At one point in his letters, Tolkien refers to Tom Bombadil as a "natural pacifist," that is, someone who doesn't take sides in the struggle between the free peoples and Sauron's forces (the good guys versus the bad guys) because he's incapable of comprehending the nature of this power struggle and what's at stake in its outcome.

In fact, Bombadil is so removed from the struggle that when he puts on the One Ring he does not disappear — and when Frodo puts on the Ring he can still see Frodo. At one point during the Council of Elrond, Tom Bombadil is mentioned as a possible Ring-bearer or as someone who might hide the Ring from Sauron. Gandalf, however, points out that he would be a poor choice because, although he could easily resist the Ring because he's so unconcerned with its power, for that same reason he could easily mislay it or even inadvertently turn it over to the Enemy or one of his servants.

Tom Bombadil, although master of wood, water, and hill, doesn't see himself as their owner or protector. Goldberry is quick to point out to Frodo that none of the land *belongs* to Tom. Tom would be affected by the outcome of the war, however, because if Sauron were to conquer Middle-earth, he would surely see himself as its owner and would undoubtedly force Tom, Goldberry, and their land to either submit to him or be destroyed. Remaining neutral in such a situation is simply not tenable. Sauron, like many modern tyrants (Kaiser Wilhelm in World War I and Hitler in World War II come to mind) would never leave Tom and Goldberry alone to lead their life in peace on the edge of the Old Forest. They have a stake in the outcome whether they participate or not in the war.

As one of the most ancient beings in Middle-earth, Tom Bombadil has seen the comings and goings of its creatures, rivers, and trees. His relationship of mastery is as the eldest who commands the respect of the youngsters — even the not-so-nice ones, such as Old Man Willow and the Barrow-wights. This relationship is, however, not one of allegiance, as evidenced by the fact that Tom leaves Old Man Willow to his own devices as soon as the tree releases the hobbits. Also, once the evil spirit flees the Barrow-mound, and the hobbits are safe and sound, Tom forgets entirely about the incident.

Tolkien also points out that Tom Bombadil, unlike wizards (discussed in Chapter 8), can learn about Middle-earth's creatures and lore without being compelled to do something with that knowledge. That sounds to me like the state of things in Eden before Adam and Eve ate from the tree of the knowledge of good and evil. In that story, God gave Adam mastery over all the beasts, birds, flowers, and fauna for the purpose of naming them and delighting in them — He said nothing about controlling or dominating them. Outside the garden, after the Fall of Man, the story is totally different. The knowledge of good and evil has led to a never-ending battle for dominance over nature and over our fellow human beings, a battle in which we are often forced to take sides against our better judgment (see Chapter 15 for much more on this scintillating subject of good versus evil).

Given Tolkien's own deeply rooted Catholicism, I wouldn't be surprised if Tolkien saw Tom Bombadil as the unfallen Adam, a human being who interacts with nature benevolently and appreciatively, secure in the knowledge of his place in God's creation.

Tom and Goldberry

Goldberry is Tom Bombadil's lovely lady. In his poem called "The Adventures of Tom Bombadil" and published in *Oxford* magazine in 1933, Tolkien tells how Goldberry and Tom originally met. It seems that Goldberry as the daughter of the River, pulled Tom under the water where he became caught in the trunk of Old Man Willow. Tom later returned home to find a Barrow-wight hiding behind his door and threatening to take old Tom down into the Barrow. In the end, Tom banished forever the Barrow-wight and took Goldberry from the river to his home, where she became his devoted wife. The poem ends with Goldberry combing her long blond hair as Tom chops willow branches (called *withies*, meaning slender, flexible branches, especially willow, from whose shape the Withywindle River undoubtedly gets it name).

According to this story, Tom is a protective spirit of the land who overcomes and ultimately tames the spirit of the river in his happy marriage to Goldberry. Perhaps through his union with this river spirit, Tom becomes not just master of wood and hill, but of water as well. In *The Lord of the Rings*, Tom dotes on Goldberry, brings her lilies and a brooch from the Barrow-mound, and she dotes on him. They are the perfect couple for protecting and enjoying the wood, hill, and water of the land they inhabit.

When Goldberry welcomes the four hobbits into the house of Tom Bombadil, her very presence and natural beauty fills them all with awe. Frodo is especially enchanted by her, feeling a joy akin to that which he felt in the presence of the Elves but that was somehow even more familiar. I like to think of Frodo's joy in the presence of Goldberry as something like the feeling one gets from sitting on the banks of a quiet river on a lovely day. Perhaps when the hobbits gaze on Goldberry, they savor the same kind of peace and harmony that so often comes from gazing into softly moving river water and feeling one with the nature around you.

Ents, Tree-herds of the Forest

The Ents are among Tolkien's most original creatures in Middle-earth. No other mythologies that I know of, Norse or otherwise, have conscious tree-like beings who tend the trees in the forests as shepherds tend their sheep. Not even the *dryads*, the wood nymphs who live in trees, are anything like them. According to Tolkien, Ents are very ancient, in the same league as Beorn and Tom Bombadil. They have hands and feet (with seven toes each) that extend from trunk-like bodies covered in a green or grey bark-like hide. They also have tall heads with hardly any neck, deep-set eyes, and long bushy grey beards that Tolkien says are "twiggy at the roots and mossy at the ends."

The Ents dwell in Fangorn Forest, which is every bit as ancient as the Old Forest where Tom Bombadil rescues the hobbits. Fangorn is located on the eastern slopes of the Misty Mountains just north of Rohan and Saruman's hangout, Isengard. Fangorn (also called Entwood) is Elvish for "Treebeard," the eldest leader of the Ents who encounters Merry and Pippin when they escape from Saruman's Uruk-hai (the really bad Orcs who can travel by day — see Chapter 10).

TRIVIA

"Until Great Birnham Wood to high Dunsinane Hill shall come..."

Tolkien made no secret of his disappointment with the prediction that Shakespeare's Macbeth would never be vanquished until the Great Birnham Wood came to Dunsinane Hill. At the end of *Macbeth,* the soldiers attacking Macbeth camouflage themselves in limbs from the trees of Birnham Wood as they move against Dunsinane Castle — thereby fulfilling the prophecy, if in only the loosest sort of way.

Tolkien thought so little of Shakespeare's solution for making this prophecy come true that after seeing the play as a schoolboy, he afterward longed to write a piece in which trees really did go to war. And that is what seems to be happening when Treebeard and his fellow Ents march on Saruman at Isengard in *The Lord of the Rings.* Now, not to be a stickler or anything, but the Ents are tree-*like* beings — not trees — going to war. It is the Huorns (Ent-like trees) who destroy the Orc army at the Battle of the Hornburg and who, properly speaking, are "trees" marching to war (see "The Relationship between the Ents and Huorns" later in this chapter for more on Huorns).

Probably the most striking feature of the Ents (besides their "tree-ness"), at least from a hobbit's point of view, is their great height: Most Ents are at least 14 feet tall. The word *ent*, in fact, means "giant" in Old English. They are also renowned for the slowness of their speech, being convinced that if something is worth saying then it is worth saying slowly and deliberately (a lesson that I for one could sure take to heart!).

According to the Ents, the Elves originally taught them to speak and instilled in them their love of languages. Although they can understand the languages of Elves and Men, the Ents speak their own: a deep, sonorous tongue, full of repetition that supposedly no one else can learn (from the sample Tolkien gives in the book, I know I couldn't handle it). Like the Elves, the Ents are very fond of verse. To the hobbits, Ents often seem to be singing to themselves.

The Ents bring out most clearly Tolkien's ecological concerns — the "green" theme of *The Lord of the Rings*. Their role as guardians of the forests is one that many today believe is the most crucial in preserving the ecology of any given environment. For me, the most impressive aspect of the Ents is the fierceness with which they preserve the ecology of the woodlands. They are by no means tree-huggers — they are fierce warriors prepared to lay down their lives for their trees (see Chapter 22 for a more complete discussion of the ecological themes in Tolkien's work).

The Ents as the children of Yavanna

Just as the Dwarves are considered the children of Aulë, the Ents are called the children of his wife Yavanna, also known as Kementari, "Queen of the Earth." Yavanna watches over the growth of all living thing in Arda — she is also goddess of the harvest, like Demeter in Greek mythology. According to the *Quenta Silmarillion* (The History of the Silmarils), Yavanna went to Manwë, the Lord of the Valar, to ask whether any of the living things she watched over would be free from the dominion of the coming elder and younger children of Ilúvatar (Elves and Men). She was especially concerned for the olvar — the growing things rooted in the earth that can't flee Ilúvatar's very mobile children.

Because of Yavanna's concerns, Ilúvatar made known his plan for what Manwë called the Shepherds of the Trees, who will protect the forests of the world. This led to a conversation between Yavanna and her hubby Aulë in which she warned him that all future children, including his beloved Dwarves, will have to contend with a power in the forest that can be stirred to great wrath. This is borne out when Saruman and his Orcs, arousing the anger of the Ents by their utter disregard of the woods, experience first-hand their destructive force at his retreat at Isengard.

The search for the Entwives

When Merry and Pippin describe the Shire to Treebeard, he immediately asks them if they've ever seen Entwives in those parts. Treebeard assumes from their description of the place that the Entwives would really take to it. It seems that Ents are a dying race because the Entwives have gone missing, and no Entings (little ones to you and me) have come along in quite some time.

As Treebeard's story goes, during the Elder Ages the Entwives became less interested in the great trees of the forests and more interested in the fruit trees and herbs and grasses of the plains. To pursue this new interest, the Entwives and the eligible Entmaidens wandered east, outside Fangorn Forest, and started gardens where they tended these trees, herbs, and grains. When Sauron returned to Mordor, the Ent gardens were destroyed and turned into the wastes known afterwards as the Brown Lands.

When the Ents went looking for the Entwives, they found the gardens destroyed and the Entwives vanished. Although the Ents asked high and low, no one knew where the Entwives had gone. Some said they went west, while others said east or south. After many unsuccessful searches for the Entwives, the Ents began to fear that they would never be reunited with the Entwives until some future dark age in which Ents and their wives have been displaced from Middle-earth. Treebeard sings a haunting Elvish lament to Merry and Pippin that speaks of the grief of the Ents and Entwives over their separation and their desire for a reunion in an unknown western land. (See Chapter 23 for more on the Ents as the romantic creatures in Middle-earth.)

The relationship between Ents and Huorns

Huorns are the ancient trees of the forest — such as Old Man Willow in the Old Forest, who at one point in the distant past started to wake up and become more Entish (which I take to mean sentient and mobile). The Huorns are important in the storyline of *The Lord of the Rings* because they are vital in winning two battles: The march of the Ents on Isengard and the Battle of the Hornburg (see Chapter 24).

Unlike the Ents, who seem gentle and reasoned — except when roused in anger — the Huorns have a darker, more brooding nature, which is most evident in Old Man Willow, whom the hobbits encounter in the Old Forest. He is a tree-being who protects himself by luring travelers in the Old Forest to him — the hobbits keep getting nudged his way, no matter how hard they try to avoid going in his direction — and then strangling them with his long branches.

The Huorns who move on Isengard and who save the day in the Battle of the Hornburg at Helm's Deep seem sinister both in their movements and the quick, stealthy way in which they dispatch with the Orcs, their greatest enemies. In the Ents, you see the positive side of a sentient tree on the move, but in the Huorns, you clearly see the dark side.

I don't know about you, but I find the idea of angry trees that can move swiftly on the attack about as frightening as anything you'd see in your worst horror movie. I guess I never recovered from that scene in Disney's *Snow White and the Seven Dwarfs* where Snow White feels that she's being chased by the spindly branches of evil-looking trees in the enchanted forest as she's fleeing the Evil Queen's huntsman! However, unlike Disney forests, where the threat seems to come from some sort of ill-defined evil within the forest itself (kind of like the scary forests in fairytales like "Hansel and Gretel"), Tolkien's forests are simply acting in self-defense, responding to the threats that come from without (see Chapter 22 for more on about Tolkien and trees).

Chapter 10

The Enemy and His Minions

*A*s any follower of fantasy or science fiction knows, the story is only as "good" as its villains are "bad." If the author fails in creating believable villains and giving a full and plausible accounting of their evil, the reader is often unwilling to buy into the premise — and won't believe in the good guys, either.

Most readers agree that Tolkien is a "master of evil," at least when it comes to creating believable and thoroughly evil villains for Middle-earth. His world contains two super-villains: Melkor, the Vala of Might who becomes Morgoth, the Dark Enemy; and Sauron, the Maia of Abomination, also known as the Dark Lord, the Lord of the Ring, or, more affectionately by his foes, the Enemy (he doesn't have any friends).

Along with the two primary villains of Middle-earth comes a whole panoply of toadies, baddies, and the minions who serve them. They are designed to tempt, degrade, and try to destroy Tolkien's heroes and would-be heroes at every turn. These nasties include such frightful demons as the Balrogs, plus Orcs, dragons, Trolls, Warg-wolves, Wights, Watchers, and giant spiders, among others.

This chapter aims to explain the significance of these evildoers in the conflicts of Middle-earth and their relevance to our own struggles and how we approach good and evil (for more on good and evil, see Chapter 15).

Melkor/Morgoth, Lord of Might and Darkness

Melkor, like the archangel Lucifer (which means "Light Bearer" in Latin) in the Judeo-Christian tradition, was called the mightiest among his fellow Holy Ones (the Ainur) who aided Eru Ilúvatar in visualizing and realizing the world by singing their themes into the Music of Creation (see Chapter 3).

Unfortunately, in a vain attempt to improve on Ilúvatar's original vision for the world to come, Melkor introduced themes of his own design into the music. These themes became dissonant when they were sung along with the musical themes of the other Ainur. In this manner, strife was introduced into the Music of Creation and into Arda, the world the Music created (see Chapter 13 for more on the whys and wherefores of Melkor dissonance).

Eru Ilúvatar invited the Ainur to descend into Arda as the Valar (the Powers) to work on constructing the world according to their music, and Melkor was among the first to go. Once there, he began at once to contend with his brother Manwë, Lord of the Valar, for kingship of the Valar and control of Arda. To that end, Melkor continued to thwart the efforts of the other Valar in fashioning Arda.

Melkor was particularly adept at playing the spoiler because he had been given a part of *all* the different powers of the other Valar. His favorite means of destruction was through extreme heat or cold. He played havoc with the elements through earthquakes, volcanic eruptions, and glaciers.

Tolkien, always keen to delineate good from evil in his works, says that when Melkor saw the other Valar take on their fair and glorious forms, his envy and malice toward them caused him to take on a dark and terrible appearance.

You always hate the one you love

For Lucifer/Satan and Melkor/Morgoth, the great object of their love — God in the case of Lucifer and the Light in the case of Melkor — became the object of their great loathing. Melkor didn't turn to darkness because he loved darkness, but rather because he loved the Light so much he couldn't cope with the fact that he couldn't have it all to himself. It was therefore the deadly combination of desire and pride that condemned Melkor to darkness. More importantly, he became jealous of anyone else whom he perceived as having the Light and wanted to deprive them of what he didn't have — the old sour grapes "if I can't have it, nobody can" syndrome.

Melkor as Tolkien's Lucifer

One way to understand Melkor's transformation into the Dark Enemy (Morgoth) is to compare it to Lucifer's transformation into Satan in the Judeo-Christian tradition. In case you've forgotten your Bible studies, the archangel Lucifer was one of God's two highest *cherubim* — a really lofty grade of archangel. Indeed, Lucifer was so prominent that his outspread wings are said to be one of the two pairs that cover the Lord's holy seat on the Ark of the Covenant (fashioned by the Hebrews to hold God's holy laws).

According to some versions of the story, Lucifer loved God so much that when God chose him to be His lieutenant in bringing order to His new earth, Lucifer was very reluctant to accept the assignment because it meant that he'd be separated from the thing he loved above all (namely, God). After a really bad case of separation anxiety, Lucifer's love for God turned into rivalry and eventually hatred that led Lucifer to the deluded belief that he could actually contend with and ultimately replace God.

As this version of the story goes, Lucifer even went so far as to corrupt a bunch of regular angels and at one point led them in an assault against God in a vain attempt to seize His throne. Needless to say, God cast down Lucifer's rebellion, during which a lot of the earth was destroyed. He separated Lucifer and his fellow angel cohorts from the light of His heavenly wisdom and condemned them forever to the fires of Hell. At this point, this fallen angel was no longer Lucifer, the Light Bearer, but Satan (Hebrew for "Adversary"). Presumably, his fellow angels became the demons of Hell.

Our fallen angel spends the rest of his time corrupting humankind, God's special children, until the end of the world — at which time, he will be thrust into the void or imprisoned in hell. Satan is able to do this through a combination of temptation and deceit, becoming especially adept at lying about God and His powers and earning one of his many nicknames: "the long-tongued liar."

So how does this version of Lucifer's fall compare to Melkor's transformation into Morgoth? Well, if you go back and substitute Melkor for Lucifer, Eru Ilúvatar for God, and Morgoth for Satan, you have Melkor's story, with one big difference: Melkor didn't love Eru Ilúvatar above all else; he loved his Light — a metaphor, perhaps, for power and his wisdom.

Melkor loved the Light of Ilúvatar so much that he wanted to possess it all for himself. However, when he discovered that he alone couldn't possess the Light (which he thought he was entitled to do as the mightiest of the Ainur), his anger became so great that it turned into a tremendous burning that Tolkien says brought him "down into Darkness." Thus, the one who desired the Light above all things was transformed into the Lord of Darkness — an important fact and crucial to understanding his subsequent behavior in Middle-earth.

The attempted rehabilitation of Melkor

Tolkien's myth also recounts a failed attempt at Melkor's rehabilitation. According to *The Silmarillion,* when Melkor was captured in the War of Powers (see Chapter 11), he was brought in chains to Valinor, judged in the Ring of Doom, and sentenced to a long term of solitary confinement in Mandos. However, at the end of this sentence, he could up for the Valarian version of parole, at which time the Valar could either pardon him or retry him for his offenses.

When the three ages were up — just after Fëanor fashioned the three Silmarils from the light of the Two Trees — Melkor sued for a pardon, vowing that he was a changed Vala who wanted to aid the other Valar in healing the hurts he had done to Arda. Manwë, the chief of the Valar and Melkor's brother, granted the pardon with the stipulation that Melkor must remain within the city of Valmar.

Although Melkor abased himself during his plea for mercy, his heart remained unrepentant and full of envy for the glory of all the beings of Aman, the Valar as well as the Elves, and desire for all their light. Melkor, however, had to bide his time before he could exact vengeance. During the initial period of probation, he was helpful to all, especially the Noldor. The Vanyar and Teleri wouldn't give him the time of day (see Chapter 4 if you need a refresher on the three groups of Elves in Aman).

Next, Melkor sought out Ungoliant the spider and wreaked vengeance on the other Valar by destroying the light of the Two Trees and stealing Fëanor's Silmarils — leaving them all, both Elves and Valar, in complete darkness.

Tolkien and the idea of irredeemable evil

You may wonder at Manwë's tolerance in pardoning Melkor after his long history of corrupting the work of the Valar in Arda. Tolkien explains this naiveté of Manwë's as stemming from his inability, as a thoroughly good being, to understand the heart of an evil one. This inability prevented Manwë from seeing that Melkor was completely devoid of love and therefore beyond redemption.

Manwë may have believed that Melkor was really repentant and rehabilitated because he wanted and needed to. Manwë knew that if his brother, who had started out with equal goodness, could fall so low as to be irredeemable, then it was possible, under the "wrong" circumstances, for him to become just as evil. And this was something that Manwë, as the king of the gods and the Vala closest to the mind of Eru Ilúvatar, was never quite able to get his mind around.

In Manwë's mistaken pardon of Melkor, Tolkien offers a modern cautionary tale about the dangers of being naive in the face of true evil and the difficulty of knowing who is beyond redemption and who can be rehabilitated. A classic example from the last century was Neville Chamberlain's underestimation of Hitler's evil and his policy of appeasing the Fuehrer's territorial aggression to the detriment of all the free peoples of Europe.

The final defeat of Melkor

The failed attempt to rehabilitate Melkor left the Valar no choice but to destroy him. But not before he — as Morgoth, the Dark Lord — inflicted a great deal of pain and suffering during the First Age (see Chapter 12).

When the Valar finally decided to move against Morgoth, at the request of Eärendil who came to Aman seeking their help (see Chapter 5), they destroyed his fortresses, cast him beyond the confines of the physical world into the Timeless Void, and in so doing Middle-earth suffered so much damage that vast regions of Beleriand sank beneath the sea.

Tolkien is very clear, though, that the end of Melkor does not mean the end of his evil. On the contrary, Tolkien assures us that the seeds of suspicion and hatred that Melkor sowed in the hearts of Elves and Men remain long after his demise, always threatening to bear dark fruit in future ages.

Sauron, the Enemy of Freedom in Middle-earth

Every great commander has to have a top lieutenant to support him, even one as wicked and reprehensible as Melkor. Enter Sauron Gorthaur — *Sauron* meaning "the Abhorred," and *Gorthaur* "Dread Abomination" in Elvish. Sauron was Melkor's first and finest lieutenant, serving as his right-hand man in all his evil deeds. In *The Lord of the Rings,* which takes place long after Melkor has been shut up in the Timeless Void, Sauron is often called simply the Enemy.

Sauron, it seems, like his evil Lord before him, was not born bad, but has spent considerable time perfecting his skill in it. Like Gandalf, Sauron is a Maia, one of the lesser, servant-type Ainur. Sauron first served the Vala Aulë, the Master Smith, before he met Melkor, who then became his real guru.

The Eye of Sauron as the ultimate "evil eye"

The belief in the power of the so-called "evil eye" to harm or even kill is widespread in the ancient cultures of Europe and Asia and still lives today among some peoples, especially in Eastern Europe and parts of the Middle East and Central Asia. According to tradition, the evil eye is a glance of envy or malice that intends to harm the one upon whom it falls. Tolkien's Eye of Sauron is the ultimate example of the evil eye, as Sauron seeks out his enemies and frightens them into submission with a look that, Tolkien says, few "could endure."

The fact that Sauron first served Aulë is important because under Aulë's tutelage Sauron learned the arts and skills of the forge that enabled him to guide the Elves of Eregion in forging the Rings of Power and to forge for himself the One Ring that controlled all their Rings.

In descriptions of Sauron, Tolkien is careful to emphasize that he is a sorcerer of great power who can assume many shapes — including very pleasing ones when it suits his evil purposes. Tolkien also stresses that Sauron rules in cruelty, twisting and misshaping whatever he controls.

This idea of an evil sorcerer ruling by brutalizing and disfiguring all that he controls — both the peoples he enslaves and the lands he commands — has its modern counterparts as well. Modern "sorcerers," such as Hitler and Stalin, among too many others, give Sauron's menace to Middle-earth its full import for today's readers. We don't need Tolkien to spell it all out in graphic detail to know how Sauron will deal with the peoples and lands of the Middle-earth should Frodo fail in his quest to destroy the One Ring.

Sauron and the forging of the Rings of Power

Only when the Valar finally sent Morgoth into the Twilight Zone of the Timeless Void did his loyal, right-hand man, come into his own. Right after Morgoth's final defeat in the Great Battle (see Chapter 12), Sauron had a momentary change of heart — yeah, right. He thought about returning to the Blessed Realm to be judged by Manwë, but after that thirty seconds passed, he decided instead to flee to what's left of Middle-earth. There, he hid out in Mordor, a gloomy, shadowy land that suited him just fine.

In time, in a new, fair appearance, Sauron came to the Noldorian Elves of Eregion as Annatar ("Lord of Gifts"). As the Elves' new pal Annatar, Sauron conned their greatest craftsmen and smiths into forging Rings of Power for the races of Middle-earth: Three Rings for the leaders of the Elves, Seven Rings for the Fathers of the Dwarves, and Nine Rings for the kings of Men. Annatar said that fashioning these rings would heal Middle-earth from the scars of war and make it as beautiful as Valinor in Aman. This particularly appealed to these Elves because they were the ones who refused to return to the Blessed Realm after the Valar defeated Morgoth in Beleriand and instead settled in Ost-in-Edhil in Middle-earth.

In return for their help, Sauron gave the Gwaith-i-Mírdain some of his secrets for forging metals that he learned from Aulë in the Blessed Realm. Of course, what he neglected to tell the Gwaith-i-Mírdain was that while they were busy fashioning the Rings of Power for Men, Dwarves, and themselves, he was forging a master Ring of Power using the volcanic fires of Mount Doom (Orodruin) in the land of Mordor. The purpose of this One Ring was to control all the ones that the Elves made, so that the thoughts of whoever wore those rings would be revealed to Sauron and come under his control.

Fortunately, the Elves discovered Sauron's evil purpose for the Rings the first time he put on the One Ring. They hid the Elven Rings of Power to keep them from his touch, so that the wearers of these three Rings did not come under Sauron's control as the others did. The Elven Rings are still subject to the One in that they will cease to function when the One is destroyed.

Sauron, much more so than his mentor Melkor, is an enemy of freedom in Middle-earth. His whole idea for creating the Rings of Power stemmed from the difficulty he had in controlling the Elves. (Men were much easier to deceive and influence because of their inordinate fear of death.) As the fair Annatar, Sauron appealed to the Elves' sense of beauty and their love of fine craftsmanship — essentially, their artistic nature — to co-opt them into fashioning the very means of their subjugation. When his scheme was discovered, and the Elven Rings were kept from him, his wrath was so great that from then on he waged ceaseless war on the Elves — first by killing the Gwaith-i-Mírdain and laying waste to the land of Eregion.

Sauron and the downfall of Númenor

Shortly after Sauron had the Rings of Power forged, his plan for the conquest of Middle-earth was interrupted by the arrival of the Dúnedain, Men from the island of Númenor in the West. Sauron hated the Dúnedain for aiding the Elves during the War of the Jewels against his master Morgoth. He also feared their power as they established more and more colonies in western Middle-earth, although he snared three of the Lords of Númenor by giving them three of the Nine Rings of Power forged for Men. Through the power of the Rings, Sauron enslaved these Lords of Men and turned them into Ringwraiths (see "The Ringwraiths, Loyal Servants of Sauron" later in this chapter for details).

During this time of contact, Sauron used subterfuge and cunning to win over the king of Númenor, Ar-Pharazôn, and wreak havoc on the Dúnedain. Sauron used the king's fear of death to convince him to worship Morgoth, and even to make war on the Valar in the Blessed Realm (see Chapter 5 for details).

Ilúvatar punished the Dúnedain's attempt to break the ban on traveling to Aman with an armada of ships by removing Aman from the Circles of the World. This caused a storm that not only sank Númenor but also destroyed Sauron's form. Unfortunately, his dark spirit survived and passed as a shadow over the sea until it reached the stronghold of Barad-dûr in Mordor. There, no longer able to take on a pleasing shape, Sauron assumed for the first time the terrifying form of the Eye of Sauron, a huge single eye rimmed in flames. This is the form that Sauron takes much later during the War of the Ring.

Sauron and the Exiles of Númenor

The Silmarillion recounts how the survivors of the disaster of Númenor made it to Middle-earth under the leadership of King Elendil and his sons, Anárion and Isildur. Together, these three Lords of the exiled Dúnedain founded the kingdoms of Arnor and Gondor (see Chapter 2 for more on these lands).

In their exile, the Dúnedain of Númenor were befriended by the Elves of Middle-earth, who were led by Gil-galad in what was left of the Grey-elven land of Lindon and by Elrond in Rivendell. Sauron was also again able to assume a humanoid shape, making him a bit more mobile than a single eye, although reportedly a very dark and terrible one (probably not any prettier than Morgoth's ugly mug). Sauron was no longer capable of generating a fair-looking shape after his shenanigans in Númenor.

Sauron attacked Gondor, took Minas Ithil (the Tower of the Moon), and drove out King Isildur. In response, the Dúnedain and Elves formed the Last Alliance against Sauron and his minions (many of which are described in the rest of this chapter). This alliance counter-attacked Sauron, winning the mammoth battle of Dagorlad just north of the Black Gate of Mordor and laying a seven-year siege to his tower of Barad-dûr.

At the end of the siege, Sauron, armed with the One Ring, was forced to come down from the tower and engage in hand-to-hand combat with Gil-galad and King Elendil. He slew both of them. But Isildur won the day by using the hilt-shard of Elendil's broken sword, Narsil, to cut the Ring from Sauron's hand. Sauron's spirit abandoned his body and fled into the wasteland.

The last act and Sauron's final destruction

It's pretty incredible when you think about it: This long and involved saga — starting with Melkor's first troublemaking in Arda and going all the way to Isildur's death and loss of Sauron's One Ring — is simply an elaborate setup for the tales told in *The Hobbit* and *The Lord of the Rings*. What you and I take as "the story" — the hobbits' finding Sauron's Ring and subsequently destroying it — is but the last act in a much larger story of the ongoing cycle of evil's emergence, defeat, and reemergence in a new form (see Chapter 15 for more on the ongoing struggle of good versus evil).

The supreme irony in the destruction of the Ring is that Sauron comes to an end because of his own evil device — Isildur's bane becomes Sauron's bane in the end. Tolkien tells us that in order for Sauron to make his One Ring sufficiently powerful to rule the other Rings of Power and thereby the different races of Middle-earth, he had to pour much of his strength and will into it. And so by simply destroying the One Ring, Sauron can be annihilated.

Sauron took this terrible gamble because, being an evil creep, it never dawned on him that someone might not be interested in the Ring's power and would destroy it rather than use it. Sauron counted on the next person who found the Ring (or whomever the Ring found) to be just like Isildur was and Saruman wants to be (a wannabe Lord of the Ring who tried to claim the Ring as his own and use its power to challenge and dethrone Sauron — see Chapter 8).

Sauron's problem is similar to Manwë's earlier dilemma, when he pardoned Melkor because as a good being he couldn't fathom the mind of evil (see "Tolkien and the idea of irredeemable evil" earlier in this chapter). Sauron has spent so much time lusting after power that he cannot fathom a being who's not in the least interested in doing the same thing. This miscalculation is what makes the hobbits such a threat to him; they are his perfect nemesis.

If not for the hobbits, Middle-earth wouldn't have the means to defeat Sauron's evil; his Ring would undoubtedly overpower and destroy anyone else with "normal" aspirations to power before he or she could ever hope to become the Lord of the Ring. As a testament to the Ring's lure, it actually does succeed in overpowering Frodo's will at the Crack of Doom. All would have been lost even then if not for the simple-minded need of Gollum to stop Frodo from possessing it (see Chapter 17 for details).

Tolkien makes clear at the end of *The Lord of the Rings* that the elimination of Sauron, like the elimination of Melkor before him, by no means spells the end of evil in Middle-earth. Evil, to use Tolkien's metaphor, is like a weed that is seeded too widely throughout the world to ever disappear entirely. All it takes for evil to sprout anew are the right soil and weather conditions.

Any gardener knows that the best way to prevent the spread of weeds is to uproot them early when they are easy to pull up. But all too often, good people, like lazy gardeners, wait too long. When they finally do go in to eradicate them (with great toil), frequently they leave the roots — making, in essence, Isildur's mistake of not destroying the One Ring when he had the chance. As a result, the evils grow back, sometimes quicker and stronger than before, requiring even more toil and effort to eradicate.

The Ringwraiths, Loyal Servants of Sauron

Everyone needs people he can really count on in times of need, even despicable old Sauron. For him, the Nine Ringwraiths, his trusty and extremely menacing sidekicks, are there to answer his every beck and call.

The Ringwraiths — Nazgûl in the Black Speech of Mordor and Úlairi in Elvish — were once Lords of Men, until Sauron gave them the Rings of Power that the Gwaith-i-Mírdain Elves made for Men. Alas, the effect that the Rings of Power had over the Men who wore them was a wee bit different from the effect of the Dwarf-Rings on Dwarves (they predominantly made the Dwarf-lords crazy for gold — see Chapter 6 for details). The Rings of Men stretch their mortal lives so thin, they waste away, making them into apparitions, wispy shadows completely subservient to Sauron and his Ring.

The Ringwraiths are Tolkien's most original and, many feel, most frightening fiends in *The Lord of the Rings*. The Ringwraiths' lives and wills are entwined with their Rings of Power. They are subjected completely to Sauron and his One Ring, and their lifespans are so warped and stretched out by the unnatural prolonging power of their Rings that they appear insubstantial, like shadows wearing hoods. Inside, they writhe in anger and hatred for themselves and for all creatures with which they come into contact.

Tolkien tells us that the Ringwraiths strike their enemies by filling them with utter terror and complete panic, causing them to freeze and *despair* — a word with special meaning in Tolkien's vocabulary (see Chapter 20 for details). They carry all sorts of nasty weapons, including the dreaded Morgul blade that wounds Frodo and nearly turns *him* into a wraith. Their poisonous Black Breath injures Éowyn and Merry after they dispatch the Lord of the Nazgûl.

The major role of the Ringwraiths is not, however, to frighten Sauron's enemies, but to seek out and retrieve his One Ring of Power. They can sense the Ring and are often seen literally trying to sniff it out. Either because their will towards the Ring is so intense or because the Ring's desire to be found is so great, when the Ringwraiths get close to Frodo, he has to contend with a tremendously strong desire to put on the Ring. The one time that he confronts the Ringwraiths and puts on the Ring at Weathertop, their terrible forms are clearly revealed to him (in contrast to their usual amorphous, dark shapes).

At the beginning of *The Lord of the Rings*, the Nine Ringwraiths disguise themselves as Black Riders to search for the One Ring in the Shire. After losing their black steeds in the flood at the Ford of Bruinen, they reappear atop huge winged beasts that have beaks and claws like birds and serpentine bodies like dragons. The Ringwraiths fly great distances on these beasts, ever scanning for the Ring-bearer and instilling terror in those below.

To me, the Ringwraiths are so scary because they are so thoroughly bent and controlled by their craving and obsession for the One Ring. Their ghost-like quality only adds to the horror because it's such a good image for someone who's given his will over to the control of something outside of himself.

Luckily, the fate of the Ringwraiths, like that of their evil Lord, is intimately tied to the fortune of the One Ring. As soon as the Ring is destroyed in the fires of Mount Doom, they are forever annihilated as well — they go poof in the air, like a mist dissipating in a breeze.

The Dragons of Middle-earth

Where would fantasy be without its dragons, the age-old enemies of many a valiant knight in legend and fairytale? Tolkien's interest in dragons may be due to the fact that Beowulf, in the epic poem that bears his name, meets his end in mortal combat with a particularly ferocious fire-breathing dragon.

In Middle-earth, dragons are the original servants of Morgoth. Most unstoppable of the dragons are the Urulóki ("Heat Serpents"), who like Beowulf's dragon wither their opponents with their fiery breath — only properly armored Dwarves are strong enough to withstand such intense heat. Tolkien mentions three of these notorious bad boys:

- **Ancalagon** the Black, the mightiest of the dragons, slain by Eärendil in the Great Battle during the War of Wrath in *The Silmarillion*

- **Glaurung** the Worm of Morgoth and the Father of Dragons, slain by Túrin Turambar in *The Silmarillion* (see Chapter 19)

- **Smaug** the Golden, slain by Bard the Bowman right before the Battle of the Five Armies in *The Hobbit*

In addition to their fiery breath, Tolkien's dragons have other dangerous qualities: their protectiveness of their hoarded treasure and their dragon-spell, or ability to put adversaries under their power through the stare of their serpent eyes. Their voices are also said to be especially beguiling, so that their words act like hypnotic suggestions that influence the hearer, although he or she can't remember what was suggested once they are free of their stare.

Dragon sickness is the possessive stockpiling of gold, jewels, and other treasures for which dragons simply have no use, being serpents who don't get out all that often, but which they nevertheless defend down to the last piece with their lives. (They are not the only ones prone to dragon sickness — I know some rich and not so rich folks who have bad cases of it.)

Dragons play no part in *The Lord of the Rings* because they are extinct by then. Smaug the Golden, seemingly the last of his kind, is dispatched by Bard the Bowman, who, armed with Bilbo's tips on the location of the vulnerable part of the dragon's underbelly, fells him near the end of *The Hobbit.* In *The Lord of the Rings,* Gandalf does comment on how fortunate it was that Thorin and Company, with Bilbo Baggins in tow, precipitated the confrontation in which Smaug is slain — for if this dragon still existed, it would have been a perfect weapon for Sauron to use against the West.

The Two Giant Spiders, Ungoliant and Shelob

All three books, *The Silmarillion, The Hobbit,* and *The Lord of the Rings,* feature creepy giant spiders in league with the Enemy. Tolkien may have been a bit of an arachnophobe, for traditionally in folklore, spiders are lucky creatures because their webs keep down insects, especially flies. They are also admired for their industriousness. (Scottish legend has it that a spider's stubborn attempts to construct a web, no matter how many times it was destroyed, inspired Robert the Bruce to renew his struggle against the British after several defeats.)

But forget folklore and children's stories like *Charlotte's Web* — Tolkien's spiders are just plain wicked. The way he describes these particular minions of the Enemy is especially creepy: They are large and they not only hide in the darkness, but actually *thrive* on the darkness.

Ungoliant and her taste for light

One giant spider, Ungoliant, in league with Melkor, attacked and destroyed the Two Trees of Aman. Tolkien says that she (like Melkor) both lusted after and simultaneously hated their light. When Melkor wounded the Two Trees, Ungoliant sucked out all their light through the gashes, poisoning their roots.

Not satiated, she then drank dry the Wells of Varda, where the light from the flowers and fruit of the Trees was stored. While gorging on the light, she belched black fumes and swelled so hideously that even Melkor was alarmed.

When Melkor and Ungoliant reached Middle-earth, Ungoliant, still hungry for the Light, demanded that Melkor feed her all the gems he'd stolen from the fortress of Fëanor. Melkor reluctantly fed her all his stolen jewels except the Silmarils. When he refused her the Silmarils, which retained the last of the Light from the Two Trees, Ungoliant tried to strangle him in her webs. Melkor let out a scream so terrible that the Balrogs, hiding in the ruins of his old haunt Angband, came running to his save his sorry behind (see "Of Balrogs, Trolls, and Orcs" later in this chapter for details). They used their whips of fire to free Melkor from Ungoliant's webs and to drive her off.

Ungoliant made her way into Beleriand and settled beneath Ered Gorgoroth (Mountains of Terror) in a lovely little valley that came to be called Nan Dungortheb (Valley of Dreadful Death) because of the terror she bred there. It seems that this valley contained a number of spider-like creatures, with whom Ungoliant mated and then promptly devoured (in good she-spider fashion). Her foul little ones remained there, ready to terrorize anyone who came their way, until Beleriand sank beneath the sea after the Great Battle.

Ungoliant headed south, looking for greener pastures. Rumor has it that at one point she got so hungry in the southern wastes of Middle-earth that she ended up devouring herself — a fitting ending for one so greedy and foul.

Shelob and her fear of light

With the sinking of Nan Dungortheb during the time of Melkor's final defeat, some of Ungoliant's offspring made it safely east to settle down in Middle-earth proper. The last of these lovelies was named Shelob ("she-spider" — *lob* is an Old English form of "spider"). She made her lair in a pass in the Mountains of Shadow connecting Ithilien with Mordor. Consequently this pass is ever after known as Cirith Ungol ("Spider Pass").

On his return to Mordor, Sauron used Shelob as a guard (he calls her his "cat") to keep the pass safe from any intruders. Shelob has no trouble devouring any creature, although she much prefers Men and Elves to Orcs.

Thanks to Gollum's deceit, Frodo and Sam are given the opportunity to meet Shelob in her lair when Gollum leads them into Mordor via the Spider Pass. Unfortunately for Shelob, Frodo and Sam remember Galadriel's parting gift to Frodo, a phial of water containing Light from Eärendil's star (see Chapter 5) mixed with water from her fountain. With the help of this special light and a powerful Elvish mantra, Sam defeats Shelob, wounding and possibly killing her, but not before Shelob injures Frodo and convinces Sam that he is dead.

The unlight of Ungoliant

Tolkien, always mindful of his language and especially his metaphors for light, was careful not to call the cloak that Ungoliant wove to hide Melkor and herself during their attack the Two Trees a *darkness*. Instead he called it an *unlight* to point out that Ungoliant's cloak was not just an absence of light but a new form of non-light or void. Tolkien invented *unlight* because he knew that the prefix *un* combined with a noun can create a new state that is not simply the opposite of the word it modifies. For example, *unrest* is not merely a lack of relaxation (no-rest) but a state of turmoil and uproar. I think it's possible to see this unlight as a active force in itself that devours light, perhaps explaining Ungoliant's seemingly insatiable hunger for light.

Eärendil's star is the last of the Silmarils, containing the last of the Light of the Two Trees of Aman, so it is poetic justice that this starlight from Galadriel's phial should blind and help destroy Shelob, the last of the foul children of Ungoliant who murdered the Two Trees. It is odd, though, that whereas momma Ungoliant hungers after the light (can't devour enough of the stuff), her daughter Shelob will have nothing to do with it. I don't know if this difference between them can be explained in terms of an adverse reaction to her mother's addiction for light or it merely points to Tolkien's quirkiness in terms of story-telling.

Of Balrogs, Trolls, and Orcs

In his long career as an evil creep, Melkor corrupted and helped fashion a great number of foul creatures. This section looks at three types that are all equally at home in the dark recesses of the world: Balrogs, Trolls, and Orcs. Balrogs and Orcs feature prominently in *The Silmarillion* and *The Lord of the Rings*. Trolls and Orcs (called goblins) appear in *The Hobbit*.

Balrogs as corrupted Maiar

As I mention in Chapter 3, Balrogs are actually Maiar, the lesser type of Valar (Powers) from Aman who gave Melkor their allegiance and were, in turn, corrupted by his evil. These humanoid creatures are intimately associated with fire, like dragons; they have fiery manes and breathe fire through their nostrils. In addition, they carry fiery whips to subdue their enemies, along with standard-issue weapons like maces and swords.

These creatures served Melkor in his northern underground fortress of Angband and Thangorodrim in Middle-earth. It was the Balrogs who rescued Melkor from Ungoliant's wrath, and it was the Lord of the Balrogs, Gothmog, who slew Fëanor (see Chapter 4).

After the Great Battle in the War of Wrath (see Chapter 12), most of the Balrogs perished when Thangorodrim was broken and Angband destroyed. One Balrog did escape Beleriand before it sank and fled east to settle in Khazad-dûm under Mount Caradhras, where it remained unknown until the Dwarves under Durin VI's leadership woke it in their digging for the scarce mineral mithril (see Chapter 6).

This Balrog, known as Durin's Bane, is the same one that Gandalf faces when the Fellowship of the Ring goes through the Mines of Moria (Khazad-dûm) to cross the Misty Mountains on their way to Mordor. The Balrog snatches Gandalf and pulls the wizard down with him using his fire-whip. After a long battle, Gandalf finally manages to destroy the Balrog by throwing him from Durin's tower.

Trolls as dumb as stones

Trolls figure prominently in Norse and Germanic legends and fairytales, where they are often associated with giants. In some Germanic legends, however, Trolls are associated with bridges, which they love to hide under — and with the devouring of human flesh, which they love even more.

Tolkien's Trolls, like their counterparts in old tales, are afraid of the least little bit of sunlight because it turns them immediately to stone — a fate that Bilbo's three Trolls, Bert, Tom, and William, in *The Hobbit* find out the hard way. Tolkien's Trolls are also very keen on consuming human flesh and are about as dumb as the stones they turn into.

Tolkien's Trolls are giants about twice the height and girth of an average human. In the War of the Jewels chronicled in *The Silmarillion*, Trolls often took part in the battles that occurred before the birth of the sun, many times accompanying their old pals, the Balrogs.

Orcs as corrupted Elves

Tolkien once characterized his Orcs as the Enemy's "foot soldiers." Accordingly, these infantrymen of evil are the most numerous of the Enemy's underlings. Tolkien got *Orc* from an Old English word for goblin or evil spirit. In the epic poem *Beowulf*, which so influenced Tolkien, the term for goblins is *orcn_as*, which are identified with, along with ogres, elves, and giants, as unmistakable kin of the original murderer, Cain.

In *The Hobbit,* Tolkien consistently refers to the Orcs as goblins, a term derived from the ancient Greek *kobalos* meaning an impudent rogue or a mischievous spirit conjured up by such a rogue. If you see Melkor as an insolent scoundrel, then this is a very fitting definition because Orcs are most certainly malicious and malign spirits.

Melkor fashioned the Orcs from the Elves that he first captured in Middle-earth and took to his dungeons in Angband. Hence, Orcs are the tortured and twisted remains of noble Elves that have gone through an insane breeding program. Orcs are hideous in form, much more stunted than the tall Elves, and are cruel by nature and as fond of human flesh as Trolls.

Perhaps the most important aspect of Orcs is that they are ferocious fighters. They love to bring pain to other creatures (it's their sole joy in life) and they fear their master's wrath more than they do their enemy's weapons.

The biggest weakness of the Orcs is their extreme vulnerability to sunlight, which greatly weakens them and causes them great pain — they must have that kind of skin that's extremely sensitive to the sun. Because of this, Orc armies are limited to battling under the cover of darkness.

To counter this weakness, Sauron, ever the inventive one, bred a new type of Orc, called the Uruk-hai (*Uruk* being Elvish for Orc). This form of Orc is somewhat larger than the original stock — as tall as Men are — is every bit as vicious, has no fear of sunlight and, therefore, is more than ready to rumble all the time.

On Werewolves, Vampires, Wargs, Wights, and Watchers

Whew! That's a little too much alliteration. The first two in the list, werewolves and vampires, are very familiar to anyone who's seen any of those great black-and-white horror films from the '30s (which may be where Tolkien got his ideas about them).

In *The Silmarillion,* werewolves and vampires appear in stories surrounding Tol-in-Gaurhoth ("Isle of Werewolves"), where Lúthien came to rescue Beren, her lover, and King Finrod from Sauron's dungeons (see Chapter 18 for details). Lúthien came to Sauron's fortress disguised as the vampire Thuringwethil ("Woman of Secret Shadow"), one of Sauron's messengers who flew between Tol-in-Gaurhoth and Angband in vampire form. Her vampire silhouette as she flew must have been truly awesome — Tolkien describes her great bat wings as having barbed joints whose fingers ended in an iron claw.

As I mention in Chapter 9, Wargs are great wolves that border on being werewolves because of their very vicious, almost human-criminal nature. In *The Hobbit* Wargs attack and tree Gandalf, Bilbo, and Thorin and Company, who all have to be rescued by the Great Eagles (despite Gandalf's best efforts to incinerate the Wargs with his pyrotechnics).

A Wight (pronounced like "white") in Tolkien's works describes a creepy creature that hangs out in barrow graves — thus the designation Barrow-wight. In *The Lord of the Rings,* the Barrow-wights are exceedingly malevolent spirits who waylay Frodo, Sam, Merry, and Pippin, take them down into the barrow graves, attempt to imprison them forever, dressing them up in funeral garb like dead princes. The hobbits manage to escape by calling on good old Tom Bombadil, who never met a Wight he couldn't banish (see Chapter 9).

Watchers are of two kinds. There is the Watcher in the Water that the Fellowship of the Ring encounter when entering the Mines of Moria. And then there are the Watchers in the courtyard of the Tower on the east side of the Mountains of Shadow that Frodo and Sam encounter right before they enter Mordor.

The Watcher in the Water is a many-tentacled monster who lives in the lake by the western entrance to Moria. This monster grabs Frodo and attempts to drag him into the water. When the company makes for the safety of the mines, this creature pulls down the Doors of Durin, permanently blocking the passage and forcing the company to go through the mines to seek the eastern passage on the other side of the Misty Mountains.

The Watchers that Frodo and Sam encounter when trying to gain entrance to Mordor are a far different kind. These enchanted, seated stone figures with gleaming eyes and three heads (looking in all the different directions) are posted on either side of the arched gate in the courtyard of the Tower. They guard the entrance to the plateau of Gorgoroth, blocking any unwanted visitors who get past Shelob's lair. Frodo and Sam break the will of these Watchers by displaying again the phial of Galadriel, flooding the courtyard with the light of Eärendil's star, and by uttering the Elf-mantras they used in holding off and subduing Shelob (see Chapter 14).

When trying to imagine the Watchers, I often picture them to be like the gargoyles that sit atop many a medieval cathedral to protect its walls from any unwanted forces. Like gargoyles, Tolkien's Watchers have animal features (the faces and claws of vultures) to make them appear ferocious. Unlike gargoyles, though, that merely appear menacing, Tolkien's Watchers have menacing powers, such as a force field that holds the would-be intruder at bay.

Part III
The History of
Middle-earth

"Look at them. If you ask me, this whole Creation of Arda Day Parade thing is just an excuse for them to go out drinking with their buddies."

In this part . . .

What major events make up the history of Middle-earth and shaped Tolkien's stories about this world? Part III attempts to answer these questions by providing you with timelines that outline the main events chronicled in Tolkien's three major fantasy works: *The Silmarillion, The Hobbit,* and *The Lord of the Rings*. This overview runs from Tolkien's more distant and legendary Valarian Ages all the way up to the Third Age, whose closing events form the basis of *The Lord of the Rings*.

Chapter 11

The Valarian Ages

*T*he *Valarian Ages* is a general name referring to the various epochs in *The Silmarillion* that precede the First through Third Ages of Middle-earth. And because the numbered ages refer to times during which the sun is the primary light of the world, the Valarian Ages refer to everything that happened before the sun first shone on Middle-earth (see Chapter 12 for more). Note that Tolkien did not refer to these periods by the term — it has been coined by others because of the prominent roles of the Valar in their events.

This chapter presents an overview of the various epochs that comprise the Valarian Ages. The purpose here is not to provide a detailed history of these epochs (there will be no test!), but to give you a feeling for the forces that Tolkien envisioned as forming the world in which Middle-earth is but a part. Hopefully, this brief introduction to these periods will give you an understanding of the basic framework from which all the other stories spring (including the ones in *The Hobbit* and *The Lord of the Rings*). If you want more information on this formative period, pick up *The Silmarillion*.

An Overview of the Valarian Ages

Tolkien began the history of his Middle-earth with the creation. Eru Ilúvatar (the "One All-father") brought the world into being according to the themes sung by the Ainur in the chorus of creation (see Chapter 13 for more). As soon as Ilúvatar finished forming the initial world according to the Ainur's songs, many of the Ainur chorus volunteered to go to the new world of Arda ("the Realm," which includes Middle-earth) to continue refining its features and fulfilling the initial vision. The Ainur were divided into two classes: the greater Valar and the lesser Maiar (see Chapter 3). All the events that took place after the Valar set the sun in the sky are a part of the Valarian Ages.

The problem with chronicling the Valarian Ages is that, unlike the numbered ages, Tolkien didn't number the years. In fact, the designations he gave to epochs in the Valarian Ages are mostly poetical: the Spring of Arda, the Days of the Bliss of Valinor, and the Noontide of the Blessed Realm. Collectively, they are called the Elder Days (not to be confused with the Good Old Days!).

One reason Tolkien didn't number the years in the Valarian Ages is because there weren't any years; another may be that he was imitating the "days" before the sun in the Biblical creation story. The Valar hadn't yet created the sun, so you couldn't count years, since by definition a year is the time it takes for the sun to return to its original position in the sky (technically, the time it takes the earth to make a complete revolution around the sun, but I doubt that the people of Middle-earth understood this, as it was eons before Copernicus). Without years, Tolkien's chronology of these ages is fuzzy to say the least. The best I can do is construct a very general timeline that simply shows the sequence of the most important events in each epoch.

The Spring of Arda

The Spring of Arda was the first epoch of the Valarian Ages. As the name signifies, this is the youthful Arda, when the Valar attempt to light the world — this first time with lamps, which give all of Arda continuous light and bring radiance and wisdom to all its beings. Despite its cheerful name, this period begins and ends in conflict, as you see in Table 11-1. The first event Tolkien recorded in the Spring of Arda is the First War against Melkor.

Table 11-1   The Sequence of Events During the Spring of Arda
Historical Event
The Valar wage the First War against their rogue Melkor to stop him from destroying their work in Arda. An Ainu named Tulkas the Strong enters the world specifically to contend with Melkor, who retreats to the Outer Darkness in the face of Tulkas's strength.
Aulë fashions the landmass known as Middle-earth between the encircling seas.
Aulë constructs the Two Lamps on giant pillars to bring light to Middle-earth: Illuin in the north of the original landmass of Middle-earth and Ormal in the south.
Yavanna sows seeds that sprout and grow into grasses, moss, ferns, and trees under the light of the Two Lamps.
The Valar go to the Island of Almaren in the Great Lake in the midst of Middle-earth and construct great mansions on the island to live in.Melkor returns from the Outer Darkness and builds his underground fortress of Utumno in the far north of Middle-earth.

Historical Event

Melkor and his servants attack and destroy the Two Lamps, destroying the pillars on which they rested and bringing their fire to earth, where it ravages much of the land and ruins the planned proportions of the world. Melkor escapes to the north.

The Valar leave Middle-earth to dwell in Valinor on Aman. This western continent is separated by the Great Sea but joined to Middle-earth in the far north by a frigid land bridge called Helcaraxë ("Grinding Ice"). Once in Aman, the Valar raise the Pelóri Mountains as a defensive shield along its east coast.

Tulkas the Strong was sent to Middle-earth specifically to fight Melkor. He makes a fascinating strongman because Tolkien his strength came from both his anger and laughter. A number of mythologies designate anger as a source of strength, but laughter is normally a sign of weakness or disrespect, yet here Tolkien portrays it as a weapon against evil. Near the end of *The Two Towers* volume of *The Lord of the Rings,* Frodo laughs out loud when Sam calls him the "famousest of the hobbits," imagining how someday people will read about their adventures in a big red book with black letters (this is not it — it's black and yellow). Tolkien says that Frodo's laughter was a sound that hadn't been heard in Cirith Ungol since before Sauron came to Middle-earth, and that it was as though the tower's stones were listening. Although Tolkien tells us nothing more about the power of this laughter, it seems as if this power, along with the light of Galadriel's phial and some basic Elvish spells, are what enable these hobbit heroes to survive their ordeal and actually enter Mordor (see Chapter 13 for more on the power of language).

As you can see in the timeline in Table 11-1, despite his early retreat, Melkor was still able to wreak havoc on Middle-earth and got the mighty Valar to retreat to Aman. This period makes it clear that evil was already a powerful force, and that the defeat of Melkor would take a very long campaign indeed.

The Days of the Bliss of Valinor

The second Valarian Age is called the Days of the Bliss of Valinor, a time of overall harmony and joy. However, the bliss was only for the those who live in Aman, for the new light source built to replace the lamps that Melkor had destroyed did not shine beyond this realm. In fact, Middle-earth, where the Elves were awakened, was as that time illuminated only by starlight. The radiance and wisdom of the light of the Valar was available only to those who traveled to Valinor. Thus, one of the major events of this age was the undertaking of the Great Journey by the Elves, who left Middle-earth to dwell in the light of Valinor, side by side with the Valar.

The Days of the Bliss of Valinor started off on a positive note. The Valar rebounded from the destruction of the Two Lamps, the marring of Middle-earth, and their retreat to Aman by creating the Two Trees as the new light source. The two 12-hour periods, during which each of the Two Trees alternately underwent a complete waxing and waning of its light, with two one-hour periods of overlap, made up the Valarian day (see Figure 11-1). The Days of the Bliss of Valinor began in the Opening Hour, when the elder Tree first began to shine. For the first time in the history of Arda, time was counted.

As you can see in Table 11-2, three major events mark this period: the awakening of the Elves, a counterattack on Melkor that led to his imprisonment, and the summoning of the Elves to come and dwell with the Valar in the Blessed Realm. For most of this epoch, things were indeed blissful. With Melkor nursing his pride in the north, the Valar were free to bring sweetness and light to Middle-earth, to sprinkle the sky with stars, and to welcome Iluvatar's Firstborn children the Elves. Like the good fairies who sought to protect Sleeping Beauty from the Bad Fairy's curse, the Valar protected the land of the Elves from the evil of Melkor. The history of Middle-earth aligns with the history of planet earth in the forces of good and evil entering a constant state of tension that often erupts in war.

Table 11-2	The Sequence of Events During the Days of the Bliss of Valinor

Historical Event
Yavanna sings into being the Two Trees of Light, Telperion and Laurelin, on the green mound called Ezellohar outside the golden gate of Valmar, the city of the Valar.
The Count of Days begins, reckoned by the hours during which the light of Telperion and Laurelin wax and wane.
Varda uses residual light from the Two Trees to rekindle the stars she had created during the Spring of Arda and to create new stars over Middle-earth, giving light to the Elves.
Ilúvatar awakens the Elves in east Middle-earth at Cuiviénen, the Water of Awakening.
During a visit to Middle-earth, Oromë the Hunter comes upon the Elves in Cuiviénen. Oromë lets the Valar know that the Elves have been awakened and sets in motion the following two events.
The Valar battle Melkor to keep Middle-earth safe for Ilúvatar's elder children. After the Battle of the Powers, Melkor is brought to Valinor and imprisoned in the Halls of Mandos.
The Valar summon the Elves to come dwell with them in Valinor (see Chapter 4).

The Cycle of Light during the Valarian Day

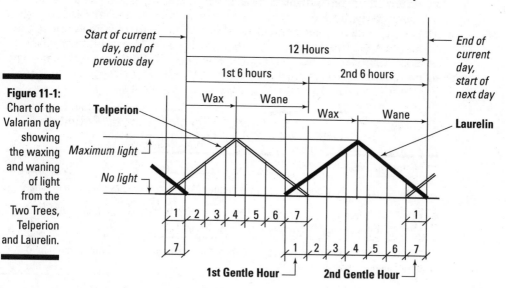

Figure 11-1:
Chart of the
Valarian day
showing
the waxing
and waning
of light
from the
Two Trees,
Telperion
and Laurelin.

Why did the Valar issue this summons to the Elves after ridding Middle-earth
of Melkor? Tolkien never said, but I believe it has to do with the issue of choice
and free will (see Chapter 19). Just as Melkor, the Vala, was given free will and
used it to mess with Ilúvatar's plans, the immortal Elves were also given the
choice to stay in Middle-earth or move in with the "heavenly hosts." Some went
to Valinor, others tried and gave up, and still others didn't make the effort. So,
from the beginning of Middle-earth, free will became a source of disunity, and
playing out the results of choices ultimately made Middle-earth an almost per-
petual battleground.

The Noontide of the Blessed Realm

The last period of the Valarian Ages is called the Noontide of the Blessed Realm.
As its name implies, this was when the radiance and wisdom of the Valar were
at their zenith. After this high noon, though, the light would never again be
as bright in Aman, culminating ultimately in a new darkness that engulfed all
of Arda — the Blessed Realm and Middle-earth as well. (After the Noontide of
Blessed Realm, the direct influence of the wisdom of the Valar on the beings
of Middle-earth would never again be as strong as it was during the Valarian
Ages — see Chapter 12 for a rundown on the Ages of the Sun that immediately
follow the Noontide of the Blessed Realm.)

It was during this age that the division of the Elves into different kindred bore very bitter fruit. As you can see in Table 11-3, this epoch began brilliantly enough with the birth of Fëanor, the most creative and gifted Elf in history (see Chapter 4). Sadly, his life coincided with one of the most tragic events in the history of Arda: the destruction of the Two Trees by Melkor and Ungoliant. Fëanor's response to this tragedy made him one of Middle-earth's most tragic figures as well (see Chapter 19 for more on Fëanor).

Table 11-3	The Sequence of Events During the Noontide of the Blessed Realm

Historical Event

Fëanor, the first-born son of King Finwë, leader of the Noldor, is born in Tirion in Aman.

Fëanor's mother Míriel dies, and Finwë marries Indis, a close kin of King Ingwë of the Vanyar. Together, they have two sons, Fingolfin and Finarfin.

The Valar pardon Melkor, release him from the prison of Mandos, but forbid him to leave Valmar, the city of the Valar.

Fëanor invents Tengwar script for writing Elvish, improving on the system developed by Rúmil. He creates the Silmarils, three jewels that contain the blended light of the Two Trees.

Fëanor quarrels with his half-brother Fingolfin and threatens him with a knife in his father's house. The Valar ban Fëanor from the city of Tirion for 12 years. Fëanor withdraws to his northern fortress of Formenos. His father Finwë vacates his crown in Tirion and joins him.

Melkor flees Valmar. By heading south to the desert region Avathar, rather than north to his hideaway at Utumno, evades his pursuers. There, he joins the monstrous spider, Ungoliant.

Fëanor joins his half-brother Fingolfin and the other Elves at a First Fruits celebration at Manwë's palace atop Mount Taniquetil. Finwë stays in Formenos, vowing to have nothing to do with the other Noldor as long as Fëanor is banned from Tirion.

Melkor and Ungoliant attack the Two Trees. Melkor wounds each tree and then Ungoliant sucks out all their light. Together, Melkor and Ungoliant flee to Middle-earth by going north over Helcaraxë. Along the way, they stop at Formenos, kill Finwë, and steal the Silmarils.

Yavanna asks to use Fëanor's Silmarils in curing the Two Trees, which she cannot recreate. He refuses. Melkor slays Fëanor's father and steals the Silmarils in his flight to Middle-earth.

Fëanor breaks the ban of the Valar by going to Tirion. There, he rouses the Noldor to rebel against the Valar and join him in going to Middle-earth to get revenge on Melkor and recover the Silmarils. He binds his sons and his half-brothers to a terrible oath of vengeance.

Historical Event

Fëanor leads the Noldorin rebels north to the port of Alqualondë. There, he demands the use of the white ships of the Teleri in order to pursue Melkor. King Olwë of the Teleri refuses. Fëanor and his band commandeer the white ships and kill many of the resisting Teleri in an incident known as the Kinslaying.

Fëanor makes his way north along the coast to avoid a storm caused by Ossë, the Maia who protects the coastal waters. When the Noldorin rebels reach Araman, the Vala Mandos (the Judge) issues the Doom of the Noldor, exiling Fëanor forever from the Blessed Realm and prophesying untold sorrow for all Noldor who follow him. Fëanor's other half-brother Finarfin abandons the march to Middle-earth and returns to Aman where he begs mercy of the Valar, assumes the crown of Tirion, and rules as King of the Noldor.

Fëanor, his sons, and their closest confederates abandon the rest of the Noldorin rebels in Araman (including Fingolfin and his children and the children of Finarfin — Finrod, Orodreth, and Galadriel). They sail the white ships of the Teleri to the firth of Drengist on the west coast of Middle-earth. There, they burn the white ships at a place thereafter known as Losgar ("Red Snow"), leaving their compatriots to die in northern wastes of Araman.

Fingolfin leads the Noldor abandoned by Fëanor over the Grinding Ice of Helcaraxë and down into Middle-earth with great loss of life.

The Valar raise the Pelóri Mountains higher, closing all passes but the one at Calacirya at the Bay of Eldamar. They erect towers to guard the Calacirya pass and hide Aman and its bay by setting enchanted isles before them, on which mariners ground their vessels.

The burning of the white ships at Losgar arouses Melkor's Orcs and Balrogs, who attack the Noldor. Dagor-nuin-Giliath, the so-called Battle of the Stars, ensues. The Noldor defeat the Orcs and Balrogs, sending them back to Angband, the fortress of Melkor, during the ten-day battle. Fëanor, however, pursues them in haste to recover the Silmarils. He is slain by Gothmog, the Lord of Balrogs.

This epoch that started out so illustriously with the birth of Fëanor, one of Middle-earth's most creative beings, ends with his death at the hands of a Balrog and the darkening of Valinor. Moreover, Middle-earth was placed under Fëanor's curse and Mandos' Doom of the Noldor. As you might expect, both curse and doom overshadow and color events in the next three epochs, the First through the Third Ages of the Sun, covered in Chapter 12.

Chapter 12

The First Three Ages and Then Some

The Three Ages of the Sun followed the era known as the Noontide of the Blessed Realm, an epoch that ended with a darkened Valinor, the Two Trees destroyed, and the death of Fëanor in his pursuit of Morgoth in Middle-earth.

This chapter gives you a quick history of the creation of the sun that heralded these first Three Ages, followed by highlights of the major events that took place during them. Keep in mind that the events described in *The Hobbit* and *The Lord of the Rings* all take place at the very end of the Third Age. Most of the events of the Third Age and all the events in the two preceding Ages, therefore, form the background material important to these two storylines.

"Here Comes the Sun . . ."

After Melkor destroyed the Two Trees, Aman went dark just like the rest of Middle-earth. Only the stars kindled by Varda over the course of the Valarian Ages provided any light at all. After a vain attempt by the Valar to heal the Trees, Telperion (the first tree) produced one last flower of silver, and Laurelin one last golden fruit.

The Vala Aulë then fashioned vessels to hold the light from this last flower and fruit: The vessel containing the silver flower of Telperion became the moon and the vessel containing the golden fruit, the sun. The Vala Varda launched the moon first (because its light came from the Telperion, the elder of the Two Trees); after it had traversed the sky of Arda seven times, she launched the sun. At the time of this very first sunrise in the west, Ilúvatar awoke the race of Men in eastern Middle-earth. From that time on, the sun was associated with the race of Men and the moon with the race of Elves. Tolkien describes this much more poetically in *The Silmarillion* where he says that the sun was placed in the sky "as sign of the awakening of Men and the waning of Elves, but the moon cherishes their [Elves'] memory."

The theme of the waning influence of the Elves in Middle-earth is one that doesn't fully develop until the Third Age chronicled in detail in *The Lord of the Rings*. The association of the Elves with the moon is a bit surprising because Tolkien normally associates Elves with the Stars (see Chapter 4). It's possible that this linking of Men to the sun and Elves to the moon is simply symbolic of their relative strength (brilliance) in the coming ages (especially at the end of the Third Age). I think that Tolkien's allusion to the moon as holding the memory of the Elves means that, although that memory has waned and become dark like the new moon, in time it will return and wax bright like the full moon (largely through Tolkien's efforts to make their stories known in his fantasy writings).

The light of the sun and moon, although derived from the remnants of the Two Trees of Valinor, is somewhat different in nature. For one thing, the light of the sun and the moon shines on all beings of Middle-earth rather than just on the beings of Aman, as was the case with the Two Trees (see Chapter 11). Although the light of the sun and moon alternates like the light from the Two Trees from which they were derived, the oscillation of their light is quite different.

The light of the Two Trees alternated in a steady rhythm, waxing and waning with no variation over each twelve-hour period. And while the light of the sun waxes and wanes following the same general pattern each day (from sunrise to noontide to sunset), the length of this period fluctuates over the year, waxing from winter to summer solstice and then waning from summer to winter solstice. And the light of the moon waxes and wanes over roughly a monthly period from dark to full moon and then from full back to dark moon.

In this way, the light of the radiance and wisdom of the Valar — although once again available to all the beings of Middle-earth, which hadn't been the case since the age known as the Spring of Arda — fluctuates in both its intensity and quality much more than was ever the case during the ages of the Two Trees known as the Days of the Bliss of Valinor and the Noontide of the Blessed Realm (see Chapter 11 for details). This greater fluctuation in the light of the Valar was reflected in their much more guarded and hands-off approach to the struggles in Middle-earth, first with Melkor and later with Sauron during all Three Ages. They directly intervened in the War of the Silmarils only at the very end of the First Age, defensively removed Aman from the physical realm of Arda during the end of the Second Age, and depended upon the Maiar they sent as wizards (see Chapter 8) to help in the War of the Ring during the Third Age.

Highlights of Events in the Three Ages

The events of the First Age are mostly concerned with the War of the Silmarils in which the rebellious Noldorin Elves attempted to defeat Morgoth and recover Fëanor's stolen Silmaril jewels. Woven into the story of this conflict is the account of the coming of Men into Middle-earth and the struggle between the Noldorin and Sindarin Elves (the ones who never left Middle-earth for the Blessed Realm). In true Tolkien tradition, the growing relationship between Elves and Men, while seemingly secondary to many the tales of this age, proves to be key to the resolution of the Silmaril conflict — such as when Eärendil the mortal mariner who visited the Valar in Aman to entreat them to intervene on behalf of Middle-earth.

The Second Age is primarily the story of the race of Men known as the Edain, who inhabited the island of Númenor — Tolkien's Atlantis — and their conflict with Sauron in Middle-earth. Sauron's co-opting of the Elves into forging the Rings of Power that become so important in *The Lord of the Rings* also takes place in the Second Age. In many ways, the Second Age is the precursor of the story taken up both in *The Hobbit* and *The Lord of the Rings*.

The Third Age concerns the reappearance of Sauron in Middle-earth and his threat to conquer it. Underlying the story is the growing dominion of Men and the waning influence of the Elves. All the events recounted in *The Hobbit* and *The Lord of the Rings* take place at the end of the Third Age.

The First Age and the War of the Silmarils

Table 12-1 lists the major historical events of the First Age. The biggest event is undoubtedly the appearance of the sun as the major source of light in the world and, along with that, Ilúvatar's awakening of the race of Men.

The remainder of this Age is mostly concerned with the downfall of major Elven kingdoms — Nargothrond, Menegroth in Doriath, Tol Sirion, and Gondolin — along with a great many battles with Morgoth. This Age ends with the Great Battle in which the Valar, Elves, Men, and Dwarves join together to destroy Morgoth's fortress and annihilate him forever.

Table 12-1	The Major Historical Events of the First Age
Date	*Historical Event*
1	The sun rises for the first time in the west; Ilúvatar awakens the race of mortal Men in the far eastern section called Hildórien.
52	With the help of the Vala Ulmo, Turgon, son of Noldorin Lord Fingolfin, discovers the secret Vale of Tumladen protected by Echarioth (Encircling Mountains) — the future site of the Hidden Kingdom of Gondolin.
56	The Glorious Battle (Dagor Aglareb) during which the Elves, led by Fingolfin and Maedhros (eldest son of Fëanor), repel Morgoth's attacks and destroy his Orcs. The allied Elves begin a siege of Angband, the Iron Fortress of Morgoth, that lasts nearly 400 years.
c. 100	Finrod founds the underground fortress Nargothrond, whose caverns are excavated and decorated by the Dwarves of Nogrod and Belegost.
126	Turgon occupies his white city in the Hidden Kingdom of Gondolin, leaving his original home in Nevrast.
c. 300	King Finrod Felagund discovers and befriends the mortal Bëor and his people near the springs of Thalos in East Beleriand. Over the next three years, the three tribes of Men migrate to Estolad (see Chapter 5).
455	The Battle of Sudden Flame (Dagor Bragollach) occurs, during which earthquakes and lava flow from Thangorodrim. Glaurung the dragon, followed by the Balrogs and armies of Orcs, comes forth and breaks the siege of Angband. During this battle, Angrod and Aegnor, two sons of Fëanor, are slain, as is Bregolas, son of Bëor, and Fingolfin, second son of Finwë. Barahir, father of Beren, saves the life of Finrod Felagund, son of Finarfin, third son of Finwë, for which Barahir earns Finrod's undying friendship and receives his ring with the crest of the House of Finwë as a token of his indebtedness to the House of Bëor.
457	Sauron captures Tol Sirion, the island in the River Sirion, where King Finrod Felagund built the original white tower, Minas Tirith (after which the second one in Gondor is named). After its capture, Tol Sirion is renamed Tol-in-Gaurhoth ("Island of Werewolves").
465	Lúthien leads Beren to her father, King Thingol in Menegroth. Thingol challenges Beren to retrieve a Silmaril from Morgoth as the price for his daughter. Beren enlists the help of King Finrod Felagund of Nargothrond.

Date	Historical Event
468	Beren and Finrod are captured by Sauron and imprisoned in the dungeons of Tol-in-Gaurhoth. Finrod dies trying to save Beren from a werewolf. Lúthien rescues Beren and together, they bury Finrod's body.
473	The Battle of Unnumbered Tears (Nirnaeth Arnoediad) occurs, also known as the Fifth Battle, during which Maedhros organizes an attack on Thangorodrim. Despite great odds, this attack almost succeeds except for the treachery of a group of men known as the Easterlings. Before his death in this battle, Huor foretells to Turgon that if Gondolin can stand a little longer, a new star shall rise from their two houses (Huor is the father of Tuor and Turgon the father of Idril, the parents of Eärendil, known as the Star of High Hope).
495	The Elves of Nargothrond under the leadership of King Orodreth (Finrod's brother) are defeated in the Battle of Tumhalad by Glaurung the dragon. Glaurung kills Orodreth and sacks the Elven kingdom of Nargothrond.
499	Túrin Turambar slays the dragon Glaurung and then commits suicide upon the discovery that his wife, Níniel, is indeed his sister Nienor.
502	King Thingol is slain by the Dwarves of Nogrod who attempt to steal the Nauglamír necklace that contains the Simaril. Melian sends the Silmaril to Beren and Lúthien in Tol Galen and then flees Middle-earth, returning to Valinor and leaving Doriath unprotected.
503	Eärendil is born to Idril and Tuor in Gondolin.
505	Beren and Lúthien die in Tol Galen. Messengers bring the Nauglamír containing the Silmaril to Dior, their son, who now rules his grandfather's Kingdom of Doriath in Menegroth. Celegorm and Curufin, sons of Fëanor, attack Menegroth. Dior and his wife Nimloth are slain along with Celegorm and Curufin, and their two young sons are left to starve in the woods. Their daughter Elwing escapes to the River Sirion with the Silmaril.
510	Morgoth's forces attack Gondolin, whose location is revealed by the treachery of Maeglin. Idril and Tuor escape with Eärendil, making their way to the mouth of the Sirion River where they join Elwing and the survivors of Doriath.
c. 525	The twins, Elrond and Elros, are born to Eärendil and Elwing.

(continued)

Table 12-1 *(continued)*	
Date	*Historical Event*
c. 560	Tuor and Idril sail west in the great ship Eärrámë ("Sea-Wing") and are not heard from again. Eärendil sails west in his ship Vingilot ("Foam-Flower") in an unsuccessful bid to locate his parents. Upon returning to Middle-earth, he is met by his wife Elwing who is carrying the Silmaril and who, disguised as a white bird with the help of Ulmo, is fleeing Maedhros and Maglor. The remaining sons of Fëanor slay the survivors of Gondolin and Doriath in hopes of recovering their father's Silmaril and kidnap their children Elrond and Elros. Eärendil and Elwing then turn around and sail to Aman where Eärendil pleads for the Valar's help in the struggle against Morgoth. The Valar reward Eärendil by making him the heavenly navigator who sails Vingilot over the skies, the Silmaril on his brow a sign of hope.
583	The Valar make war on Morgoth in Middle-earth with the help of the Elves of Aman in the War of Wrath and the Great Battle. The Valar defeat Morgoth's Orcs, Balrogs, and dragons, destroying the mountains of Thangorodrim and his fortress of Angband. They remove the remaining two Silmarils from Morgoth's iron crown and hurtle him into the void beyond the confines of the world. Maedhros and Maglor steal the Silmarils from the camp of the Valar. Burned by the Silmarils, Maedhros casts himself into a chasm in the earth, and Maglor jumps into the sea. As a result of the Great Battle, most of Beleriand sinks under the sea. Many of the Elves of Beleriand sail west to return to Aman. Some, such as Círdan, Gil-galad, Galadriel, Celeborn, and Elrond, elect to remain in Middle-earth.

The Second Age and the Sinking of Númenor

Table 12-2 shows the major historical events of the Second Age. This age is mostly concerned with the rise and fall of Númenor, the island nation that the Valar provided for the Edain who help the Elves during their long struggle against Morgoth in Beleriand. As I point out in Chapter 2, the story of the fall of Númenor is Tolkien's thinly disguised Atlantis.

The Second Age also sees the continuation of Morgoth's evil in the hands of his loyal steward Sauron. Sauron first deceived the Elves of Eregion by pretending to be a healer who wanted to mend the hurts that Morgoth's evil has done. He deceived the last king of Númenor by urging an attack on Valinor as the antidote to human mortality (see Chapter 16). Fortunately, at the end of this age, the Faithful (the Men of Númenor who came to Middle-earth with Elendil and his two sons Anárion and Isildur,) stand in alliance with the Elves. Together, they defeat Sauron, if only for a time.

Table 12-2	The Major Historical Events of the Second Age
Date	**Historical Event**
1	The Elves found Lindon and Grey Havens in Middle-earth.
32	The group of Men known as the Edain, loyal to the cause of the Elves during the War of Silmarils, reach the Island of Númenor. Elros, the mortal son of Eärendil and Elwing, rules as King Tar-Minyatur, the first King of Númenor.
442	King Tar-Minyatur dies; he was mortal brother to Elrond Half-elven.
500	Sauron, having survived the Great Battle, reappears in Middle-earth.
750	A group of Noldorin Elves found Eregion (Hollin) in Middle-earth.
1000	Sauron founds his kingdom in the eastern land of Mordor and begins building his fortress, Barad-dûr ("The Dark Tower").
1200	Sauron appears in the guise of Annatar ("Lord of Gifts") to the Elves of Eregion. The Men of Númenor begin to colonize the western shores of Middle-earth.
1500	The Elven smiths, under the leadership of Celebrimbor, begin forging the Rings of Power according to Sauron's designs.
1590	The Elven smiths complete the Rings of Power — three for the Elves, seven for the Dwarf Lords, and nine for the Lords of Men.
1600	Sauron forges the One Ring of Power to control all the other Rings of Power in the fires of Mount Doom (Orodruin). Celebrimbor perceives Sauron's treachery.
1693	Sauron makes war on the Elven-smiths. Celebrimbor hides the Three Elven Rings.
1697	Sauron destroys Eregion and kills Celebrimbor. The Dwarves shut the Doors to Moria. Elrond founds Rivendell.
c. 1800	Númenor begins to dominate the western coast of Middle-earth.
2251	The Ringwraiths, also known as the Nazgûl, the slaves of the Nine Rings of Power forged for Men, appear in Middle-earth.
2280	Númenóreans found the port of Umbar in the south of Gondor.
2350	Númenóreans found the port of Pelargir at the branching of the Sirith and Anduin Rivers.
3255	Ar-Pharazôn, last King of Númenor, illegitimately seizes the throne of Queen Míriel.
3262	King Ar-Pharazôn invades Mordor, captures Sauron, and takes him back to Númenor as a prisoner.

(continued)

Table 12-2 (continued)

Date	Historical Event
3310	Under the influence of Sauron, Ar-Pharazôn begins building an armada with which to attack the Valar in Aman.
3319	Ar-Pharazôn invades Valinor. Ilúvatar removes Aman from the Circles of the World (the Change of the World), causing Númenor to sink. The Faithful flee to Middle-earth.
3320	The Númenórean Faithful found the Realms in Exile in Middle-earth: Elendil founds the Kingdom of Arnor in the north of Middle-earth. His sons Anárion and Isildur found the Kingdoms of Gondor and Ithilien in the south. The Seeing Stones (palantíri) are divided among the new kingdoms. Sauron's spirit returns to Mordor.
3430	The Last Alliance of Men and Elves forms under the leadership of King Elendil, Elrond, and Gil-galad.
3434	The Last Alliance of Men and Elves defeats Sauron's forces in the Battle of Dagorlad. The Alliance lays siege to Sauron's tower of Barad-dûr.
3440	Anárion, eldest son of King Elendil, is slain during the siege of Barad-dûr.
3441	Sauron comes down to do hand-to-hand combat with King Elendil. Sauron slays both Gil-galad and Elendil, but Isildur fells Sauron by cutting the One Ring from his hand with the hilt-shard of Narsil, the broken sword of Elendil.

The Third Age and the War of the Ring

In the Third Age, Sauron's spirit — preserved by Isildur's refusal to destroy the One Ring in Mount Doom — rises again in Middle-earth to threaten the freedom of all its peoples. The major events of the Third Age and Sauron's rise are listed in Table 12-3. Note that although more than 3,000 years are chronicled, the tales and stories that Tolkien tells in *The Hobbit* and *The Lord of the Rings* all take place within the last 200 years of the Third Age.

Also keep in mind that the year T.A. 1601, in which King Argeleb II officially ceded the Shire to the hobbits, is year 1 in the hobbit system of dating, known as Shire Reckoning (S.R.). The year 3021 — in which Bilbo, Frodo, Gandalf, Galadriel, and Elrond sail from the Grey Havens for the Undying Lands — is the year S.R. 1421. Unlike the rest of the Reunited Kingdom which counts the next year as the first year of the Fourth Age (F.A. 1), the hobbits continue to use Shire Reckoning. So, when Tolkien tells us that in the year S.R. 1485 Sam set sail from the Grey Havens to join Frodo in the Undying Lands after the passing of his beloved wife, Rose, it was the year F.A. 64 according to the Reunited Kingdom calendar.

Table 12-3	The Major Historical Events of the Third Age
Date	*Historical Event*
2	Isildur plants a seedling of the White Tree in Minas Anor (later renamed Minas Tirith). He vacates Gondor to assume rule over his father's Kingdom of Arnor. On his way north, Orcs attack his company and the Battle of Gladden Fields ensues. The One Ring abandons Isildur, and he is slain by Orcs. The One Ring is lost in the River Anduin.
c. 1050	Wizards come to Middle-earth. Círdan the Shipwright entrusts Narya the Elven Ring of Fire to Gandalf the Grey. An evil power comes to the Greenwood Forest, which Men rename Mirkwood Forest.
c. 1100	Sauron comes to Dol Guldur in Mirkwood Forest disguised as the Necromancer. The Wise, led by Gandalf and Elrond, mistakenly think that a Ringwraith has taken residence there.
c. 1300	The Ringwraiths reappear in Middle-earth. The Lord of the Ringwraiths, known as the Witch-king, goes north to Angmar.
1601	The hobbits migrate west of the Brandywine River and are granted the Shire by King Argeleb II of Arthedain. They name this year 1 in their system of Shire Reckoning.
1974	The North-kingdom falls when the Witch-king conquers Fornost, its capital.
1975	An army of Men and Elves defeats the Witch-king at the Battle of Fornost. The Witch-king escapes and flees south.
1980	The Witch-king goes to Mordor and gathers the other Ringwraiths to him. The Balrog of Moria slays Durin VI.
2000	The Ringwraiths attack and besiege Minas Ithil.
2002	Minas Ithil falls to the Ringwraiths and becomes known as Minas Morgul.
2463	Déagol finds the One Ring in the River Anduin near Gladden Fields. Sméagol (Gollum) murders his friend Déagol for the Ring.
2470	Sméagol, known as Gollum, takes the One Ring deep into the Misty Mountains.
2745	Orcs overrun Osgiliath in Gondor.

(continued)

Table 12-3 *(continued)*

Date	Historical Event
2845	Sauron seizes the seventh Ring of Power given to the Dwarves from Thráin II.
2941	Bilbo Baggins finds the One Ring in Gollum's cave.
2951	Sauron begins rebuilding Barad-dûr. He sends three Ringwraiths to reoccupy Dol Guldur. Elrond reveals Aragorn's true name and heritage and gives him the heirlooms of his house, including the shards of the sword Narsil and the ring of Barahir. Aragorn and Arwen meet for the first time in Rivendell.
3001	Frodo inherits the Ring and Bag End from Bilbo, who goes to stay at Rivendell.
3008	Gandalf reveals the true identity of Bilbo's Ring to Frodo.
3018	Frodo, Sam, Merry, and Pippin go to Rivendell and join the Fellowship of the Ring.
3019	The War of the Ring begins, ending with the destruction of the One Ring in Mount Doom. Aragorn Elessar is crowned King of the Reunited Kingdom and marries Arwen Undomiel (Evenstar).
3021	The Keepers of the Three Rings, Gandalf, Galadriel, and Elrond, along with the bearers of the One Ring, Bilbo and Frodo, sail to the Blessed Realm of Aman.

Our historical knowledge of Middle-earth doesn't end when the Ring-bearers sail away to Aman. In Appendix B in *The Lord of the Rings*, Tolkien includes a short chronology of the major events of the first 120 years of the Fourth Age. It begins by listing S.R. 1422 as the first year of the Fourth Age in the Shire — although the hobbits continue to count years according to Shire Reckoning. This short chronology concludes with the death of King Aragorn and Legolas and Gimli sailing to Aman in S.R. 1541 (F.A. 120).

For those who aren't history buffs, one dating system is more than enough. Tolkien's additional Shire Reckoning is likely an extra vexation. I'm sure that Tolkien added this alternate system to reinforce the idea that this all reflects the hobbits' perspective on events, especially in the Third Age.

In Tolkien's dating system, with the exception of the First Age where the beginning is marked by the all-important event of the first sunrise, the ages (Second, Third, and Fourth) are not initiated by important events that kick off the new age but by important events that close the previous one. For example, the Third Age starts after Isildur defeats Sauron by cutting the Ring off his hand at the close of the Second Age. So, too, the Fourth Age starts immediately after the Ring-bearers sail to Aman at the close of the Third Age.

Part IV
The Languages of Middle-earth

The 5th Wave By Rich Tennant

ⓒRICHTENNANT

"...and remember, no more Elvish tongue twisters until you know the language better."

In this part . . .

Where does language fit into Tolkien's Middle-earth, and what part does it play in its tales? Part IV deals with these questions and attempts to provide some insight into the overriding importance of language in Tolkien's fantasy world. This part also introduces you to some of the actual languages and linguistic thinking that influenced Tolkien when he went about inventing languages for some of the beings of Middle-earth. It also acquaints you with some of the basic components of the Elvish languages on which so much of his fantasy world depends.

Chapter 13

Tolkien and Language

· ·

In This Chapter

▶ The importance of language in Tolkien's fantasy world

▶ How Tolkien made the sounds of his languages reflect the character of their speakers

▶ Singing the world into being: the creation of Arda

▶ The magical power of words in the tales of Middle-earth

· ·

No reader of Tolkien's fantasy works can ever doubt the importance of language to this author, even if he or she is unaware of Tolkien's background as a longtime student of languages and Professor of Anglo-Saxon. Not only are his works full of foreign-sounding terms, but they often give multiple names for the same characters and places. This approach can be especially daunting given the sheer number of characters and lands in *The Lord of the Rings*. On top of this, Tolkien felt compelled to create different languages for the various peoples featured in his Middle-earth sagas in order to make them more believable. You can find passages in which characters suddenly go spouting off in their own "native" tongue — some of which Tolkien never bothered to translate for those of us not up on our Entish or High Elvish.

This chapter evaluates the general significance of language in Tolkien's fantasy works by looking first at Tolkien as the linguist of Middle-earth and considering how his search for the history of words may well have been the genesis of Middle-earth. It then moves on to explore the euphonic ("sweet-sounding") aspects of Tolkien's languages. The chapter concludes by examining the power of language in Tolkien's fantasy world: as the primary process through which the world comes into being and as the way some of his characters manipulate their environment.

Tolkien as a Linguist

Dictionaries define a *linguist* as a person who is accomplished in languages, especially someone who speaks several languages. By this definition, Tolkien was a consummate linguist, having learned more than a dozen languages and teaching one of them — Anglo-Saxon. In addition, Tolkien invented several languages, many of which are featured in his tales of Middle-earth.

Keep in mind that none of the languages that Tolkien invented for his Middle-earth mythologies is fully formed. You can learn the vocabulary and syntax rules for some of his more complete languages, such as Quenya, the so-called High Elvish. But you can't actually speak or write anything you want in any of these languages because, even where Tolkien fully developed the grammar, he didn't have the opportunity or need to develop a full vocabulary as well. See Chapter 14 for more on specific languages he created for Middle-earth.

The etymological mythmaker

Etymology refers to studying the history of a word by tracing its development from its earliest known sources, analyzing its components, and tracking down its cognates to a common ancestral source. In many ways, Tolkien was a consummate "etymological" mythmaker. He often seems to have developed his stories as explanations of the history of particular terms.

I can't help but wonder if all of Tolkien's myths recounted in the *Quenta Silmarillion* (History of the Silmarils) of *The Silmarillion* stem from his fascination with the sound of the name *Éarendel* in Cynewulf's poem *Crist:*

```
Hail Éarendel, the brightest of angels sent to the world of men
```

(See Chapter 1 for Old English version of this line.) Éarendel was an Old English term for a ray of light that seems also to have signified the morning star (Venus) with its Christian symbolism related to John the Baptist and Christ. I believe that Tolkien saw the potential in this name for developing a pre-Christian myth that later would be fulfilled in the gospels.

In the *Quenta Silmarillion*, though, the reader learns that Eärendil (Tolkien's spelling of Éarendel) was the brightest angel (messenger) because he wore the sole-surviving Silmaril on his brow — a jewel that carried the last vestige of the blended light of the Two Trees of the Blessed Realm. Eärendil was sent by the Valar of the Blessed Realm and sailed over Middle-earth in his ship Vingilot ("Foam-Flower") as a symbol of promise and hope to all people that they may yet prevail against evil, even as the Valar prevailed over Morgoth by ejecting him into the void (see Chapter 5 for more on Eärendil's story).

One can easily see how the story explaining the significance of Eärendil and his appearance over Middle-earth could spawn stories about how the Silmarils came into being and how the Elves and Morgoth contended over them in a long war in Middle-earth — as well as later stories of how Men rose and fell in Númenor and battled the reemerging evil of Morgoth's lieutenant Sauron.

Whether the myth of Eärendil was the real genesis of the many other sagas recounted in *The Silmarillion, The Hobbit,* and *The Lord of the Rings* is not nearly as important as understanding how the history of a word can indeed generate myth. Tolkien was a great storyteller because he demonstrated over and over the process by which people create their treasured myths — a process that can begin with the origin and history of one name or term.

Invented language and its need for a mythology

Tolkien clearly believed that fabricating a language was a futile business if you weren't also willing to create a history or mythology for it to express. This was the basis of Tolkien's criticism of Esperanto, the language invented to facilitate communication between all the peoples of the world and that few people learn and fewer bother to use. In Tolkien's estimation, constructed languages such as Esperanto are doomed from the get-go because they have no history or legends, just syntax, grammar, and a way of building vocabulary. Pretty boring stuff for most of us. By contrast, Tolkien's rich mythologies provide not only contexts for characters to express feelings and thoughts, but also histories explaining how their languages evolved.

One important example of language history in Tolkien's tales is the story of the prohibition on the older form of Elvish called Quenya, spoken by the Elves in Aman, and how this ban in Middle-earth affected the acceptance and development of a younger dialect called Sindarin (see Chapter 14 for more on the differences between Quenya and Sindarin).

According to *The Silmarillion,* the Elvish language split in part because of a political decision — a prohibition of the older language. The King of Doriath, learning of the slaying of his Telerin kin in Aman by the Noldorin rebels under Fëanor, forbade the use of their language, Quenya, within his kingdom in Middle-earth (see Chapter 4 for details). Underscoring this split with the older form of Elvish (supposedly spoken by the Valar as well in Valinor), the King of Doriath even changed his name from its Quenyan form, Elwë Singollo, to its Sindarin form, Elu Thingol.

Because of the ban, Quenya ceased to develop in Middle-earth. Unlike Sindarin, it became a "dead" language, reserved for writing only. Given this political climate, it's always interesting to note when Tolkien has one of his Noldorin Elf characters break Thingol's ban and use Quenya.

One example of defiance of this ban occurs in *The Silmarillion* when Aredhel, the White Lady of the Noldor who was forcibly wedded to the Sindarin Elf Eöl, named their child Lómion (Quenyan for "Child of Twilight"). The child's father, however, gave him the Sindarin name Maeglin ("Sharp Glance"), the name the boy took and used when he betrayed the Noldorin Kingdom of Gondolin.

Another example of flouting the ban occurs in *The Lord of the Rings* when Galadriel bids farewell to the Fellowship by singing a song, now generally known as *Namárië* (Quenyan for "Farewell"), which Frodo recognizes as being in the "language of Elven song" (Quenya) and speaking of things seldom heard of in Middle-earth (the song laments the loss of Valinor).

Galadriel's quoting of *Namárië* is one of the few instances of more than a simple phrase or two of Quenya in *The Lord of the Rings,* where the Elves primarily use Sindarin. By inserting the *Namárië* in an otherwise Sindarin environment, Tolkien not only subtly introduces the bad blood between the Noldorin and Teleri Elves and all woes in Aman and Middle-earth, but also gives us a sweet taste of what's been lost because of the ban. Tolkien concretely demonstrates how compelling a constructed language can be as the centerpiece of a convincing history and legend.

Euphony in Tolkien's Languages

Euphony (Greek for "sweet-voiced"), meaning a pleasing or sweet sound or acoustic effect, is an important concept in understanding Tolkien's invented languages for Middle-earth. For Tolkien, a language's euphonies or lack thereof reflected the character of its speakers. In the plainest of words: the good guys' languages sound pretty, and the bad guys' sound ugly.

In *The Lord of the Rings,* Elvish is supposed to be very euphonic, whereas the so-called Black Speech of Mordor is very harsh. Compare, for example, the names of Shagrat and Grishnákh, two particularly nasty Orcs, with those of Gildor and Elrond, two particularly exemplary Elves.

Although no one would expect Shagrat to be among the top ten baby names for next year, I somehow doubt that Gildor will make it either. My point is that euphony is in the "ear" of the beholder. Like Tolkien, I have studied a few different languages and do prefer some over others — usually the ones that as a native English speaker I can pronounce more correctly and understand more easily. But I don't judge them as more or less beautiful sounding; I just realize that they utilize different sets of related sounds.

For example, contrast the sound of the Elvish greeting Frodo uses when he meets Gildor in the Shire with the Black Speech inscribed on the inside of the One Ring (see Chapter 21). Frodo's Elvish greeting goes like this:

```
Elen sκla lumenn' omentielvo!
```

This translates as "A star shines on the hour of our meeting," a very elegant and Elf-like way to say howdy. Now look at the Ring's inside inscription:

```
Ash nazg thrakatulûk. Agh burzum-ishi krimpatul.
```

This translates as "One Ring to bring them all and in the darkness bind them" — not a very nice thought and, according to Tolkien, a particularly nasty way to express it. When Gandalf utters aloud this inscription at the Council of Elrond, it practically makes the Elves' ears bleed.

Now, I don't know about you, but to my ears, the Elvish greeting is most agreeable. It's almost Italian-like; its open vowel sounds give it a sort of lilting, almost musical quality that's very pleasing. This phrase is, however, a little difficult for me to pronounce. For me, the end of the phrase is somewhat like a tongue-twister and trips me up if I try to say it over and over again.

In contrast to the lilting Elvish, the sounds of the Black Speech phrase is pretty guttural. The harshness, apart from its dire meaning, comes from its throati-ness: If you say it over and over, not only will the Dark Lord come and take you to Mordor, but you'll get a really sore throat. Tolkien engineered the phrase to be the antithesis of euphony. (I can well imagine that after doing a few takes as Gandalf uttering this inscription at the Council of Elrond for the Special Extended DVD Edition of *The Fellowship of the Ring*, Sir Ian McKellen had a really scratchy throat.)

Nevertheless, just hearing the sounds of Black Speech with the more guttural tones and staccato-like phrasing than Elvish doesn't convince me of its evil. I've chanted Tibetan sutras that use some phrasing every bit as guttural — that to the untrained ear might sound as dark as Black Speech — even though they are expressing unending love and compassion for all beings.

The Power of Sound

For me, the real beauty of Tolkien's rapport with language is his clear under-standing that language is primarily spoken sound, and that it is fundamentally powerful. In fact, if you remember, spoken sound is so great a power that it is how Tolkien's world was created.

In addition to the creation story in which the Ainur literally sing the world into being, Tolkien's tales are full of characters doing amazing things with the sound of their voices. Any study of Tolkien's languages is incomplete if it doesn't include a basic exploration of the power of sound in his works.

Singing the physical world into being

As with so many other elements in his fantasy works, Tolkien was not entirely original in his idea that the universe was brought into being through sound. Perhaps the closest real-world example of singing the world into being is the

Ancient Egyptian religion. The god Thoth, creator of magic and writing and teacher to mankind, was thought to have created the world with his voice alone (uttering magical words or some sort of vocal spell, no doubt).

Later, the idea of a direct link between sound and the manifestation of the universe found its way into the theories of Pythagoras, the Greek mathematician and mystic. He expressed this relationship as the Music of the Spheres, in which each planet moving through solar system creates its own sound, and together they create harmonious music.

Pythagoras was also a pioneer in establishing a direct relationship between particular numerical quantities (such as string length or wave lengths) and musical tones. Pythagoras's concept of the ratios inherent in musical harmonics was much later applied to the relationships of the orbits of the planets around the sun by the German astronomer Johannes Kepler, who saw in these relationships a divine geometry and celestial harmony.

Two concepts are central to all these ideas, including Tolkien's myth about the Ainur singing the world into being: Sound is vibration and sound is a powerful transformative energy. Because all physical objects vibrate, sound can influence them, either by matching or competing with their *resonance* — the rate at which they naturally vibrate. If that sounds far-fetched, think of a diva shattering a glass with her voice, or high winds vibrating a bridge until it shakes itself apart. Both of these instances involve matching the resonance of an object and then increasing the object's vibration until it disintegrates.

At its heart, Tolkien's creation myth makes use of both of these central concepts. The voices of Ilúvatar's Ainur sing the themes by which the phenomena of the world — water, air, and earth — are realized. In other words, their musical themes establish the vibratory rate for all the things that will come into being in the universe.

Tolkien tells us that it was a single Ainu who introduced discord into the Music of Creation: Melkor, the mightiest Holy One, who shared the powers of all the others and therefore undoubtedly knew the resonance of their themes. Melkor introduced discord not because he was a naughty boy (he became that way in spades later on), but out of his concern that Ilúvatar's music didn't pay attention to the need for the void or empty space, without which all the wonderful things the other Ainur sang about would be glommed into one — perhaps the condition of the universe prior to the Big Bang.

So, Melkor created his own (spaced out) theme that introduced a competing vibration into the music of creation, one that you and I and the rest of the Ainur perceive as discord because it doesn't jibe with the harmony of the other voices — it was Melkor's competing vibration that was the origin of all evil in our world. In other words, evil exists because of Melkor's hubris in assuming that Ilúvatar had overlooked this need, and because he took it upon himself to fill this void and create this space his own way.

After the Ainur finished composing the Music of Creation (including Melkor's own "Variation on the Void"), Eru Ilúvatar, like Thoth in the Egyptian creation myth, brought the whole thing into being by uttering the single magic word *Eä* ("Let it be!"). The way I see it, with this one, powerful word, Eru Ilúvatar sent out a pulse that vibrated all the sounds called for in the various themes sung by his Ainur. As each physical phenomenon came into being, it naturally assumed the resonance given to it in the original music, so that ever after it continues to vibrate at that rate, producing that sound and thereby contributing to the overall celestial harmony.

Singing a mythical world into being

I love Tolkien's myth of the physical creation of the world and think that his idea of evil as a vibration that competes with the natural resonance inherent in created phenomena is pure genius. Nevertheless, the idea of singing a world into being can be understood in another metaphorical sense as well, and I think it's important to explore it, too, however briefly.

As mythmaker for Middle-earth, Tolkien became in essence its bard, or *scōp* (that latter an Anglo-Saxon term for poet, related to our *shape*). Bards performed stories orally in medieval courts. One could say that Tolkien sang Middle-earth into being through the power of his words in *The Silmarillion, The Hobbit,* and *The Lord of the Rings.* In doing so, Tolkien was a part of a long tradition that included both *Beowulf* and *Sir Gawain and the Green Knight,* epic poems with which Tolkien's academic career is most associated.

The worlds conjured up in *Beowulf* are the realm of the Geats in Southern Sweden and the Anglo-Saxon homeland of Denmark, set in an era when monsters and dragons still raised their ugly heads to challenge heroes. In *Sir Gawain and the Green Knight,* the world is that of legendary King Arthur's court at Camelot, complete with Queen Guinevere and the Knights of the Round Table. In *The Lord of the Rings,* Tolkien created a fairytale realm replete with giants (Ents), little people (hobbits), fairies (Elves and Dwarves), goblins (Orcs), wizards, knights, kings, and evil sorcerers (Saruman and Sauron) thrown in to boot. Who could want anything more from a world where heroes still fight for right against insurmountable odds?

The Power of Words

Many myths and fairytales reflect the concern of ancient peoples with the power of words, often in the form of curses and spells, and with the power that one's enemies would gain by knowing one's true name. This concern appears in a number of folktales, legends, and religions, including the ancient Egyptian religion where the name was considered a constituent of power and identity on a par with other parts of the soul. It seems to have peaked in the Israelites, who refused to utter the name of God and instead said *Adonai* ("Lord") whenever the four letters of His name appeared in scriptures.

Along with the power that comes from knowing another's true name comes the power that one derives from naming oneself. A hero often finds his strength and purpose (or fate) through coming to know his true name or identity. (See of Túrin Turambar in Chapter 19 and Aragorn in Chapter 17.) Here, I discuss the magical properties that Tolkien assigned to certain words and of the power ascribed to the voices of Gandalf and Saruman.

The power of spiritual words

When I was a kid, I was entranced by the magic word *Abracadabra,* used to make magic tricks happen, and by *Open Sesame,* which Ali Baba used to gain entrance to the treasure cave of the forty thieves. The idea of magic words uttered at the appropriate time and by the appropriate person is almost as prevalent in folklore and legend as the idea that he who knows your true name has power over you.

In *The Lord of the Rings,* these magic words are more spiritual in nature, are mostly in Elvish, and are often connected to the all-important myth of Eärendil as the Star of High Hope (see Chapter 5) and to Varda, Queen of the Valar, Star Queen and Kindler, and Elbereth Gilthoniel — because she put the stars in the night sky to light the way of the Elves.

One big exception to the use of Elvish for magic incantations in *The Lord of the Rings* is the inscription on the One Ring, which although inscribed in Elvish letters actually record Black Speech and are an evil mantra when spoken aloud (see Chapter 21 to see the inscriptions and "Euphony in Tolkien's Languages" earlier in this chapter for more on Black Speech).

In the Western spiritual traditions with which Tolkien was very familiar, spiritual words are uttered in a number of different forms, including Gregorian chants, the recitation of the rosary and the Hail Mary prayer in Catholicism, and the Jesus Prayer in Eastern Orthodox Christianity.

In the Eastern traditions, one widespread form of uttering spiritual words is the recitation of mantras (*mantra* is ancient Sanskrit meaning "mind protection"). Scholars think that mantras originated as the magic words that the Hindu Brahmin priests said at crucial times in their performance of Vedic fire sacrifices to various gods. In time, the term meant sacred recitations that mendicants pronounced as part of their meditation. It was in this form that *mantra* became a part of Buddhist meditation practice, reaching a pinnacle in Tibetan Buddhism, where not only priests but also laypeople recite mantras as part of their practice. The most famous one is

```
Om Mani Padme Hum
```

In Middle-earth, a comparable mantra might be what Sam and Frodo cry when they break the will of the Watchers at the Tower of Cirith Ungol. To get past them and through the gate to Mordor, Sam cries out something that he remembers drove away the Black Riders at the Woody End in the Shire:

```
Gilthoniel, A Elbereth!
```

Frodo then cries out

```
Aiya Elenion Ancalima!
```

These mantras, hailing first Varda as the Star Queen and then Eärendil as the Star of Long Light, not only protect the minds of Sam and Frodo and enable them to pass by breaking the Watchers' concentration, but they also cause the keystone to tumble at their feet and bring the entire arch down in ruin. Here again is the power of resonance, a vibratory power that causes the arch to crumble. The resonance of the two mantras obviously disrupts that of the Watchers and their archway, showing how a mantra can protect one from evil.

Controlling others through voice

Even if you've never been hypnotized, you're probably aware of hypnotism's power (how else to explain infomercials?). Hypnotism relies on the seductive power of the voice to exert control and plant suggestions in someone's mind that he or she then acts on. In a similar way, Tolkien's wizards Gandalf and Saruman are able to control others through the power of their voices alone — a kind of Jedi-mind trick. (Sauron, too, seems to have a similar power; he is a Maia like Gandalf and Saruman, though he is not technically considered a wizard.) In Saruman the White, who betrays the alliance to Sauron, this voice control is most dangerous. Saruman relies on the power of his voice to entice and influence others almost as much as a modern politician.

In the "Voice of Saruman" chapter in *The Two Towers* volume of *The Lord of the Rings,* Gandalf and Théoden confront the White wizard, who is trapped in the Tower of Orthanc after the attack of the Ents and Huorns (see Chapter 22 for details). Tolkien is careful to point out both the power and seductiveness of Saruman's manner of speaking. Saruman's voice is "an enchantment," and those who hear him can't remember what he said afterward, though they vividly remember how delightful his voice was and how much they agreed with what it said. In contrast, the voices of others sound harsh and angry. Most who listen to Saruman are literally spellbound by his voice. Fortunately, its effect lasts only as long as he speaks and does not affect the mind and will of stronger characters such as Gandalf and Théoden.

In our world, the problem of voices holding us spellbound, cajoling while deceiving, usually by telling us what we want to hear, is far greater than in Middle-earth. Our "wizards" use mass media to influence many more people than ever before possible. Where are our Gandalfs and Théodens to stand up to them, question their authority, and break their spells?

Chapter 14

The Tongues of Tolkien

To make his fantasy world as complete as possible, Tolkien developed an entire history of languages for it. This chapter takes a cursory look at some of the linguistic aspects of Tolkien's Middle-earth, in particular the relationship between Old English and the languages of hobbits and Men, as well as the dialects of Elvish, the most fully developed of his invented languages.

First up is a look at why the language of the hobbits seems so English in terms of their names and their manner of speaking. Next, I consider the influence of Old English (also called Anglo-Saxon, the language Tolkien taught at Oxford) on the names of characters and places in *The Hobbit* and on those of the Horse Lords of Rohan in *The Lord of the Rings*. Finally, the chapter ponders Quenya and Sindarin, the two major dialects of Elvish that Tolkien created for his most beloved Middle-earth inhabitants. This last section offers some basic information on pronunciation and writing systems.

Why the Hobbits Seem to Speak English

Many readers just take it for granted that because Tolkien was English, hobbits, his heroes, naturally speak that as well. In fact, nothing could be farther from the truth: Hobbits, despite the fact that they inhabit the British-sounding place called the Shire, don't know a word of the King's English.

Hobbits actually call the place where they live Sûza, and the characters we know and love as Sam and Ham Gamgee, as far as hobbits are concerned, are in fact named Banazîr and Ranugad Galbasi — Ban and Ran Galpsi, for short. And as for the word *hobbit*, they wouldn't know it from *rabbit* or *wombat;* they refer to a member of their kind as a *kuduk.*

So what's with all this Sûza, Ban, Ran, and kuduk stuff? To paraphrase Professor Henry Higgins from *My Fair Lady*, "Oh why can't the hobbits learn to speak English?" The reason is really quite simple: By not having the hobbits speak English, Tolkien perpetuated the fiction that he was not the author of *The Hobbit* and *The Lord of the Rings*, but merely their translator. Tolkien supposedly translated these stories from the Red Book of Westmarch written by Bilbo and Frodo (who knows what the hobbits actually called it?).

You may wonder why Tolkien wanted to be regarded as *translator* of stories about Middle-earth rather than *creator*. I think that as a linguist and scholar, the role of translator felt comfortable and allowed him to show off his language chops. At any rate, it enabled him to add Appendix F to *The Lord of the Rings*, which explains the translation of hobbit speech into English — which he does so well that hobbits seem as English as teatime and kidney pie.

Old English and the Languages of the Men of Middle-earth

According to Tolkien's linguistic history of Middle-earth, the main language group of Men is called Adûnaic, a word Tolkien translates as Westron. This language was spoken by the Dúnedain of Númenor and originated from the speech Men learned from the Elves east of the Misty Mountains (giving it a distant connection to the original tongue of the Elves). When the Númenórean exiles reached Middle-earth near the end of the Second Age, their Adûnaic mingled with the tongues of Men already dwelling there. The resulting hybrid language is known as Common Speech (or Westron), which the hobbits adopted when they came to dwell in the Shire (er, Sûza).

Although Tolkien's Common Speech is rendered in English in *The Hobbit* and *The Lord of the Rings*, it seems to have kinship with Anglo-Saxon, the Old English Tolkien studied and taught — especially character and place names.

Along with Anglo-Saxon, Tolkien mixed in Norse names and terminology. The Norse comes in most clearly in the names of Dwarves: Many are adopted from a list of Dwarf names in the Old Icelandic epic called the *Prose Edda*.

The strongest link between Anglo-Saxon and *The Hobbit* occurs in the runic writing on Thror's map that is reproduced at the front of all editions of the book. *Runes* refer to an ancient alphabet used by various Northern peoples between the late 2nd and 13th centuries. Runes were normally engraved on wood, metal, or stone — accounting for their general squared-off appearance. The word *rune* means "mystery" and "secret" in Old English and Norse. According to Norse legend, the original runic alphabet was revealed to Odin, king of the gods, while he hung upside-down for nine nights from the World Ash Tree, Yggdrasil. Scholars, however, believe that it was adapted from a Latin alphabet in use in Italy around 200 BCE (Before Common Era).

The original Norse runic alphabet is called the Elder Futhark — *futhark* describes the order of the first six letters: f, u, þ, a, r, k. The þ, called a *thorn*, is pronounced like "th." The form of runic alphabet Tolkien used in Thror's map in *The Hobbit* was an adaptation of the Elder Futhark for representing the sounds of Anglo-Saxon, which are a little different from Old Norse. As you can see in Figure 14-1, this form of the runic alphabet, called the Anglo-Saxon Futhorc, had a few more than the original 24 letters.

Note: You can use Figure 14-1 to decode the inscription on this book's title page, as well as the instructions on Thror's Map at the front of *The Hobbit*.

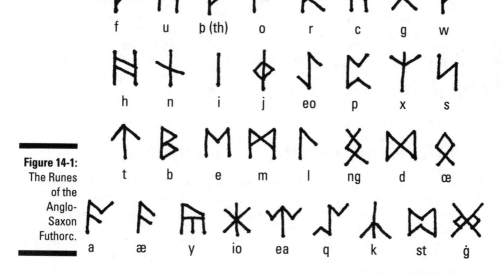

Figure 14-1: The Runes of the Anglo-Saxon Futhorc.

f   u   þ (th)   o   r   c   g   w

h   n   i   j   eo   p   x   s

t   b   e   m   l   ng   d   œ

a   æ   y   io   ea   q   k   st   ġ

In *The Lord of the Rings*, most of the Anglo-Saxon influence is evident in the people and places of the Rohirrim, the Horse Lords of Rohan. For example, Théoden, the King of Rohan, means "chief," "prince," or "lord" in Old English. Grima Wormtongue, the king's traitorous counselor, means the "fierce" or "grim" one with a "serpent's tongue." Likewise the Mark, short for Riddermark and an alternate term for Rohan, comes from the Anglo-Saxon *mearc*, denoting a "bounded territory," and Meduseld, the golden hall of King Théoden, would signify a "mead-hall" to any thirsty Anglo-Saxon.

The Anglo-Saxon influence on many of Rohan's personal and place names gives them a rougher, more barbaric feel than those of their neighbors to the south in Gondor. This association was undoubtedly intentional on Tolkien's part. The Anglo-Saxon naming of the Horse Lords enables Tolkien to reference his beloved Anglo-Saxon while providing a contrast to Gondor's Westron terms that hark back to the original language of Númenor and ultimately to Tolkien's finest language creation: Elvish.

Quenya and Sindarin: The Languages of the Elves

High Elvish, which Tolkien terms Quenya, is reputed to have its roots in Finnish, a non-Indo-European language (not related to most European languages), whereas the Grey-elven speech of Middle-earth, called Sindarin, owes more to Middle Welsh. Although I don't speak Finnish, and my early Welsh is a bit rusty, I am aware of some of Finnish sounds and syntax from studying *The Kalevala,* the Finnish epic song cycle whose myths in part inspired Tolkien's Middle-earth sagas.

All the studies I've seen that analyze the relationship between Finnish and Quenya point to a very loose connection between the phonology (the sounds of a language) and grammar of the two languages and a minimal correlation between their vocabulary. It is clear that Tolkien had a thing for Finnish — superficially, the sound of Quenya seems to follow Finnish in its liberal use of vowels and a tendency to end words in vowels. (Neither language likes lots of consonants together — that's much more like Welsh.)

Guide to Middle-earth Pronunciation

One of the more daunting tasks for the reader of Tolkien's fantasy works is knowing how to pronounce all those foreign terms (and I do mean foreign — Quenya 101 is not being offered down at the local junior college). To make the task a little easier, I cooked up a table that covers most of the sounds that might trip you up. Table 14-1 starts with the diphthongs —vowels that glide together to produce a new sound — followed by vowels and then the potentially more troublesome consonants.

Table 14-1	Guide to Pronouncing Elvish Terms
Letter(s)	*Pronunciation*
ae and ai	Pronounced *eye* so that *Ainur* is pronounced *"Eye-noor"* and *Dúnedain* is *"Dun-e-dine"*
au or aw	Pronounced like *ou* in *found* and *ow* in *how* so that Sauron is pronounced *"Sour-on"*
ei	Pronounced like *ey* in *"grey"*
ui	Pronounced like *ui* in *"ruin"* so that the *Anduin* is pronounced *"An-duwin"* and you say the last syllable really fast

Letter(s)	Pronunciation
ie	Not a diphthong — pronounce both the *i* and *e* so that *Nienna* is pronounced *"Ni-enna"*
ea and eo	Not diphthongs — pronounce both *e* and *a* and *e* and *o*. The separation of these letters is usually marked with either a dieresis (two dots) as in *Tol Erresëa* (Erresëa has four syllables) or an acute accent as in Théoden, pronounced *"The-o-den."*
a	Pronounced like the *a* in *father*
e	Pronounced like the *e* in *were* (a kind of weak "uh" sound). Note that *e* is always pronounced even at the end of Elvish words, usually indicated by a dieresis as in Manwë and Aulë (both two syllables).
i	When it is at the beginning of a word, pronounced like *y* so that *Iarwain* is said as though it were spelled *"Yar-wine."* Otherwise pronounced like *i* in *machine*.
o	Pronounced like *o* in *for*
u	Pronounced like *u* in *brute*
c	Always pronounced like *k* and never like *s* so that *Cirith Ungol* is pronounced *"Kirith Ungol"*
ch	Pronounced like *ch* in *Bach* and never like *ch* in *church*
g	Pronounced like *g* in *get* and *give*
qu	Pronounced like *qu* in *queen* and never like *ke* as in the Spanish expression *"Que pasa?"* According to Tolkien, *qu* represents the sound *cw* in Quenya (*cwēn* is the Old English spelling of *queen*).
v	Pronounced like *v* in *victor*
w	Pronounced like *w* in *white*
y	Pronounced like the consonant *y* in *"you"* in Quenya and similar to the vowel *u* in *"Luke"* and exactly like the vowel *ü* in the German *füllen* in Sindarin — *y* had a similar sound in Old English where *fyllen* (to fill) was pronounced like the German *füllen*.

Tolkien came up with some rules on how to accent his words. To me, they read like those incomprehensible grammar rules English teachers are so fond of (surprise, surprise). Maybe you can make some sense of them:

✔ If the word has two syllables, accent the first syllable as in *RINGwil*, unless the word has an accent mark that indicates a long vowel on the second syllable, as in *MuzGÂSH*.

✔ If the word has more than two syllables, accent the second-to-last syllable when that syllable contains a long vowel marked by an acute accent
(as in ó) or circumflex accent (as in ô), as in *NúmeNÓrë*, a diphthong
(such as *ae, ai, au, ei,* and *ui*), as in *FinDUIlas*, or a vowel followed by
two or more consonants, as in *NaerAMarth*.

✔ If the word has more than two syllables, and the second-to-last syllable
contains a short vowel, accent the third-to-last syllable as in both
anCAlima and *TaNIquetil*.

Tolkien's Scripts and Letters

Tolkien also created two different scripts for representing his invented languages: a system known as the Tengwar ("letters") and a system known as
the Cirth ("runes"). The Tengwar letters were created originally by a Noldorin
Elf named Rúmil and then later improved by Fëanor (see Chapter 4).

The letters in Fëanor's system do not represent an alphabet in our strictest
sense of the word — that is, a set of letters and other characters arranged in
a routine order (such as A to Z). Instead, the Tengwar are consonantal signs
that in Fëanor's system are arranged both by type of sound and by general
letter shape. As Tolkien was quick to point out, the sounds assigned to the
Tengwar may vary according to the language for which they are used.
Tengwar can render Middle-earth tongues, such as Quenya, Sindarin,
Westron, and Dwarvish — and modern ones, such as English and Finnish.

The Cirth system is obviously based on the runic alphabet used by Northern
European tribes such as Vikings and Anglo-Saxons. (See "Old English and the
Languages of the Men of Middle-earth" earlier in this chapter.) However,
Tolkien's Cirth are much more complex than the 24 simple signs developed
by his Norse and Germanic ancestors. The Cirth uses almost three times the
number of runes than the Norse Futhark, topping out at 60 symbols.

According to Tolkien's mythology, the Cirth were developed in Beleriand by
the Daeron, a Sindar Elf. Like the runic alphabets of the Vikings, the Cirth
were supposedly used to inscribe names and memorials in wood or stone.

Fëanor's Tengwar script

Table 14-2 shows the Tengwar script arranged a traditional tabular format
with the 24 primary letters (numbered 1-24) arranged in four series across
the columns (I-IV) and the six grades (1-6) down the first six rows. These primary 24 letters are created through skillful combination of two basic strokes:
one called a *telco* ("stem") and a curved shape called a *lúva* ("bow").

Table 14-2

Fëanor's Tengwar

	I	II	III	IV
1	1 Tinco - t	2 Parma - p	3 Calma - c/k	4 Quesse - kw
2	5 Ando - d/nd	6 Umbar - b/mb	7 Anga - ngw	8 Ungwe - g/ng
3	9 Thúle or Súle - th	10 Formen - f	11 Harma or aha - kh or s	12 Hwesta - khw
4	13 Anto - nt	14 Ampa - mp	15 Anca - nk	16 Unque - nkw
5	17 Númen - n	18 Malta - m	19 Noldo - _g	20 Nwalme - ngw
6	21 Óre - r	22 Vala - v	23 Anna - y	24 Wilya or Vilya - w or v
	25 Rómen - r (trilled)	26 Arda - rd	27 Lambe - l	28 Alda - ld
	29 Silme - s	30 Silme Nuquerna - s	31 Áre, Áze, or Esse - r, z, or ss	32 Áre Nuquerna - r, z, or ss
	33 Hyamen - h	34 Hwesta Sindarinwa -hw	35 Yanta - y	36 Úre - w

As you can see in Table 14-2, each of the letters in a particular series (running down the columns) uses a similarly shaped bow — either doubled or single or open or closed — with a different length of stem. You may also notice that each of the grades in the first six rows uses the same type of stem, even though the bow differs in orientation and being open or closed going from one series to the next. Tolkien, I mean, Fëanor shows true genius in creating this arrangement (it no doubt helped boost Elven literacy).

The letters in the three rows beneath the sixth grade (traditionally separated by a rule) represent the extra sounds used in the different Elvish dialects: the letter shapes don't fit the simple stem and bow pattern. I find these shapes to be the ones that really add interest to Elven script (the simple stem-and-bow letters are a little too monotonous in their close resemblance to one another).

Vowel marks in the Tengwar

Of course, no language is complete without a way to mark the vowels in its words (although Hebrew comes pretty close). To indicate vowels, Tengwar uses marks called tehtar ("signs"). These marks are normally placed above an associated consonantal sign or, if no consonant is available, over a special long or short "carrier." In the cases of diphthongs such as "au" and "ui," the vowel marks are place over the consonant úre (number 36 in Table 14-2, which looks like our "o" and is pronounced like our "w" or "y").

For stand-alone vowels, a long or short carrier is used depending on whether the vowel is short or long — the short carrier appears to the left of this paragraph. Long vowels, according to Appendix E of *The Lord of the Rings,* are pronounced no differently from short vowels in Sindarin, but are terser and more closed in the Quenya dialect — just the opposite of our long vowels, which are held longer and usually more open.

The long carrier (shown left), used for long vowels, is just a little more than twice the height of short carrier (think: long stroke for long vowels and short stroke for short vowels). Table 14-3 shows the tehtar for each of the major vowel sounds of "i," "e," "a," "o," and "u" in Quenya and Sindarin. Note that, given the frequency of "a" at the end of Quenyan words, the tehta for "a" was sometimes written as a circumflex (^) over the consonant or carrier instead of as a triangle made of three dots as shown in Table 14-3.

Table 14-3		The Tehtar (Vowel Marks) of Tengwar		
i	*e*	*a*	*o*	*u*
●	／	∴	ρ	ꝰ

Vowel marking in Quenya and Sindarin

Unsurprisingly, Tolkien wasn't content to just create one system for applying the tehtar vowel marks in both Elvish dialects. No, no, that would have been far too simple. Instead, he made one marking system for Quenya and another for Sindarin. Here are the rules:

✔ In languages such as Quenya, in which most words end in a vowel (specifically, the vowel "a" in Quenya), you place the vowel mark (tehta) over the consonant *preceding* the vowel's position in the word.

✔ In languages such as Sindarin in which most words end in a consonant, you place the vowel mark (tehta) over the consonant *following* the vowel's position in the word.

If the word has no preceding or following consonant in the right position, you add a short carrier (unless the vowel is long) and then place the tehta over it.

Just in case Tolkien's grammar rules for tehtar placement are clear as mud, see Figure 14-2, which hopefully makes the difference clear as a bell (though I still consider this a fussy and unnecessary complication on Tolkien's part).

In the left column in Figure 14-2, I show the Quenyan way to write the word *El* (the word for both "star" and "Elf") and *tara* ("noble" or "high"). In the right column, you see the Sindarin equivalents: Note that in Sindarin *tara* drops its final vowel and becomes *tar,* as in Tar-Minyatur, the title of Elros as the first King of Númenor.

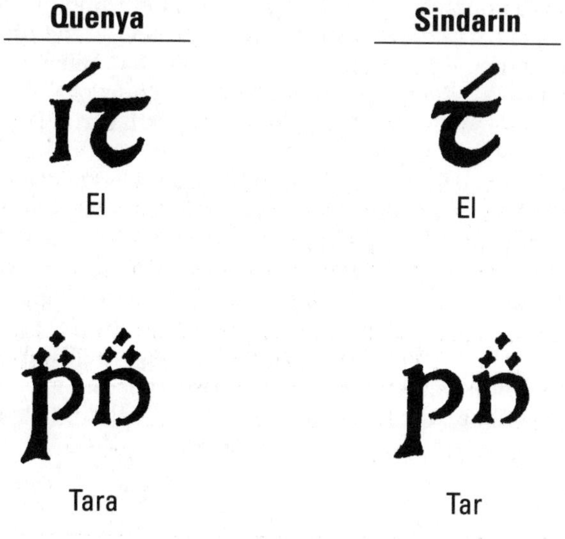

Quenya   **Sindarin**

Figure 14-2:
Tengwar for "star/Elf" and "noble," showing the difference between Quenyan and Sindarin vowel markings.

Because the word *El* contains no preceding consonant over which to position the vowel, as is required by the Quenyan vowel-marking convention, I added a short carrier and placed the e-tehta over it. However, because in Sindarin the vowel mark goes over the consonant that follows the vowel, I don't have to add a carrier to the Sindarin form — I simply place the e-tehta over the lambe to write the same word.

The second example of *tara* and *tar* shown in Figure 14-2 illustrates the situation for which Tolkien developed the two systems of vowel marking. The a-tehta over the *tinco* and *órë* in the left-hand, Quenya column give you *tara*, whereas the single a-tehta over the *órë* in the right-hand, Sindarin column gives you *tar*, the Sindarin form of the word that lacks the final vowel. To write the word *tara* using the Sindarin system of vowel marking would require the addition of a final short carrier with an a-tehta. Because so many words in Quenya end in final vowels, the Quenyan system of vowel marking makes it much easier and quicker to write this dialect in Tengwar characters.

English is more like Sindarin, so in the Tengwar inscription at the bottom of the title page of this book, I placed the vowel marks over the consonant that follows the vowel's position in the words. This is consistent with the way that Tolkien rendered his English inscription written in Tengwar at the beginning of the three volumes of *The Lord of the Rings*.

Tolkien's Cirth script

Figure 14-3 shows the Cirth script that Tolkien also developed for writing the various languages of Middle-earth. The arrangement of the runic characters and numbering them from 1 to 60 is a sequence that Tolkien calls the Angerthas Daeron — Daeron being a minstrel in the court of King Thingol of Doriath in Beleriand who originally devised the Cirth script for Sindarin.

This sequence uses some of the same principles as the arrangement of the Tengwar, in which strokes and shapes reverse to indicate shifts in sounds. You may notice that some of the letters have two sound values separated by a dash, as in number 29, r-j, and number 30, rh-zh. In such cases, the letter(s) to the left of the dash indicates the value of the Cirth in the supposed older system developed by the Sindarin Elves, whereas the letter(s) to the right of the dash indicate the sound value given to the Cirth by the Dwarves of Moria. In a few cases, the sound value is enclosed in parentheses: This indicates sound values used only by the Elves, whereas those that are followed by an asterisk indicate values used only by the Dwarves.

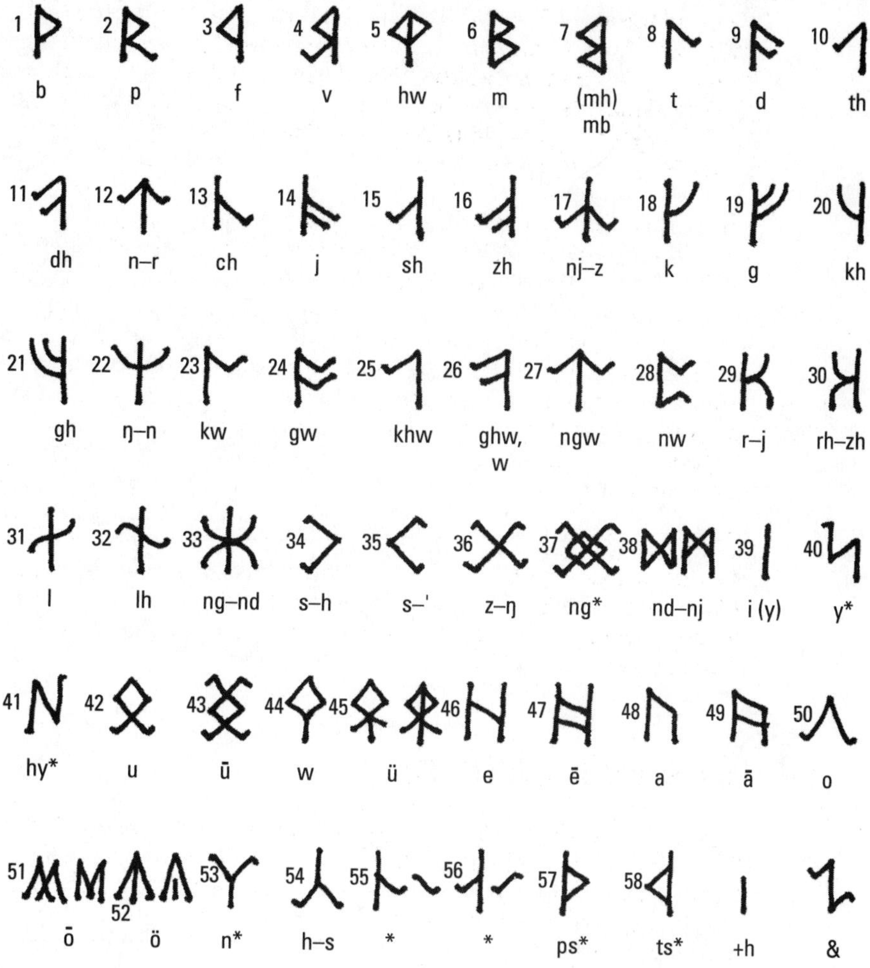

1 b	2 p	3 f	4 v	5 hw	6 m	7 (mh) mb	8 t	9 d	10 th

11 dh	12 n–r	13 ch	14 j	15 sh	16 zh	17 nj–z	18 k	19 g	20 kh

21 gh	22 ŋ–n	23 kw	24 gw	25 khw	26 ghw, w	27 ngw	28 nw	29 r–j	30 rh–zh

31 l	32 lh	33 ng–nd	34 s–h	35 s–'	36 z–ŋ	37 ng*	38 nd–nj	39 i (y)	40 y*

41 hy*	42 u	43 ū	44 w	45 ü	46 e	47 ē	48 a	49 ā	50 o

51 ō	52 ö	53 n*	54 h–s	55 *	56 *	57 ps*	58 ts*	+h	&

Figure 14-3:
Tolkien's Cirth script arranged in the Angerthas Daeron sequence.

() indicates cirth used only by Elves.
* indicates cirth used only by Dwarves.

As far as writing samples using Tolkien's Cirth script are concerned, there is only one. It occurs in Chapter IV of Book Two of *The Fellowship of the Ring*, called "A Journey in the Dark." There, the Cirth appear on the slab for Balin's tomb, which the Fellowship discovers on their trek through Moria. Reportedly, the Cirth were also used in the Book of Marzabul, which recounts the last stand of the Dwarves against the Orcs and the Watcher in the Water (sea creature that nearly nabs Frodo when the Fellowship enter Moria).

Part V
The Themes and Mythology of Middle-earth

"I think a lot of the themes in Tolkien's work must have come from his experiences at Oxford University. Particularly the roles of Brewski, Keeper of the Keg, Spaz the Geek, and Shagrat, Lord of the Wedgie."

In this part . . .

What lessons do Tolkien's stories about Middle-earth have to teach us? Part V attempts to answer this question by analyzing the more prominent themes found in Tolkien's myths and legends. These themes run the gamut from the problem of the ongoing struggle of good and evil to the issue of gender roles and the place of sex in Middle-earth. The chapters in Part V form the heart of this book — they are your personal invitation to explore the potential meanings and morals in Tolkien's work and make them your own.

Chapter 15

The Struggle Between Good and Evil

The central issue of Tolkien's fantasy writing is the struggle between good and evil, particularly in the stories of the war against Melkor in *The Silmarillion* and against his protégé Sauron in *The Lord of the Rings*. This chapter begins by looking at the nature of evil as exemplified by Melkor and Sauron and their assaults on Middle-earth during the first Three Ages. It then looks at Tolkien's idea of good versus evil and his views on the final outcome of the struggle at the end of the world. Finally, it explores the personal struggle against evil dramatized in Frodo's quest to destroy the Ring, with a special look at what all us "little guys" can do in the face of evil.

The Nature of Evil

In each of its Three Ages, the peoples of Middle-earth were threatened by a great evil force that tried to subjugate them (see Chapter 12). In the First Age, Melkor posed the primary threat to the freedom and well being of the Elves, Dwarves, and later the Men who joined them in Beleriand.

Prior to the War of the Silmarils, Melkor had been intent on controlling the light of the world by destroying the Two Trees and then stealing the remaining light of the Trees contained in the Silmarils. During the War of the Silmarils, he added the goal of annihilating all the Elven and human kingdoms of Beleriand, reducing all of them to servitude. Melkor's evil was a blend of hatred of the light (see Chapter 10 for why) and a desire to be the sole lord of Middle-earth.

During their long struggle against Melkor in Middle-earth (which lasted more than 500 years), Elves and Men referred to him as Morgoth Bauglir ("The Black Enemy and Constrainer"). As this name implies, Melkor's brand of evil was especially related to confinement, both physical and mental. Melkor's physical confinement came in the form of the darkness of his underground fortress of Angband; the mental version came from sowing dissension and self-doubt among Elves and Men (refer to the story about Túrin Turambar in Chapter 19 for an example).

After Melkor's defeat and final elimination at the end of the First Age, Sauron assumed his role as chief enemy of the creatures of Middle-earth. During the Second Age, he concentrated on subjugating Elves, Dwarves, and Men through forging the Rings of Power (see Chapter 10). Near the end of the Second Age, Sauron helped bring about the destruction of the island of Númenor when he was partially defeated in Middle-earth by survivors of the Númenórean deluge who established kingdoms there.

During the Third Age, Sauron's spirit survives, protected by the existence of the One Ring, now lost but not destroyed. Through its power, his evil influence returned to Middle-earth and grows stronger. At the end of the Third Age, during the years chronicled in *The Lord of the Rings,* Sauron wages war against the free peoples of Middle-earth, intent upon subjugating them all to his rule.

Sauron takes the cause of spreading evil more into the political arena. He attempts to spread darkness primarily through conquering all the independent lands of Middle-earth. He seeks to deny access to the light not by destroying and controlling its sources like Melkor, but by binding all people in the darkness of enslavement. Just as natural darkness reduces the varieties of color and form into a single black mass, Sauron's metaphorical darkness threatens to reduce all the different varieties of beings and cultures in Middle-earth — the Elves, hobbits, Dwarves, and Men — into a single, amorphous class of nameless slaves under his never-sleeping eye.

Sauron's particular brand of evil may seem familiar to readers of George Orwell's *1984.* Orwell's vision of modern England under the totalitarian regime of English Socialism (Ingsoc) and within constant watch of Big Brother's telescreens is suggestive of the type of regimentation and oppression that the various peoples of Middle-earth would experience if conquered by Sauron and placed under his watchful eye.

Good versus Evil

Tolkien was clear in the stories of *The Silmarillion* and *The Lord of the Rings* that the struggle between good and evil is never-ending. No sooner did the Valar vanquish Melkor than Sauron emerged in Middle-earth and forged the Rings of Power to bring it all under his control. If history in the first Three Ages are any indication, one can assume that no sooner do the heroes of *The Lord of the Rings* vanquish Sauron at the end of the Third Age than a new, perhaps worse promoter of evil will arise in the Fourth Age (though Tolkien gives us no indication of this in his brief chronology of the Fourth Age).

Not only do the seeds of evil continue to sprout and grow in Middle-earth, but the dark conditions in which they flourish continue to spread. As the sources of light diminish over the different Ages of Middle-earth, it becomes easier to deny the power of light and tout that of darkness. This expansion has fostered a loss of hope and a lack of faith that helped defeat the various Elven kingdoms in Beleriand, and later Númenor. After that, it sapped the strength from the exiled kingdoms of Arnor and Gondor.

In our world, a feeling of growing darkness can give rise to ennui and defeatism. Inherent in this defeatism is the sense that evil is stronger and somehow more real than goodness. This is, of course, the precise opposite of the truth as many, including Tolkien, see it: Evil cannot prevail over goodness because evil is just a denial of the only true and fundamental wisdom: God, in the Judeo-Christian and Islamic vocabulary; Enlightenment in the Buddhist.

In other words, the light may be hidden or blocked, thereby allowing darkness to grow, but it cannot be destroyed. All you have to do to regain the light is remove whatever obscures it, be it Melkor's or Sauron's evil. The great thing is that the moment you remove whatever blocks the light, it immediately flows again, illuminating the world as brightly as before.

Of course, as *The Lord of the Rings* so aptly points out, removing the obstacles to the light is often very difficult and comes at a very high price. More importantly, even though the light returns as strong as before once the obstacles are removed, the damage caused by their evil lingers, sometimes long after.

Shadows of evil

Tolkien often used the word *shadow* in relation to evil and evil characters, even going so far as to refer to Sauron as the Shadow. As the darkness created by an object blocking out light, a shadow lacks substance. Shadow can also mean a faint representation, in the sense of "he is only a shadow of his former self." And shadow can refer to darkness and gloom, as when Aragorn tells Celeborn and Galadriel that Gandalf has fallen "into shadow" in Moria.

Tolkien's calling Sauron the Shadow is an effective way of getting across his dark, evil aspect while reinforcing the insubstantiality of his evil. Same goes for Sauron's good buddies, the Ringwraiths, or Nazgûl (see Chapter 10 for details). The Ringwraiths, too, are just dark shapes that instill great fear, even though they seem to lack any substance. Consider that when Merry stabs the Lord of the Nazgûl, his hauberk (coat of mail) gives the only indication of where to try to wound him.

The threat of becoming a shadow like one of the Ringwraiths or Sauron himself is one that particularly menaces Frodo as the bearer of the One Ring. After the Lord of the Nazgûl wounds Frodo with the Morgul-knife, Gandalf notices that Frodo is becoming slightly transparent. As the Ring's evil power becomes stronger as Frodo nears Mordor, this process of turning into a wraith becomes more pronounced — Frodo is literally becoming a shadow.

In Frodo's struggle against turning into a wraith, Tolkien illustrates one process of becoming evil (metaphorically descending into shadow). It is not a process that happens all at once — it progresses gradually over time, like Frodo's very gradual fading. Some critics suggest that Frodo's initial disgust toward Gollum — his criticism of Bilbo's pity towards him, and his revulsion at the idea that Gollum is at heart a hobbit — are due to Frodo's fear of what *he* could become. In this view, the evil that Frodo carries can separate him from his own self and all he holds dear. In the end, the power of Ring, especially given Frodo's continued use of it, corrupts him and convinces him that he can stand against Sauron and be the new Lord of the Ring.

I feel that Tolkien's notion of "wraithing," that is, gradually giving yourself over to a controlling power until you're just a shadow of your former self, helpless before the evil influence, is very compelling and particularly applicable to modern life. Note that the power causing the "wraithing" doesn't have to be as symbolic as the Ring: it can be any of the thousand-and-one addicting influences that rob people of their humanity. The key idea here seems to be that this process of becoming evil renders all of its "wraiths" into indistinguishable shadows, robbing them of individuality and personality.

Tolkien and the last battle against evil

In the Norse mythology that so influenced Tolkien's writings, the final battle that ends the world is called *Ragnarok,* the Doom of the Gods (or Twilight of the Gods). This great conflagration not only destroys the Norse gods of the higher realm of Asgard, such as Odin and Thor, but also ends up destroying all of Midgard (our world of "Middle-earth") as well. But from the ashes of this final battle, a new, more beautiful world eventually rises.

Ragnarok is quite unlike the Christian notion of Armageddon in the Book of Revelation. There, the angels of God overwhelm and cast down the Devil and his beasts just before God creates a new heaven and earth — it's not even a fair fight. In Ragnarok, the gods face giants and other fell beasts knowing they will be killed in the process. In other words, the Norse gods face the Last Battle as any Viking hero would: ready and happy to die if necessary. In this Norse version of the end of the world, both good (the forces of world order) and evil (the forces of chaos) annihilate each other. The few survivors establish the new world.

Despite Tolkien's firm personal belief in a Day of Judgment, though, his fantasy works show no such certainty, only hinting at the possibility of a Last Battle and a new world to follow. His clearest reference is in the Dwarves' belief that at death they will wait in the Halls of Mandos until the Last Battle, at which time they will come out and help their father Aulë fashion a new world. Other than that suggestion, Tolkien gives only vague references to a day when the world is changed or made anew.

But I imagine that if pushed to depict the Last Battle in Middle-earth, he would fashion something closer to Ragnarok than Armageddon. I base this assumption on the way in which Gandalf and Aragorn face the Battle of Morannon ("Black Gate") near the end of *The Lord of the Rings* (see Chapter 24). Here, they decide to face the Enemy and his great forces right outside the Black Gate of Mordor — not from any naive notions of victory but to buy necessary time for Frodo to destroy the Ring in the fires of Mount Doom.

They know full well that the chances of Frodo succeeding are remote, and that even if he does they may not live long enough to see it. Nevertheless, like the Norse gods at Ragnarok, they're ready to battle the enemy in the face of almost certain defeat. The biggest difference between the heroes of the Battle of Morannon and those of Ragnarok is that Aragorn and the others show none of the good old Norse Gods' relish for the fight and little of the Rohirrim's delight in a warrior's death.

Rather, the warriors of the Battle of Morannon seem quite resigned to their fate. They face this tremendous challenge with all the fear and trepidation of modern, non-professional soldiers. In fact, I see Tolkien's attitude in *The Lord of the Rings* towards war and battling evil as very contemporary. In most of the battles, good guys are far outnumbered by bad guys, and their chances of victory are usually slim to none. Ignoring for the moment the adolescent battle banter between Gimli and Legolas, Tolkien's warriors are serious about their jobs, especially Gandalf and Aragorn. The only exceptions seem to be the Théoden and the Rohirrim (they are like landlocked Vikings anyway — see Chapter 5).

Tolkien's attitudes toward warfare in *The Lord of the Rings* closely resembles the outlook prevailing since World War I: War is hell, the world is a dangerous place, and the forces of evil are everywhere and numerous. Just as fewer of us are certain that good always triumphs over evil, heroes such as Gandalf and Aragorn are far from certain about the success of their desperate venture to prevent Sauron's total domination of Middle-earth.

Tolkien's heroes fight with little assurance of victory in their particular struggle, to say nothing of a final triumph of good over evil in a much later Last Battle. They fight knowing that they *must* resist evil to preserve the islands of light in Middle-earth and to arrest the spread of darkness, even with no guarantee of success. In them, I see a blend of Viking courage with a lot of 20th-century ambiguity over the final outcome of the good/evil question.

Frodo Lives!

I first encountered Tolkien in the form of "Frodo Lives" graffiti sprayed on buildings at the University of Illinois as part of the anti-war protests in 1968. In my ignorance, I thought that Frodo must be some new guerrilla warrior like Che Guevara, having seen many a "Che Lives" poster in the dorms.

For those of you too young to know what the heck I'm talking about, Che Guevara was a martyred hero to the New Left known for his advocacy of peasant revolutions and guerilla warfare to liberate the developing countries of Central and South America — after his death, supposedly at the hands of the CIA, Che was prominently featured, in his fetching black beret, on a poster with the heading "Che Lives."

Imagine my surprise to discover that Frodo was no South American revolutionary and that "Frodo Lives" referred to the end of Volume II *(The Two Towers)* of *The Lord of the Rings,* where Sam finds out, much to his relief, that Shelob's sting has only rendered Frodo unconscious and not killed him after all. I remember distinctly finishing *The Two Towers* — I had not yet purchased *The Return of the King* and had to run right out and immediately purchase it.

Now many years and studies later, the motto "Frodo Lives" seems less like a cry of victory over Shelob and much more like a call to everyman to pick up Frodo's quest against evil. As I point out in Chapter 17, Frodo is an unwilling hero. He is the common man — that is, hobbit — who does what he must do, reluctantly undertaking an almost impossible quest against great evil.

Frodo's quandary is much like our own, and therefore it is with his burden and hardships that most readers empathize. Few if any of us are superheroes on the scale of Gandalf, Théoden, and Aragorn. We're much more like the humble hobbits of the Shire — though we are more aware of the extent of evil and danger than they are.

The personal struggle against evil in the world is more on the scale of "Frodo Lives" than "Che Lives." Each of us, like Frodo, must decide how to bear the burden that the world lays at our doorstep. Each of us has to consider what steps, if any, he will take against the evils of our times. You may feel as small as a hobbit in the face of the challenges — and maybe even less courageous than the hobbit heroes of Middle-earth. But if you take a stand against evil, even at the risk of failure and of being an unsung hero, then in essence the motto "Frodo Lives" will never be untrue.

Chapter 16

Immortality and Death

• •

In This Chapter

▶ The pros and cons of Elven immortality

▶ The human desire for immortality and the debate over the Doom of Men

▶ The fear of death and how the Enemy exploits it

▶ The significance of a mortal life and the hope held out by death

• •

In most fantasy and science fiction, death is a mere backdrop to the plot action, occurring more often than not in great battles or as a result of personal combat between hero and villain. Death itself, however, is seldom dealt with on a philosophical level, and discussion of what happens after death is normally entirely absent.

This is not so with Tolkien's fantasy writings. Immortals and mortals — Elves and Men, respectively — not only co-exist in Middle-earth, but also interact on an ongoing basis. Moreover, Tolkien turns their fundamental differences in life expectancy into a wedge driven between them, one that the great villains Melkor and Sauron exploit whenever possible to their advantage.

This chapter looks at the significance of immortality and mortality in *The Silmarillion* and *The Lord of the Rings*. It begins by comparing the interaction between Tolkien's immortal Elves and the mortal race of Men to that of gods and humans in classical mythology. It then explores immortality as exemplified in the Elves, both its pros and cons. Finally, it examines the issue of human mortality and how the fear of death — and especially what, if anything, lies on the other side of it — makes us more vulnerable to evil.

Relations Between Immortals and Mortals in Middle-earth

In traditional folklore and mythology, the immortal beings who interact with mortal men are anthropomorphic (human-like) gods and goddesses, such as Odin and Freya in the Nordic pantheon and Zeus and Aphrodite in the

Greek. In Greek mythology, in fact, the gods not only meet humans, but on rare occasions mate with them as well, producing special heroic, if mortal, offspring. For example, the Greek hero Perseus was the son of Zeus, king of the gods, and the mortal Danae (to whom Zeus appeared as a shower of gold).

In Tolkien's world, the gods — that is, the Valar or Powers — do not meet or interact with mortal Men on a regular basis. But they do interact with the Elves, some of whom actually live among the Valar in Aman. Only one union ever occurred between any of the beings of Aman and the Elves: the marriage of the Maia Melian and Elu Thingol. They met in Middle-earth when Melian was wandering east in Beleriand and Thingol was migrating west to Aman.

The Silmarillion does, however, chronicle a long history of interaction between the Men of Middle-earth and the Elves of Beleriand — and later between the Men of Númenor and the Elves of Tol Erresëa in Aman. Elves refer to Men, Eru Ilúvatar's second-born, as the Engwar ("the Sickly") or the Fírimar ("the Mortals"), for although Men live for hundreds of years, they all do eventually sicken and die. By contrast, the Elves, the Elder Children of Ilúvatar, do not know any sickness or form of natural death. The only way that Elves can die is by being slain or by succumbing to a wasting disease in which they become too weary of living in the world to go on.

In the annals of Middle-earth, Tolkien chronicled but a few Elf/human unions: Lúthien and Beren, Tuor and Idril, Elwing and Eärendil, and Aragorn and Arwen. Unlike Greek mythology, where all such offspring are mortal (although many are great heroes), not all of the children from these Elf/human unions are mortal (see Chapter 5 for more on these unions).

The Immortality of Elves

So, who wouldn't want to live forever like the Elves — free of disease and with no worries about getting old, wrinkled, and senile? Sounds like heaven to anyone like me, looking a little long in the tooth (holding age 29 for 25 years is no easy business). However, Tolkien's Elven immortality has given me a whole different attitude towards living forever. I think that, given the choice, I might just be one of those oddballs who opt for a mortal life.

After all, you have to admit that immortality presents unique problems. First, you have the problem of deciding what you want to be when you grow up . . . *for the rest of eternity.* Then you have to wonder when, if ever, you get to retire from that job you've been doing for the last four or five thousand years. No matter how many interests you have and how much you love your job, you'd surely get a wee bit bored with it all after, say, the first ten millennia.

On top of mundane and personal concerns, consider the wider ecological problems in supporting an immortal race. Overcrowding and overpopulation are bound to occur when no one of any generation dies. Just contemplate the sheer size, not to mention the cost, of a family reunion for, say, a favorite aunt and uncle's 5,000th wedding anniversary!

Finally, consider the factor of immortality that most affects the Elves: the weariness of contending with the world's never-ending problems and the ongoing cultural and political decay. For the Elves, immortality can be every bit as much a chore as a joy. This is especially true for the Elves that are under the Prophecy of the North or Doom of the Noldor (see Chapter 22) in Beleriand and Middle-earth proper. Each group must witness, stand up against, and resist the repeated evils of Melkor and, in Middle-earth, Sauron.

Worst of all, from the Elves' point of view, must be in seeing that no matter how much and how long you struggle against evil in Middle-earth, it continues to reappear, seemingly getting stronger and stronger each time. This is a condition that Galadriel calls "the long defeat," which very well may echo Tolkien's feelings on the secular history of our world.

Elven Death in Middle-earth

On the odd occasion, Elves do actually die — they are either murdered or they sicken from weariness with living in the world. But even death isn't an escape — the spirits of dead Elves go to Mandos, the Houses of the Dead, to await the end of the world. Or, theoretically, Elves can return to a new life in Middle-earth. This is Tolkien's version of reincarnation in Middle-earth, though none of his Elven characters who die are reborn in this manner, and Tolkien never explains how an Elf would return to life in Middle-earth.

If you thought that struggling perpetually against evil in Middle-earth is tiresome for an Elf, try imagining the boredom that sets in after waiting a couple hundred thousand years in Mandos for the world to come to an end. Wouldn't it be just your luck to be one of those Elves who finally gives in and dies of world-weariness, only to get immediately reincarnated and sent back to Middle-earth to face its tedium and struggles all over again?

In some ways, this fate of dying of ennui and then being sent back to the world to experience the same thing all over again is reminiscent of Sisyphus, the mythical founder and first king of Corinth. He is said to have been so cunning that he chained up Thanatos, the god of death, so that the dead could no longer reach the underworld. As punishment, Zeus sent Sisyphus to the underworld where he is forced to forever roll a block of stone up a steep hill, and then once it tumbles back down, to roll it back all over again. It makes me tired just thinking about it.

The death of Míriel Serindë

Although *The Silmarillion* mentions the Elven death of world-weariness, Tolkien offered few examples. One that stands out is that of Míriel, the mother of Fëanor (one of the most famous Elves of all time — see Chapter 4 for details). In Aman, Míriel fell in love with Finwë, the leader of the Noldor, and their marriage was very happy until she bore their first child, Fëanor.

Unfortunately, bearing Fëanor sapped all of Míriel's strength and spirit — Tolkien says that after her son's birth, she longed for release from the world. Here the world-weariness is a kind of Elven post-partum depression, an exhaustion caused by giving her strength to her extraordinary child (see the nearby sidebar for a comparison to Buddha's mother). Finwë tried to save her by putting her under the gentle care of the Vala Irmo in the gardens of Lórien (see Chapter 3). But despite all efforts to heal her melancholy, Míriel died, and her spirit departed and silently entered Mandos, the Halls of Awaiting.

The death of Fëanor

Fëanor's death came at the hands of Gothmog, the Lord of the Balrogs (see Chapter 10), when Fëanor led an Elven host against Melkor in the Battle of the Stars. Tolkien says that as he lay dying, Fëanor was blessed with the "fore-knowledge of death." He was able to see that no power of the Noldor would overcome Melkor in his fortress of Angband and Thangorodrim. Nevertheless, he bound his sons to an oath to avenge their father and recover his Silmaril jewels from anyone who had them, no matter the cost (see Chapter 19 for my analysis on tragic consequences of this oath).

TRIVIA

The death of Buddha's mom, Queen Maya

Míriel's death after giving birth to a great son who consumed her spirit in the process is suggestive of the death of Buddha's mother, Queen Maya. After giving birth in a grove of trees on her way to her father's home, Queen Maya suddenly sickened and died within five days. The child, Prince Siddhartha, the future Buddha, was left in the care of his aunt. It is said, though, that some time after his enlightenment, Buddha visited his mother in heaven and preached his Dharma (truth) to her to ensure her liberation in a future life.

The Buddhist idea that giving birth to a being as great as the Buddha takes all the mother's strength and results in an early death is surely mirrored in the story of Queen Míriel's son Fëanor. Unfortunately, Fëanor was destined for as much tragedy as greatness (see Chapter 19). However, both Buddha as the Enlightened One and Fëanor as the Spirit of Fire were examples of beings of exceptional inner light who quite literally burned out their mothers during their births.

The rainbow body of Tibetan saints

The idea of a person's body being consumed at death has its own tradition in our world. According to Tibetan Buddhists, at death the bodies of certain highly trained lamas (teachers) and saints dissolve into light, leaving behind as relics only their hair and nails. The bodies of a few very special yoga practitioners such as the Saint Milarepa are said to completely dissolve into a rainbow-hued light at the moment of death.

Of course, the immediate consumption of Fëanor's body by his spirit in its haste to escape is very different from the rainbow-colored lights that gradually consume the body of a Tibetan yogi. Nevertheless, there is some correspondence in the idea of extraordinary beings whose spirits consume their bodies rather than leaving them to the natural process of decay.

Fëanor's spirit was so fiery that when he died, it burned his body to ash as it sped west to Mandos, appearing "like smoke" as it went. This description is similar to the death of Saruman near the end of *The Lord of the Rings*. There, Saruman's spirit rises from his body like a great mist, appearing "like smoke from a fire" that lingers for a moment before being dissolved by a cold blast of western wind. According to Elven belief, Fëanor's spirit remains in the Halls of Awaiting until the end of the world, at which time he will once again come forward and finally explain how he made the Silmarils.

The death of Finrod Felagund

The death of King Finrod, also known as Felagund ("Cave Hewer"), in Sauron's dungeons is another example of an Elf's death by slaying. His tale also sheds a little light on funeral customs among the Elves.

King Finrod, known as the fairest of the Noldorian Elves, was Galadriel's brother and also a great friend to the new race of Men. His death is bound up with Beren and Lúthien's attempt to recover one of the Silmarils stolen by Melkor (see Chapter 18). Finrod accompanied Beren on his quest to recover the Silmaril (and thereby win the hand of the lovely Lúthien) in order to honor the oath he swore to Barahir, Beren's father, when Barahir saved Finrod from certain death during the Battle of Dagor Bragollach. The oath was sealed with the gift of Finrod's ring, which became an heirloom of Beren's house that eventually passed to Aragorn.

During this quest, Sauron waylayed Beren and Finrod, who were disguised as Orcs, and brought them to Tol-in-Gaurhoth. There, Sauron contended with Finrod in a singing contest (see nearby sidebar) in which they tried to outdo each other by chanting songs of power. Ultimately, Sauron bested Finrod, stripped him and Beren of their Orc disguises, and threw the pair in the dungeons.

There, Finrod died from wounds received while slaying a werewolf Sauron sent into the dungeons to kill Beren. As Finrod died, he told Beren that it would be a long time before he returned among the Noldor and that it might be that they would never meet again in death or life. When Lúthien finally came to rescue Beren, she found him mourning the death of his friend Finrod. Together, they buried Finrod's body on the green hill of Tol-Sirion, the name of the island before Sauron came to it. At the end of the story, Tolkien tells the reader that Finrod's grave remained green and inviolable until the island sank when Beleriand was sundered at the time of the final defeat of Melkor.

What's so interesting in the story of Finrod's death is that Finrod did not remain in the Halls of Awaiting. Instead, he returned to Aman and dwells there with his father Finarfin. As high king of the Noldor who refused to join Fëanor in his quest for the stolen Silmarils, Finarfin has never tasted death and continues to live in bliss in the Blessed Realm, ruling over the remaining Noldor from the great city of Tirion.

The singing contest in *The Kalevala*

The singing contest between Sauron and Finrod may have its roots in another singing contest of which Tolkien was well aware. It occurs between the hero Väinämöinen and the young minstrel Joukahainen in the Finnish epic poem, *The Kalevala*. This collection of poems was assembled by Elias Lönnrot in the 1800s from the ancient oral tradition of Finnish rune singers.

In the third poem in this cycle, Väinämöinen, the original human being, is challenged by the youthful Laplander minstrel Joukahainen to a singing contest. The much elder Väinämöinen betters the upstart by literally singing him into a swamp till he's up to his neck in muck. To get free, Joukahainen promises Väinämöinen the hand of his sister Aino (which distresses her so much she later commits suicide).

In *The Kalevala*'s contest, just as in the one between Sauron and Finrod, each side takes turns singing a magic-wisdom song, attempting in each round to better his opponent. Väinämöinen wins his by chanting songs about the world's creation that bests Joukahainen's superficial understanding of the world and its origins. Sauron wins his by chanting songs of treachery, including that of the Elven Kinslaying (see Chapter 4), that best Finrod's songs of integrity, trust, and freedom. (For more on the power of language in Middle-earth, see Chapter 15. For more on the role of Finnish in the high Elven language of Quenya, see Chapter 14.)

In reuniting Finrod after death with his father, Tolkien shows us the closest thing to a reward in the afterlife that exists in his works. Aman may not be the Heaven of the Christian scriptures, but it is the closest thing to it. Obviously, Finrod's blissful end in being reunited walking free under the trees with his father is a far better fate than being confined in the Halls of Awaiting till the end of the world, as were Fëanor's mother Míriel and Fëanor himself.

Human Death in Middle-earth

Although the creator Eru Ilúvatar considered mortality to be his special gift to humankind (his younger children), this was one present that most Men of Middle-earth would just as soon have returned unopened. It doesn't help the situation at all for Men to know that Ilúvatar's Firstborn, the Elves, received the gift of immortality. In other words, Men got rooked.

On top of the gift of death — certainly *not* one that keeps on giving — Ilúvatar gave Men frail bodies that fall prey to disease, hunger, and a host of other ills, as well as, ironically, a keen love of life and a full knowledge of the limited span of their years (this deal just kept getting better and better).

You can imagine the problems the Valar had at the beginning of the Second Age in trying to sell the Men of Númenor on the benefits of this "package" deal. The Men complained about how good the Valar and their buddies — the immortal, never sick, always blissful Elves — had it in Aman. The dialog between the messengers (angels) of the Valar and the Men of Númenor is one of the more fascinating and significant encounters in *The Silmarillion*.

In this meeting, Men argued against their fate of mortality, complaining that even the Elves who participated in the revolt against Valinor still live forever, whereas the Men who aided the Valar in the defeat of Morgoth still die — the old "give death to those that deserve it" gambit. The Valarian messengers rubbed a little salt on the wound by admitting that they really were clueless when it came to understanding Ilúvatar's thinking regarding death — especially as a gift for one's children. Nevertheless, they are certain that Men's fate lay outside the Blessed Realm, which remained strictly off limits.

Men then countered by saying that the situation wasn't fair because one of their own kind, Eärendil the Mariner, never knew death (the old "you did it for one, so you have to do it for all" gambit). The Valarian messengers replied that Men knew very well that Eärendil's was a special case. He was allowed to select his fate (he chose to be immortal for his wife's sake — see Chapter 5), but at the cost of never again being allowed to return to Middle-earth. (I'm not at all sure that having to continually sail over Middle-earth for all time is preferable to death anyway — that old Sisyphus thing.)

The Valarian messengers reminded the Men — and us — that whether they liked it or not, death was their fate, and that it couldn't be opposed without it becoming a restraint on their freedom and free will. Hard as it was, Men had to trust Ilúvatar and hope that in time, Ilúvatar would reveal his purpose in fating Men to death even while instilling in them a deep attachment to life.

Exploiting Men's fear of death

Most of us are like Woody Allen, who said, "It's not that I'm afraid to die, I just don't want to be there when it happens." It's not the fact of death so much as the awareness of death's inevitability that shakes us. In *The Silmarillion*, Tolkien attributes this fear to Men's lack of trust in Ilúvatar's plan — which Morgoth and Sauron exploited every chance they got.

Nowhere is this exploitation of the human fear of death clearer than in *The Akallebêth* (The Downfall of Númenor) in *The Silmarillion*, the story of Sauron's corruption of Ar-Pharazôn, the last king of Númenor (see Chapter 5). Sauron conned the king into assaulting the Blessed Realm of Aman by spreading the lie that merely by reaching those hallowed shores he would gain immortality. (The Valar's messengers contradicted this lie by explaining to the Dúnedain that Aman was called the Undying Land because the immortal Valar and Elves dwelt there — not because the land conferred immortality.)

Balder's sea funeral

In a very popular Norse myth, the gods attended the funeral of Balder, the gentle god of spring and son of King Odin and Queen Frigg. Balder's ship, Hringhorni, was so large that the gods had to call on the help of a giantess named Hyrokkin (wounding Thor's male pride and making him so furious that he almost boinked her on the head with his hammer). Once the ship was finally afloat, and the bodies of Balder and his wife Nanna (who had died in grief at the funeral) were on board, Thor consecrated the ship with his hammer while the gods set it aflame. Unfortunately, Thor inadvertently kicked a Dwarf named Lit, who just happened to get in the way of his foot, into the funeral pyre, immolating him with Balder and Nanna (and adding new meaning to his name).

Balder's death signaled the start of Ragnarok, the Last Battle that marked the Twilight of the gods and the end of Midgard (Middle-earth) — as did the launching of the ship named Nagflar upon the ocean. This Viking ship, made entirely of the nail-clippings of the dead whose relatives did not cut their nails prior to burial, carries giants ready to make war on Valhalla. Tolkien did not have Boromir's companions pare his nails prior to launching his funeral ship, so Boromir's nails too are used in the completion of the Nagflar and therefore help to hasten the end of the world.

Nevertheless, Ar-Pharazôn and those among his supporters who feared death above all things wanted to believe Sauron's lie. In fact, they needed to believe it so much that they were prepared to force the Valar to grant them immortality at the points of their swords. Talk about "storming heaven"! Such extreme fear of death is present in our society in those who resort to any means of extending the life of a loved one, no matter the cost in terms of continued suffering or reduced quality of life.

In the story of Sauron's turning Ar-Pharazôn to worship Melkor as the Giver of Freedom — the one who would release Men from death — Tolkien seemed to be warning that the fear of death can actually end up constraining freedom and defeating the purpose of free will. And it seems true that whenever the fear of death grows so excessive that avoiding it becomes the guiding light of your life, you're no longer free to choose how you live and in a very real sense are no longer living fully. It's like the line from Baz Luhrmann's film *Strictly Ballroom:* "A life lived in fear is a life half lived."

The death of Boromir

Only one character among the nine in the Fellowship of the Ring dies: Boromir, son of Denethor, the Steward of Gondor. Boromir is the character who struggles the most regarding the Ring of Power, and his death comes right after his "sin" of trying to steal the Ring from Frodo. With his heroic death, fighting the mighty Uruk-hai Orcs, Boromir atones for this sin (see Chapter 20 for more on Boromir).

Of interest here is the way Boromir's compatriots Aragorn, Legolas, and Gimli honor his heroism by attempting to give him a proper burial. Their first impulse is to bury him underground or to raise a barrow-mound over his body. Legolas, however, points out that they have neither the time nor the tools. He then suggests they raise a cairn over him (a heap of stones raised up normally as a memorial). Gimli points out that there are few stones about. Finally, Aragorn decides to place Boromir's body in one of the Elven boats with his weapons and those of his vanquished foes and send it over the Falls of Rauros.

The three put his Elven cloak under his head, his helmet to his side, the shards of his sword and his broken horn on his breast, and the swords of his enemies at his feet. They then lead the boat into the middle of the Lake of Mist and let it go. According to later tales in Gondor, Boromir's funeral boat survived the Falls of Rauros, went down the River Anduin, past the ruins of Osgiliath, and out into the Great Sea, perhaps headed for the Blessed Realm.

What's most interesting about Boromir's funeral is how it resembles the funeral of Scyld Scefing in Tolkien's favorite Anglo-Saxon poem, *Beowulf* — and corresponds with what we know about Viking funerals. In the case of the mythical Scyld, his body, laden with treasures, goes out on a boat into the sea, and we are told that none could tell where it ended up.

Normally, great Vikings heroes or royalty are buried in barrow-mounds, many of which are found in the outskirts of Viking settlements on the coast. In them are bodies laid out in their finest, surrounded by their riches, in the midst of an actual Viking ship (some being very large). The Viking ship in the barrow-mound is both a symbol of wealth and prestige and the way the dead can traverse the underworld of Niflheim.

Viking sea funerals may well have occurred from time to time, though they probably involved cremating the body by setting the ship aflame, an element entirely missing from Boromir's (see nearby sidebar). Setting your comrade free in a ship without first immolating his body, thereby leaving it open to plunder, would probably not seem at all right to the Viking way of thinking.

The deaths of Aragorn and Arwen

Aragorn, King of the Reunited Kingdom, restores the line of great Kings of Númenor that started with Elros, the first King of Númenor. Elrond, the twin brother of Elros, is the father of Aragorn's Elven wife Arwen, known as Undomiel ("Evenstar"). Aragorn not only restores the greatness of his ancestors in the way he rules his kingdom, but also in the way he dies.

In Appendix A of *The Lord of the Rings,* Aragorn chooses the time of his passing, informing Arwen that their son Eldarion is ready for kingship and that he (Aragorn) is ready to go. Arwen, of course, tries desperately to talk him out of it, but Aragorn is resolute. He knows the natural span of his life is almost up and that if he doesn't go willingly, he will shortly be forced to go in a state that Tolkien calls "unmanned and witless."

In going to the House of Kings to die by his own will, Aragorn repeats the rite of the early Kings of Númenor who laid down their lives and relinquished the kingdom to their sons willingly when they reached the sum of their days.

This tradition of trusting in Ilúvatar's gift of death by dying willingly is one that the latter kings of Númenor violated. They clung to their lives at all costs, denied their sons the throne even if they were mature and ready to rule, and gave up their lives only when old age caused their bodies and wits to fail.

The spiritual tradition of graceful death

When Tolkien wrote that the Kings of Númenor willingly laid down their lives when they reached the sum of their days, he was keying into a long spiritual tradition in which advanced practitioners sense the onset of death and prepare themselves and their followers for the event. In the Zen tradition, it's common for masters to dictate a death poem prior to their passing. In the Tibetan tradition, lamas often sit in meditation and die as calmly as they lived. In medieval Christian accounts, deaths of Saints was often accompanied by phenomena such as special lights, smells, and sounds — and by miraculous preservation of the body and/or hallowing of the place of death.

Aragorn's going to the House of the Kings to lie down and pass away after bidding Arwen farewell is a similarly graceful exit. Tolkien communicates the spiritual power in his passing with an eloquent description of Aragorn's splendor in death (captured beautifully in Peter Jackson's movie *The Two Towers* in the foreshadowing of the death of Aragorn and mourning of Arwen).

Aragorn's decision causes Arwen much sorrow, but through it she finally understands the pain of Ilúvatar's gift of mortality to Men. In his final words, Aragorn counsels Arwen not to despair over his death but to trust that their final fate lies beyond the Circles of the World. Tolkien says that in death, Aragorn's appearance blends the beauty of his youth with the spirit of his maturity — both the wisdom and dignity of age were apparent.

Arwen then takes leave of her children — Eldarion, the new King of the Reunited Kingdom, and her daughters — and journeys back to Lórien, once ruled by Galadriel and Celeborn. There, she lies down and dies on Cerin Amroth ("Amroth's Mound"), where she and Aragorn originally pledged their undying love for one another (that old "plight thee my troth" thing). Tolkien tells us that her burial mound, covered in lovely golden Elanor and white Niphredil flowers, will stay evergreen until the world is changed, all remembrance of her life is forgotten, or Elanor and Niphredil no longer bloom in Middle-earth (for more on Aragorn and Arwen's romance, see Chapter 18).

The Hope in a Mortal Life

Now it's high time to look closer at the significance of human mortality in Tolkien's Middle-earth. Remember that, as a Catholic, Tolkien felt he already knew the answer to the human quandary over death: the Gospel of Jesus Christ.

The problem was that his characters lived well before Christ and the procla-
mation of the "good news" — just as his audience live way after (making us in
some ways as far removed from this hope as his characters are).

If death is the wage of original sin — the price humans pay for the initial dis-
obedience of Adam and Eve — then Christ was the one who paid for our sin
with his life, thus canceling the debt we owe and freeing us from death. But if
you follow Tolkien's thinking that human mortality is the *eucatastrophe* (see
Chapter 1), that happy misfortune that brought God out of Heaven and down
to Middle-earth as the Messiah, then Christ is also the final installment on the
gift of God's grace.

Tolkien's answer to death as a Christian

Remember that the Valarian messengers had no answer for the human concerns
with death (see "Human Death in Middle-earth" earlier in this chapter). The
only thing that they could tell Men was to be patient and to trust that in the
fullness of time, Eru Ilúvatar would give them the hoped-for answer. But what
an answer that turned out to be: God deigned to become Man in order to experience what it's like to live under the shadow of certain death and to love life
in spite of this certain darkness. Otherwise, how would God as an immortal,
eternal being ever really understand the anguish of his finite, mortal children?

In Christ's Passion, God's experiences fully the gift of mortality that he gave to
Adam and Eve and all their descendents. But surprise, surprise: Death turns
out to really be a gift that keeps on giving — for out of death comes new life,
a life eternal, signified by Christ's resurrection. And with this resurrection
comes the further promise of the eventual return of God one day to make
the world anew, healing all its fractures and wounds.

In this context, consider what Sauron's One Ring of Power represents for mortal
Men: The Ring rules, finds, and brings them in — then binds them all in darkness. The debate over what exactly the One Ring symbolizes (nuclear weapons,
technology, secularism) is endless (and drove Tolkien nuts). I am happy, however, to throw another log on the fire of this controversy.

What if the Ring of Power symbolizes human fear of death? Fear of death in
mortal Men acts like a Master Ring, controlling all the other Rings of Power
that enslave us — lust, greed, violence, jealousy, and so on. Sauron therefore
fosters an ignorance of death as Ilúvatar's gift among men in order to keep
the One Ring powerful and in control of all the other Mortal Rings of Power,
which he so willingly doles out to the Lords of Men.

Seen in this light, Christ then becomes God's Ring-bearer, taking up the quest to bear the fear of death and then, through the sacrifice of his own life, forever destroy it. On Good Friday, Christ destroyed this One Ring with his death, and his labored bearing of the cross to the hill of Golgotha is not unlike Frodo's attempt to carry the Ring up Mount Doom. On Saturday, Christ descended into Hell to free the captives bound there; on Easter Sunday, he emerged from the tomb, forever breaking the bonds of death. In *The Lord of the Rings,* the Ring is destroyed on March 25th — during the Easter season.

Christ then ascended to heaven with a promise to return, at which time the world will be made anew, and death will become a thing of the past. Using Tolkien's imagery of creation through song, perhaps we will all join in singing the music of a new creation, with each type of being adding in his own part and telling his own tale. The choir of all the Valar, Maiar, Men, Elves, and Dwarves would make some beautiful music — this time free of Melkor's discord and the disharmony of his minions of evil.

The problem, however, lies in the interim — the time between Christ's ascension and his return. Tolkien was well aware that in the intervening millennia since Christ's sacrifice, many Men no longer hear the Music of Creation, and even fewer acknowledge its Composer. Instead there is a new Dark Lord named Science, with Technology as its first lieutenant, and together they claim mastery of our Middle-earth. Like Melkor and Sauron before them, they maintain that they are the Lords of Freedom promising to free us from death if we will only give them our undying and total allegiance. Instead, under their guidance, our fear and uncertainty about death, and our rush to hedonistic pleasure to hide that fear, continue to grow (see Chapter 22 for more on Tolkien's view on science and technology).

Bearing your own Ring of Power

In attempting to resurrect the metaphorical and poetic language of mythology in his writings on Middle-earth, Tolkien may be trying to give us a way to hear the Music of Creation and thereby know its Composer. In ennobling his characters and showing how some of them can maintain hope in the darkness of their pre-Christian world, he may be signaling a possible way for us to follow in our post-Christian one.

If, for the moment, you entertain my notion that the Ring of Power that binds you in darkness is your fear of death, then even if you're like Frodo and find it a burden that you weren't prepared to carry, it still is one that you must take up and attempt to dispose of. For if you don't, the power of that fear will consume you and turn you into a wraith, who stretches his lifespan out as long as he can but is not really alive, and you will ever be its slave.

And I imagine that Tolkien had in mind each and every one of us when he has Frodo, to his own utter surprise, pipe up at the Council of Elrond and say, "I will take the Ring, although I do not know the way." And remember Elrond's response to these surprising words: "I think that this task is appointed for you, Frodo, and if you do not find a way, no one will." (For more on Frodo's quest and its potential implications in your life, see Chapter 17.)

Of course, although bearing this mortal Ring of Power is a task appointed to all, you need not follow a particular path in order to destroy it. As a devout Catholic, Tolkien found his way through his faith in the Christian good news. As a committed Buddhist, I try to find my way in the practice of the Buddha's Dharma. The important thing is not the particular path you take to Mount Doom, but that you find a vehicle that gives you the strength to undertake the voyage and guides you in your passage even if you "do not know the way."

And for those times when the darkness seems too oppressive and the fear too overpowering to go on, I invite you to look to the east right before dawn, or to the west after dusk. With any luck, you'll catch sight of Eärendil's Star of Hope — the blended light of the Two Trees of Wisdom and Mercy, the brightest of the messengers sent over Middle-earth, and its light will help guide you on your way.

Chapter 17

The Heroic Quest

*W*ithout heroes and their quests, the world would be deprived of many of its most entertaining and important myths and legends. Contrary to the sentiments expressed in Tina Turner's title track for the movie *Mad Max Beyond Thunderdome,* human cultures *always* seem to need another hero, by whose deeds greatness and virtue can be judged. Tolkien obliges this need by creating both classic and, for want of a better word, common heroes whose quests not only move story elements along, but also underscore key virtues that the author would have us emulate. This chapter begins by exploring the general characteristics of a heroic quest in folklore and myth and investigating the qualities of some representative heroes. The chapter then changes gears and looks at the more prominent heroes in *The Hobbit* and *The Lord of the Rings:* Aragorn, Tolkien's classic hero, and the most unlikely of heroes, the hobbits.

The Nature of the Heroic Quest

A *hero* is defined as an illustrious warrior who shows great courage and is widely admired for his achievements and noble character. This noble character is often an example of semi-divine parentage or superhuman strength. A *quest* is an act of seeking (from the Latin *quaestus,* "having sought") — more specifically, a chivalrous enterprise involving some sort of adventurous journey, as in a medieval romance.

The heroic quest takes many forms in traditional mythology and in modern myths such as Tolkien's. Some heroes, such as Arthur of Camelot and Aragorn of Middle-earth, seek their kingdom and recognition as the rightful king.

Others, such as Jason of the Argonauts and Tolkien's Beren, must recover some priceless thing. Jason had to recover the Golden Fleece to obtain his rightful kingdom of Thessaly, and Beren the Silmaril for the right to marry the love of his life, the Elf-princess Lúthien (see Chapter 18). Other quests, such as that of Odysseus (Ulysses) of the Odyssey, are more modest: to return home safely and save his wife from suitors. Frodo's primary motivation in taking the Ring to Mount Doom is to save his home, the Shire. Yet although he does save it and its way of life, he is never able to find peace there again, as Odysseus did in Ithaca.

The ultimate object of some quests — those of Gilgamesh of Mesopotamia and Sir Perceval of Camelot, for example — is ephemeral. Gilgamesh sought immortality after his closest friend Enkidu died in his place. Sir Perceval sought the Holy Grail, which Christ used during the Last Supper and which received the blood from the wound in his side on the cross. The recovery of the Grail was deemed necessary to restore the integrity of the Round Table, which had been shattered by Queen Guinevere's infidelity, and to prove the full spiritual realization of the Knights of the Round Table.

The common denominator in all heroic quests is that the hero is in search of something, and to find it, he or she (yes, Virginia, there are female heroes — see the story of Beren and Lúthien in Chapter 5) undertakes a journey, usually a long, dangerous one involving many challenges that enable the hero to demonstrate strength, ingenuity, and virtue.

As I indicate with the last two examples of Gilgamesh and Sir Perceval, not all heroic quests end as expected. The quest for an unpossessable mystery does not necessarily translate into failure on the part of the hero. Gilgamesh returned to Uruk a much wiser and more just king, though still mortal. Perceval achieved holy enlightenment but Camelot fell with the defeat of King Arthur by Sir Mordred (Arthur's nephew, in some legends — in others, Arthur's son by his sister Morganna).

Tolkien turns this particular heroic formula on its ear by making the major quest in The Lord of the Rings to destroy the One Ring of Power successful, even though Frodo, the main hero who is to carry it out, fails to complete this task. In contrast, Aragorn, the classic hero of The Lord of the Rings, achieves the object of his quest and is no way a failure; he attains his kingdom and wins Arwen's hand, fulfilling more than most other Tolkien characters the fairytale formula of living "happily ever after."

The Nature of Tolkien's Heroes

Most heroes of traditional mythology are, if not semi-divine in nature, with one parent being a bona fide god or goddess, at least from royal or noble families. In Tolkien's mythology, the closest thing to semi-divine heroes are the ones who descend from Melian the Maia, one of the lesser divine powers, who married the Elf-lord Thingol (see Chapter 4). Their progeny include Lúthien, Melian's daughter and the wife of Beren; Eärendil, Melian's great grandson; Melian's great-great-grandsons Elrond and Elros; and Elrond's daughter Arwen, who marries Elros's distant descendent, Aragorn.

Other Tolkien heroes do have noble or royal backgrounds. These include Elven heroes such as Finrod Felagund, Galadriel, and Legolas; the Dwarf-heroes Thorin Oakenshield and Gimli; and human heroes such as Théoden, Elendil, Isildur, and Aragorn. Of particular interest, however, are the notable heroes who have no pedigree whatsoever: the hobbits. These include Bilbo, the hesitant hero of *The Hobbit,* as well as Frodo, Sam, Merry, and Pippin in *The Lord of the Rings.* Tolkien's hobbit heroes cut across the traditional heroic type in mythology, pointing to a more modern conception of a hero, one who undertakes a great quest more out of necessity than a sense of adventure or personal aggrandizement. This unusual kind of hero, however, is just what's required to achieve the very unusual quest that Tolkien sets up in *The Lord of the Rings:* to destroy (rather than recover) the object of desire, the One Ring of Power.

Before considering how the hobbits play the heroes' parts in the very atypical quest to destroy the Ring, I want to take a look at Tolkien's more classic hero, Aragorn, and then consider Bilbo's somewhat curious heroics in *The Hobbit.* Understanding how these two heroes function in Tolkien's works can provide a basis for seeing both the classic and novel aspects of the heroics embodied by the hobbits Frodo, Sam, and Gollum.

Aragorn as Tolkien's Classic Hero

Aragorn falls somewhere between the classic British heroes Robin Hood and King Arthur. In his guise as Strider, a Ranger of the North who wanders Middle-earth, defending the peace against Sauron's agents, Aragorn is like Robin Hood, who tried to uphold justice in Sherwood Forest against the evil King John and his lackey, the Sheriff of Nottingham. As Isildur's heir to the Kingdom of Gondor, Aragorn is like King Arthur, who must prove his right to his kingdom while protecting it from its enemies.

Aragorn as Strider

Aragorn as Strider protects Eriador and Gondor from the king's enemies in his absence, just as Robin Hood protected England from King John's injustices until John's brother, King Richard the Lionhearted, returned from the Crusades. The difference is that Strider himself is the absent king. Strider is really protecting the lands of Middle-earth for himself as Elessar, the King. Part of the tension of Aragorn's story is his struggle to emerge as the rightful king while providing this protection. As leader of the Fellowship of the Ring, he must shepherd and aid Frodo, the Ring-bearer, with the heroic task. As the Ring quest proceeds, Tolkien gradually releases Aragorn from his secretive role as Strider the Ranger and reveals him more as the king in quest for his throne.

VOCABULARY
abc

Gilraen's lament

Gilraen left Rivendell after Aragorn was grown, and at the final meeting between mother and son, she utters a couplet, which Tolkien calls a *linnod,* that plays on the word for hope. Gilraen's linnod is a lament that uses Aragorn's given name Estel ("hope"). She says (in Elvish, mind you), "I gave the Dúnedain Hope, I kept no hope for myself" (my translation). In the first half of the verse, Tolkien capitalized Estel to indicate Aragorn, but in the second part, he lowercased it to indicate that Gilraen retained no hope for herself. The play on words is furthered by the fact that the verb *onen* that Tolkien used at the beginning of the linnod means "I gave" in the Sindarin dialect of Elvish, but "I begot" in the Quenyan.

Aragorn as Estel, son of Gilraen

As the unrecognized but rightful king, Aragorn's story parallels in some ways the myth of King Arthur. Like Arthur, Aragorn grew up unaware of his royal blood and his right to his kingdom. Unlike Arthur, however, Aragorn was not a foundling brought up by foster parents, but a ward of Elrond, reared by his own mother Gilraen in the safety and anonymity of Rivendell. And whereas Arthur discovered his royal right to kingship by retrieving the Sword in the Stone, Aragorn learned of his royal heritage from Elrond when he returned to Rivendell for his twentieth birthday.

Up till then, Aragorn was known as Estel ("Hope"), the name his mother Gilraen gave him — perhaps in hopes that he would fulfill that role for his people, the Dúnedain. At their meeting, Elrond revealed Aragorn's true name and heritage: Aragorn son of Arathorn, Isildur's heir, Lord of the Dúnedain. Elrond also gave Aragorn two heirlooms:

✔ **The Ring of Barahir:** This is the ring the Elf-king Finrod Felagund gave to Barahir, Beren's father, as a token of undying friendship between the Elven House of Finwë and the mortal House of Bëor (see Chapters 4 and 5). It carries the crest of the House of Finarfin (Finwë's third son), which depicts two intertwining serpents with emerald eyes, heads joined beneath a spray of golden flowers with one serpent upholding the spray and the other attempting to devour the flowers.

✔ **The Shards of Narsil:** These are the pieces of King Elendil's sword that broke under him when Sauron felled him in Mordor. Isildur, Elendil's sole surviving son, cut the One Ring of Power from Sauron's hand with the hilt-shard of Narsil.

Elrond keeps the third heirloom, the Scepter of Annúminas, symbol of the kings of the northern kingdom of Arnor, from Aragorn until his coronation as King of both Arnor and Gondor (called the Reunited Kingdom).

Aragorn as Isildur's heir

Like King Arthur, Aragorn's kingship is bound up with a sword. Arthur's sword Excalibur came from the mysterious Lady of the Lake. Aragorn's Narsil (Elvish for "Red and White Flame") belonged to his ancestor King Elendil and was preserved for him by the Elves of Rivendell. Unlike Excalibur, Aragorn's sword is broken, which, whether Tolkien intended it or not, is an apt symbol for the state of Aragorn's kingdom: Arnor has ceased to exist, and Gondor is in steady decline. The task for Aragorn is to reforge his broken kingdom — much as the Elves of Rivendell reforge the shards of Narsil into a new sword that Aragorn takes into battle. (The reforged sword is renamed Andúril — Elvish for "Flame of the West.") The theme of the broken sword also appears in the Norse legends of Sigmund, whose son Sigurd inherits his father's shattered blade, which is re-forged (see Chapter 21 for more on *Volsung Saga*).

The myths of Arthur and Aragorn have other parallels, though Tolkien was careful to change those elements that didn't suit the greater story he was telling. The closest one is that both Arthur and Aragorn were tutored by wizards: Arthur by Merlin the Magician, and Aragorn by Gandalf the Grey. According to Tolkien, Aragorn met Gandalf shortly after leaving Elrond and Rivendell at the age of 20. Gandalf became a close friend who taught Aragorn much wisdom during his 30 years of wandering Middle-earth as Strider the Ranger. But Gandalf's counsel ends when Aragorn is crowned King of the Reunited Kingdom, whereas Merlin counseled King Arthur well into his reign.

Treading the Paths of the Dead

In *The Lord of the Rings,* Aragorn's quest to regain his kingdom doesn't really begin until after the breakup of the Fellowship of the Ring — until then, he was dedicated solely to aiding Frodo destroy the One Ring. Afterward, Aragorn completes tasks that prove his prowess in battle and his steadfastness as a leader (primarily with King Théoden at the Battle of the Hornburg — see Chapter 24 for details).

The act that ensures Aragorn's right to rule Isildur's kingdom and identifies him beyond all doubt as his heir is a bit unusual. In the Arthurian myth, Arthur's pedigree was proven by his ability to remove the sword in the stone. Tolkien cooked up something far more complex and macabre. Aragorn saves the city of Minas Tirith from Sauron's forces during the critical Battle of Pelennor Fields by commandeering the black ships of the Corsairs of the port of Umbar and sailing them into the harbor outside Minas Tirith just in the nick of time. But to take over the ships, Aragorn must perform one little tiny errand — to travel the Paths of the Dead and enlist the help of the dead oath breakers from Isildur's time.

The tale of the Paths of the Dead in *The Lord of the Rings* has overtones of Celtic kingship lore. In it, Tolkien introduces a seer named Malbeth — shades of Macbeth, I'd say. Back when the last King ruled from the northern capital of Fornost, Malbeth prophesied the day when the dead who broke their oath to King Isildur to come to his aid against Sauron would be reawakened by his heir at the black stone of Erech. Isildur brought the stone of Erech to Gondor from the island of Númenor, and it was there that the "oath breakers" first swore an oath of allegiance to him.

The stone of Erech is vaguely reminiscent of the Lia Faíl stone at Tara, the hall of the ancient kings of Ireland. This stone was supposed to cry out when touched by the rightful king of the Emerald Isle. Tolkien's stone of Erech enables the rightful king to reawaken and summon the dead oath breakers to fulfill their promise to fight against Sauron. Thus, the stone of Erech legitimizes Aragorn's claim to be Isildur's heir and King of Gondor in a way that the heirlooms he receives from Elrond could ever do.

The return of the rightful king

It is significant that after the victory at Pelennor Fields — brought about by Aragorn's unusual commandeering of the ships of the Corsairs of Umbar, with the help of the phantom oath breakers — all in Gondor consider Aragorn the sole and rightful king. This includes Faramir, the sole survivor (after Denethor's demise) of the Stewards, who were officially charged with ruling Gondor in the king's place until his return. As if that weren't enough, Aragorn clinches the deal by proving himself a true healer in Gondor's House of Healing. He uses the herb athelas (kingsfoil) to save the lives of both Éowyn and Faramir, thus proving the words of the soothsayer Ioreth, who declares that the "hands of the king are the hands of a healer."

After Aragorn's coronation, Tolkien further underscores Aragorn's right to rule and reassure the reader of the success of his reign. The new king finds, with Gandalf's help, a sapling on the mountainside from the now withered White Tree of Gondor. This tree is a descendent of Nimloth the Fair of Númenor, in turn a descendent of Galathilion of Tirion and the Tree of Light, Telperion of the Blessed Realm of Aman (see Chapter 5 for more on the tree's history). With the flowering of the renewed White Tree of Gondor in the first summer of King Aragorn and Queen Arwen's reign, Aragorn fulfills his quest to become the true and just king in the best tradition of this type of mythology.

Bilbo as the Hesitant Hero

In *The Hobbit,* the book that introduced hobbits to the world, Bilbo Baggins is anything but your classic hero. In place of a knight errant, going about looking for adventures in which to prove his strength and virtue, you find a curmudgeonly old hobbit who only wants to be left alone in his very well-to-do and comfortable hobbit hole.

Bilbo agrees to go on the Dwarves' quest to regain their kingdom under the Lonely Mountain and their treasure (now guarded jealously by Smaug the dragon), but only after discussing such mundane details as the risks involved, who covers out-of-pocket expenses, and terms of remuneration. To me, such humdrum considerations seem more suited to a business seminar than a heroic quest to slay a dragon and take back a great treasure. In addition to Bilbo's "what's-in-it-for-me" approach and his reluctance to get involved in adventures away from home is the matter of his billing in the whole enterprise. Gandalf, who engineers Bilbo's involvement with the Dwarves' quest, advertises him as a burglar ready to go into Smaug's lair and steal back the lost treasure.

Bilbo, the thief of Thorin's company

By turning Bilbo into the "professional thief" of the quest, Tolkien characterizes him as a "hero for hire" — far different from his nephew Frodo, or any of the other hobbits in *The Lord of the Rings* adventures, for that matter. As the Dwarves' quest progresses, Bilbo actually turns into a rather respectable thief, both effective and upstanding. In this way, he is a bit like the Persian Ali Baba in the *Arabian Nights* tale "Ali Baba and the Forty Thieves." A big difference is that Ali Baba, who stole the bandits' treasure after learning the secret password to their cave ("Open Sesame"), became a thief because he was poor and needed the gold. Bilbo is far too well off for loot to be his motive.

It's interesting, though, that both Ali Baba and Bilbo justify their thievery by noting that what they're attempting to pilfer is itself stolen booty. Bilbo at least can say that his stealing is in the service of the rightful owners of the treasure. The Dwarf-lord Thorin Oakenshield, who hires Bilbo as the burglar for the company, is indeed the heir of King Thrór, the Dwarf king who originally amassed the treasure (see Chapter 6 for details).

The point here is that Bilbo is a far cry from a typical hero (leaving aside the Ali Baba comparison). However, the quest Bilbo is actually part of is far different from the one he thinks. More than just a reluctant burglar in the pay of a pack of Dwarves, Bilbo turns out to be a pivotal figure in the fate of Middle-earth.

Bilbo and Gollum's ring

When Tolkien first wrote and published *The Hobbit,* Bilbo was not slated to play such a crucial role in the history of Middle-earth. Although Bilbo was always meant to find the creature Gollum's magic ring, which conveys invisibility on its wearer, this particular magic ring was not originally Sauron's One Ring of Power, lost thousands of years prior when Isildur was ambushed and killed on his way north to the Kingdom of Arnor.

As originally conceived, Gollum's ring was just a plot device that enabled Bilbo to become invisible whenever he needed to be in order to go about his burglaring business (what better device for getting in and out of a dragon's lair undetected?). Only when *The Lord of the Rings* was commissioned as a sequel to *The Hobbit* did Tolkien decide to make Gollum's ring into Sauron's One Ring of Power.

To suit the Ring's new, more daunting identity, Tolkien went back and modified the encounter between Bilbo and Gollum in *The Hobbit* so that instead of winning the Ring in a game of riddles with Gollum, Bilbo finds the Ring in Gollum's cave after the Ring abandons its longtime bearer. Through this plot change, Bilbo becomes inadvertently enmeshed in a much larger and more significant quest: the quest to save Middle-earth from Sauron's reemergence, as told in *The Lord of the Rings*.

In light of this larger quest, Bilbo's participation in destroying Smaug, the last dragon in Middle-earth, and helping the Dwarves regain the Lonely Mountain takes on added significance. In losing Smaug, Sauron loses a powerful weapon. By helping the Dwarves regain their Kingdom under the Mountain, Bilbo creates allies that eventually help fight Sauron's forces during the War of the Ring (see Chapter 24 for details).

In finding Gollum's magic ring, Bilbo becomes the unwitting bearer of the One Ring of Power until he bequeaths it to his only heir, Frodo Baggins. This innocent passing of the Ring from one generation to the next is different from Isildur's conception of it as a precious heirloom to be passed down to all his descendents. It is the only known instance of the Ring being freely willed to another instead of stolen through murder. Freely giving the Ring to Frodo, although far from easy to do, is surely a testament to Bilbo's indomitable spirit — one that grows immensely on his quest to the Lonely Mountain. In this act is a self-effacing hobbit heroism that, though far different from the heroics of Men, Elves, and Dwarves, proves ultimately to be the key to Ring's undoing.

Frodo as the Unwitting Hero

Frodo Baggins, the main character of *The Lord of the Rings,* becomes its unwitting hero when he's adopted by Bilbo Baggins (his cousin, but known affectionately as "uncle"). Frodo is an only child and an orphan — like Tolkien himself — who comes to live with Bilbo at Bag End at the tender age of 21 (hobbits don't come of age until they reach 33). After Bilbo's surprise exit from his 111th birthday party — which happens also to be Frodo's 33rd birthday — Frodo inherits his entire estate, along with his magic gold ring, which Gandalf barely persuades Bilbo to leave behind. The ring is the Ring, of course, and Frodo is saddled with the responsibility of taking it to its destruction in Mordor.

Frodo is, then, a "drafted" hero. Even Bilbo, who goes kicking and scream-
ing on his adventure with the Dwarves, does it for the adventure itself and
its potential reward. Frodo, however, begins his quest much more out of
necessity — it's brought upon him as necessary to save the Shire that he
loves so well. A hero involuntarily burdened with a quest is the farthest thing
from the knight errant looking for dragons to slay. Although at times Frodo hankers for adventure — he wants very much to go with Bilbo when he leaves the
Shire — Tolkien is also careful to show Frodo's reluctance to be the savior of
the Shire when Gandalf reveals to him the true identity of the Ring and its
danger.

Tolkien in no way presents Frodo as a young headstrong hero aching for a fight,
but rather as a reluctant one full of trepidation and self-doubt. Frodo seems
to me more of a modern-day hero — who does his duty for lack of another
choice — than a typical fantasy or legendary hero, who does it for the challenge
and test of his prowess. I think this is part of what makes *The Lord of the Rings*
so very different from other fantasy tales. If a typical fantasy writer had written the tale, he or she would undoubtedly have made Aragorn and not Frodo
the main hero who confronts and destroys Sauron (as Aragorn's ancestor Isildur
did before him). With Frodo, Tolkien does his own take on confronting evil
(see Chapter 15) and gives us a more accessible model for our own heroics
(for more on each of us as Ring-bearers, see Chapter 16).

Frodo's courage and internal struggle

Throughout his quest to take the Ring to Mordor and destroy it, Frodo faces
an internal struggle with the Ring's evil and his own self-doubt. A pivotal point
occurs at the Council of Elrond when, to his own surprise, he finds himself
volunteering with his famous expression, "I will take the Ring, though I do not
know the way."

During the journey, Frodo many times manifests a courage that he doesn't
know he has. He shows courage at Weathertop where, instead of being para-
lyzed with fear, he stabs the Lord of the Ringwraiths. Later, after crossing the
ford of Bruinen at the border of Rivendell, he defies the Black Riders who've
come to take him back to Mordor. The problem is that Frodo's first impulse
whenever he needs to summon his courage is to put on the Ring and use its
power. He actually does put the Ring on prior to confronting the Ringwraiths
at Weathertop and stabbing the Lord of the Nazgûl. He also resorts to putting
it on when Boromir tries to take it from him at Amon Hen.

Frodo first becomes aware of the Eye of Sauron searching him out when he's
sitting on the Seat of Seeing at Amon Hen wearing the Ring. In this encounter,
you begin to see the seriousness of Frodo's internal struggle, for he is not
sure whether his response to Sauron is "never in your wildest dreams" or
"Chief, I'm on my way." When he finally realizes that he must take off the Ring
or risk Sauron getting a fix on his location, he still wrestles with the decision
to take it off.

In a very telling description, Frodo is said to be "writhing" during this struggle. Suddenly, Tolkien tells us, Frodo becomes aware of himself again and takes off the Ring in the nick of time. This is where Frodo makes the decision to go it alone to Mordor, saying, "I will do now what I must." Of course, Sam won't let him go alone. As he perseveres toward Mordor, you see Frodo morphing from simple Ring-bearer into wannabe Lord of the Ring. As he and Sam get closer to Mount Doom, the seat of the Ring's power, its influence weighs heavier and heavier on Frodo, and he becomes increasingly possessive of it (that old "My Precious" thing). Despite the terrible internal struggle, Frodo finds the courage and the stamina to continue on to the bitter end.

Given Frodo's ongoing struggle between Ring-bearer and Ring master, I wonder whether his words "I will do now what I must" really mean that he has to go on alone to Mordor in order to destroy the Ring or in order to confront Sauron for its mastery?

Frodo's Christ-like suffering

It doesn't take a biblical scholar to feel some similarity between Frodo's struggle to carry the Ring up Mount Doom and Christ's struggle to carry his cross to Calvary. By the time Frodo reaches Mount Doom, he is so weighed down by the power of the Ring and despair over its destruction that Sam carries him and the Ring up the path to the Crack of Doom — shades of Simon the Cyrenian bearing Jesus' cross to Golgotha.

Any parallel, intentional or not, between Frodo and Christ ends when Gollum attacks Frodo on the path in their second-to-last encounter. Gollum's effort to wrest the Ring from him re-ignites Frodo's will, showing how stern and powerful he has become under the Ring's influence. In prophetic and commanding words, Frodo fends off Gollum, warning that if he ever touches him again, he will be cast into the Fire of Doom.

Unlike Christ, who at the height of his trial on the cross submits his will to God's and commends his spirit into His hands, Frodo, at the climax of his ordeal with the Ring, exerts his own will first by choosing not to complete the quest, saying, "I will not do this deed." With this declaration of will, Frodo claims the One Ring as his own and puts it on to openly reveal himself to the Eye of Sauron.

One can only surmise that at that point Frodo is prepared to directly challenge the Dark Lord for the title of Lord of the Ring. The idea that Frodo could best Sauron in a contest of evil, even wearing the Ring, is hard to believe. More likely than not, the Ring is simply using Frodo to get back to its master by revealing its whereabouts.

The great irony of this situation is that the moment Frodo feels as though he's finally mastered the Ring by claiming it and deciding against its destruction is precisely when the Ring takes completely mastery of him and turns his will into its will. Frodo's failure at Mount Doom is the polar opposite of Christ's victory on the cross, wherein Christ masters his suffering and death by submitting his will to this fate.

Frodo as the failed hero

Frodo's failure at Mount Doom is unlike anything found in folklore. Although mythology is full of tragic heroes undone by hubris after achieving greatness (such as Oedipus and Jason of the Argonauts) and heroes who are ultimately defeated in their final quests (Beowulf and King Arthur), I know of no other hero who, just at the point of achieving the quest, turns against it and abandons it.

This begs the question of whether Frodo can even be considered a hero. But he is a hobbit of great courage and stamina despite his collapse at the end, for a hero of lesser character and courage would not have made it as far as he did without succumbing to the Ring's power. I see the cause of Frodo's breakdown not as a lack of will but rather as an overabundance of it (the will amplified and used by the evil of the Ring).

One can only speculate on why Frodo fails right when he's poised to succeed. Personally, I think it has to do with Tolkien's idea of providence and eucastrophe (see Chapter 1) and the idea that none of us can succeed alone — especially not through the power of our *will* alone. (See the sections on Sam and Gollum later in this chapter.)

Frodo as the wounded hero

If you consider the One Ring as some kind of weird psychic amplifier that boosts your willpower and turns it to its own, then Frodo does extraordinarily well in reaching the Crack of Doom — one can only imagine what the Ring would have done in the hands of more strong-willed characters such as Galadriel, Aragorn, Gandalf, or Boromir.

What's more, the ordeal of the Ring haunts Frodo long after he returns to the Shire. And there, instead of being received as a hero, he's actually shunned in favor of his more boisterous companions Merry and Pippin, who are welcomed back as natural leaders. Although he is instrumental in saving the Shire from Sauron's domination, Frodo is never really able to be comfortable there again.

In this way, Frodo is a lot like war heroes who never become fully reintegrated on returning home and are ever after haunted by their war service. Tolkien certainly knew something about this, given that he was in the trenches of France during the First World War. He also undoubtedly encountered many such heroes after the Second World War, years during which he worked diligently on the writing of *The Lord of the Rings*.

Even as the other hobbits in the Fellowship find their places in the reconstructed Shire, Frodo remains alienated and often plagued by illnesses — which recur on the anniversaries of his encounter with the Ringwraith on Weathertop and his failure to destroy the Ring. Finally, upon completing his memoirs — the supposed source of *The Lord of the Rings* — he departs Middle-earth forever upon an Elven white ship, headed for the Blessed Realm (see Chapter 19 for more on the fate of the Ring-bearer).

Sam as the Common Hero

As the saying goes, "behind every good man stands a good woman." In this case, standing behind Frodo Baggins is Sam Gamgee. No character in modern literature is as a true and good a servant as Sam is to Frodo. Ostensibly Frodo's gardener at Bag End, Sam ends up playing a perfect Friday to Frodo's Robinson Crusoe.

Tolkien himself commented in a letter to his son Christopher on Sam's emergence as a *real* hero of *The Lord of the Rings*. All I know is that no one could ever ask for a more faithful friend and companion than Sam. He is tireless in caring for Frodo's physical and psychological needs — not to mention the childlike enthusiasm with which he greets each new positive experience (seeing the Elves in Rivendell and Lothlórien and the oliphaunts in Ithilien) and the resolve with which he faces so many negative ones.

Sam is both common as the dirt in which he gardens and as bright as the rhymes he can recite verbatim at any time. Above all, Sam has a dogged determination to fulfill his duty to Frodo. His biggest problem on the quest to destroy the Ring is having to share his beloved master with Gollum. When Frodo takes Gollum on as guide and attempts the reclamation of the Sméagol part of Gollum's warped and split personality, Sam's jealousy flares, showing a little more human side of an otherwise very saintly hobbit.

Sam's undisputed heroism shows when he defeats the giant spider Shelob (see Chapter 10) and then, thinking Frodo is dead from her bite, takes up the Ring to continue the quest. Despite Sam's doubt regarding his ability to succeed where Frodo has failed, he takes up the Ring anyway out of sheer love for Frodo and respect for his sacrifice. Here, we see the time-honored image of the warrior picking up the fallen hero's standard, vowing to fight on to victory, and in so doing honoring his comrade's sacrifice.

After rescuing Frodo from the Orc tower (Frodo has only been knocked out cold by Shelob's venom), they enter Mordor, and Sam again shows the depth of his devotion. When Frodo is too demoralized to go on he carries Frodo on his back to the foot of Mount Doom. In visualizing this, I think of the classic image depicted on those old St. Christopher medals: the saint carrying the Christ child on his shoulders as he fords the stream (Christopher comes from the Greek, meaning "Christ bearer").

Whether at his master's side in Rivendell, on the slopes of the erupting volcano after the destruction of the Ring, or helping Frodo back to health in the Shire, Sam is one of the most sincere and humble heroes in all of literature — one whom few could emulate, but all would want by his side. I think of Sam as Tolkien's ideal, the everyman Christian who is readily willing to follow his master to the very fires of Hell and back, if need be.

Gollum as the Unintentional Hero

Probably no more unlikely literary hero can be found than Gollum (see Chapter 7), who saves Middle-earth by taking the Ring from Frodo's hand (along with his forefinger — ouch!) and destroying it in the Fires of Mount Doom (himself along with it — ugh!).

On the one hand, Gollum is corrupted beyond redemption by his association with the Ring (which he bore for more than 470 years, compared to Bilbo's meager 60 years and Frodo's paltry 18). On the other hand, Gollum is one tough cookie in resisting the Ring's evil as much as he does, especially considering that he killed his friend to get it. It's a wonder he has any of his original Sméagol personality left by the time we meet him in *The Lord of the Rings*. This resilience is probably because of his hobbit ancestry — his people are from the Stoors clan of hobbits— and his limited use of the Ring (he only used it to be invisible while catching fish). Gollum shows the Sméagol side of his personality most clearly when he plays the riddling game with Bilbo in his cave under the Misty Mountains and when he adopts Frodo as his master, agreeing to lead him and Sam to Mordor and swearing loyalty to them by his Precious (the Ring).

The oath Gollum takes, sworn on his Precious, is crucial to understanding what happens later with Frodo on Mount Doom: Sméagol swears to never let Sauron have the Ring and that, if need be, he will save it. He is as good as his word, for that's exactly what he does when he bites off Frodo's finger and takes the Ring into the Crack of Doom. On some level, Gollum surely understands that when Frodo claims the Ring and puts it on, in very short time Sauron's Ringwraiths would be there to reclaim it for their master.

I'm convinced that in some odd way (and Tolkien has a rather odd sense of humor), Gollum's death in the volcano's bowels is not just the accidental demise of one who lost his footing in the delirium of once again holding the object of adoration. I think of it as a kind of Ragnarok-type death — the hero goes down literally in flames of self-sacrifice rather than surrender to defeat at the hands of the enemy (see Chapter 20 for more).

Chapter 18

Chivalry and True Love

You have to travel pretty far and wide to find someone who doesn't down deep believe in true love, whether or not that person has experienced it in his or her life. This subject must have been near and dear to Tolkien because he devoted an inordinate amount of time to writing one particular tale of true love and chivalry: that of the mortal Beren and the Elf-princess Lúthien.

More than any other tale in *The Silmarillion,* the story of Beren and Lúthien is a romance in the original sense of the word: a tale based on legend, chivalric love, and adventure, with a touch of the supernatural thrown in. So vital was this love story to Tolkien that he saw fit to reprise it in *The Lord of the Rings* in the story of the mortal and future king Aragorn and the Elf-princess Arwen, Elrond's daughter. Unfortunately, Tolkien did not weave this tale into the larger story of the War of the Ring; the details of Aragorn and Arwen's love story occur only in the fifth section of Appendix A of *The Lord of the Rings.* Fortunately, the director Peter Jackson did find an effective way to integrate this love story into his movie version of *The Lord of the Rings* so that a wider audience could enjoy and benefit from it.

This chapter looks at Tolkien's view of true love as demonstrated in the stories of Beren and Lúthien and Aragorn and Arwen and compares them to traditional chivalric love popularized in the Middle Ages and to romantic love in our modern age. At the heart of this comparison are the ideas that true love is a goal worthy of the greatest heroic quest (see Chapter 17) and that love is true insofar as the lovers are willing to sacrifice for that love and undergo the trials that fate has in store for them.

Courtly Love in the Age of Chivalry

A most novel idea sprang up in the latter years of the Middle Ages, or medieval age: a concept called *fin' amors* (literally "fine love"), or courtly love. Troubadours in all the best courts in Europe sang about it. Courtly love expanded the code of *chivalry,* the knight's idealistic code of behavior that called for actions of high honor, generosity, and courtesy on and off the battlefield. Chivalry was most important for the so-called knight errant — a knight off on a quest for his lord in which he proves his bravery and loyalty. In this situation, the knight errant is expected to be particularly chivalrous toward all the ladies in the court he's visiting.

Courtly love played on these high-minded ideals of chivalry and extended it as a spiritual practice proving a knight's chastity and purity towards ladies of the court, especially married ladies of higher rank. These women were strictly off-limits, of course, except in song and poetry — at least, they were if a knight knew what was good for him.

As portrayed in minstrels' lays (narrative ballads), courtly love often spoke of the knight's humiliation before the lady he loved and about love as a process of spiritual improvement. Many ballads are about a valiant knight who vanquishes all his enemies on the battlefield, only to be vanquished himself by his love for his lady. Given the piety of Christianity in medieval society, many of the lays that spoke of *fin' amors* also referred to making homage to the lady, as though she were an object of worship. They put her almost on the same footing as the Madonna, the mother of Jesus, herself the object of intense adoration throughout the 14th century. Suffice to say, this kind of courtly love gave whole a new meaning to putting your "lady on a pedestal."

This extremely idealistic view of love as a chaste and spiritual adventure, while providing great material to the troubadours of the time, was never even close to the norm in real, everyday castle life. Marriages were almost always arranged and were highly political and financial affairs, involving among other things the bride's dowry. However, even if impractical in daily life, chivalrous love continued to color the perception of true love with a rosy tint, and its influence began to appear in great works of literature of the time.

One of Tolkien's favorite works was the anonymous epic poem *Sir Gawain and the Green Knight.* Another was *Perceval, or the Story of the Grail* by Chrétian de Troyes. In both poems, the lady of high rank was none other than Queen Guinevere, Arthur's lady. In *Sir Gawain,* the knight championed the lady's honor against the insults of the Green Knight, who came uninvited into Camelot to test the bravery of Arthur's knights and frighten Queen Guinevere. In *Perceval,* the knight defended Guinevere's honor when another knight took Arthur's cup and spilled its contents all over her. Both poems extol the chaste knight who championed his lady and fought for her honor —though Perceval was less chaste by far than Gawain, and even Gawain was tempted by a mysterious lady of the castle where he had been given refuge.

Romantic Love in the Modern Age

At first glance, our modern idea of romantic love, the stuff Hollywood and soap operas thrive on, may seem light years from the chivalrous or courtly love of the Middle Ages. On closer inspection, though, you have to admit that they share a few important traits. For one thing, both are very idealistic (the more jaded might say unrealistic). For another thing, both are thoroughly grounded in a belief in love at first sight and praise the virtues of the lover along with the feelings that he or she arouses.

With chivalrous love, though, the amorous feelings were of a more spiritual nature, whereas romantic love is more sensual. Another big difference is that chivalrous love tended to be centered on an unattainable lady (one who was already married or of a higher rank) while romantic love usually focuses on an equal, or at least a lady within reach, and hopefully unmarried.

Another huge difference is that romantic love doesn't require any test of its truth beyond its own existence. In chivalry, a knight had to prove his love for his lady, and consequently his loyalty to his liege lord, by championing her in combat or by performing a great quest to protect her honor. In romantic love, the lover gets away with simply sending flowers.

Tolkien's True Love

According to a letter from Tolkien to his son Christopher, his own love story with Edith Bratt, the love of his life and wife of 55 years, was the source for his greatest tale of true love, that of Beren and Lúthien in *The Silmarillion*. Tolkien met his wife-to-be when he was but a lad of 16, and she a young lady of 19, and they both lived in a Birmingham boarding house.

But once their covert love was discovered, Tolkien, still a minor and a ward of a Catholic priest, Father Francis Morgan, was forbidden by the good Father to see Edith again until he was 21. Heartbroken, he nevertheless obeyed the injunction (except for one clandestine meeting that was witnessed and duly reported to Father Francis). Like the loyal knight who performs superhuman feats for the love of his lady, Tolkien kept true to his vow to Father Francis and did not contact Edith again until he was 21.

But by then Edith was engaged to be married, having decided by the long silence that Tolkien no longer loved her. Tolkien rushed to her side and persuaded her to break off the engagement. They were married a year after he graduated from the university (with honors in English, surprise, surprise). That same year, 1916, Tolkien was shipped to the battle front in France, where he took part in the horror and carnage of the Battle of the Somme.

Returning to England the following year, after suffering a bout of "trench fever," Tolkien was reunited with Edith. In his letter to Christopher, he recounted how, after recovering his health in the Yorkshire village of Roos, he conceived of the love story of Beren and Lúthien while visiting a small woodland glade of hemlocks. There, he said, Edith danced and sang for him under the moonrise, a vivid image that inspired Beren's meeting his love Lúthien, daughter of King Thingol, and Aragorn meeting Arwen, daughter of Elrond.

When Edith died in 1971, Tolkien ordered a simple granite tombstone with her name, Edith Mary Tolkien — followed by the name Lúthien and the years of her birth and death, 1889-1971. When he passed away two years later, his children ordered an equally simple granite tombstone for him with his name — followed by the name Beren and his birth and death years, 1892-1973.

The Love Story of Beren and Lúthien

Tolkien's love story of Beren and Lúthien in *The Silmarillion* combines motifs from a wide variety of myths and legends. In it, Tolkien penned his version of the fairytale of Rapunzel ("Rapunzel, Rapunzel, let down your hair"); his own upside-down versions of the Greek myths of Jason and Medea and Orpheus and Eurydice; and a host of vampires and werewolves in the best (or worst) tradition of Hollywood horror flicks. Throw in a loyal dog, the wolfhound Huan of Valinor who met his end in a battle with a wolf worthy of Fenris the Wolf (in Norse mythology, at Ragnarok Fenris not only devoured the sun but also slay Odin, king of the gods) — and you've got yourself a love story like no other.

The tale of Beren and Lúthien is really two stories: The Quest of the Silmaril — Fëanor's cursed gems brought to Middle-earth by Morgoth (see Chapter 4) — and the Lay of Leithian, the "Song of the Release from Bondage."

The first story contains a common fairytale element: A father figure sets up an impossible quest designed to get rid of the young upstart suitor who threatens him or his kingdom in some way. The father figure disguises (rather thinly) his true motive by telling the young upstart that he must accomplish a "little" quest to prove himself worthy of his heart's desire.

In the myth of Jason and the Argonauts, the father-figure was Jason's evil uncle Pelias, usurper of Jason's rightful throne as King of Iolcus. He challenged Jason to recover the Golden Fleece from the land of Colchis at the end of the earth, and *then* he would surrender his throne to Jason (the real object of Jason's quest). In Tolkien's myth of the Quest of the Silmaril, King Thingol of Menegroth challenged Beren to recover a Silmaril from Morgoth before he could win the hand of Thingol's only daughter Lúthien (the real object of Beren's quest).

In both cases, the father figure hedged his bet: Although his real goal was the elimination of the upstart rival, he wouldn't really have minded too much if his rival achieved the impossible quest because its object was a thing beyond price. The Golden Fleece was said to be able to cure any disease. (Jason, by the way, means "healer" in Greek — see Chapter 5 for more on this myth.) The Silmarils, made from the blended light of the Two Trees of Valinor (see Chapter 4 for more on the Silmarils), were the last remaining vestiges of the Light from the Blessed Realm of Aman.

Of course, there's just one little hitch to each quest. The Golden Fleece was kept in a tree in the barbaric land of Colchis at the end of the earth and guarded by a terrible dragon. The Silmarils were kept in Angband, the impenetrable underground fortress of Morgoth, the Lord of Darkness, and set in his iron crown that he never took off.

Both tasks were so daunting that the heroes called in the cavalry. Jason called on twelve of the greatest Greek heroes (including Hercules) and had Argus, the greatest shipbuilder, build Argo, their famous craft. Beren called on King Finrod Felagund, Elf-king of Nargothrond, who was indebted to Beren's father. Finrod found ten brave and loyal Elf warriors to go with them.

Nevertheless, in both myths, it was not the merry boys of Sherwood Forest who ensured that the Robin Hoods won the day, but the Maid Marians of the tale. In Jason's case it was Medea, the only daughter of King Aeëtes of Colchis. For Beren, it was Lúthien, the only child of King Thingol.

The power of love

Beren fell head-over-heels in love with Lúthien the very moment he caught sight of her dancing at moonrise one evening in a glade in the woods of Neldoreth. In the Greek myth it was Medea who fell madly, who-is-that-guy in love with Jason the moment he appeared before her father's court. The fact that the hero fell hopelessly in love with his helpmate in the quest in the first tale and the helpmate fell desperately in love with the hero in the second marks the critical difference between one of the greatest love stories ever told and one of the greatest tragedies (check out Euripides' play *Medea* for more).

Both Lúthien and Medea were women of great power. Lúthien had the power of song — she could sing spring into being, sing down the battlements of Sauron's dungeons in Tol-in-Gaurhoth, and sing Morgoth to sleep. Medea (who was called a witch) had the power of potions. She concocted a draught to put the Fleece's guard-dragon to sleep and poisoned the bridal gown she later presented to her husband's bride-to-be, the Princess of Corinth (a marriage made to advance Jason's political career for which Medea feigned acceptance but actually exacted her vengeance).

Both Lúthien and Medea were totally devoted to their heroes. Lúthien's love for Beren was so great that she willingly rushed to save him from Sauron's dungeon, helped him retrieve the Silmaril from Morgoth's crown, followed him in death to the Halls of Mandos, and even gave up her Elven immortality to become a mere mortal like him. Medea's love for Jason was such that that she was willing to cut up her younger brother's body into little pieces and throw them into the sea to slow down her father's pursuing ships — later she killed her own children and flung their lifeless bodies at the feet of their father as the final act of revenge for his repaying her unwavering love with a marriage of political convenience to the Princess of Corinth.

Both myths demonstrate the immense power of love: Beren and Lúthien's love defeated death and escaped its bondage, whereas Jason and Medea's tragic tale shows the power of an unrequited love to exact unbelievable vengeance and suffering. Just as surely as Beren used his love for Lúthien as inspiration to achieve greatness, Jason used Medea's love for him as merely a means to achieve his political goals. In the endings, it was the selfless versus the selfish qualities of the love that made all the difference in the world.

Love and death

In the love story of Beren and Lúthien, the Lay of Leithian the "Song of the Release from Bondage," was perhaps even more important than that of the Quest of the Silmaril. It seems certain that Tolkien modeled parts of this second part of the love story after the myth of Orpheus and Eurydice. In this myth, Orpheus, the son of the muse Calliope and the best musician in the world, was inconsolable upon the death of his lover, Eurydice. He descended into the Underworld of Hades to retrieve her and bring her back to the land of the living. In the Lay of Leithian, Lúthien went to the Houses of the Dead to retrieve Beren after his death during the Quest of the Silmaril.

In the tale of Orpheus and Eurydice, Orpheus gained entrance into the Underworld ruled by the god Hades and his Queen Persephone by charming the three-headed dog Cerebus, who guarded the nether regions, with his playing of his lyre and his singing. In the Lay of Leithian, Lúthien gained entrance into the Houses of the Dead by bidding Beren to linger there until she could come to say her final farewell and then willing her spirit to separate from her body, whereupon it flew to the Houses of the Dead.

Orpheus played and sang so sweetly of his grief over the loss of Eurydice that Hades wept and Persephone shed a single tear. In the Lay of Leithian, Lúthien knelt before Mandos and sang a song of sweet sorrow bemoaning the fates of both of the children of Ilúvatar — the sadness of the race of Elves and the anguish of the race of Men. As she sang, Tolkien says her tears fell on the feet of Mandos like "rain on stones," and Mandos was moved to great pity.

Moved to pity by Orpheus's song, Hades let him reunite with the shade of Eurydice. He also allowed Eurydice to follow Orpheus back to the world of the living on the condition that Orpheus not turn to look at Eurydice until she had completely left the Underworld and reentered the land of the living. But just before they reached the light from the sky, Orpheus lost faith and turned back to make sure that Eurydice was following him. Because she was still a shade, he couldn't hear her footsteps as they ascended the long passageway up from the Underworld. In so doing, Orpheus lost Eurydice forever.

Lúthien and Beren's fate was not so tragic. Mandos, moved to pity by her song, appealed to Manwë, Lord of the Maiar, on their behalf. Manwë interpreted the will of Ilúvatar by offering Lúthien a decision: Either she could dwell in Valinor forever — but without Beren, who would have to move out of the Houses of the Dead and beyond the Circles of the World — or she could become mortal and return with Beren to Middle-earth. Given the decision between an immortal life without any cares and hardships but also without her true love and between the brief life of a mortal with limited happiness but shared with her true love, it was no contest. She immediately chose to return as a mortal to Middle-earth with Beren. They settled on Tol Galen, the Green Isle, in Ossiriand and lived happily in their love until the end of their days.

Tolkien ended the story by emphasizing that although Lúthien was the only Elf to die and leave the confines of the world, her choice of mortality forever joined the two children of Ilúvatar, the immortal Elves and mortal Men. He also highlighted the fact that Lúthien became the forebear of others in whom the Elves see her likeness. These descendents include Elwing, her granddaughter, and Arwen, her great-great-granddaughter — and the subject of another love story between an Elf-princess and a mortal (see next section).

In evaluating the moral of the story of the Lay of Leithian — the Song of the Release from Bondage — one naturally asks which of the two lovers was released from bondage? Was it Beren, who died completing the impossible task of retrieving a Silmaril for King Thingol in order to gain Lúthien? Or was it Lúthien, who died in order to go to the Houses of the Dead to bid Beren a final farewell and plead their case to the Lord of Death?

Keep in mind that Beren, although allowed to return to life in Middle-earth, was still subject to a second, permanent death. His conundrum was like that of Lazarus, whom Jesus raised from the dead, but who then had to look forward to a second, more lasting death. I don't know about you, but in my book, this is not really a release from the bondage of death. It's more a postponement of the death sentence; you could even call it double-jeopardy, having to die twice (isn't dying once bad enough?).

Lúthien's choice to forego immortality to be with Beren is not what you'd call a release from the bondage of death, either. It's more like an innocent taking on the death sentence of their culpable partner in order to be with him. Another way of evaluating her choice is to say that Lúthien preferred to live on borrowed time with Beren in Middle-earth than live eternally alone in the Blessed Realm. If you adopt Tolkien's attitude toward the fate of Elven immortality as a kind of curse, and human mortality as a gift (see Chapter 16), Lúthien may well have been the one who was released from the bondage — not of death, but of never-ending life.

There is another way to consider their situation as a release from the death's bondage. Perhaps the bondage they were freed from was not death but the *concern* about dying. I like to think of their love as so pure and strong that it enabled them to transcend any concern for dying as long as they shared the same fate, be it immortal in the Houses of the Dead or mortal beyond the Circles of the World — together they could face anything.

Beren and Lúthien Reprised: The Love Story of Aragorn and Arwen

Tolkien loved to reprise his themes. Each version used many of the same elements while bringing them forward into a new and sometimes more complex or often more restrictive environment (for more on the history of Middle-earth as a long defeat, see Chapter 1).

The love story of Aragorn — Isildur's sole heir to Arnor and Gondor, and Arwen, the only daughter of Elrond, master of Rivendell — reprises the love story of their ancestors Beren and Lúthien. The most interesting thing about this is how much Aragorn and Arwen's story consciously refers back to that of Beren and Lúthien's. You almost have to know Beren and Lúthien's story to make full sense of Aragorn and Arwen's.

In *The Lord of the Rings,* Aragorn sings part of the song of Lúthien Tinúviel ("Nightingale" or literally "Daughter of Twilight"), a song that tells of the initial meeting of Beren and Lúthien in the glade in the forest of Neldoreth. And this is precisely how Aragorn first met Arwen: The day after Elrond reveals to Aragorn his true, royal ancestry, Aragorn is walking by himself at sunset in the woods around Rivendell, singing (you guessed it) the Lay of Lúthien when, it seemed, Lúthien herself appears before him.

After staring at this vision in shock for some time, Aragorn calls out to her by the name Tinúviel that Beren used when he first laid eyes on Lúthien. Arwen asks him who he is and why he called her by that name. Aragorn replies that she appeared to him just like Lúthien Tinúviel, of whom he was just singing.

Arwen explains that she's often compared to Lúthien, though she doesn't yet reveal Lúthien as her ancestor. She tells Aragorn that she is not Tinúviel, but she may yet share her fate — which prefigures the love that she will feel for this mortal stranger. Aragorn then reveals his identity as Isildur's heir, to which Arwen responds that in that case they are distantly related, for she is the daughter of Elrond (refer to the genealogy in Chapter 4 for more on how Aragorn and Arwen are distant relations).

After this initial meeting, Aragorn's mother Gilraen tries to discourage him from pressing his love for Arwen — to no avail, of course. She tells him that he's way out of his league, is aiming too high even for a descendent of kings, and that it isn't right for mortals to mix with Elves (the old *West Side Story* "stay with your kind, one of your own kind" thing). When Aragorn responds that this isn't the first time this kind of thing has happened (after all, he was singing the Lay of Lúthien), Gilraen says that that happened a long time ago in a happy age before the race of Men had diminished. She also mentions that Aragorn needs Elrond's goodwill to regain his kingship and that she doesn't think that Elrond will be pleased with the idea of his only daughter following in the footsteps of Lúthien by marrying a mere mortal.

This is where the father figure is supposed to enter into the action and set an impossible quest for the young upstart Aragorn, but Tolkien reformed this part of the fairytale to account for Elrond's special relationship to Aragorn. After all, Elrond has been a foster father to Aragorn and although he is far from enthusiastic about Aragorn marrying Arwen, he has a genuine interest in helping Aragorn regain his throne and save Middle-earth.

Yet Elrond also has a special reason for not wanting Arwen to marry a mortal and, perhaps, become one herself. He himself was the child of a marriage between an Elf-princess and a mortal (albeit a very special one) and as a consequence lost his parents and his twin-brother, Elros, to human mortality. When his parents Elwing and Eärendil came before the Valar, they and their children were allowed to choose which fate they wanted: mortal human or immortal Elf. Only Elrond chose immortality and is therefore permanently separated from his family. His parents are destined forever to fly through the heavens carrying the Silmaril as a symbol of hope, and his only brother has gone beyond the Circles of the World after long reigning as the first king of Númenor (see Chapter 5 for details). If Arwen chooses mortality to marry Aragorn, Elrond will lose his only daughter in exactly the same way. Elrond does everything he can to discourage the match without actually forbidding it, perhaps wisely realizing that there is no way to stop true love.

Many years pass between the initial meeting of Aragorn and Arwen and their next. After about thirty years of traipsing around Middle-earth as the Ranger Strider, Aragorn meets her again by chance when he comes to Lothlórien and she has returned to the house of Galadriel, her grandmother. There, on a green hill called Cerin Amroth, they pledge their undying love.

When Elrond learns of this, he tells Aragorn the next time he sees him in Rivendell that the only way he will ever marry Arwen is after he has fulfilled his fate and regained his kingship. Elrond is aware of being in a lose/lose situation with Aragorn: Should Aragorn fail to regain his kingship, Sauron will take dominion over Middle-earth, and Rivendell will be lost. Should Aragorn succeed in winning back his kingdom, Elrond will surely lose his daughter to mortality and ultimately be parted from her forever as he was from his parents and brother. The sadness of Elrond adds another dimension to the bittersweet nature of the Elf/human relationship. Tolkien underscores the sacrifice on Elrond's part, which adds greatly to the nobility of this Elven character and to the depth of this love story.

After the successful conclusion of the War of the Ring and the crowning of Aragorn as King Aragorn Elessar of the Reunited Kingdom, Aragorn and Arwen live as "happily ever after" as mere mortals can, reigning long in complete love for one another. It is only when Aragorn at last comes to the end of his days and lays down his life (see Chapter 16) that Arwen feels the full impact of her choice of a mortal life and the human bitterness over death and realizes exactly what she has sacrificed for the love of her life. Aragorn, nevertheless, urges Arwen as one who helped him defy both the power of the Shadow and the Ring not to despair before the final test of death.

In the end, Tolkien's boy named "Hope" (in Elvish, Estel, Aragorn's original name) lives up to his name by holding out hope for all mortals who must die and go beyond the Circles of the World. Arwen in great sorrow returns to Lothlórien only to find it deserted — Galadriel has left with Arwen's father for the Undying Lands, and King Celeborn has taken the rest of the Galadrim east into Mirkwood. There in Lothlórien, she faces her utter loneliness and lies to down to die on the green hill of Cerin Amroth, where she and Aragorn first pledged their love.

In the tale of Aragorn and Arwen I see a maturing of the theme of being released from the bondage of death that Tolkien introduced in Beren and Lúthien's love story. Here, the Elven and human lovers are released from the bondage of death by fully facing and feeling their sorrow over each other's death without giving in to despair and without giving up on the hope that death can never be an end to true love.

Chapter 19

Fate and Free Will

. . . .

In This Chapter

▶ The roles of fate and free will in Tolkien's fantasies

▶ Fëanor and his fate in light of his creation and curse of the Silmarils

▶ The tragic story of Túrin Turambar, the "Master of Fate by Fate Mastered"

▶ The collective fate of the Ring-bearers in *The Lord of the Rings*

▶ The fate of the Elves in the Age of the Dominion of Men

. . . .

*I*n Tolkien's works the theme of fate and free will ranks right up there with death and immortality and faith and redemption. I'd even venture to say that they're all interrelated. Tolkien goes to great lengths to point out when a character is facing fate (often using the term *doom*) or when an event seems fated.

This chapter looks at fate versus free will first by exploring a couple of important myths in *The Silmarillion:* the story of Fëanor, the most talented Elf in history and his misfortune with the Silmaril jewels, and the tragic tale of the mortal Túrin Turambar, who in trying to master his own fate becomes mastered by it.

The chapter analyzes the idea of collective fate and discusses how it affects or limits free will in *The Lord of the Rings*. It compares the shared fate of all the Ring-bearers to that of all the Silmaril holders. The chapter concludes by considering the fate of the Elves at the end of the Third Age and the beginning of the Dominion of Men in the Fourth Age.

Fate and Free Will: A Matter of Choice

The question of what's fated in our lives versus what we're free to choose is very important and possibly as old as human culture itself. The answers developed in mythologies, philosophies, and religions run the gamut from "everything is free will and nothing is fated" to its opposite. What is of most interest in terms of Tolkien's myths is the grey area in between the action being carried by a character's will rather than his circumstances and the time in which he either fulfills or overcomes his destiny.

As in many traditional myths, sometimes Tolkien's characters seem positively carried away by fate, helpless and hopeless before the onslaught of a destiny not altogether of their own making. These characters — such as the Elf-lord Fëanor and the mortal Túrin Turambar ("Master of Doom") — I deem tragic heroes. They contrast with the successful, mythic heroes who fulfill a greater destiny for which they seem uniquely fashioned (see Chapter 17).

Who can say whether Tolkien's tragic heroes are more controlled by outside forces and exercise less free will than the non-tragic ones? It may be instead that his tragic heroes exercise their wills a little bit too freely, that is, in ways that run counter to their "greater" destinies and actually play into the hands of more constrained or tragic fates. If so, ironically they are in a way more tightly controlled than successful heroes, who freely match their wills to the greater destinies in which they participate.

Between what will be and what shall be

I want to do a little word research and define some of the terms, such as *doom* and *fate,* that Tolkien uses extensively in his writing. First off, Anglo-Saxon (Old English) makes a distinction between the concepts of what *will* be and what *shall* be. In modern English, these verbs are not well differentiated. To us, "I will do it" and "I shall do it" say the same thing. But in Old English, the former statement would mean "I want or intend to perform this action" whereas the latter meant "I ought or find it necessary to perform this action."

In Old English, the verb *willan* — from which we get both the noun *will,* as in "free will," and the auxiliary verb *will,* as in "you will go" — meant "to be willing" or "to wish." The verb *sculan* — from which we derive the auxiliary verb *shall,* as in "you shall not steal" — meant "ought," "to be necessary," or even "must be." The difference, although subtle or nonexistent to our ears, is significant when considering fate and free will in Tolkien, for often what a character wants to do (*will* do) is not at all what he ought to do (*shall* do).

A couple of other terms that often pop up in Tolkien's stories about fate and free will can use some explanation: the seemingly synonymous words *doom* and *fate.* Doom (spelled *dōm* in Old English) had not just the modern connotation of "bad fortune" and "disaster," but also "judgment." This is seen clearly in the term *dōmdaeg* ("Doom's Day"), the Old English way of saying "Judgment Day," as in the Last Judgment of the New Testament. Interestingly enough, it also occurs in the term *dōmgeorn,* literally "doom eager," which was an adjective that meant "eager for praise or glory" — a commodity for which all heroes in literature are quite willing (if not able).

Although we use *fate* (from the Latin *fatus*, meaning "that which is spoken") to mean destiny, the Old English term for destiny is still with us, though with a very different connotation: *weird*. Spelled *wyrd* in Old English and meaning "fate," "chance," and "destiny," this term is related to the past tense of *weorþan*, meaning "to become" and to the Latin *vertere*, meaning "to turn" (as in *revert*, to "turn back," and *invert*, to "turn inward"). In days of yore when you referred to *the old weird woman*, you meant the sooth-sayer — she who saw your fate and predicted your future (what *will* be and what *shall* be) — and not some old kook. Of course, because many a soothsayer may have been on the odd side, to the say the least, you can see how *weird* has come to denote the "strange," "odd," or even "cracked" (isn't that totally weird?).

The problem with the term *doom* in Tolkien is that it doesn't always mean "bad fortune" or "disaster" as we naturally think of it. Tolkien used it whenever a judgment — good or bad — was involved. Thus, the circle where the Valar sit in judgment was Máhanaxar, the "Ring of Doom," without meaning that they only made pronouncements of death and catastrophe. Understanding this helps make sense of a line in the love story of Beren and Lúthien: When Lúthien first looked on Beren, "doom fell upon her," and she instantly loved him. Here, Tolkien probably meant that she made a very favorable *judgment* about him and then fell head-over-heels in love. Tolkien certainly didn't mean that the moment she laid eyes on him a catastrophe struck her up the side of the head, but she went ahead and loved him anyhow. (The great thing about this use of *doom* is that both meanings are implicit — whereas Lúthien is aware only of her decision to love Beren, the reader is aware of how this decision also sealed her fate of living a mortal life.)

Understanding *doom* more in its "judgment" sense rather than its "disaster" sense also lends a new understanding to Mount Doom, the volcano where Sauron's Ring was forged and the only place it can be destroyed. As much "Mount Judgment" as "Mount Misfortune," it is a place of trial and testing for our hobbit heroes (especially Frodo) as well as downfall (especially for poor Gollum — see Chapter 17 for more).

Fate personified

In Greek and Norse mythology, fate was personified as three sisters. For the Greeks, the fates were called the *Moîrai* (the "Apportioners," or the Furies):

- **Klotho** ("Spinner") spun the thread of one's life at its beginning.
- **Atrophos** ("Unbending" or "Unchanging") wove the thread of one's life into a tapestry recounting its actions.
- **Lachesis** ("Allotter") cut the thread of one's life at its end.

In Norse mythology, these three sisters were known as the *Norns:*

- **Urd** ("Fate," related to *wyrd* in Old English) was old and decrepit and focused her one-eyed gaze backward on the past.

- **Verdandi** ("Being") was young and fearless and fixed her gaze on what was right before her.

- **Skuld** ("Necessity"), heavily veiled and inscrutable, turned toward the opposite direction of her sister Urd and held an unopened scroll.

For the Greeks and the Norse, the Three Fates were not subject to the will of the gods — though sometimes the gods were able to sway their judgments a wee bit. Also, by profession, both sets of sisters were weavers or spinners of cloth that told the story of one's birth, exploits, and death (the Moîrai spun their threads into cloth on a loom, whereas the Norns spun theirs into webs).

Tolkien used this image in *The Silmarillion* for the Vala Vairë, "the Weaver" and the spouse of Mandos (also known as Námo, "the Doomsman"). It is Vairë who weaves all the events that have ever taken place into storied webs that cover the halls in the Houses of the Dead (see Chapter 3).

While Vairë records the fate of all beings, her mate Mandos actually prophesies the fate of others. The most important example is the so-called Prophesy of the North, also affectionately known as the Doom of the Noldor, by which Mandos predicted the dire fate of the rebellious Elves under Fëanor's command (see "The Tragedy of Fëanor and the Silmarils" later in this chapter). This was, however, as close as Tolkien got to personifying fate. His Christian sensibilities may have prevented him from finding any place for the Three Fates in Middle-earth, though he was surely familiar with their influence in the mythologies on which his "modern" myths depended.

The power of the curse

Before looking at how fate and free will work in some of Tolkien stories, I want to examine one other element important to most myths about fate. This element is found especially in those featuring a tragic hero who is trapped into fulfilling a doom (in both senses of judgment and catastrophe) that he doesn't intend: the good old-fashioned curse.

The word *curse* has two complementary meanings: a prayer or invocation for harm to befall one's enemies (also known as an imprecation) and the evil or misfortune that befalls another (known as the cursed) seemingly as a result of such an imprecation. Though Tolkien did not go in for personifying fate (a job better left to God in his estimation), he was fairly big on curses.

The most significant curses occur in *The Silmarillion* in the myths of Fëanor and Túrin Turambar. In the story of Fëanor, it was the Curse of Mandos on the Noldor that drove the tale. Mandos issued the curse in response to Fëanor's leading his people in rebellion against the Valar and to the Kinslaying of the Teleri at Alqualondë. In the story of Túrin, Morgoth's curse on the entire family of Húrin (Túrin's father) drove the tale.

The Tragic Fate of Fëanor

In many stories, the critical factor in determining whether the main character becomes a great hero like Aragorn in *The Lord of the Rings* or a tragic figure like Fëanor in *The Silmarillion* is simply how he responds to his fate. In traditional Greek drama, the tragic hero, although marked for greatness (usually through some auspicious birth — see Chapter 17 for more) possesses a tragic flaw, a basic character flaw which dooms him to his disastrous fate. In Tolkien's tragic myth of Fëanor, as in the Greek myth of Oedipus Rex, the tragic flaw is arrogance and a quick temper (hubris for short).

Although Tolkien does not specify a particular fate for Fëanor, he makes it clear from the story of his birth and his early achievements that Fëanor was an extraordinary Elf shaped for greatness (see Chapter 4 for details). This potential greatness was marred by Fëanor's temper and quickness to anger as evidenced in the quarrel he had with his half-brother that got him banned from Tirion, and in his later orchestration of the Noldorin rebellion against the Valar, and of the commandeering of the white ships at Alqualondë that resulted in the Kinslaying of the Teleri.

Fëanor reached the height of his hubris when he had his seven sons swear to vengeance on whoever possessed his stolen Silmarils, the pride and joy of his creativity. Instead of vowing vengeance on Morgoth alone, the one who murdered his father and stole the Silmarils, Fëanor's curse included any who touched the jewels and was the cause of much suffering among the Elves and Men of Middle-earth (see Chapter 12).

In the end, Fëanor's anger and pride not only got him killed by the captain of Morgoth's Balrogs, but eventually also brought violent deaths to all of his sons and countless other Elves and Men. Fëanor, blinded by hubris, allowed his desire for revenge to overpower his natural creativity. As a result, his name is linked to a long history of vengeance and bloodshed that blemishes his great accomplishments, including the Silmarils, the palantirí ("Seeing Stones"), and the Tengwar letters (see Chapter 14).

What happened to Fëanor happened to countless other tragic heroes in literature, including such notables as Sophocles's Oedipus and Shakespeare's Macbeth. In the beginning, their great destinies (fate) bestowed much choice (free will) on them. Then, the choices they persisted in making out of hubris diminished their freedom, ultimately chaining them and others around them to a tragic, unalterable fate.

The Tragedy of Túrin Turambar

Tolkien's story of Túrin Turambar in *The Silmarillion* is the closest thing to a Greek tragedy that you'll encounter in his writings — it's a regular Middle-earth *Oedipus Rex*. I don't make this comparison only because both Túrin Turambar and Oedipus innocently became entangled in incestuous relationships (Túrin married his sister Nienor; Oedipus married his mother Iocasta). In fact, much more compelling than the incest themes are the parallel curses on their fathers, which doomed their sons to do such unpardonable, though unwitting, acts.

The curse of the father visited on the son

A curse on the father that determines the fate of a son is a common theme in tragic myths. In the Oedipus story, Zeus doomed Oedipus's father King Laïus of Thebes to die at the hand of his own son because of a curse by Pelops, a very famous mortal honored by the gods as few mortals ever were. Laïus had killed Pelops's only son Chrysippus (that old "eye-for-eye" thing).

In the Túrin Turambar story, Morgoth cursed Húrin's family (who had aided the Elves in their war on him), chaining Húrin to a stone chair on the high place of Thangorodrim from which he could literally witness the destruction of all his family members. Morgoth placed this curse on Húrin's family after capturing Húrin at the Battle of Unnumbered Tears (see Chapter 12).

Will the real hero please stand up?

In the Oedipus myth, trying desperately to escape fate ended up being the very mechanism by which Oedipus fulfilled it. This theme is missing from the Túrin Turambar tale. However, both share another fundamental mythological element: that of the protagonist knowing who he is while remaining unknown to his enemies.

On the most basic level, this story element appears in some myths as an ongoing struggle on the hero's part either to know his true identity and name or to hide them from an enemy. This theme can also be expressed, as it is in both the Oedipus and Túrin Turambar myths, as an ongoing case of mistaken identities. How else, I ask you, are you going to go so far as to marry your own mother or sister, for heaven's sake?

In the tragedy of Oedipus, this question of identity was crucial. In response to King Laïus's question about whether he would ever have an heir, Apollo's oracle at Delphi told Laïus that he would indeed have a son but would die by his son's hand (by the way, note that there's nothing in this particular prophesy about the son marrying his mother after slaying his father). As soon as this son was born, King Laïus and Queen Iocasta immediately had a trusted slave leave the baby Oedipus to die in the wild in order to escape the fate decreed by Apollo (which, of course, as any fool knows, cannot be evaded).

Naturally, in trying to evade the fate decreed for Laïus — to die by the hand of his son as repayment for killing Pelop's son — Laïus and Iocasta set in motion the whole tragedy involving their son. To ensure that no one would rescue the child whom they were about to expose to the elements, they bound his feet together with an iron pin, maiming him (Oedipus means "Swollen Footed" in Greek).

But the slave, instead of exposing Oedipus to die as commanded, gave the child to a foreign shepherd (after all, how could the child possibly harm his father if he was reared in a foreign land?) This shepherd took the child to the childless King and Queen of Corinth, who raised Oedipus as their own child and heir to the throne of Corinth.

All went well until one day the young and impetuous Oedipus (filled with more than just a touch of hubris in all its senses) encountered a drunken man who taunted him about his "true" parentage. Naturally, Oedipus went to the oracle at Delphi to ask about that. The oracle responded only that one day he would kill his father and defile his mother's bed (*now* the fate contained the double-crime of patricide and incest).

In horror, Oedipus fled, vowing never to return to Corinth, where he might harm the folks he believed were his father and mother. On the road, he encountered King Laïus, who just happened to be on his way to ask the oracle another question (probably "how do I get rid of this curse I'm under?"). Oedipus's hubris got the best of him when he arrogantly refused to allow the older man to pass before him at the narrow crossroads. Laïus, deeply offended by this young stranger's insolence, got into a quarrel that quickly turned violent, resulting in Oedipus's slaying his real father.

After that ugly incident, one thing led to another until Oedipus found himself the hero of Thebes, having saved the city-state from a terrible monster known as the Sphinx, and married to the widowed queen, Iocasta. As King of Thebes (his rightful kingdom, but very wrongfully gained), Oedipus then slowly learned his true identity as the murderer of his father and the husband of his mother. The knowledge of the enormity of his crime, plus the fact that instead of outwitting his fate he had literally run into its arms, crushed the once mighty lord — a fate that Túrin very much shares with Oedipus.

Know yourself

According to tradition, the doors of the Temple of Apollo at Delphi, the site of the god's oracle, held two inscriptions: "Know Thyself'" appeared on one side and "Nothing in Excess" (literally "nothing too much") on the other. In the cases of Oedipus and Túrin, both aphorisms apply, for if they had been able to check their excessive hubris, they might have both had a chance to know who they really were, without the tragic consequences that they and their kin suffered.

Túrin: When the master becomes the thrall

You may wonder at the word *thrall* in that heading. It comes from the Old English word for "servant" or "slave." Tolkien used this word frequently in *The Silmarillion* to mean slave. *Thrall* survives in Modern English only in the form *enthrall*, meaning to "enslave" in the sense of being captivated or enchanted by someone or something wonderful. Tolkien's hero Túrin Turambar tried desperately to be a master of his own fate, but ended up becoming its slave, a process in which Túrin became very much *enthralled* with his power to create his own destiny.

In contrast to the Oedipus myth, where the hero's ignorance of his own identity was the critical element in the tragic chain of events, the ignorance of others regarding Túrin's true identity formed the vital element in his story. The myth of Túrin is like no other, for in its brief course the hero went by no fewer than six different names:

- ✔ **Neithan** "The Wronged"
- ✔ **Gorthol** "Dread Helm'
- ✔ **Agarwaen, Son of Úmarth** "Bloodstained son of Ill-fate"
- ✔ **Mormegil** "The Black Sword"
- ✔ **Wildman of the Woods**
- ✔ **Turambar** "Master of Doom"

The myth of Túrin Turambar is, to say the least, one of Tolkien's more complex myths. Briefly, it is a story of a child who was fostered by the Elves in the kingdom of Doriath after his father was captured in the disastrous Battle of Unnumbered Tears (see Chapter 12). His mother committed Túrin to the care of King Thingol and Melian while she and her daughter Nienor remained behind, oppressed in the land of Dor-lómin.

When Túrin came of age, in the best heroic style, he donned the finest heirloom of his father's house of Hador (see Chapter 5), the Dragon Helm of Dor-lómin, and went to defend Doriath from Morgoth's Orcs and other fell creatures. During this time, his mother and sister still refused make the more and more dangerous trip from Dor-lómin to Doriath.

One day, upon his return to Menegroth from the front, one of the counsels of King Thingol insulted Túrin and his kin, taunting him about his unkempt looks and the wildness of the women. In the best tradition of hubris, Túrin responded by throwing a wine cup at him and then confronted him on the street the next day. Túrin literally chased the man until he fell to his death.

In this incident, Tolkien combined Oedipus's response to the taunt about his parentage and his murder of his father at the crossroads. Afterwards, Túrin went into the wild, joined up with a band of outlaws, and became their leader (funny how that happens so easily in these myths), renaming himself Neithan, "The Wronged."

Túrin's initial acts of hubris, murder, and exile were just the beginning of a long, downhill series of unfortunate encounters (and aliases). The most interesting thing is that once Túrin became an outlaw and assumed his first alias, he essentially kept running for the rest of the tale. When he was brought to Nargothrond to the court of King Orodreth (his brother King Finrod Felagund having already died trying to help Beren recover the Silmaril), Túrin became very angry when he discovered that his real name had been revealed to the Elves (at that moment, he was going by the lovely alias Agarwaen, Son of Úmarth — that is, "Bloodstained son of Ill-fate").

Túrin feared being exposed because he believed that others having knowledge of his true name would hasten Morgoth's curse that specified that his father would witness the destruction of all his family and from which he was trying to hide. Just the opposite turned out to be true: His great enemy the dragon Glaurung saw to it that Túrin's sister Nienor knew neither Túrin's true identity nor her own, making it possible for her to fall in love with him and become his wife under the new name Níniel ("Tear Maiden") that Turin gave her. Then, when the dragon, mortally wounded by Túrin, wanted to exact its revenge, all he had to do was reveal their true identities (see Chapter 5).

Whereas the Oedipus Rex tragedy warns against coming to a tragic end through ignorance of who you really are, the tragedy of Túrin Turambar points out the danger of hiding who you really are from others. In both cases, however, the heroes were incapable of achieving a greater, non-tragic destiny (even though both were fashioned for greatness) because neither could exercise the will to give up pride and arrogance.

The Power of Collective Fate

Individual destiny is not the only kind of fate encountered in the great myths of the past. For example, prominent in the Norse myths that Tolkien studied so well is the tale of Ragnarok, the final battle in which the gods are fated to be defeated and the world ends. During this last battle, the gods of Asgard are doomed to valiant defeat at the hands of giants and monsters. The doom of the gods during Ragnarok is a shared fate that none of the individual gods, regardless of their particular powers or deeds, can escape.

Tolkien's mythology, especially in *The Lord of the Rings,* also tells of different types of collective fate shared by all the individuals in a particular group, regardless of their individual powers and exploits. In the concluding sections of this chapter, I examine two of these: the fate of all who bear one of the Rings of Power and the fate of the Elves at the end of the Third Age.

The fate of the Ring-bearers

All the beings who at one time or another are Ring-bearers *and* survive the War of the Ring share the same fate: They leave Middle-earth forever and journey to the Undying Lands of the Uttermost West at the end of the Third Age. Ring-bearers in this category include the following characters:

- **Elrond** who bears the Elven-Ring Vilya, the Ring of Air
- **Galadriel** who bears the Elven-Ring Nenya, the Ring of Water
- **Círdan the Shipwright** and then **Gandalf** who bear the Elven-Ring Narya, the Ring of Fire
- **Bilbo, Frodo,** and **Sam** who bear the One Ring of Power

Near the end of *The Lord of the Rings,* Sam accompanies Frodo on an outing to the Woody End, in the Shire's East Farthing. This is where, three years prior, they and Merry and Pippin encountered a band of Elves led by Gildor Inglorion of the House of Finrod. The Elves scared away a Black Rider who was very close to discovering the hobbits in the woods. Gildor's Elven band was on its way to the Grey Havens to go west to the Blessed Realm.

Now Frodo and Sam encounter another band of Elves making their way west, this one led by Elrond and Galadriel. Among their host is a very tired, 130 year-old Bilbo Baggins (it is September 22nd and therefore both Bilbo's and Frodo's birthday). Here, Frodo reveals to Sam that he is joining Bilbo, Elrond, and Galadriel on their journey to the Grey Havens.

Frodo explains to Sam that it's not yet Sam's time to join the Ring-bearers in their fate, though he may at some later time. Sam can remain in

Middle-earth because in bearing the Ring such a short time, he is still relatively whole. The presumption here is that both Bilbo and Frodo are too deeply wounded and divided by their experiences with the One Ring (remember what it did to Sméagol/Gollum?) to enjoy the peace they helped to restore to Middle-earth.

Frodo then goes on to make a speech which I feel speaks to the fate of many (contemporary) heroes and how they do not always get to enjoy the life they fought so hard to preserve. Frodo sums these feelings up to Sam by saying that although he helped to save the Shire, it was not saved for him.

When the troupe of hobbits and Elves get to the Grey Havens, they are met by the Elf Círdan the Shipwright, who welcomes them aboard the white ship bound for Aman. They are also greeted by Gandalf, who, bearing the Elven-Ring Narya openly for the first time, is joining them for the journey back to Aman and his home in Lórien (Chapter 2). Pippin and Merry appear to say farewell and accompany Sam back home to Bag End.

Many years later, upon the death of his beloved wife Rosie and after a long and productive life as Mayor of Hobbiton and gardener extraordinaire, Sam returns to the Grey Havens and, as the last of the Ring-bearers, follows Frodo to the Blessed Realm. Personally, when contemplating the question of whether Frodo is ever made whole in the Blessed Realm (a question I raise at the end of the section on Frodo in Chapter 7), I like to think that he is — just as soon as he's reunited with his beloved Sam. I picture them sitting with Gandalf on the Green Mound of Ezellohar, watching the sunset and all smoking in their pipes the closest thing to that great pipe weed Old Toby that they can come by in the Blessed Realm.

The fate of the Ring-bearers is truly bittersweet: Bitter in that they are denied the ability to enjoy the Middle-earth that they all fought so hard to save from destruction; sweet in that they are headed for the Blessed Realm where they all have a chance to rest and, in the case of Frodo, to become healed. Of this band of seven, only Gandalf and Galadriel have ever been to Aman before — for the rest of them it is a new experience.

Círdan the Shipwright was originally supposed to go to Aman with the main group of the Teleri Elves during the Great Journey during the Days of the Bliss of Valinor (see Chapter 11) but remained behind to lead a small contingent on the west coast of Beleriand. During the Second and Third Ages, Círdan dwelt at the Grey Havens. Sometime during the Fourth Age, the age of Dominion of Men, he finally makes it to Aman by boarding the last white ship out the Grey Havens headed for Aman.

I find it particularly beneficial to contrast the ultimate fate of those who bore Sauron's One Ring of Power with that of those who bore Fëanor's Silmarils. Despite bearing an object of great and corrupting evil (see Chapter 21), Bilbo, Frodo, and Sam are given the chance to find peace in the Undying Lands.

Contrast this with the fate of the bearers of Fëanor's Silmaril jewels, objects of great and uplifting good, who with the exception of Eärendil and Elwing, find no peace in Aman and are imprisoned for the duration of the world in the halls of Mandos with no hope of healing.

This comparison reminds me that it's not the relative purity or impurity of the objects we carry (that is, the burdens we bear) that determines our ultimate fate, but the purity or impurity of our hearts as we bear them.

The fate of the Elves in the Age of Men

During the Council of Elrond, when the fate of the One Ring is being discussed, the council members ask what would happen to the Elven-Rings of Power should their plan to unmake the One Ring succeed. Elrond explains his belief that once the One Ring is gone, the power of the three Elven-Rings will falter rather than be set free, and that many of the fair things of Middle-earth "will fade and be forgotten."

Under the Age of the Dominion of Men, ushered in by the destruction of Sauron through the unmaking of his One Ring, among the fair things that do undoubtedly fade and are in danger of being forgotten (at least until Tolkien came along) is the fair race of Elves. In fact, one way of interpreting *The Lord of the Rings* is to see it as Tolkien's explanation of why so few of us ever see the fair Elves in our world.

As Galadriel hints in Lothlórien after refusing to take the Ring Frodo offers her, she is destined to diminish and go into the West. For those Elves who do not follow her (including her husband, the remnant of her people who migrate from Lothlórien to Mirkwood Forest, and Legolas's people in the northern part of Mirkwood), the fate of diminishing importance in the world of Men seems unavoidable.

Celtic legends continue to speak of a tall, shining race of the fairy mound *daoine sídhe* (Gaelic, pronounced "dee-*nya* shee"), which is invisible to most mortals except during Samhain (pronounced "*sow*-in" — our Halloween) and Midsummer Eve, the evening of the summer solstice. But in other traditions, the Elves shrank both in stature and significance. Later ages diminished the Elves further, shriveling them down to the size of the wee people or pixies and, worse, associated them with the dark dwarves and gnomes of Germanic myth. As the final blow to their memory in modern times, the once noble Elves have been reduced to lawn statuary and children's cartoons.

If not for Tolkien and his enchanting tales about the Elves in his books on Middle-earth, this fair race might possibly have been fated to remain forever submerged in this most ignoble state, where their true beauty and significance for our lives would be in danger of totally vanishing from our world.

Chapter 20

Faith and Redemption

In This Chapter

▶ The roles of faith and hope in Middle-earth

▶ The great sin of despair according to Tolkien

▶ Atonement and redemption in Middle-earth

Many of the great myths of mankind are essentially stories of great faith — not just faith in a greater destiny, but faith in the love, kinship, and friendship of others. Of all of Tolkien's books, none shows his concern for the power of faith (he often calls it hope) better than *The Lord of the Rings*. Throughout, this book juxtaposes the themes of hope and despair, demonstrating what can be accomplished against great odds by means of the simple virtues of trust and mercy. It also illustrates how easily things can go awry and how evil can creep in when one loses hope and begins to despair.

This chapter examines the themes of faith and redemption in *The Silmarillion* and *The Lord of the Rings* with an eye toward understanding how they help the human spirit survive the many trials and tribulations of our contemporary world. It begins by looking at the role of faith in Tolkien's writings and then moves on to examine a couple of the numerous examples of how trust undermines Sauron's threat to Middle-earth and how its polar opposite despair bolsters Sauron's threat, almost bringing him victory.

The Role of Faith in Tolkien's Work

To understand the fundamental role of faith in Tolkien's writings, you have to hearken back to his treatment of good and evil. According to the *Ainulindalë* (The Music of the Ainur), the first book of *The Silmarillion*, dissonance first crept into the Music of the World when Melkor became impatient with the void and passionate to fill it. Melkor lost faith in Ilúvatar's plans to fill the void, and in his plan to use Melkor to achieve his design. The first sin, according to Tolkien's mythology, was not pride but *doubt* — a lack of trust in the order of things and the way they would ultimately play out.

This lack of faith runs like a thread through many of the tragic stories in the other books of *The Silmarillion*. For example, Fëanor's quarrel with his half-brother Fingolfin led to Fëanor's being banned from Tirion and set in motion a long list of tragedies — all because Fëanor lacked faith in his father's love. Túrin's mother sent him away to be fostered by the Elves of Doriath because she didn't trust the Easterlings and feared that they would carry off her son into servitude. Later, she refused to join him in Doriath, lacking faith in her ability to safely guide herself and his sister there from Dor-lómin.

But in contrast to these and other *Silmarillion* stories, Tolkien also wrote many in which hope and love win the day. You see hope in the stories of the friendship between the Elf-king Finrod Felagund and the Men of the House of Bëor, especially in the way Finrod honored his debt to Beren's father by aiding Beren in his quest for the Silmarils. Finrod gave up his life to save Beren from one of Sauron's werewolves. You also see hope at play in the love story of Beren and Lúthien: It guides Lúthien to follow Beren, even in death, all the way to the Halls of Mandos (see Chapter 18).

Pity saves the world

From faith in oneself and one's world comes charity for others. In Tolkien's story of Sauron's defeat, charity (which Tolkien calls pity and I think of as compassion or mercy) literally saves Middle-earth. Each hobbit Ring-bearer — Bilbo, Frodo, and Sam — is stopped at some point by compassion from slaying Gollum.

Compassion restrains Bilbo from doing in the poor old guy when he first finds the Ring in Gollum's cave and is desperate to escape him. Compassion comes into play when Frodo begs Faramir to stop his men from shooting Gollum as he poaches fish in the Forbidden Pool.

When Faramir urges Frodo to abandon Gollum and not follow him into Mordor, Frodo replies that he has promised to protect Gollum and to go where he leads him. Frodo asks Faramir if he would have him, in Tolkien's words, "break faith" with Gollum? This is interesting because Gollum is just about to break faith with Frodo and Sam by taking them to Cirith Ungol, the lair of the monstrous spider Shelob.

The last and most important time that compassion saves Gollum occurs on Mount Doom. Gollum has just attacked Frodo in a desperate attempt to prevent him from taking the Ring to the Crack of Doom. Sam sends Frodo on to complete his mission while remaining behind to deal with Gollum for the last time.

As Gollum begs for his life, Sam has no internal debate about whether Gollum *deserves* to die for his treachery at Cirith Ungol and now again on Mount Doom. Sam is convinced that finishing him off is the only *safe* thing to do.

Nevertheless, Tolkien says that some feeling deep in Sam's heart restrains him, even though he is unable to find words for how he feels. In a critical instant of mercy, Sam curses Gollum, orders him to be gone, and goes on up to attend to Frodo.

Note that Tolkien is very clear in this encounter that Gollum deserves death, but mercy stays Sam's hand (although he can't name that feeling at the time). Here, Tolkien is presenting the reader not with the concept of justice, the retribution that a criminal merits, but with the concept of mercy, the clemency that an offender has not earned but is granted nonetheless.

This theme of mercy rather than justice is one that Tolkien weaves in earlier in *The Lord of the Rings*. In typical word play, Frodo complains "what a pity" it is that Bilbo didn't kill Gollum when he had a chance. Gandalf replies that it was "pity and mercy: not to strike without need" that not only prevented Bilbo from murder, but quite possibly saved him from further wounding by the Ring's evil, which eventually enables him to give it up. Bilbo is the only Ring-bearer besides Sam who willingly gives up the Ring to another.

The idea that mercy saves us and justice doesn't is particularly difficult for modern audiences to identify with. We live in a world in which there seems to be precious little justice, so that more often than not we're tempted to see justice as a much more worthy, even if unreachable, goal than mercy. Mercy is often seen as a sign of weakness; justice, a sign of strength.

In contemplating their relative merits, it may be helpful to remember that our words *salvation* and *safe* are related. They come from the Latin *salvus,* meaning "healthy" and "secure" (*health* is related in turn to the Greek *holos,* meaning "whole" and "hale"). In my description of Sam's pity for Gollum, I italicized the word *safe* — Sam feels that killing Gollum would be the safe thing to do. But the truth is just the opposite: Slaying Gollum before he can fulfill his destiny would be unhealthy not just for Sam, but for all Middle-earth (see "Gollum's Atonement" later in this chapter).

Without pity for Gollum, the One Ring would never have been destroyed in the fires of Mount Doom, and Middle-earth would surely have been conquered by Sauron. By the time Sam shows this last act of mercy, despite his "better" judgment, the Ring has already taken Frodo. When attacked earlier by Gollum, Frodo prophetically warns the shrinking creature that if he ever touches him again, "you *shall* be cast into the Fire of *Doom*" (italics mine — see Chapter 19 for more on *shall* and *doom* in Tolkien's vocabulary).

By the time Frodo reaches the Crack of Doom to cast the ring into its fires, he shows a kind of righteousness — he feels entitled to challenge Sauron and claim the Ring as his own. This is reminiscent of Isildur's claim on the Ring as his rightful *weregild* (see Chapter 5).

In the nick of time, Gollum disabuses Frodo of this outlandish conceit by struggling with him for the Ring and taking both the Ring and himself to their mutual doom (in the sense of judgment and justice) in the fires below. Afterwards, awaiting their end on the side of Mount Doom, Frodo admits to Sam that Gollum's part was essential in completing the quest and for that reason he is worthy of their forgiveness (perhaps coming from compassion or charity).

The Sin of Despair

In Tolkien's world, the cardinal sin is not something as common and mundane as pride, lust, anger, or any of the other deadly sins — it is instead the sin of despair. As Gandalf explains at the Council of Elrond, despair is only for those who can see the end of an enterprise without any doubt. Underlying Gandalf's argument is the fact that none of us (save God, in Tolkien's view) can see the final end of the events in which we are placed. Therefore, we do not have the right to despair, although things may look bleak and the chances seem slight for the outcome we hope for.

"Where there's life, there's hope . . ."

On the journey from Henneth Annûn to Cirith Ungol, Sam counters despair with the old Gaffer's aphorism, "Where there's life, there's hope" — and then adds in typical hobbit fashion, "and a need of vittles." Ostensibly, Sam is trying to get Frodo to take a bite to eat. But Tolkien is reinforcing that we must all resist giving in to despair, although it is difficult, given the enormous problems we create for ourselves.

As essentially a child of the 20th century (he was born in 1892), Tolkien was keenly aware of widespread despair. Writing much of *The Lord of the Rings* during World War II and the early years of the cold war, he experienced firsthand events that at times surely tempted him to despair of humanity's ability to ever live in peace.

Denethor's despair

For everyone living in the cold war's uncertain aftermath, it's all too easy to lose faith in the future, constantly assailed as we are with problems whose solutions are ambiguous at best. When you are most prone to despair, remember the Old Gaffer's aphorism — and make sure that you get a few vittles in you as well. You might also remember Tolkien's cautionary tale of Denethor, the Steward of Gondor, and how his despair ended up taking his life and nearly taking the life of his only remaining son Faramir.

Frodo and his conception of justice over pity

The discussion between Gandalf and Frodo about pity versus justice regarding Gollum is crucial to understanding why Frodo fails at Mount Doom. Remember, Frodo begins carrying the Ring with the attitude that having it dumped on him is unjust. The Ring then may then use and amplify Frodo's attitude towards this injustice to ultimately control him, separating Frodo from the natural compassion that he shows throughout most of the story and replacing it with a strong sense of righteousness. The Ring uses this righteousness (a sense of entitlement) to get Frodo to challenge Sauron by claiming his Ring (which Frodo bore with great suffering) as his own rather than just throw it away into the fires of Mount Doom.

In *The Return of the King,* the third volume of *The Lord of the Rings,* Denethor is the aging Steward (custodian or keeper) of the Throne of Gondor. He is holding it until the day when the rightful king returns, if ever. During the War of the Ring, Denethor uses the Seeing Stone (palantír) of Minas Tirith to look into the future and see his city's fate in the upcoming Battle of Pelennor Fields (see Chapter 24) as well as the fate of the West in defeating Sauron. Unfortunately, Sauron makes sure that Denethor sees only the future events that Sauron wants him to see. These include the black ships of the Corsairs of Umbar sailing up to Minas Tirith to turn the tide in the battle.

What Denethor is not shown in the palantír is that Aragorn will have commandeered these ships — they will turn the tide of the battle in favor of the West. Without this vital information, Denethor convinces himself of the folly of resisting the enemy at the gates of Minas Tirith. In his despair, he attempts to immolate (burn to death) both himself and his ailing son Faramir. Gandalf saves Faramir from the fire and tries to dissuade Denethor from suicide. Denethor ignores Gandalf's words, lights his funeral pyre anyway, and lies down on it — and then reveals the palantír he's been using to see the future. (It is said that ever afterward, anyone who looks in the palantír sees only the two aged hands of Denethor surrounded by flames.)

When considering the message in this tale, please remember that when you think you have all the facts about your future and you're certain that there is no hope for the future, you may not have all the facts or, more likely than not, you may not be interpreting them correctly — like Denethor's reading of the black ships. If, as Tolkien says, despair is for those who know the future beyond doubt, you would do well to remember how difficult it is to know anything that certainly in life, especially those things that haven't come to pass. And in that little doubt, strangely enough, you may find your way back to hope.

Acts of Redemption

The Lord of the Rings is full of stories that point to the power of faith and imply redemption for those who lose it along the way. You could see the Fellowship of the Ring as a ring of faith that counters the Ring of Power. Even though the Fellowship breaks up before destroying the Ring, the bonds of trust among its members continue long after the Ring is gone.

In this section, I examine two acts of redemption in *The Lord of the Rings* and discuss how Boromir and Gollum's deaths atone for their earlier acts of faith-lessness.

Boromir's redemption

Of all the members of the Fellowship of the Ring, Boromir is the one who most lacks faith in the wisdom of the decision of the Council of Elrond to take the Ring to Mordor to be destroyed. As far as he can see, this folly is tanta-mount to hand-delivering it to Sauron — they might as well put the Ring in a box with a pretty ribbon around it.

Boromir's doubt grows as the Fellowship comes to the western side of Nen Hithoel ("Lake of Mist"). There, he confronts Frodo while they are separated from the rest of the company. His lack of faith turns to despair when Frodo refuses to "lend" him the Ring to use in defense of Minas Tirith. Frodo naturally flees Boromir's madness, resolving to go on alone to Mordor (although he can't escape Sam, despite his best efforts).

By the time Boromir comes to his senses, Frodo has slipped on the Ring and is long gone. Boromir, regretting his actions and words, calls to Frodo in vain. When Boromir returns to the company, he makes light of his encounter with Frodo, saying only that he became angry with the hobbit, who disappeared before his very eyes. Before splitting up to find Frodo, Aragorn asks Boromir to look after Merry and Pippin. Thus ends *The Fellowship of the Ring,* the first volume of *The Lord of the Rings.*

The Two Towers begins with Aragorn hearing the horn of Boromir from the top of Amon Hen. By the time Aragorn finds him in Parth Galen ("Green Sward"), Boromir is mortally wounded, and Merry and Pippin are gone, having been abducted by the Uruk-hai against which Boromir had tried in vain to protect them.

In a death scene much briefer than the one in Jackson's movie version, Boromir admits that he tried to steal the Ring from Frodo and asks forgive-ness. With his dying breath, Boromir asks Aragorn to go to Minas Tirith and save his people and declares that he has failed. Aragorn disagrees by telling him that he has conquered and gained a rare victory. He also tells Boromir to be at peace, for "Minas Tirith shall not fall." Boromir smiles and then dies.

Tolkien follows this touching death scene with a description of Boromir's sea-funeral (described in Chapter 16) that shows us that Boromir has found peace and has indeed atoned for attacking Frodo. The Elven boat — bearing Boromir's body, broken shield, horn, and weapons of the many enemies he slew in his last battle — passes safely down the Falls of Rauros and sails down the Great River, past Osgiliath, through the Mouth of Anduin, heading west (towards the Blessed Realm) to the open sea under the stars.

Although Boromir does fall prey to his fears, Tolkien shows how he overcomes and redeems himself by laying down his life for the hobbits, Merry and Pippin. His show of valor and courage in their defense redresses his previous shortcomings, making him, in my opinion, the most human of the heroes in *The Lord of the Rings*.

Gollum's atonement

Gollum starts out his Ring-bearing days with one great big strike against him: He murders his friend Déagol, who found the One Ring in a tributary of the Anduin River. From the descriptions of Gollum and the One Ring, it seems that for Gollum, the Ring is simply a bright and shiny gold band with the great magical property of making him invisible to his enemies. (In this gold lust, Gollum resembles the *Volsung Saga*'s Dwarf Andvari, who lusted for his magic golden ring that made more gold — see Chapter 21).

Until Bilbo happens upon Gollum in his cave more than 400 years later, Gollum is quite isolated and completely enslaved to his lust and need for the Ring. Through Gandalf's words to Frodo, Tolkien makes sure we're aware that the Sméagol/Gollum split in his personality (which makes him refer to himself more often than not as "we" and "us") mirrors a love/hate relationship. As Gandalf says to Frodo, "Gollum both loves and hates the Ring as he loves and hates himself."

Sméagol/Gollum's internal struggle is amazing considering the power of the One Ring (see Chapter 21) and the long time he bears it. As I argue in Chapter 17, Gollum is the unintentional hero of *The Lord of the Rings,* sacrificing himself and the Ring in fulfillment of the oath he swore to Frodo to never let Sauron have it. In his final encounter with Sam, Gollum begs Sam to let him live "just a little longer," telling him that he is lost, for when the Precious (Ring) goes, Gollum will go as well. In fighting Frodo for the Ring and taking it into the Fire of Mount Doom, Gollum atones for his many sins, including the initial slaying of his friend Déagol.

Gollum's murder of his friend for the Ring hearkens back to the biblical story of Cain and Abel — the first murder. Oddly enough, the Cain and Abel story is also the story of the first redemption of a sinner. As you may recall, Cain (Adam and Eve's firstborn) killed his younger brother Abel after God rejected Cain's sacrifice of the fruits of the earth and accepted Abel's, one of the finest sheep in his flock. After confronting Cain with the enormity of his sin, God condemned him to be a fugitive who would live in fear for his life — much like Gollum, who was forced to leave his folk and go into seclusion in the Misty Mountains. In extreme remorse for his sin and its dire consequences, Cain asked God if his iniquity was too great to be forgiven. In response, God vowed seven-fold vengeance on anyone who would slay Cain and put upon him His sign, marking him as having received God's mercy.

Instead of a "mark of Cain," Gollum carries the mark of the One Ring, until reclaiming the Ring from Frodo's hand and sacrificing himself in the Fire of Doom. In his death, which saves Middle-earth from Sauron's domination, Gollum also saves himself from the Ring's domination. He buys his own freedom and the freedom of all Middle-earth with his death (which he predicts shortly before, when begging mercy from Sam), while at the same time atoning for his murder, treachery, and unfaithfulness.

Chapter 21

Ring-related Myths

The Rings of Power in Tolkien's *Lord of the Rings* are compelling symbols that continue to stir the imaginations of readers, along with the many fans of the Peter Jackson movie trilogy. This chapter looks at the mythology of the Ring in Tolkien's work and compares it with other, older symbolism and mythologies having to do with rings.

The chapter begins by exploring the symbolism of rings, especially from medieval times to the present. It then goes on to take a closer look at the power of the Rings over the beings of Middle-earth and compares this with the things that tend to reel us in and bind us in darkness. The chapter concludes by examining older Norse and Germanic ring sagas, evaluating their influence on Tolkien's conception of Sauron's One Ring of Power, and looking at possible meanings for modern mankind's One Ring.

Ring Symbolism

The ring, a circular form with neither beginning nor end, is an age-old symbol of eternity, unity, and perfection. Traditionally, rings, especially those inscribed with magic or holy words, were reputed to protect the wearer. For example, for medieval Christians, rings inscribed with the names of the Holy Family or the Three Magi were supposed to protect the wearer from the Evil Eye and the plague (for more on the Evil Eye and Sauron, see Chapter 10).

Rings made of special metals were believed to have healing properties. In particular, rings fashioned by melting the first five silver coins placed in the Church's communion plate while saying prayers were said to cure cramps. These "cramp rings" could also be made from coins donated by five unmarried members of the opposite sex, although the most effective were said to be made from old coffin fittings (not exactly my first choice for jewelry).

Rings were and still are symbols of fidelity. Often, an oath of fealty (loyalty) to a feudal lord was sworn on a ring presented by the lord to his new vassal. In fact, the homage ceremony was very much like the modern-day marriage ceremony; it was customary for the vassal and the lord to clasp hands during the recitation part, and the ceremony was sealed, literally, with a kiss.

The oaths to the lord were often sworn in church, or on the lord's estate, and often upon holy relics of saints that the lord or his family had picked up on a crusade to the Holy Land. Typical oaths were promises of faithfulness every bit as all-encompassing as those exchanged by a bride and groom: One Anglo-Saxon version reads something like "I shall be true and faithful, and love all that he loves and shun all that he shuns . . ."

In addition to the pledge of loyalty sworn on rings, a lord also rewarded faithful and victorious knights with war bands — arm-rings of gold and silver. This practice gave rise to the expression *a ring-giving lord* found in epic poems, such as *Beowulf*, to which Tolkien devoted much study. These war bands symbolized the mutual bond between lord and vassal and were expressions of the lord's pleasure with the vassal as his knight.

Nowadays, the custom of bestowing rings as symbols of fealty is reserved mostly for engagements and weddings. Many believe that the engagement ring tradition, in which the woman promises fidelity until she and her future husband are married, is a holdover from the lord-to-vassal ring exchange. The custom of exchanging wedding rings during the wedding ceremony seems to be relatively recent. It was unknown in England until the 19th century, although the newlyweds would sometimes exchange rings afterwards. Today, no wedding ceremony is complete without it.

In *The Lord of the Rings*, you can see that Tolkien uses rings both as magic talismans and as symbols of fidelity. And although the magic carried by his Rings of Power varies according to the race for which they were intended, they were forged for the single purpose of forcing the wearer into undying fealty to none other than the king of all baddies — the Dark Lord Sauron.

The Powers of Tolkien's Rings

In case you've forgotten, Celebrimbor and his Elven smiths fashioned 19 Rings of Power: three for the Elves, seven for the Dwarves, and nine for Men. They made all this jewelry for Sauron, who was disguised as a "good guy" named Annatar, Lord of Gifts. Annatar talked up how he wanted to help heal the hurts that Middle-earth had suffered (he first went to Elrond and Gil-galad with that story, but they would have none of what he was selling).

By the time the Elven smiths of Eregion discovered that Sauron was no Lord of Gifts and had secretly forged a master Ring to control the Rings of Power they had created, they had already given him the Dwarves' and Men's Rings. Fortunately, they still had the three Elven-Rings, so although the fates of these three Rings are tied to his One Ring, their magic is free of his evil.

The Power of the Elven-Rings: Vilya, Nenya, and Narya

Because the Elven-Rings of Power are unsullied by Sauron's hands, they do not corrupt their bearers as do the ones for Dwarves and Men. Indeed, the Elven-Rings, named Vilya, Nenya, and Narya, protect their bearers from the Eye of Sauron (similar to the medieval rings that warded off the Evil Eye).

Originally, Celebrimbor gave the three Rings of Power to the Elf-lords Gil-galad, Galadriel, and Círdan. Before Gil-galad died at the hands of Sauron at the end of the Second Age (see Chapter 12), he gave his Ring, Vilya, the blue sapphire Ring of Air and most powerful of the three, to Elrond. When Gandalf came to Middle-earth, Círdan the Shipwright gave him Narya, the red Ring of Fire, to help him with his upcoming trials in Middle-earth and to reawaken the hearts of those in a world grown cold.

Elrond and Galadriel's Rings not only protect them from the Eye of Sauron but also protect their Elven kingdoms from his evil and prevent their peoples from succumbing to the Elven disease of world weariness (see Chapter 4).

It's interesting to note that unlike Sauron's Ring, which renders the wearer invisible, the Elven-Rings are *themselves* invisible on the bearer's finger. Only Frodo can see the Ring on Galadriel's hand when it catches the rays of Eärendil's star; she explains that he can see it because he bears Sauron's Ring and has already seen his Eye. When Galadriel asks Sam if he noticed the Ring on her hand, he says only that he saw a star between her fingers. So, too, none of the Fellowship notices that Gandalf is wearing Narya until he appears at the Grey Havens just prior to boarding the white ship.

Although Sauron wants these three Elven-Rings of Power to control the Elf-lords and, in turn, all their people, it's unclear how these Rings would have done so — that is, how they would ". . . bring them all and in the darkness bind them." Because the Elven-Rings were not tainted by Sauron's touch, we will never know exactly how Tolkien intended these Rings to corrupt and control the Elves. If I had to venture a guess, it probably had would deepen the Elves' propensity to become weary of the world's trouble — the only disease that affects them (see Chapter 4).

The Rings' Powers over Dwarves and Men

Whereas the Elven-Rings of Power are benign and even beneficial to the Elves, the ones designed for Dwarves and Men are not. The Dwarf-Rings generate a lust for gold so intense that nothing else in the world matters.

The seven Dwarf-Rings' power to snare their lords by generating intense desire for more gold is not entirely original. Andvari's ring in the *Volsung Saga* was said to have the power to create more and more gold in the hands of a Dwarf; this is why Andvari was so reluctant to turn it over to Loki (see "Ring-related Sagas in Norse and Germanic Mythology" later in this chapter).

The nine Rings of Power for the Lords of Men seem to convey immortality, which is what Men want most — but at a terrible cost. The Lords who wore these Rings became neither living nor dead. They turned into the Ringwraiths, enslaved to Sauron's will and the power of his One Ring.

The Power of the One Ring

Unlike the other 19 Rings, Sauron's One Ring is just a plain gold band with no stone. The only indication that it is the One Ring is that when heated, inscriptions appear on it (see Figure 21-1). The outside inscription reads

```
One Ring to rule them all, One Ring to find them
```

and the inside one goes

```
One Ring to bring them all and in the darkness bind them
```

Both inscriptions are in the highly cursive and extremely beautiful Tengwar letters (see Chapter 14). But in this case, they transcribe the Black Speech of Mordor, and therefore the words are very harsh-sounding to hear.

Tolkien's idea of engraving the One Ring with a powerful incantation is right in line with the old custom I mentioned of engraving a ring with magic words. However, instead of protecting the wearer, this spell bewitches and subdues.

We know from Gandalf that the One Ring contains much of Sauron's power and evil. In Sauron's hands, the Ring controls all the other Rings of Power, enabling him to perceive and control the wills of their wearers. The only exceptions to this are the three Elven-Rings that he never touched. Nevertheless, Elrond says at the Council of Rivendell that the Elven-Rings are still linked to the One Ring, and that he believes that should the One Ring be destroyed, the three Rings may well lose their powers as well.

The Magical Inscriptions on the One Ring of Power

Outside Inscription:

*Ash nazg durbatulûk * Ash nazg gimbatul*

Inside Inscription:

*Ash nazg thrakatulûk * Agh burzum-ishi krimpatul*

The biggest problem with Sauron's One Ring is that it exerts an evil influence over almost anyone who wears it. While seeming only to render its wearer invisible, the One Ring amplifies the wearer's desires and uses them to control him.

In many ways, the One Ring gains mastery over its bearer just like any addiction — food, sex, drugs, rock n' roll, you name it. The Ring seems to intensify the wearer's desires — usually high-minded desires for the good guys in the tale, such as saving Middle-earth and restoring justice. At the same time, it masks fears and hesitations. As time goes on, the Ring-bearer relies more and more on the power of the Ring to accomplish his needs and gives up more and more of his own will in return. This "wraithing" process continues until the personality of the Ring-bearer completely fades out, leaving only dependence on the Ring.

This addictive trap is why powerful figures for good, such as Gandalf and Galadriel, refuse to take the One Ring when Frodo offers it to them. Gandalf knows that his desire to save Middle-earth would be greatly aided by the power of the Ring. He also realizes that the Ring's power would use his desire to pursue these high-minded goals to ultimately enslave him to its power. Galadriel is aware that possessing the Ring could prevent the fate she fears most for her and her people: dwindling away into the wee folk that will eventually fade from memory. At the same time, she understands that the price would be to totally lose herself, becoming a terrifying and beautiful goddess who inspired both love and fear and demanded the worship of all.

The only one who seems completely immune to the Ring's corrupting influence is Tom Bombadil. When he puts on the One Ring, he does not disappear, and when Frodo puts it on, Tom can still see him even though he's invisible to Sam, Merry, and Pippin. It may be that Tom escapes the Ring's influence because he harbors neither the desire nor fear that the Ring requires in order to control him. Unfortunately, Tom also lacks the drive to save Middle-earth from peril and is therefore an unfit custodian or bearer for the One Ring (see Chapter 9).

In his immunity to the Ring's evil, Tom is literally one of a kind, for even the hobbits with their rather modest and mundane desires and fears fall prey to the Ring. As I argue in Chapter 7, the hobbits fortunately are of such humble ambition that they can bear the Ring far longer than the other beings of Middle-earth before being taken by its evil. This is why only they can destroy the One Ring (see Chapter 19 for more on the hobbits as Ring-bearers).

Ring-related Sagas in Norse and Germanic Mythology

Tolkien was by no means the first mythmaker to put a powerful ring at the center of his story. He was well aware of the mythological themes surrounding magical rings in medieval Scandinavian and German sources, which also inspired the 19th century operatic cycle by Richard Wagner titled *Der Ring des Nibelungen (The Ring of the Nibelung)*.

The *Volsung Saga* told the heroic and tragic story of the family of Volsung, the grandson of Odin and king of the Huns — in particular, Volsung's son, the great hero Sigmund, and the latter's posthumous son Sigurd. Their tales apparently were sufficiently popular among Anglo-Saxons that an early form of Sigurd's part of the story was quoted (using the name Sigemund) within Tolkien's favorite epic poem *Beowulf,* when a minstrel sang its song for Beowulf and his warriors.

The story of the Nibelung family told in the medieval German *Nibelungenlied* uses many of the same characters as the *Volsung Saga* (although the German versions are a little different). This work was apparently based on much older traditions. The *Nibelungenlied,* however, seems more historical and less mythological than the *Volsung Saga,* though both tell essentially the same story. When Richard Wagner adapted the stories of the *Nibelungenlied* and the *Volsung Saga* for *Der Ring des Nibelungen,* he re-mythologized it so that it appeared much more like a dragon-slaying heroic tale from the age of *Beowulf* than a medieval romance epic of chivalry and courtly love.

By the way, both the *Nibelungenlied* and the *Volsung Saga* include tales of a hero's broken sword that must be reforged (shades of Elendil's sword Narsil reforged as Andúril for Aragorn). And both tell the story of a Dwarf who has a magic gold ring upon which he lays a curse when it's stolen from him.

The ring of the "Volsung Saga"

The ring of the *Volsung Saga* is called Andvarinaut ("Andvari's loom") because in the hands of the Dwarf Andvari, the ring can produce more gold. This ring is sometimes associated by mythologists with Draupnir, a Dwarf-made arm ring of the chief Norse god Odin's that cloned gold rings like itself, thus producing an ever-increasing hoard of treasure. When Loki, the trickster god, stole Andvari's ring to make *wergild* (gold paid for the wrongful killing of another), Andvari cursed the ring and the treasure that went with it, declaring that it will be a bane for all who possess it.

Andvari's curse on his magic ring is similar to Fëanor's curse on the Silmarils in *The Silmarillion.* With Tolkien's Rings of Power in *The Lord of the Rings,* there's no parallel curse because the Rings have a built-in curse of enslavement and control. Andvari's curse on his magic ring was every bit as effective as Fëanor's was on his Silmaril jewels, for everyone who possessed the Andvarinaut was loathe to give it up, and all who see it are quite willing to kill to possess it.

Although Tolkien's One Ring is not cursed like Andvari's ring (it is more like the curse itself), it does share some of the same negative characteristics. For one thing, no one who bears the One Ring ever gives it up easily, and few do it willingly. Only Bilbo and Sam give the Ring up by their own free will, and it is quite a struggle for Bilbo at that. Gollum, of course, kills to possess it the moment he sees it in Déagol's hand. And Boromir is ready to take the Ring from Frodo by force if necessary when he confronts him at Parth Galen.

Wagner's ring cycle

Richard Wagner's operatic version of the story of the *Nibelungenlied* was first performed at Bayreuth in 1876, a scant 16 years before Tolkien's birth. Wagner, like Tolkien, was attempting to reintroduce his people to their mythological heritage by bringing them a heroic saga, each of which just happened to involve a ring of power.

Wagner's four-part version of the Nibelung ring quest reflects the romantic longings of Europe in the latter half of the 19th century, just as surely as Tolkien's *Lord of the Rings* reflects Europe's postmodern longings. From the opening scene in the first part *Das Rhinegold,* with Rhine-maidens playing in the water before the lustful Alberich the Dwarf, until the final scene in *Götterdämmerung* when Brunnhilde takes the ring from Sigfried's dead hand, places it on her finger, and rides his steed Grane into the flames of Sigfried's funeral pyre, Wagner's myth is full of romantic longing for love gained and then lost. From the opening scene at Bilbo's 111th birthday party in *The Fellowship of the Ring* until the final scene in *The Return of the King* of the Ring-bearers' wistful departure from the Grey Havens, Tolkien's myth expresses postmodern longings for an older, steadfast way of life, which has been lost and never quite regained.

In Wagner's saga, the ring takes on some decidedly modern features that may well have influenced Tolkien's One Ring. In Wagner's retelling, the Rhinegold was a goldstone from which a gold ring could be forged that enabled its owner to control the world. The catch was that only one who completely renounced love and all its pleasures could ever take the Rhinegold and fashion it into such a ring.

Well, this was an offer far too good to refuse for a certain Dwarf named Alberich (Andvari's name in the German version), who was far too much of a troll to win anyone's affections anyway. Therefore, he was quite willing and able to curse all love, steal the gold, and forge the ring that let him rule the world (the old "if you can't have love, you might as well have power" philosophy).

As with Wagner's magic ring, Tolkien's was forged by a skilled smith who had renounced all love and cared only for power. Sauron was first an apprentice to the Vala Aulë the Smith before serving Melkor (see Chapter 3). Likewise, Tolkien's One Ring, like Wagner's, enables its master to control the world. Indeed, the fact that Sauron needs only to regain the One Ring in order to be assured of total mastery over Middle-earth is the major plot device operating throughout *The Lord of the Rings*.

One big difference between the two ring myths is that in Tolkien's tales, the heroic characters fight constantly to destroy Sauron's One Ring rather than to use it against him. Tolkien's approach to a ring that can control the world is the sensible "get rid of it by any means, for heaven's sake" rather than the more predictable "fight fire with fire" by using the Ring against its maker. And instead of everything going up in smoke at the end of the final act, as in the *Götterdämmerung*, the fate of Middle-earth is somewhat more hopeful — only Sauron, his evil tower of Barad-dûr, and his minions suffer that fate.

The Power of the One Ring in Modern Life

The big question that seems to come up in any discussion of Tolkien's Rings of Power is: What does the One Ring symbolize in our lives? Almost from the inception of *The Lord of the Rings*, readers have debated the symbolism of the One Ring, often to Tolkien's dismay.

The most common answer that readers and book critics come up with seems to be nuclear weapons. And naturally enough, for the longest period of the book's published life, the world endured a terrible nuclear arms race with nuclear deterrent strategies that threatened the existence of everyone on the planet. The threat of nuclear war controlled world politics and very definitely threatened to bring us all in the darkness and bind us. Plus, just as the One Ring is linked with the fires of Mount Doom, nuclear weapons burn with the same fire as the sun. Not to mention that the name of the element used as nuclear fuel — plutonium — comes from the god of the underworld (Pluto), bringing to mind the fires of Hell.

The other big candidate as the symbol of the Ring in modern times is technology. Our ever-growing dependence on the technology we create and the widening separation from nature fits nicely with many of the themes in *The Lord of the Rings*. You see Tolkien's comment on the gulf between nature and technology in the war between Saruman and the Ents of Fangorn Forest. I often think of Saruman as the perfect technocrat (his name could be translated from Old English as "Science Man" or "Crafty Man"). For him, understanding and control go hand in hand (for more on Saruman, see Chapters 8 and 22).

If you consider the full force of the Ring's inscription (refer to the earlier section "The Power of the One Ring" if you need a refresher), technology does seem to fit very well. After all, it is definitely something that's beginning to rule us all. Considering all the Big Brother-type listening devices, satellites, and hidden cameras everywhere you go, technology surely seems quite capable of finding us all. For all its bright points, modern technology, at least as a spoiler of our environment, does threaten to bring us all into the darkness and bind us there (see Chapter 22 for more on the ecological themes in *The Lord of the Rings*).

The only problem with pegging technology as the One Ring is that according to Tolkien's myth, the One Ring is far too powerful for anyone to wield and must be therefore be destroyed. Not only is it extremely unlikely that mankind will abandon technology, it's probably far too late for that anyway. If we are to survive, surely we must find a way to use technology to correct past mistakes as well as learn how to use technology wisely in partnership with the planet. Our reliance on technology doesn't seem open to the solution of simply casting it back into the fires of Mount Doom, so to speak.

In the end, I don't think the One Ring has one particular meaning for our modern world. In Chapter 16, I argue that the fear of death could possibly be the One Ring of Power — I now encourage you to examine what desires or fears control *you* in the way the One Ring controls the beings of Middle-earth. Then maybe you can evaluate how you manage to bear your One Ring and eventually determine how and when you'll eliminate it. For your inspiration in this task, you can always look to Tolkien's story of how peoples face and eliminate together the threat to their world.

Chapter 22

Ecological Themes

Any ecological or "green" themes found in Tolkien's fiction are the result of Tolkien's modern mind looking at a very modern situation. After all, until very recent times, Europeans (whose ancestors these beings of Middle-earth are supposed to be) saw nature primarily as a hostile force to be conquered rather than a fragile web of interdependent life in danger of unraveling.

This chapter looks at the ecological themes Tolkien tucked into his stories about Middle-earth. It considers the fouling of the Shire by Sharkey's men during the War of the Ring as an ecological crisis. It also examines the healing of the Shire and compares it to our attempts to clean up our world. The chapter concludes with a look at the Ents' marching to war on Isengard, and how that can signify nature's rebellion against our continuing disregard of our environment.

The Fouling of the Shire

Because all Tolkien's stories about Middle-earth take place well before the Industrial Revolution, you may find the notion of ecological crisis there a bit bizarre. You'd think that probably the worst polluters in Middle-earth would be fire-breathing dragons, such as Glaurung and Smaug the Golden, but dragons are all extinct by the time of the War of the Ring in the Third Age.

Tolkien has a way of making the primary evil-doers, Melkor in Beleriand and Sauron in Middle-earth proper, appear as the worst polluters of all time. His descriptions of their realms conjure up images of dead zones or no-man's lands, with all the warmth and life of slag heaps and waste dumps. Mordor in particular is almost devoid of living things. Frodo and Sam have difficulty even finding decent water to drink. The entire area gives the impression of the desolation after a war or plague.

But it's not Mordor that shows Tolkien's great concern for the environment so much as the Shire and the devastation done to it during the War of the Ring. When Sam looks in Galadriel's mirror, he sees a terrible vision of the Shire's future, a preview of the eco-damage that Sauron's rule could bring to all of Middle-earth. The mirror shows Sam's neighbor Ted Sandyman cutting down trees that don't need felling, followed by the horrific vision of some sort of red brick, smoke-belching, factory-like mill (with lots of busy folks at work) that has replaced Sandyman's water-powered mill. The final horror for Sam is the sight of Bagshot Row all dug up, and the Gaffer bringing down bits of junk in a wheelbarrow.

The "semi-industrialized" future for the Shire is like something out of a Dickens novel. Unfortunately for Tolkien's hobbit heroes, they return to a Shire that's very much as prefigured by Galadriel's magic mirror. The Old Mill is indeed replaced by a mill with an immense chimney that not only spews out black smoke but discharges stinking waste into the water below, which Farmer Cotton says reaches all the way to the Brandywine River. In addition, they find that all the trees along Bywater Road have been cut down, including the Party Tree under which Bilbo gave his farewell speech on his 111th birthday.

The hobbits also discover that Bagshot Row, the area on the Hill where Sam and the old Gaffer live, has become a gravel quarry, and Bag End above can't be seen for all the sheds and hovels that have been put up. All Sam can say after bursting into tears at the sight of the felled Party Tree is that seeing their home violated in this way is worse than Mordor because they can remember how it was before it was ruined. Frodo says the fouling of the Shire is indeed a "work of Mordor."

Frodo and Sam discover that the man behind this destruction is called Sharkey — or the Boss, as he's affectionately known to his ruffian henchmen — and then that Sharkey is none other than Saruman himself (see Chapter 8 for more on Saruman). After his defeat and imprisonment by the Ents at Isengard, Saruman comes to the Shire to spread his polluting ways and exact his revenge on the hobbits, whom he holds responsible for wrecking his home at Orthanc (see "When the Ents Go to War" later in this chapter).

Sharkey's curse

When Frodo and the three other Travelers (the name the hobbits give Frodo, Sam, Merry, and Pippin upon their return) confront Sharkey/Saruman at Bag End and demand that he leave, the wizard tells them that he has done much to the Shire that they will find difficult to mend or undo in their lifetimes. When the other hobbits call for Sharkey's death rather than exile, he replies that if they stain the Shire with his blood, it will wither and never be healed again. Here, Sharkey is both the polluter who wantonly spoils the environment and the technocrat who curses the land.

The fouling of the Shire shows real contempt for the environment and utter disregard for its care, stemming from a profit motive like the one that has been so hard for environmentalists in our age to counter. The profit motive surfaces when Pimple, Farmer Cotton's sarcastic name for Lotho, of the so-called Sackville-Bagginses, starts buying up property all over the Shire, including Sandyman's Old Mill, while selling pipe-weed to Saruman in Isengard. (This explains the pipe-weed that Merry and Pippin find after the Ents attack Isengard.) Then strange men that the hobbits call ruffians appear from the south and start felling trees and planting pipe-weed in their place. Eventually, Pimple names himself the Chief, and he and his men start making new rules and tossing hobbits in prison. The irony, as Tolkien points out in Farmer Cotton's story, is that as the Shire under the Chief starts producing more pipe-weed for export to Isengard, the hobbits suffer their first ever pipe-weed shortage.

Unlike Lotho (the self-appointed Chief of the Shire), Saruman/Sharkey, the real Chief behind it all, is not motivated to pollute the Shire by a simple desire for quick profit and power. Saruman seems driven rather by a more sinister and longstanding contempt for the environment stemming from his elevated view of his own knowledge and his ability to divorce this knowledge from ethics. Out of this comes his brand of Machiavellian philosophy in which "the ends justify the means" (see Chapter 8 for more on this).

In the long run, it may be the scientists and technocrats who have adopted a Saruman/Sharkey-type philosophy towards knowledge who are more of a threat to the environment than the Pimples of the world. After all, a Pimple can be swayed to stop fouling his nest just by making it worth his while economically not to do so, whereas a Sharkey is quite another matter. His fundamental approach to knowledge is the problem, for it enables him to stand apart from his environment and adopt a superior stance to it. Until a technocrat like Saruman can integrate his extensive knowledge into a philosophy that does not put control above the preserving integrity of the ecosystem, he will, in the words of Frodo, do the work of Mordor.

The irony is that Saruman/Sharkey originally has no intention of doing Sauron's bidding, any more than a technologist starts out intending to harm the environment. As Frodo says, Saruman thinks he is doing his own work, but all the time he's doing the work of Mordor, just as most scientists see themselves as simply in the business of increasing the overall knowledge of the world, with no intention of contributing to the degradation of its environment.

Healing the Shire

In Tolkien's Middle-earth, Sharkey's curse foretells that much of the environmental damage he's done may not be reversible during the hobbits' lifetimes. This, of course, is just as true in our Middle-earth, where much of the environmental degradation we're responsible for will take long years to repair, assuming that we even try. Some of the injury that we've caused, such as the extinction of species, is irreparable. Other environmental problems, such as global warming and the impairment of the ozone layer, may be mended, but will take long decades, perhaps beyond most of our lifetimes.

In terms of healing the environmental damage done to the Shire, the hobbits are of one mind; they labor together to quickly remove the blights from their countryside, an effort known as the scouring of the Shire. They pull down all the structures put up by Sharkey's ruffians, including the new mill. They fill in the gravel pit on the Hill, plant a garden on it, and clear Bag End. Finally, they restore Bagshot Row by putting new hobbit holes on the back of the hill (lined with brick taken from some of Sharkey's dismantled structures). This new development of hobbit holes is simply known as New Row, although many hobbits wanted it named either Battle Row or Better Smials (for Old English *smygel,* "a burrow"); unofficially, it is known as "Sharkey's End," a pun referring to where Saruman/Sharkey met his demise.

The damage done to the trees of the Shire is not so easily fixed. Luckily, Sam remembers the box that Galadriel gave him as one of his parting gifts in Lothlórien. This box contains a single nut-shaped seed with a silver shell and a fine grey dust that Sam uses to restore as many of the felled trees as possible: At the base of each tree that he replants across the Shire, he places a single grain of the Lothlórien dust. In the place where the Party Tree stood, he plants the silver-coated seed.

The following spring, all the trees that Sam planted have grown as though they had been planted twenty years prior (that was some kind of pixie dust that Galadriel put in Sam's gift box!). Where Bilbo's Party Tree once stood sprouts a beautiful mallorn tree sapling. The only tree of its kind east of the sea and west of the Misty Mountains, Sam's mallorn has silver bark and golden flowers — a cross between the silver tree Telperion and the golden tree Laurelin in Aman. In addition to the bounty of the trees, the crop harvest that year (Shire Reckoning 1420) is more plentiful than ever, including both corn (called wheat in the United States) and pipe-weed. The barley and malt harvested that year make such outstanding ale that ales ever after are compared to it.

Regrettably, our world lacks anything like Galadriel's magic dust for quickly repairing the ecological damage we're inflicting on our Shires. It even seems these days that we lack the will of the hobbits to pull together to clean up the damage and make amends for the hurts that we've allowed our ruffians to do to our communities in the name of progress and profit.

For me, this overall lack of will to retake and scour our Shires as much a "work of Mordor" as the continued fouling of the environment is. For without such a will, even the discovery of Galadriel's magic soil would not save us from eco-catastrophe.

When the Ents Go to War

For many readers, including me, one of the most intriguing stories in *The Two Towers* volume of *The Lord of the Rings* is the encounter between Merry and Pippin and the Ents when they march to war against Saruman in Isengard (see Chapter 24). In this war against Saruman — who, in the words of the Ent leader Treebeard, has no regard "for growing things except as they serve him for the moment" — Tolkien shows the power of nature to fight back against the ecological injustices perpetrated against it. Beyond simply a more satisfying version of Shakespeare's marching forest in *Macbeth* (see the sidebar in Chapter 9 for more on this), I see a cautionary tale in the Ents' war of Mother Nature someday rising up and giving us the boot for our utter disregard for the growing things of her realm.

The Ents, who are the shepherds of Middle-earth's forests, are as much the children of Yavanna (Tolkien's goddess of the livings things and our equivalent to Mother Nature) as the Dwarves are the children of her mate Aulë the Smith. In Middle-earth biology there are two types of living things: olvar, the growing things rooted in the ground, and kelvar, the mobile living things.

Remember that as soon as Aulë fashioned the Dwarves, Yavanna went immediately to Manwë, king of the gods, with her concern regarding the threat these brutish and highly mobile beings posed to her olvar (especially the trees). Manwë assured Yavanna — addressing her as Kementári ("Queen of the Earth") — that her trees would grow tall enough in Middle-earth to house his great eagles and that they would be protected by the "Shepherds of the Trees." Afterwards, Yavanna returned to Aulë and warned him that his children would have to contend with a power in the forests of Middle-earth whose anger they aroused at their own peril.

Treebeard arouses this very wrath in the Ents at the Entmoot in Derndingle where, in a rather hasty manner (after only three days — Ents do and say everything with painstaking deliberation), they decide to march on Isengard. You can hear the anger in the songs they sing as they march, vowing to repay their neighbor for all his treachery against the forests they're sworn to protect. Aided by the Huorns (the actual forest that marches against Saruman under the Ents' leadership), they imprison Saruman in his tower, drowning and destroying all of his underground works by diverting the waters of the Isen River into the ring of stones.

Tolkien's tale of the Ents' war against Isengard ends well. The Ents not only stop Saruman and his Orcs from further damaging the forests, but eventually, after the War of the Ring, they convert Isengard into the Treegarth of Orthanc — a garden that surrounds the Tower where Saruman once imagined ruling the entire world.

Now that Yavanna's Ents have faded into myth, the question before us is: Who will now act as the shepherds of her forests? With no Ents around, who is willing to stand up and save the olvar from the wanton destruction of human development? And what happens if there are too few of us protecting, as the Ents do, what's left of the old forests and the world's green belts?

I would venture to guess that at such a juncture Mother Nature's wrath will be roused in a far greater way than when her Ents marched against Saruman. If we are ever stupid enough to get to that point, we may well find ourselves imprisoned in a far drearier and dismal place than Saruman does at Orthanc, when he is surrounded by the mighty Ents and Huorns throwing themselves against his fortress. In our hearts, we all know it's most unwise to fool with Mother Nature, as she will undoubtedly someday turn around and give us our comeuppance.

Chapter 23

Sex and Gender

Sex sells. Everybody knows that — why else would I have a chapter called "Sex and Gender" in a book on Middle-earth? If this is the case, however, why on earth are Tolkien's books so popular with men and teenage boys? His fantasy is about as unsexual as you'll find in the genre. There's no character the least little bit like Barbarella here.

This chapter examines the role of sex in the love lives of Middle-earth men and women, including Ents, Elves, and Dwarves. It leaves aside any thought of Orcs because that's disgusting. The chapter also looks at the patriarchal nature of Middle-earth societies and evaluates the rather rigid, traditional gender roles Tolkien set up for his men and women. It examines the gender role reversal of Éowyn who, for a moment, definitely breaks out of the traditional role for which she is otherwise destined. The chapter concludes by assessing the significance of Faramir, the sole male character in *The Lord of the Rings* who seems to cut against the traditional Middle-earth machismo.

Sex in Middle-earth?

You know you're in trouble when the most romantic creatures in *Lord of the Rings* are the Ents — the tree-like beings can't keep their minds off their missing Entwives. The most lurid passages in the book are those of the Ent leader Treebeard telling Merry and Pippin of the days when there were fair Entmaidens (ah!) among them. Treebeard describes the lusciousness of one particular Entmaiden named Fimbrethil ("Slim Birch"), also known as Wandlimb the Lightfooted. One can easily imagine the old Ent recounting with a gleam in his eye the loveliness of Fimbrethil with her smooth, young bark and her lithe, young stem and branches.

Outside of that juicy part, *The Lord of the Rings* is really lacking in spicy romance. In places, the book concerns itself with the courtly, rather disembodied, chivalrous love of Aragorn and Arwen. But their romance is literally relegated to a small section in Appendix A of *The Lord of the Rings* (see Chapter 18 for more on this kind of PG-rated love in Middle-earth).

One of the only flesh-and-blood romances among the other main characters that's even hinted at in *The Lord of the Rings* is the one between Sam Gamgee and Rosie Cotton. Rosie is only briefly mentioned as the sister of Sam's buddies Nibs and Nick Cotton in the second-to-last chapter of *The Return of the King*. Tolkien gives this innocent hobbit romance a lot less attention than Peter Jackson does in his movies — it's really a stretch to turn this novel into date-night movie material. Besides that, there are only the unrequited romantic longings that Éowyn feels towards Aragorn, but he only has eyes for Arwen. Aragorn's rejection ends up motivating Éowyn to disguise herself as the male warrior Dernhelm and go off into battle (see "Gender Role Reversal" later in this chapter for details on her days as a Valkyrie).

The dark side of desire

It's somewhat predictable, given the overt lack of sex and romance outside the sphere of the very chivalrous love that Tolkien depicts in his fantasy works, that the dark side of sexual desire should take its place. This is most clear in a couple of related stories in *The Silmarillion,* in which certainly lust and in one case perhaps even sexual assault take place.

The first is the story of Eöl and Aredhel. Eöl was a Teleri Elf who lived by himself in Nan Elmoth ("Valley of the Star-dusk") in the very woods where Thingol first saw and fell in love with the Maia Melian. Aredhel was the daughter of Fingolfin, high king of the Noldor in Hithlum (see Chapter 4 for more on Thingol and the Noldor family tree). She dwelt with her brother Turgon, the lord of the hidden kingdom of Gondolin.

Against her brother's wishes, Aredhel went to visit her kin in east Beleriand and ended up wandering into Nan Elmoth. There, Eöl spied her, but instead of being filled with love as Thingol was upon seeing the light shining from Melian's face, Eöl was filled with *desire* when he saw her shining figure.

Eöl's feelings for Aredhel were far different from the pure, chaste, chivalrous love that Tolkien's other male lovers feel when they first see their soul mates — including Thingol and Melian, Beren and Lúthien, and Aragorn and Arwen. Those guys would never dream of taking advantage of the lady they spied upon from afar.

This was not the case with Eöl. Instead of making his presence known to Aredhel (as the other men did when they abruptly came upon their ladies in a glade), Eöl snuck back to his house in the woods after putting enchantments around the area so that Aredhel, unable to find her way out, was led directly to his doorstep.

About Aredhel's first meeting with Eöl, Tolkien says only that he welcomed her, let her into his house, and took her as his wife — and afterwards her kin heard nothing of her for a very long time. But Aredhel "was not wholly unwilling" in the matter, a dubious comment to say the least and easily interpreted to mean that she was somehow forced to stay with him and become his de facto wife — perhaps what we call a common-law wife.

The taking and imprisonment of Aredhel is followed by the story of her only child with Eöl, a son called Maeglin. Maeglin ("Sharp Glance" in the Sindarin dialect of Elvish) was the name Eöl gave the boy — his mother named him Lómion ("Child of Twilight" in the Quenyan Elvish dialect).

While Eöl was away visiting the Dwarves, Maeglin and his mother eventually escaped his clutches, stealing away from Nan Elmoth to return to the hidden kingdom of Gondolin. There, King Turgon welcomed his nephew and embraced him as kin. But Maeglin began to desire Idril Celebrindal, Turgon's only child and Maeglin's first cousin (Tolkien indicates that union between first cousins was as verboten among Elves as it is between humans).

When Ulmo sent Tuor to Gondolin to warn Turgon of the impending doom of his kingdom, Idril fell instantly and deeply in love with the handsome stranger, dashing Maeglin's chances of ever having her. In revenge, Maeglin betrayed the whereabouts of Gondolin to Melkor after Melkor promised to give Idril to Maeglin when the hidden kingdom had fallen. Tolkien made sure that the treachery was properly rewarded: Tuor killed Maeglin before escaping with Idril via her secret passageway (see Chapter 5).

Tolkien's stories of the disastrous love of Eöl and his son Maeglin, fueled by lust rather than chaste and chivalrous love, contrast starkly with his closely related stories of true love. Tuor and Idril escaped the fall of Gondolin with their only child Eärendil despite Maeglin's treachery. Later, Eärendil fell in love with and married Elwing, only daughter of Beren and Lúthien, Tolkien's favorite true-love couple (see Chapter 18). Elrond, one of Eärendil and Elwing's twin boys, fathered Arwen Evenstar, the true love and eventual wife of Aragorn, who together form the last of Tolkien's true-love couples.

Tolkien's lesson here on love seems pretty clear: Love based primarily on physical desire has no future, whereas love based on chivalrous love (much like Tolkien's love for his wife, Edith — see Chapter 18) renews itself generation after generation. One problem for modern audiences is that the likelihood of experiencing a chaste and chivalrous true love is relatively small — they don't call it a fairytale romance for nothing — while that of having a relationship based primarily on lust is all too probable.

Somehow, I think that Middle-earth could have used a little more of that old Ent-passion-for-the-lithesome-Entwives energy and a little less of the maiden-worshipped-on-the-hill-under-moonlight stuff. In my opinion, a more balanced approach to sexuality and desire would act as a more effective counterweight to the energy of lust alone, simply because it is more realistic and more in tune with the lives that we now live.

Middle-earth as a Man's Men's World

On the surface, Middle-earth seems to be a complete world. It's only when you take a closer peek at it that some gaps become apparent. Two of these — the lack of formal religion in Middle-earth and the scarcity of women — have been noted by critics of his work.

In a letter to Houghton Mifflin, his American publisher, Tolkien responded to both these criticisms. To the first one regarding the lack of religion, Middle-earth was a monotheistic world of "natural theology" whose historical climate did not call for the establishment of temples and religious rites. ("Natural theology" is a Catholic doctrine that states that God's world proclaims His divinity even to those who aren't yet aware of the Gospel of Christ.) To the second criticism, on the lack of women in *The Lord of the Rings,* he declared that it didn't matter and that it wasn't true anyway. Another of Tolkien's responses to this latter criticism was that it was a wartime story and mainly men are involved in war (at least, combat).

Personally, I find it oppressive to have to follow Tolkien's lead and write "Men" to refer to the collective race of human beings that includes both male and female genders. This may be because my generation has been sensitized to sexism, at least in its more blatant forms (and you have to admit that using "Men" when "humans" are indicated is a pretty blatant one).

The lack of female characters and heroes in particular in Tolkien's fantasy work is not nearly as important as the gender roles he reinforced in the male and female characters he did create. It's precisely in this area that Tolkien pulled a few surprises, despite the superficial sexism abounding in the many cultures of Middle-earth.

Gender roles in Middle-earth

As an author writing about a fantasy world in a totally imaginary time, Tolkien was free to create societies based on models other than the standard patriarchy. For instance, he could have fashioned matrilineal and matriarchal societies for Middle-earth, or even all-female societies like that of the mythical Amazons had he so chosen. Tolkien preferred instead to create rather typical societies: Men hold all the power, run all the governments, and do almost all the fighting (of course, because men cause the wars in the first place, perhaps it's only fitting that they have to go off and fight them).

In all the histories of Arda and Middle-earth that Tolkien created, no woman ever rules a kingdom by herself. This is interesting because when he was born his own nation of Great Britain was ruled by Queen Victoria, one of the prominent queens in its history — and by Queen Elizabeth II, one of the longest ruling queens, when he died. Moreover, both queens had husbands in the role of consort who were thus ineligible to become king.

Tolkien's one mortal queen, Míriel, who did end up inheriting the crown (she was the only daughter of Tar-Palantir, one of the last kings of Númenor) was not allowed to rule on her own. Ar-Pharazôn, the last king, forced Queen Míriel to marry him and cede him her power. Galadriel, the one woman character Tolkien created who genuinely desires to wield power and rule a kingdom, rules Lothlórien only in tandem with her husband Celeborn (it seems that even the Elves aren't as liberated as you might imagine).

Gender Selection among the Valar

The *Ainulindalë* (The Music of the Ainur) book in *The Silmarillion* contains a very mysterious passage in which Tolkien describes how the Valar — his equivalents of gods and goddesses (see Chapter 3) — choose their gender at those times when they want to take on forms that Elves could see. According to my understanding of it, most of the time the Valar do not need bodies, which would be like clothing to them.

This must mean that normally the Valar go around Aman "naked" (making it the original nudist colony). They don't really have any form and therefore don't have any gender either. But when they want to make themselves visible to the Elves, they decide which gender to "wear" based on their temperament. Now, at their inception, when the Valar were still among the other Ainur, they were simply the thoughts of Eru Ilúvatar (the One All-father). When these thoughts entered the world as Valar, their shape was influenced by their knowledge of the world of Arda.

I find this topic very interesting because of Tolkien's clothing analogy (which he calls *raiment* to make it sound appropriately old-fashioned). But just think about this for a second: When you or I are naked, that's precisely when our gender is most manifest, but when the Valar are naked, that's when their gender is most hidden. This means that for the Valar, in a sense, the clothes literally make the man — or woman, as the case may be.

Tolkien must have understood this for he went to great lengths in the same passage to liken gendered embodiment for the Valar to our situation in which our clothing may reveal our gender, but it certainly doesn't determine it.

Tolkien's complex passage on Valar gender selection is most insightful. He seems to saying that gender is fundamentally a matter of our temperament (the way we are "from the beginning") rather than the equipment, the "raiment" or physiological differences, we take on. As many sociologists and psychologists assert, our gender is not a simple matter of having the right paraphernalia — it has a lot do with our natural dispositions as formed by an intricate interplay between genes and environment.

Unlike the Valar, of course, we can't simply change "clothes" if one day we discover that we've put on a gender that's incompatible with the our understanding of the world. As anyone who's dealt with gender issues will tell you, it's a complex matter, filled with many subtleties having to do with how successfully one can navigate between differences in his/her temperament and her/his physiology.

Gender Role Reversal

Despite the overwhelmingly patriarchal character of Middle-earth, Tolkien does manage to come up with a couple of characters who question the strict gender roles that their respective societies have mapped out for them. One of them is Éowyn, niece of King Théoden of Rohan, who hides her female gender and becomes the male warrior Dernhelm ("Secret Helmet") so that she can go fight at the Battle of Pelennor Fields (see Chapter 5). Another is Faramir, a Ranger of Gondor and son of its Steward, Denethor. Faramir has no enthusiasm for war and a great love and appreciation of culture, such as it is for Númenórean exiles in Middle-earth. He eventually falls in love with and marries Éowyn (after her Dernhelm days are over).

Both Éowyn and Faramir cut against the traditional roles set forth for them by their respective societies. Éowyn's rough-and-tumble land of the Rohirrim ("Horse Lords") is a little less civilized than Faramir's. Although she is called a shield maiden of Rohan (presumably a woman who holds or guards the shields of the other male warriors), she's neither expected nor allowed to ride into battle with her brother Éomer or her uncle King Théoden — instead, she is continually left behind and in charge until the lords return. Before Faramir "tames" her, and she falls in love with him, she wants only to vie with the Riders of the Mark and sing their battle songs — in other words, she just wants to be one of the boys.

Faramir's natural sensitivity cuts a little less against his society's expectations, in part because he's rather highborn. As a member of Gondor's upper class, he's probably expected to be somewhat more refined than the average guy you'd meet in Minas Tirith. Nevertheless, Faramir is a far cry from his elder brother Boromir, who fights with the gusto you'd expect from a Viking warrior.

In terms of masculine gender roles, one big difference between Boromir and the younger Faramir is in their attitudes towards power, the most masculine thing you can have in Middle-earth of the Third Age — or any other age for that matter. Boromir longs for the power of the Ring borne by Frodo to defend Gondor against the Enemy, whereas Faramir rejects the One Ring and sends Frodo on his way.

Faramir's rejection of the love of war — and the code of the warrior who fights for the love of it — goes hand in hand with his natural proclivity towards culture. Gandalf taught him to read, and he seems to know more about the Númenórean heritage of his people than even Aragorn. I think it's safe to say that this guy's definitely in touch with his more feminine side, at least compared with the other Men of his society.

It's surely no coincidence that Tolkien paired Faramir, the most sensitive guy in Gondor, with Éowyn, the shield maiden of Rohan. In fact, I think that their union is based on the assumption that true peace can only be based on what we modern people tend to think of, rightly or wrongly, as feminine virtues — what Tolkien has Éowyn call a life of healing and a love of all things that grow.

The encounter between Éowyn and Faramir that precipitates their surprising declaration of love takes place right after the destruction of Sauron is announced. At the walls of the White City outside the Houses of Healing, Faramir asks Éowyn if she loves him. Instead of the gushy, poetic type of response that Tolkien gives us in similar scenes with other couples, Éowyn replies that she had wanted another — remember, she has it bad for Aragon and only goes off to war as Dernhelm when she thinks he is dead. She rejects Faramir, saying that she wants no man's pity (in other words, "If I can't have the king, I'd rather be on my own, thank you very much").

This conversation continues as a kind of duel between the "sensitive" guy and the "hard-edged" shield maiden. Faramir cautions Éowyn not to reject pity when it comes from "a gentle heart," but that he does not pity her and would love her even if her dream of becoming Aragorn's wife and the Queen of Gondor had come true (though I think Arwen would have had a thing or two to say about that). This is all it takes to change Éowyn's heart and make her declare her love for Faramir. On top of that, she rejects her shield maiden days forever, declaring her intention to become a healer and dedicate her life to peacemaking rather than warmaking. She ends her declaration of love for Faramir with the admission that she no longer desires to be a queen.

I think Tolkien was insightful in realizing that Éowyn's love interest in Aragorn is intimately tied to her desire for power and that her realizing this frees her to see her true feelings towards both Faramir and her earlier shield maiden tendencies. But I must admit to a little disappointment in the idea, implicit in her no longer desiring to be queen, that all the women of Middle-earth must give up their ambitions for power to remain "feminine."

Call me modern, but I would rather see a Middle-earth where women can be anything they want — including power-holding monarchs and not just good-looking ladies on the king's arm. I'd rather the so-called "feminine" virtues of healing and nurturing were more integrated into the power structure. In some ways, Tolkien's not-so-original but nonetheless important point — that the way of peace is the way of healing and nurturing — is, in my opinion, blunted by its adoption solely by the one woman in all Middle-earth who aspires to play as an equal in a man's world and by a man who already "gets it."

Part VI
The Part of Tens

The 5th Wave   By Rich Tennant

"...and last week I crafted these 3 Rings of Power and a pair of drop earrings to die for."

In this part . . .

What are the top ten battles of the War of the Ring? Where are the top ten Web sites that you can visit to get more information on Tolkien and his fascinating world of Middle-earth? What are the top ten differences between Peter Jackson's movie versions of *The Lord of the Rings* and Tolkien's books? These are the questions that this modest Part of Tens attempts to answer.

Chapter 24

Top Ten Battles in the War of the Ring

• •

*T*echnically, the War of the Ring starts in mid-June of the year 3018 of the Third Age (T.A. 3018), when Sauron's forces attack the ruined city of Osgiliath in the south in Gondor and King Thranduil's Woodland Realm in the north in Mirkwood Forest. But the bulk of the fighting and the major battles occur in rapid succession during early in T.A. 3019. These battles are important milestones in the struggle between good and evil (see Chapter 15).

As you can see by the following battle dates, all the major battles really take place within a matter of weeks in March, some of them only days apart. The only exception is the all-important Battle of Bywater in November 3019, marking one of the few times that blood is shed in the Shire and the very last of the hostilities associated with the War of the Ring.

1. Ents March on Isengard (March 2)

The first theater of war centers on Saruman's treachery and Isengard's attacks on the Western Alliance. On February 25, 3019, Saruman's forces attack Rohan and kill Théodred, the only son of King Théoden of Rohan, in the First Battle of the Fords of Isen. Coinciding with Saruman's unleashing of his Uruk-hai and other Orc forces on the Rohirrim at Helm's Deep, the Ents under the leadership of Treebeard attack Isengard in retaliation for the wizard's wanton destruction of the trees of Fangorn Forest.

The Entmoot in which the Ents decide to march to war against Saruman at Isengard ends the afternoon of March 2. By nightfall, accompanied by a host of Huorns, the Ents reach Isengard and begin their attack. By the morning of March 3, the Ents and Huorns complete their destruction of the evil works of Isengard (in part by diverting the course of the River Isen), and Saruman in prison at Orthanc is joined by the traitorous Gríma Wormtongue.

2. Battle of the Hornburg (March 3-4)

On March 2, Théoden and his Rohirrim ride west to engage Saruman's Uruk-hai and Orc forces. Upon hearing of the defeat of his defensive forces at the Second Battle of the Fords of Isen, Théoden moves his troops to the ancient fortress of Helms Deep. There, they are assailed by an army of Isengard some 10,000 strong, outnumbering the Rohirrim by about five to one.

Gandalf rides off to find and regroup the remaining Rohirrim forces and to seek the help of the Ents at Isengard. Meanwhile, Saruman's forces eventually breach the walls of Helm's Deep with a primitive explosive, whereupon the defenders retreat to the Hornburg, the citadel at the top of Helm's Deep. All during the night of March 3, the defenders continue to hold the Hornburg until the Orcs breach its gate with another incendiary device. Théoden leads a cavalry charge ("Forth Eorlingas!") that repulses the attackers. In the nick of time on the morning of March 4, Gandalf returns with the Rohirrim forces under Erkenbrand ("Chief Torch"), and they finish off Saruman's forces with the help of the Huorns.

3. Assaults on Lórien (March 11, 15, 22)

On March 6, Aragorn reveals himself to Sauron using the palantír of Orthanc. In response to this revelation by Isildur's heir, Sauron accelerates his planned attacks on the Western Alliance. On March 11, he sends his forces out of his old hangout of Dol Guldur at the eastern edge of Mirkwood Forest to attack Galadriel and Celeborn's Elves in Lothlórien. The Elves repel this attack and two subsequent attacks by Sauron's forces on March 15 and 22.

4. Battle for the Ships at Pelargir (March 13)

On March 8, Aragorn, accompanied by Legolas and Gimli, sets out on the Paths of the Dead to reach the Stone of Erech where, as Isildur's heir, he is able to compel the spirits of the Oathbreakers (those who proved false in Isildur's battle against Sauron in the Second Age) to follow him to the Port of Pelargir. There, on March 13, the ghosts of the dead under Aragorn's leadership commandeer the black ships of the Corsairs of Umbar. Aragorn then sets sail up the River Anduin to reach the besieged city of Minas Tirith.

5. Battle of Pelennor Fields (March 13-15)

On March 13, Faramir, son of Denethor the Steward of Gondor, is wounded by the vanguard of Sauron's forces that overrun the ruins of Osgiliath on the 12th. On the following day, the enemy breaches the Rammas Echor ("Great Encircling Wall") that encloses the Pelennor fields, and the defenders of Gondor retreat to Minas Tirith. Sauron's forces then besiege that city.

In the wee hours of the 15th, the forces of the Lord of the Ringwraiths break the Great Gates to the city. Gandalf stands alone against him when the horns of the Rohirrim are heard. At dawn, the Rohirrim under King Théoden arrive and join the battle on the Pelennor fields. Théoden is killed when the winged beast that the Lord of the Ringwraiths is riding spooks his horse.

Upon the death of Théoden and the wounding of his niece Éowyn, Éomer leads the Rohirrim into battle against the advancing reserves of the enemy only to be cut off by these forces, which include the cavalry of the mûmakil (Oliphaunts). Before it's too late, the black ships of the Corsairs arrive at the landings at Harland just south of Minas Tirith. The troops under Aragorn relieve Éomer and, with the help of the other forces of Gondor, they ultimately turn the tide and achieve victory.

6. Battle under the Trees (March 15)

While Gondor is battling for its life in the south, the northern forces of Sauron out of Dol Guldur attack King Thranduil (the father of Legolas and king of the Woodland Realm) in the northern part of Mirkwood Forest. Known as the Battle under the Trees, Thranduil's forces repel the forces of Dol Guldur, which then attack Lothlórien a second time.

7. Battle of Dale and the Siege of Erebor (March 17-27)

While King Thranduil and his Elves battle Sauron's forces in Mirkwood Forest, Sauron's allies, the Easterlings, attack the Men and Dwarves of the north in Dale and Erebor (the Lonely Mountain). During the three-day battle, known as the Battle of Dale, both King Brand of Dale and King Dáin of the Dwarves (Thorin Oakenshield's heir) are slain, and the combined forces of Men and Dwarves have to take shelter under the Lonely Mountain.

Sauron's forces then besiege Erebor, although they are unable to breach its gate. On March 27, when news of the victory over Sauron and his dark forces arrives (see "Battle of Morannon" that follows), the Dwarves and Men are able to break the siege and rout the disheartened Easterlings.

8. Battle of Morannon (March 25)

To buy valuable time for Frodo, Aragorn leads the remaining forces of the West to engage in a hopeless battle at the Morannon, the Black Gate of Mordor. Aragorn's forces are badly outnumbered and surrounded. Just as they are nearly engulfed, the Ring is destroyed, and the Nazgûl suddenly retreat, making a beeline for Mount Doom followed right behind by the great eagles.

Upon the destruction of the One Ring at Mount Doom and the annihilation of Sauron with it, all of Sauron's Orcs are destroyed in the ensuing melee. The remaining Men allied with Sauron then become completely dismayed and either flee or surrender to Aragorn's troops, giving them an easy victory.

9. Destruction of Dol Guldur (March 28)

With the destruction of Sauron, Celeborn and Galadriel lead the Elven forces out of Lothlórien against Sauron's old fortress of Dol Guldur, where Galadriel throws down the walls and destroys its dungeons. After their victory, Celeborn and Thranduil meet in the forest — which they rename Eryn Lasgalen, the Wood of the Greenleaves. Thranduil claims the northern portion of this forest as his realm, and Celeborn claims the southern, renaming it East Lórien. With the passing of Galadriel into the Uttermost West, Celeborn leaves East Lórien and goes to dwell with the remaining Elves in Rivendell.

10. Battle of Bywater (November 3)

Returning to the Shire, Frodo, Sam, Pippin, and Merry discover that ruffians under the leadership of a murky character called the Boss have taken the place over and been busy making some disastrous changes (see Chapter 22). On the afternoon of November 2, Pippin and Merry rouse a group of hobbits and engage in a small skirmish with the ruffians and shoot one of their leaders.

The following morning, just outside the village of Bywater, the hobbits gather to meet the ruffians who prepare to make a last stand. Reinforcements under Pippin's command arrive from Tuckborough, giving Merry sufficient hobbits to engage the enemy. During the battle nearly seventy of the ruffians are killed and are buried with the hobbit dead in a mass grave on the hillside with a garden around it. After the victory, Frodo, Sam, Merry and Pippin go to Bag End to confront the Boss, who they discover is none other than Sharkey, also known as Saruman. As they are about to force Saruman to leave, Gríma Wormtongue kills him in a fit of rage, but is himself shot as he flees, so the last villains in the conflict meet their end and the War of the Ring concludes.

LOTR Project
theonering.com

Chapter 25

Top Ten Online Middle-earth Resources

● ●

As you're by now undoubtedly aware, there's always more to learn about Tolkien's Middle-earth. In order to help you delve a little deeper into particular areas of Tolkien- and Middle-earth-related lore, I've put together my Top Ten list of Middle-earth Web sites. They run the gamut from language sites to the official Tolkien Page and *The Lord of the Rings* movies sites. Enjoy, and when you visit, be sure to tell them Greg sent you!

1. Encyclopedia of Arda

Number one on my list has to be the magnificent Encyclopedia of Arda. This site is jam-packed with information on all aspects of Tolkien's fantasy world (an offline and CD-ROM version of the site is even available for sale). Among its many resources are a chronicle of the major events that take place within any given year of the First, Second, Third, or Fourth Age, a list of old and rare English words that Tolkien uses in his texts, and an interactive calendar that converts any date in our modern Gregorian calendar to its equivalent date in the different calendars Tolkien devised. The site also includes extensive alphabetical lists to just about every single character, race, location, language, poem, plant, and animal mentioned in either *The Silmarillion* or *The Lord of the Rings*.

    www.glyphweb.com/arda

2. The Lord of the Rings Maps

The Lord of the Rings Maps Web site has the greatest and most imaginative maps covering all the various lands of Middle-earth and also offers some great posters for sale. The maps are categorized into seven different categories: *The Lord of the Rings; The Hobbit;* The Shire; Gondor, Rohan, and Mordor; Beleriand; Planet Tolkien; and Númenor.

    lotrmaps.middle-earth.us

now LOTR · lotrproject.com

3. Lord of the Rings.net

Lord of the Rings.net is the official Web site for Peter Jackson's outstanding movies inspired by *The Lord of the Rings*. It's full of great movie trivia, beyond-the-scenes interviews, information about where the movies are playing, and how to order the DVDs. The site has links to the official shop, where you can purchase movie merchandise, including facsimiles of some of the different movie props, and to the auction Web site where you can bid on the real things.

www.lordoftherings.net

4. Lord of the Rings.com

The stated goal of Lord of the Rings.com Web site is the same as this book — to encourage readers of all ages and backgrounds to experience the power and beauty of Tolkien's Middle-earth by actually reading his books about it! This site contains great news and message board pages along with FAQs where you get an enormous amount of info, all of it relevant to learning more about Tolkien and the significance of his contributions to literature and thought.

www.thelordoftherings.com

5. Tolkien Online

Tolkien Online is a Web site devoted to the fans of *The Lord of the Rings* books and movies. It has a message board, where you can converse on a wide variety of topics, and a place for you to post your own Middle-earth-inspired poems or stories. Check out this enchanting Web site or, better yet, take a look and then become a member.

www.tolkienonline.com

6. Houghton Mifflin's Official Tolkien Page

Here's the place to go when you're ready to take the plunge and actually read *The Lord of the Rings* or you've finally worn out your best old set of paperbacks.

Houghton Mifflin's Official Tolkien Page offers every imaginable edition and set of *The Lord of the Rings* books. This site also contains links to pages where you can purchase a biography of Tolkien or buy any of his other fantasy works including *The Hobbit* and *The Silmarillion*.

`www.houghtonmifflinbooks.com/features/lordoftheringstrilogy`

7. The Tolkien Archives

The Tolkien Archives is a special feature of *The New York Times*, no less. This delightful and thoroughly entertaining site includes links to *Times* stories on Tolkien and his works. It also offers trivia quizzes where you can test your knowledge of Middle-earth (which should be pretty extensive after reading this book) against the best.

`www.nytimes.com/specials/advertising/movies/tolkien`

8. A Tolkien Dictionary

Visiting Bob Ireland's Web site, A Tolkien Dictionary, is like stumbling upon a vast, comprehensive, and interactive index to all the characters, places, and things covered in *The Silmarillion* and *The Lord of the Rings*. Ireland includes the etymology of each term along with a brief definition.

`www.quicksilver899.com/Tolkien/Tolkien_Dictionary`

9. Amanye Tenceli

Amanye Tenceli ("The Writing Systems of Aman") is the place to go if you want to learn how to write and interpret the Tengwar described in Chapter 14. This beautiful and educational site includes basic information on the Tengwar (Rúmil's, called Sarati, and Fëanor's), instruction in a number of styles of Tengwar calligraphy, as well as wonderful Tengwar illuminations, including a lovely version of the Sindarin version of the hymn "Elbereth Gilthoniel" and the Quenyan poem *Namárië*.

`hem.passagen.se/mansb/at`

10. Ardalambion

Ardalambion ("The Tongues of Arda") is the most extensive Tolkien language Web site you can find on the Internet. This is the site to visit if you want to really know just how many languages Tolkien created. Instructive and engaging, it contains not only information on Middle-earth languages, but also the invented languages of his youth, including Animalic, Nevbosh ("New Nonsense"), and the only known and untranslatable quote in Naffarin.

www.uib.no/people/hnohf

Chapter 26

Top Ten Ways the "Lord of the Rings" Books Differ from the Movies

● ●

Rarely, if ever, are avid fans of any book completely happy with its transition to the big screen, and *The Lord of the Rings* is no exception. As of this printing, only two of the three *The Lord of the Rings* movies by Peter Jackson have been released: *The Fellowship of the Ring* and *The Two Towers*. Here then are the top ten differences between the two that bug me the most.

Note that these differences are arranged in chronological order and represent only a small portion of the differences between the storyline and tone in Tolkien's first two books and Peter Jackson's movies. The first six items have to do with differences between the movie and book version of *The Fellowship of the Ring* and the last four, *The Two Towers*.

1. The Forming of the Hobbit Company to Accompany Frodo

The forming of the hobbit company of Sam, Pippin, and Merry to accompany Frodo on his quest to take the One Ring to Rivendell differs considerably in the movie and the book versions. In the movie version, Frodo and Sam, on their way to meet Gandalf in the village of Bree, encounter Pippin and Merry being chased by Farmer Maggot after having just pilfered his fields. In the book, Sam and Pippin accompany Frodo on his way to meet Merry who is waiting for them at Crickhollow, Frodo's new house in Bucklebury (part of an elaborate ruse to cover Frodo's disappearance from the Shire).

Ironically enough, in the book Farmer Maggot actually gives Frodo, Sam, and Pippin sanctuary at his farmhouse and then gets the hobbits safely to the Bucklebury ferry without being seen by the Black Riders (where Merry is waiting to take them across the Brandywine River to the relative safety of

Frodo's new house). And Frodo is the one reluctant to accept Farmer Maggot's hospitality, remembering the time when he was caught pilfering Farmer Maggot's mushrooms and was chased by his dogs.

The movie version of this encounter and the forming of the hobbit company makes Merry and Pippin into buffoons who provide hobbit comic relief. In the book version, Pippin and Merry are serious co-conspirators with Sam in an attempt to not let Frodo go on his Ring quest alone and Frodo himself provides the comic relief (after safely depositing the hobbits at the Bucklebury ferry, Farmer Maggot produces a basket of mushrooms that his wife has prepared for Frodo).

2. Tom Bombadil and Goldberry in the Old Forest

Missing entirely from the movie version of *The Fellowship of the Ring* is the encounter between the hobbit company and the evil of Old Man Willow and the Barrow-wights in the Old Forest that feature prominently in the book. Having cut the peril of Old Man Willow and the Barrow-wights, the movie has no need to introduce the characters of Tom Bombadil, who rescues the hobbits from both of these dilemmas, and his lady, Goldberry. Although the movie works without their presence, I miss them because they added to my enjoyment of Middle-earth and to my understanding of what is good in their world and what is at risk if Sauron succeeds in subjugating Middle-earth.

3. Frodo Encounters the Ringwraiths at Weathertop

In the movie version of the encounter between the Lord of the Ringwraiths (the Witch-king of Angmar) and Frodo on Weathertop, Frodo puts on the Ring and then simply recoils from the wraith until he is trapped against a rock and the Witch-king can wound him in the shoulder. Frodo here is passive, merely reacting to his fear by trying to get out of harm's way.

In the book, Frodo, although still powerless to resist putting on the One Ring, very actively and bravely resists the attack of the Witch-king. After putting on the Ring, Frodo actually throws himself forward and — while crying aloud "O Elbereth! Gilthoniel!" — stabs the Witch-king in the foot with his sword. The book version demonstrates Frodo's failure to resist the power of the Ring while at the same time showing his courage in the face of great evil. Hence, the book version weaves in important themes that continue to play out in his quest to destroy the Ring in the Crack of Doom.

4. Frodo's Flight to the Ford of Bruinen to Escape the Ringwraiths

In the movie version of the flight to the Ford of Bruinen, Arwen carries Frodo across the ford on her horse; she then turns to confront the Black Riders on the other side of the stream and conjures up the torrent in the Bruinen River that carries away the Black Riders.

In the book version, Frodo crosses the ford and confronts the Black Riders alone (on the white horse named Asfaloth, which belongs to the Elf Glorfindel). He brandishes his sword and commands the Black Riders to return to Mordor. When the Riders taunt him, saying with they will return with him and the Ring, Frodo declares that they shall have neither and calls upon the power of Elbereth and Lúthien the Fair. The River then rises in response to Frodo's call and dispenses with the Black Riders.

In the book, Tolkien again shows Frodo resisting the evil of the Ringwraiths and calling upon the power of the forces of good. In the movie, Jackson shows us Frodo relying upon the power and courage of others to save him from evil.

5. The Forming of the Fellowship of the Ring at the Council of Elrond

In the movie version of the forming of the Fellowship of the Ring at the Council of Elrond, each of the eight members to accompany Frodo on his quest pipes up, declaring his support of Frodo and volunteering to be part of the Fellowship ("You have my axe," "And my bow," and so forth). In the book version, Elrond appoints each member of the Fellowship (with the exception of Merry and Pippin, who are both adamant about going) and sets the total number at nine to match the nine Black Riders.

The movie version emphasizes the courage and willingness of each of the individual members to accompany Frodo on his dangerous quest. The book version emphasizes the authority and responsibility of Elrond to pick the most able and representative body of cohorts to ensure the success of their desperate mission.

6. The Breaking up of the Fellowship of the Ring

Both the movie and the book version of *The Fellowship of the Ring* end with the breaking up of the Fellowship of the Ring and the death of Boromir. This takes place after the Fellowship lands their Elven boats on the right shore of the lake Nen Hithoel. In the book, the Fellowship must decide whether to turn west and go to Gondor to help in the wars there or turn east to go to Mordor to seek out the fires of Mount Doom. It is when Frodo goes off by himself to decide the fate of the Fellowship that Boromir confronts him and attempts to steal the Ring.

In the movie, there's no question of Frodo deciding between going to Gondor and Mordor. Indeed, the question is simply whether or not Frodo should abandon the Fellowship and go alone to Mordor. When the power of the Ring takes over Boromir and he tries to steal it from Frodo, this seals the deal and Frodo tries to slip away alone while the Uruk-hai begin their attack on the Fellowship (of course, Sam catches up before Frodo can get his boat across to the eastern shore). In the book, Frodo doesn't get the idea of going to Mordor alone until after Boromir tries to steal the Ring, and Frodo then uses the Ring to escape and go to the hill of Amon Hen where the Eye of Sauron nearly discovers the whereabouts of the Fellowship before Frodo has the good sense to take it off.

7. The March of the Ents Against Saruman at Isengard

The decision of the Ents to march on Isengard and confront the evil of the Wizard Saruman is a major event in *The Two Towers*. In the movie, the hobbits Pippin and Merry engineer this event by getting Treebeard to carry them south toward the Wizard's tower where the Ents can see first hand the extent of the destruction Saruman has done to the nearby forests.

In the book, Pippin and Merry are catalysts of this event only in the sense that they discuss with Treebeard the events of war as far as they know (the hobbits actually know next to nothing about Saruman and Isengard). Treebeard then takes the lead in telling them that although he is uninterested in events as faraway as Mordor and the Shire, Saruman is a neighbor who has to be dealt with. Treebeard then organizes the Entmoot (the meeting of the Ents) in which after relatively little deliberation (for Ents), they decide to march on Isengard. Treebeard then decides to take Pippin and Merry with them, figuring that they may be of some help, although the helpless hobbits have no idea what they're in for.

8. The Battle of the Hornburg at Helm's Deep

The movie version of the Battle of the Hornburg at Helm's Deep handles the setup and conclusion of the battle quite differently from the book. The movie has King Théoden reluctant to engage his people in a war with Saruman and ordering Éowyn to lead the people of Rohan from Edoras to Helm's Deep while he attends to an isolated attack by Orcs riding wargs. In this film version, Aragorn and Gandalf thoroughly disagree with this defensive strategy, urging the king instead to meet the enemy directly.

In the book, King Théoden is on his way to the front at the Fords of Isen (where his son Théodred was recently killed) when Gandalf meets him and urges the king to retreat with his forces to Helm's Deep until he (Gandalf) is able to gather the scattered Rohirrim and get help from the Ents in Fangorn Forest. In the book, Théoden has no reluctance to engage the enemy; the only reason he doesn't is Gandalf's insistence that the forces of Saruman are too large to meet head on.

The two versions also differ in which forces Gandalf brings to Helm's Deep to save the day at the Battle of Helm's Deep. According to the movie, Gandalf brings the forces of Éomer to save the day on the second morning by breaking the siege right after Théoden leads his cavalry charge out of the Hornburg. (According to a subplot of the movie, the treacherous counselor Wormtongue has engineered a feud between Théoden and his nephew Éomer that caused him and his men to be exiled from Edoras.) In the book, Gandalf brings the Rohirrim forces under Lord Erkenbrand (Éomer fights in the Battle of the Hornburg right beside Aragorn) to break the siege, and the Ent-like trees, the Huorns, come unbidden to dispose of the routed Orc troops.

9. Faramir Encountering the Hobbits and Gollum

One of the most confusing movie changes for me happens near the end of *The Two Towers,* when the Ranger Faramir (Boromir's brother) encounters Frodo, Sam, and Gollum. This event occurs right after the three have been unable to enter the Black Gate of Mordor and are doubling back south to find the crossroads that leads to the only other way into Mordor, Cirith Ungol ("Spider's Pass"). From the book, we know that Faramir and his men lead Sam and Frodo to their hideaway in the cleft of Henneth Annûn ("The Window on the West"). This waterfall is above the so-called Forbidden Pool where Faramir's men almost shoot Gollum until Frodo intervenes.

In the book, Faramir decides to let Sam, Frodo, and Gollum go on their way to Mordor from Henneth Annûn (after they swear not to return there unbidden). In the movie, Faramir and his men take the three of them all the way back to the ruins of Osgiliath (the city on the Anduin River, near Minas Tirith) instead, where a winged Ringwraith appears. Frodo nearly surrenders the Ring to him and then nearly throttles Sam. Because none of these events occur in the book, the movie account of Faramir letting the hobbits go free from Osgiliath rather than from Henneth Annûn is quite perplexing.

10. The Stairway of Cirith Ungol

The movie version of *The Two Towers* ends at a considerably different place from the book, leaving us right at the point where Gollum is leading Sam and Frodo to the Stairway of Cirith Ungol ("Spider's Pass"). In one of the last scenes of the movie, Sam and Frodo are walking along through a woods and Sam begins musing about how he and Frodo are living one Mr. Bilbo's adventures. He speculates how in time people will gather around the fire to hear the story of Frodo and the Ring, calling Frodo "the famousest of the hobbits."

In the book, the same conversation takes place between Frodo and Sam but in a very different location and with very different ramifications. Frodo and Sam are climbing the twisting stairs of the Cirith Ungol about to enter the dark pass when they have this conversation in the book. When Sam mimics a child asking to hear the story of Frodo and the Ring again, the book says that Frodo laughed "a long clear laugh from his heart." Tolkien says that this sound had not been heard in that place since Sauron had come to Middle-earth and that it was as though all the rocks around them were listening.

In the book version of this conversation, Sam actually likens the adventure that he and Frodo are living to the legends of Beren and Eärendil and their involvement with the Silmaril jewel (see Chapter 5). This causes Sam to suddenly remember that the phial Galadriel gave Frodo as his parting gift contains light from this selfsame jewel and to realize that they are still in the same tale. As those of you who've read *The Two Towers* already know, Sam's recalling of Galadriel's star-glass is critical to the outcome of the danger they're just about to face in the Spider's Pass. For those of you who've haven't, you'll just have to get yourself to a screening of Peter Jackson's *The Return of the King* as soon as you can to find out what I'm talking about.

Index

●●